D0874044

Wake Up The Echoes

Notre Dame Football

Wake Up The Echoes

Notre Dame Football

by

Ken Rappoport

STRODE PUBLISHERS, INC.
HUNTSVILLE, ALABAMA 35802

To Bernice
My Queen Of Love And Beauty

Contents

Foreword

Introduction

1. The First Hurrah 11
2. The Father Of Notre Dame Football 18
3. The Boy From Syracuse 25
4. A Boy's Education 38
5. Air Power 46
6. Cattle, Oil Wells, And Football 56
7. The Pied Piper 71
8. Free Spirit 101
9. Famine, Pestilence, Destruction, And Death 116
10. One For The Gipper 140
11. Undefeated, Untied, And Unbelievable 146
12. Just Plain Hunk 165
13. Return Of The Horseman 178
14. Hello, Columbus. . .Good-bye, Ohio State 189

15. A Notre Dame Man .... .209
16. Some Great Days For The Irish .... .235
17. Shaking Down The Thunder .... .253
18. The Fainting Irish .... .285
19. Cardiac Special .... .308
20. ...And Still The Winner! .... .331
21. "Coaches Don't Build Houses" .... .344
22. No Joy In Mudville .... .360
23. The College Superbowl .... .371
24. Unhooking The Horns .... .380
25. Old Notre Dame Will Win Over All .... .395
26. Winning One For Ara .... .404
    Epilogue .... .410
    Appendix .... .413

Foreword

Anyone attempting to compile a volume on the history of Notre Dame football to the complete satisfaction of Irish fans everywhere is immediately confronted with a monumental task. How many words are needed to adequately describe the indefinable Notre Dame spirit? Where do you begin, and how well can any one writer capture the essence of the tradition? What players do you spotlight and how many more must you necessarily omit from detail because of space limitations?

Individual works have been written on the brilliant Knute Rockne, the acknowledged mastermind of college football. Books have been published on the late and great Frank Leahy, several of which sadly lacked both the attention and dedication to the man's real contributions to Notre Dame and the collegiate game, while still other works could yet concern themselves with the fabulous era of Ara Parseghian, or the storied list of Notre Dame All-Americans or the aggregate of an unprecedented nine championship seasons.

These are just some of the problems faced by Ken Rappoport as he labored to put together one of the most comprehensive volumes of Notre Dame football ever undertaken. Yet he was able to touch all bases with a writing skill that does do justice to the excitement, frustration, and joy inherent in the basic structure of human nature and of athletic skill and competition. His endless hours of research into the imposing massive shelves of Notre Dame football material resulted in rich dividends. His industrious approach to literally hundreds of personal interviews gives this book an authenticity nowhere else recorded. He has relived the glorious as well as the disappointing moments with a sense of impartial journalism that should be the standard for all who attempt such projects. Indeed, this is a book to be enjoyed not only by those interested in Notre Dame and its football legends, but by college football fans everywhere.

E. W. Krause
Athletic Director
University of Notre Dame
Notre Dame, Indiana

Introduction

Some time ago, a small statue of the Rev. Edward Frederick Sorin was stolen from the Notre Dame campus. From time to time the university received postcards from all parts of the world: "Having a good time, wish you were here. Sorin." The statue was eventually returned—in a rowboat, dancing lazily on the campus lake. In terms of history, the caper truthfully fit the man. For Sorin was a traveler. Without him, it is possible that Notre Dame never would have been founded. And of course there would have been no Notre Dame football team.

Father Sorin, a young priest with the physique of a giant and an even larger appetite for adventure, was a member of a seminary in France before he struck out for America, determined to bring the gospel to the religious poor. Accompanied by several brothers of the Congregation of the Holy Cross, Sorin crossed the Atlantic in a rough boat trip that took 39 days and plenty of heavenly courage. From New York, Father Sorin and his hardy associates took off for the missionary station of St. Peter's near Vincennes, Indiana. They reached Indiana by canal boat, by horse and cart, and by foot, surviving storms and robbers, and eventually set up a school. Sorin concluded in a note back to his superior at Le Mans, France: "Tell me, are we not men of faith?" This was 1841.

By 1842 the missionary school was flourishing, and the Holy Cross men—sparked by Sorin's fiery spirit—hoped to expand to a college. They were offered a tract of 900 acres near South Bend, and Sorin and his brothers hastily took up the offer. They made the 250-mile trip in 10 days and upon their arrival, knelt in the snow to pray and dedicate their future work to Notre Dame (Our Lady). Through the offices of a Methodist state senator, Sorin got his coveted charter for The University of Notre Dame du Lac ("Our Lady of the Lake") on January

15, 1844.

Sorin was the fighting spirit of Notre Dame for many years after that. When the school's working capital was reduced to fifty cents he got money by selling his horses. When a nearby dam produced a festering ground for cholera, Father Sorin and his team of brothers razed it with crowbars. When fire leveled every building on the campus except the church in 1879, Father Sorin personally began the task of rebuilding. Taking up the first wheelbarrow Sorin commented: "If it were all gone, I should not give up."

Father Sorin advanced in the Congregation of Holy Cross from provincial to superior general, but Notre Dame was still his favorite place. And the feeling from its population was always reciprocal. In a way Sorin became the Knute Rockne of his time.

"His words could be exploited as a continuing source of inspiration and a lesson in the strength of humility, a tireless reminder that there would be no Notre Dame but for the indomitable will and toil of the founder and his breed," notes Chet Grant, the highly regarded Notre Dame historian.

Sorin laid the foundation for others to build on. And what a towering structure has evolved! In any terms, the history of Notre Dame is staggering—richly enhanced, of course, by its gigantic football legends. As with Sorin's painful work, nothing came easily for the Fighting Irish either. Religious persecution occurred on the football field. In fact, the very nickname was given to the team by scornful opponents. Since Northwestern students applied that disrespectful sobriquet in 1889, the term "Fighting Irish" has taken on a bit more luster. And very few have actually taken the fight out of the Irish.

The "Notre Dame Victory March" jazzed up the tempo and became everybody's victory march. Rockne established a tremendous rhythm in college football in his time, and Notre Dame became everybody's school.

Father Sorin no doubt would have enjoyed the intensity that his successors produced. In fact, he would have fit right into the Notre Dame scheme.

Six years before Sorin's death in 1893, football was born at his school. Years later football made Notre Dame world famous. But to get to the position of No. 1, the Fighting Irish had to struggle. It was not easy, but they made it. Father Sorin would have liked their style.

The First Hurrah

On November 23, 1887, sports history was made at Notre Dame, but the metropolitan newspapers in the area chose to ignore it. Instead, the sports pages were crammed with other news. Bankrupt won the Produce Exchange Handicap at the New Orleans track. The Cincinnati baseball team denied reports of a sale. Jake Schaefer, Sr., defeated George Slosson, 200 to 120, in the cushion-carom billiard tournament in Chicago. George Ryder knocked out Slippery Breen, a Chicago featherweight fighter, in 31 "fierce" rounds at Boston. There was no mention of the first Notre Dame football game.

If Chicago was not very excited about it, there was no waning interest in South Bend. Campus fever sizzled.

"For some days previous to Wednesday, great interest had been manifested by our students in the football game which had been arranged between the teams of the Universities of Michigan and Notre Dame," reported the *Notre Dame Scholastic.*

Mornings were sometimes free periods for the students, and usually they stayed in bed, studied, or took a walk. But on this particular morning, they went directly to the campus playground to witness the first exhibition of intercollegiate football at their school. The Notre Dame band gave musical support to the Notre Dame players, and the students vocalized from the sidelines, "Rah, rah, Nostra Domina." Their fervor, however, was soon dampened by Michigan's superior forces. And the game ended at the half with Michigan in front, 8-0.

The game itself was not considered so much a contest as a lesson. It had been scheduled between the schools for the sole purpose of providing instruction for the Notre Dame players.

11

The *Scholastic* reported on November 26, 1887:

"The home team had been organized only a few weeks and the Michigan boys, the champions of the West, came more to instruct them in the points of the Rugby game than to win fresh laurels. The visitors arrived over the Michigan Central railroad Wednesday morning, and were taken in charge by a committee of students. After spending a few hours 'taking in' the surroundings, they donned their uniforms of spotless white and appeared upon the campus. Owing to the recent thaw, the field was damp and muddy; but nothing daunted, the boys 'went in' and soon (Michigan's W. W.) Harless' new suit appeared as though it had imbibed some of its wearer's affinity for the soil of Notre Dame. At first, to render our players more familiar with the game, the teams were chosen irrespective of college. After some minutes' play, the game was called and each took his position as follows:

"University of Michigan—Full Back: J. L. Duffy; Half Backs: J. E. Duffy, E. McPherran; Quarter Back: R. T. Farrand; Centre Rush: W. W. Harless; Rush Line: F. Townsend, E. M. Sprague, F. H. Knapp, W. Fowler, G. W. De Haven, and M. Wade.

"University of Notre Dame—Full Back: Harry M. Jewett; Half Backs: Joseph E. Cusack, (Captain) Henry Luhn; Quarter Back: George R. Cartier; Centre Rush: George A. Houck; Rush Line: Francis Fehr, Patrick Nelson, Edward A. Sawkins, Frank H. Springer, Thomas O'Regan, and James T. Maloney.

"On account of time, part of only one inning was played, and resulted in a score of 8 to 0 in favor of the visitors. The game was interesting and, notwithstanding the slippery condition of the ground, the Ann Arbor boys gave a fine exhibition of skillful playing. The occasion has started an enthusiastic football boom and it is hoped that coming years will witness a series of these contests. After a hearty dinner, the Rev. President Walsh thanked the Ann Arbor team for their visit, and assured them of the cordial reception that would always await them at Notre Dame. At 1 o'clock, carriages were taken for Niles, and, amidst rousing cheers, the University of Michigan football team departed, leaving behind them a most favorable impression."

The spark of football thus was planted at Notre Dame, and it did not take long for it to catch on. One week after the game with Michigan, a meeting was held on the Notre Dame campus to form a rugby football association. Brother Paul, the father of athletics at the university, was named president of the association and later managed the first four Notre Dame teams. It was Brother Paul who suggested that campus teams be organized, and he was instrumental in securing the first uniforms. The *Scholastic* noted that the uniforms were made up "of canvas jackets and trousers, stockings of the best quality of wool, and jersey caps. The trimmings are brown and black."

Frank Fehr, one of the players from the first Notre Dame team, once reflected: "We had only 11 starters and a substitute or two. We played in white duck pants and shirts that laced up the front, and we had no equipment, such as shoulder pads, headgears, etc. We used baseball shoes with football cleats. We had no coach. In fact, we did not know the game, and learned it only after watching other teams play. Then we copied their plans, which consisted almost entirely of the flying wedge. Several times we had to finish a game with only 10 men.

"Considering the lack of pads, the game was somewhat murderous. All our yardage came from mass formation from which we tried to bull our way for five yards and a first down. We had three downs to make five yards, the required distance for a first down. I'll never forget meeting teams like Michigan and Northwestern with one reserve. In 1889, we beat the Wildcats 9-0 and came mighty close to finishing the contest with ten men. One of our ends injured an ankle and our only substitute had to fill the position."

Organized college football in America was less than 20 years old when Notre Dame took up the sport. It was a bold move, since most Catholic colleges and universities had not looked upon football with any favorable degree. After Princeton and Rutgers met in the first intercollegiate game in 1869, football was slow gaining favor with secular schools, and it was many years before such institutions as Georgetown, St. Louis, and Holy Cross found it palatable.

Before football made its indelible mark in the Notre Dame scheme, it was preceded by other recreations. Father Edward Frederick Sorin, founder of the university, was an expert at marble shooting and enjoyed tackling the students at this competition. As early as 1843, advertisements to students stressed

13

This hardy group represented Notre Dame in its first football game, against Michigan in the fall of 1887.

"facilities for recreation and physical exercise." Numbered among the recreational pursuits were wrestling, tag games, fishing, hunting, boating, and hiking. By the 1860s some of the Notre Dame population competed in boat races, in baseball, and soccer.

Describing a soccer match, the *Notre Dame Scholastic* reported in 1867: "A group of 70 students of the university interested themselves in a game of football the other afternoon from one o'clock until 5:30. The game consisted of kicking the ball around and kicking each other in the shins."

Father Thomas J. Walsh, president of Notre Dame from 1881 until his untimely death at 40 in 1893, was one of the main supporters of football at the school. It was during his reign that the sport was given birth and allowed to flourish under the influence of Brother Paul, a far-visioned religious man who was a member of the Congregation of Holy Cross, the university's founding group. With these two buoyant energies, it was inevitable that football would never die at Notre Dame, even though it took a hiatus during the 1890 and 1891 seasons.

In 1888 Notre Dame challenged Michigan to two games and lost both, 26-6 and 10-4, on successive April days. The first game was played on Friday, April 20, in the Green Stockings Ball Park in South Bend. It was spiced by wrangling over the rules, and a fellow named Sprague, from Ann Arbor, refereed. "The game was very exciting, and included much kicking of the ball and rushing by men of the team," noted the *Notre Dame Alumnus*.

The second game on Saturday, April 21, was played on the Notre Dame campus and was no less argumentative. Sprague played for Michigan the second day, and an injured Michigan player served as the referee. And a reporter for the *Notre Dame Scholastic* pointed out in his game story that an apparently legal Notre Dame score was disallowed while Michigan was given a touchdown that was questionable.

Still, no hard feelings resulted. Said the *Scholastic* reporter: "We were impressed by the manly bearing and courteous conduct of the Michigan players and we hope that next year will bring another friendly contest for football honors."

The 1888 season was not a total loss, however. On December 6, Notre Dame defeated the Harvard School of Chicago 20-0 and thus recorded the first victory in its history.

By 1889 the team had smart, new uniforms—with old gold and sky blue the primary colors. The initials "ND" were emblazoned on the breasts of the jackets and the visors of the caps. With all the accoutrements and all the talent, all that was needed at this point was perhaps a guiding light. Suggested the *Scholastic*: "What the football eleven needs most now is a coacher. They are all strong men and work hard, but do not play as scientifically as they might. If a good man were obtained for two or three weeks, there would be great improvement."

However, no bona fide coach was immediately forthcoming. The early Notre Dame teams were led either by recent graduates or men from other schools who were working for postgraduate degrees at Notre Dame. The "coach" usually played.

Some of the early Notre Dame football players were recruited from Catholic Institute Associations, Young Men's Catholic Clubs, and similar social athletic organizations. Others were so-called "tramp" athletes who went from school to school and spent more time on the football field than in the classroom. They came from as far away as Washington, Texas, and Michigan to join forces with the "Catholics," as the team was sometimes called by midwestern sports editors.

Along with the aforementioned players on the original team, the Notre Dame squads of the 1880s included Edward C. Prudhomme, Joseph L. Hepburn, Gene Melady, and Dezera Cartier and contributed to the nation businessmen, physicians, high army officials, judges, and capitalists. Prudhomme was the Notre Dame captain when the football team made its first trip, a 100-mile journey to Evanston, Illinois, to play Northwestern in 1889. It was here that the name "Fighting Irish" was born, although originally cast as an unflattering remark by scornful Northwestern students. Frank Fehr, the Notre Dame center, recalled the circumstances:

"We were leading Northwestern, 5-0, at the half only to hear the Northwestern fans chanting 'Kill the Fighting Irish—Kill the Fighting Irish'—as the second 45-minute half opened. From that time on, the name stayed with Notre Dame athletic teams. Funny thing about it—we had only two Irishmen on the squad. We never had over two Irishmen on the team at the same time the first three years we played."

The game with Northwestern marked the beginning of a traditional rivalry, although the first contest in the series was not born of good will. Not only were the fans unfriendly, but the Northwestern players were downright mean. "According to one version, Notre Dame players were still being returned to campus in ambulances a week later," said one writer. They could not take the fight out of the "Fighting Irish," however. Dezera Cartier kicked the first field goal in a midwestern college game, and Notre Dame defeated Northwestern 9-0.

Football was pushed to the sidelines in 1890 and 1891, and gentler pursuits took over at Notre Dame. The Sacred Heart Church was dedicated and filled with art work. It also held a 300-year-old altar and the largest bell in the nation. Notre Dame boasted possession of the oldest painting in America, one of the largest magnets in Indiana, a collection of historical sacred vessels, and had the honor of being the first college in America to be lighted with electricity. Famous people came to look over the growing institution: Daniel Doughtery, the orator; Carl Schurz, the German democrat and reformer; James G. Blaine, who was campaigning against Grover Cleveland for the presidency; and Chief Justice Chase.

The school started giving out the Laetare Medal, a distinguished award to the Catholic judged outstanding in a particular year. Poets, soldiers, historians, scientists, architects, and authors won the award. To celebrate the opening of a campus building, a Greek play *Oedipus Tyrannus* was performed. A South Bend newspaper commented that the audience enjoyed it, even though they could not understand it.

The Father Of
Notre Dame Football

In the 1890s Notre Dame attracted a wide crossbreed of America's muscular young men. Some were itinerants who came just to play football, then left. But more representative of the flock in those days was Francis E. Hering, considered by many to be the father of Notre Dame football.

When he arrived at South Bend in 1896, it is possible that he had more football acumen than had been accumulated at Notre Dame since the start of the sport there in 1887. Hering had won letters under Amos Alonzo Stagg at Chicago University and had coached at Bucknell. These credentials allowed Hering to virtually take over Notre Dame football in his first year. He was at once proclaimed coach, captain, and quarterback of the 1896 team, a move no one at the school dared to challenge or ever regretted.

Hering was a poet, orator, and magazine writer, but these intellectual talents faded in comparison to his historical contribution as Notre Dame's first full-time football coach. Hering built his team of 1896 into one of the leaders of early midwestern athletics. He developed such standout players as Angus McDonald, Jack Mullen, John Farley, and John Eggeman. By 1897 and 1898, Hering's last two years, Notre Dame was meeting and beating such teams as Michigan State, DePauw, and Illinois.

Hering was all too perfect for the Notre Dame job. He enhanced his position there by teaching English and studying law. He took little money for his efforts, rather accepting cuts of beef from the Notre Dame farm as part of his salary. Even his

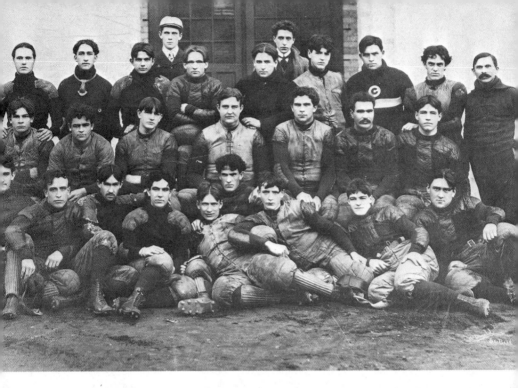

Francis E. Hering, the "father of Notre Dame football," is shown with one of his teams of the 1890s. That is Hering in the last row with the cap.

bearing was wonderful, noted one writer: "He had the jaw of a fighting man and the brooding look of a poet."

Hering's appearance at Notre Dame gave some stability to a football program that was drifting in no purposeful direction. Prior to his guiding force, there were no coaches of his impact. After two years' absence, football was picked up again at Notre Dame in 1892, and it was not until 1894 that some leadership was provided. James L. Morison was the coach in 1894 and H. E. Hadden in 1895, but both made few waves on the football program.

Recounting the misdeeds and mismanagement of those pre-Hering seasons, the *Notre Dame Scholastic* complained that the Fighting Irish did not make proper use of all their players. According to the *Scholastic*, the substitutes did not receive encouragement because regulars were kept in the games most of the time: "There have been plenty of good substitutes for the varsity—men who could step in at any stage of the game and put

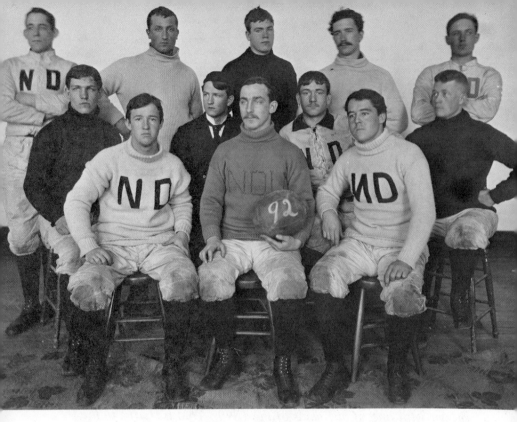

The players of 1892 in their handsome varsity sweaters. Foot-ball had been dropped for two years, but they picked it up again.

Interest in football during the early years was strong at Notre
Dame, as witnessed by the size of the 1893 squad.

up a hard, snappy fight. These are substitutes we should have at hand every year, for no one knows when some of them will force his way on the varsity. They should be given a chance in the early games of the season and not (be) reserved on the sidelines all the time. There is neither honor nor pleasure in standing idle along the sidelines with a suit on. Piling up big scores looks well in the papers, but it will not develop substitutes when they are needed in a close game."

The Fighting Irish managed to have winning seasons in 1894 and 1895, but the *Scholastic* and many others wondered how they did it. In 1895, aside from captain Daniel V. Casey and a few others, no one else was vaguely familiar with football. Noted the *Scholastic*: "The others were simply beginners. They tackled high, fouled without discretion, fumbled whenever there was a chance and were utterly ignorant of what line play, interference and team work meant. Those that watched the first few practice games expressed regret at the slump athletics had apparently taken at Notre Dame."

When Morison and Hadden coached, Notre Dame's opponents included such "forgettables" as the Illinois Cycling Club,

The boys of fall, circa 1894. They served under Notre Dame's first coach, James L. Morison.

The 1895 Notre Dame team: "They tackled high, fouled without discretion, fumbled whenever there was a chance and were utterly ignorant of what line play, interference and teamwork meant."

Indianapolis Artillery, Chicago Physical and Surgical, Northwestern Law, and Rush Medical. When Hering made his dramatic entrance, more respectable opponents appeared on the Notre Dame schedule, including Chicago University, Purdue, DePauw, Michigan State, Illinois, Michigan, and Indiana. Against such formidable opposition, Hering's teams compiled a 12-6-1 record in three seasons.

At this point, football had reached such a level of importance at Notre Dame that Hering even had an assistant—James J. McWeeney, a onetime heavyweight wrestler with the Chicago Police Department and a worker on the Notre Dame farm. McWeeney's rugged philosophies were constantly being imparted to the Notre Dame ballcarriers: "Go into the line with your free fist doubled. You won't have to use it. Your opponents will get the message." When Hering retired after the 1898 season, McWeeney took over as coach for one year.

Notre Dame became so bullish that Amos Alonzo Stagg's famous Chicago University team was forced to throw in a ringer or two for their games in order to subdue the Fighting Irish. If

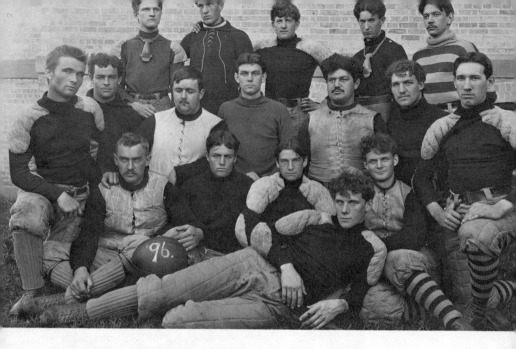

The 1896 team—one of the early leaders in Midwestern athletics.

the contests were usually one-sided in Chicago's favor, they were not easy in the sense of physical strain. The *Chicago Tribune* once reported: "(John) Farley and other Notre Dame players were taken out for rough play."

Notre Dame never lacked for inventiveness or daring. The Fighting Irish gave the midwestern fans one of their first looks at the revolutionary field goal, then a dropkick worth five points. After the 1897 game, won 34-5 by Chicago, the *Tribune* said with astonishment: "The game was the most remarkable of all games in the West on one account. . .for the first time the Princeton place-kick was successfully made in a regular game. The Maroons have been practicing among themselves on the new kick of the Tigers, but when the men from Hoosierdom made the formation for its trial on the Chicago 30-yard line, the defenders were puzzled. There was a hitch in the Notre Dame signals and the men fell into position that looked like a preparation for a punt, and yet it was not the conventional formation. A whisper of 'fake kick' came from the sidelines but when Mullen (captain John Mullen) took the ball and placed it on the ground a thrill of pleased surprise went around and grew into loud applause when (Mike) Daly kicked the pigskin calmly between the uprights."

The Boy From Syracuse

At the turn of the century a 'strapping young man from Syracuse, New York, entered Notre Dame with ambitions of becoming an engineer. He had arranged to work his way through school by waiting on tables and set up residence in St. Joseph's Hall.

The boy from Syracuse worked intensely but also found time for recreation such as football on the hall campus. Someone noticed that his talents far exceeded his playmates'. When questioned, the boy acknowledged that he had played football in high school—but "not much."

He was persuaded to join the Notre Dame football team at Cartier Field and in a short time became the star fullback—and perhaps the best fullback in the entire country. His name was Louis Salmon, but he was better known as Red Salmon, due to a shock of fiery red hair.

"Salmon punted, kicked off, and drop-kicked from the field and for points-after," says Chet Grant in his book *Before Rockne At Notre Dame.* "He was a breakaway potential on kickoff and punt returns. He was a first-rate blocker. He was reputed to be the only linebacker to stop the great Willie Heston of Michigan consistently even as the Wolverines dominated the scoreboard. A Western press association circulated his halftone with the caption of 'Greatest Back in the West.' At the time when it was a red-letter event for a Western Conference or a Michigan star to breach the ivy walls of Walter Camp's All-America lineup, Red Salmon of tiny Notre Dame made the third team."

Salmon's stature in Notre Dame annals can be certified by

25

The 1900 varsity—Pat O'Dea's first team at Notre Dame.

the performance of Fighting Irish teams during his time as a player. From 1900 through 1903, Notre Dame compiled an enviable record of 28-6-4, including an undefeated, once-tied season in 1903 where the opposition scored no points in nine games. Newspaper writers of the day described this sturdy, 5-foot-10, 170-pound figure in terms of wonder. "Salmon, the mainstay of his team, tore the Purple line as if made of wet paper," said one Chicago writer after a typical performance by the irrepressible redhead. "When Salmon was forced to punt, the ball went 65 yards," said another. "When not crashing line or skirting ends, he was on the interference pulling a companion to the front. . .on defensive also a star," noted one more.

Typical of Salmon's efforts was an extraordinary iron-man performance against Fielding "Hurry Up" Yost's great Michigan team of 1902. The all-conquering Wolverines won the game 23-0 that October day, but Salmon won the hearts of the 1,600 fans at Toledo, Ohio's, old Armory Park and the respect of Michigan. The rugged fullback carried the ball 10 times on one drive, averaging over five yards a carry, and took Notre Dame to the shadow of the Michigan goal line. Salmon had been unstoppable and apparently would have crossed the goal line except that he slipped in an extremely muddy field on the last down of the explosive series. This performance was against a team that was in the midst of a five-year unbeaten streak, a team that was recognized as the giant of the nation. It would be a long time

26

before Salmon's performance was challenged in Notre Dame football lore.

"Captain Salmon was the bright and shining light on the Notre Dame eleven," reported the *Toledo Blade* after that game. "Too much cannot be said of the red-headed fullback. His line bucks have never been exceeded on any gridiron. He was a tower of strength for the Hoosiers. It was a great game and one that will be remembered for many years to come. Notre Dame need not be ashamed of the showing she made."

Michigan's players, expecting to beat Notre Dame by a much larger score, were "chagrined at the outcome," according to a spectator. Aaron B. Cohn, who played football at the Ohio Law School and later became a judge, remembered watching Notre Dame's dynamo in action. "The Michigan players didn't hesitate for a second to place the credit for Notre Dame's superlative showing where it belonged—squarely on the bull-like shoulders of one Red Salmon, captain and fullback for the Irish. This worthy son of Hercules did everything in the first half but uproot the goal posts and pound the Wolverines over the head with them."

Because he was a man of depth and deep religious feeling, Salmon's ferocity at football seemed unnatural at times. Once

The mighty 1903 Notre Dame team—undefeated and unscored on.

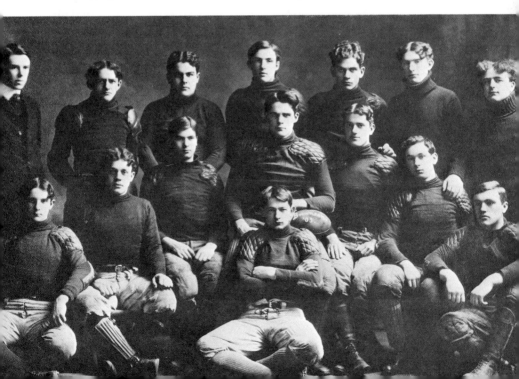

Coach Pat O'Dea (last row, far right) and Red Salmon (middle row, second from right) were instrumental in Notre Dame's successes of the early 1900s.

he got into a football suit, Salmon unleashed fierce energies and passions. The same Aaron Cohn who witnessed him in that significant Michigan game of 1902 also was on hand when Salmon later came to Toledo with a semipro team. This is what he saw:

"Salmon returned to Toledo with the South Bend Studebakers to meet the Toledo Athletic Association. He was the same old Red Salmon, even more so. The TAA had on their roster such local names as 'Dirty Louie' Hadding, Andy Jankowski, Joe Taylor, 'Mother' Kruse and the Tattersall brothers. Harry Shepler was their manager. During this contest, Salmon once hit 'Dirty Louie' so hard that fans thought he'd never get up. But Louie did get up and later in the afternoon, he returned the compliment with such force and enthusiasm that Red had to be helped to his feet. That it was none other than 'Dirty Louie' who helped Red to his feet drew more comment than the game itself, as is proved by the fact that I still don't know which team won."

Salmon was described "as handsome as a movie star" by

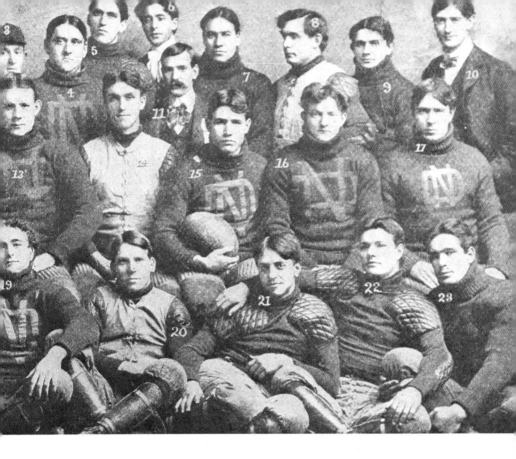

one observer—apple cheeks, "startling" blue eyes, and unblem-
ished, translucent skin to go along with his flaming red hair. His
modesty exceeded his good looks. When South Bend newspapers and students persistently identified him as "Sammon,"
there was no attempt on his part to seek a correction. First,
Salmon himself felt that he was not good enough to make the
varsity, but fate soon took him in that direction. A story from
Dr. W. W. Halloran, class of 1903, confirms this:

"I think I was the first one to tackle him. I was captain of
the St. Joe Hall team and asked Red if he ever played football.
He said, 'Not much,' so we put him on the second team. We
kicked off. He got the ball. I hardly touched him. And everyone
else was on the ground. He was on the goal line standing up.
The next day he was playing fullback for the varsity."

Salmon not only played, he helped coach the varsity when
there was no one else around to do it. Pat O'Dea was the Notre
Dame coach in 1900 and 1901, leading the Fighting Irish to 14
victories in those two years. But he quit after his meteoric

29

career. There was no coach at the beginning of the 1902 season, and the team was put together by Salmon and some of the other regulars. A little later in the year James Farragher, a tackle on the 1901 team, was hired as coach and produced six victories. Farragher was again on the scene in 1903, but much of the credit for Notre Dame's first full undefeated season went to Salmon. The only blemish on the record that year was a scoreless tie with Northwestern, as Notre Dame produced a point accumulation of 292 to 0 in nine games. "In 1903, the material was good but there was no coach (at the beginning of the year)," said the *Notre Dame Alumnus*. "There was a fear that this material would go to waste. Captain Salmon worked hard with his men, coaching them as well as playing himself. It was thought that the task would be too much for 'Red', but he came out on top, producing the most successful eleven that had ever represented Notre Dame until that time."

After Salmon's graduation in 1903, he became the full-time coach. But he had a mediocre 5-3 season in 1904 because of a lack of talent and the frequency of injuries. Of his excellent team of the year before, Salmon had lost the entire backfield, both tackles, one end, and one guard. And to make matters worse, only 16 of his squad of 25 in 1904 were eligible by their classes to play.

By 1905 Notre Dame had a new coach in Henry J. McGlew, who had been Salmon's teammate from 1900 to 1903.

Former player Red Salmon (second row, far right) took over as coach of Notre Dame for the 1904 season.

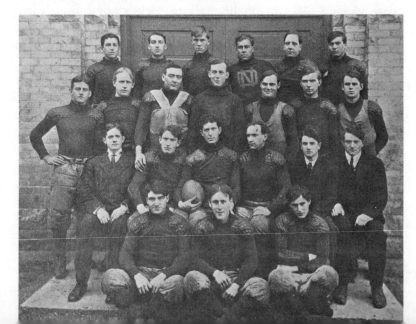

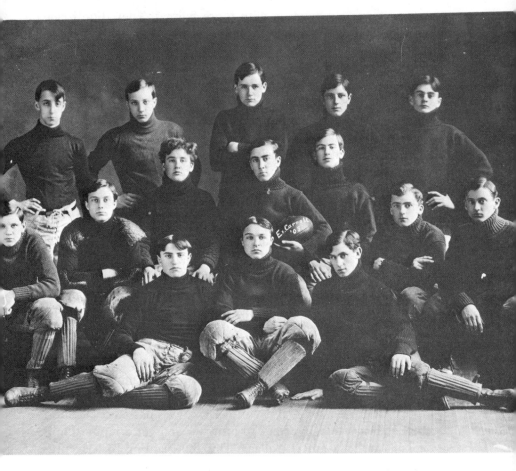

The 1905 team hoped to join the Western Conference but was passed over and told in effect to grow up and get a reputation.

McGlew fared no better than his predecessor, but he did produce Notre Dame's biggest game point total in history—an embarrassing 142-0 victory over American Medical. After a 25-minute first half, during which the Fighting Irish took a 121-0 lead, the second half was shortened to only eight minutes. This allowed the American Medical team time to eat before catching a train for Chicago. The score would have been even more ridiculous if Notre Dame had a good extra-point kicker. The Fighting Irish scored 27 touchdowns but missed 20 extra points.

Dominic Callicrate, who played in that historic game for Notre Dame, recalls: "Well, they were medical men and of course it was a recreation with those fellows. They didn't care whether we ran up 150 or 300 points. They were all good sports and they liked the game just to play it."

Callicrate, a lively 90-year-old who lives in Portland, Oregon, was a bright star on the Notre Dame horizon in those years. "He was a halfback, especially notable for his open field running," says Chet Grant, the Notre Dame historian and one-time football player. "He was brilliant. He captained the 1907 team. I had a chance to visit with him at a reunion a number of years ago. He's a handsome man with a dry and yet lively wit."

Callicrate followed Salmon as the Notre Dame hero in the early 1900s. He remembers Salmon as "a bearcat. . .a very tough, hard-running back. . . very hard. . .a champion." He remembers himself as a runner who never ran out of gas. "I'll say this. My best work was running. I had a lot of wind. I mean a lot. I used to run quite a bit. In other words, I didn't smoke, and I didn't burn myself out before I got into the game. I had good wind, and I could navigate at a pretty good rate. Off-tackle was my specialty, but I could mix it up."

The era in which Callicrate played, 1905 through 1907, marked a significant point in time, both for Notre Dame and for football. The Fighting Irish hunted for bigger game and hoped to join the distinguished Western Conference when Michigan dropped out in 1905. "But Notre Dame was passed over as too small and was told in effect to grow up and get a reputation," explains writer Francis Wallace. This the Fighting Irish eventually did, taking some hard knocks along the way. Also during Callicrate's time at Notre Dame, football underwent startling rules changes. The most significant was the legalization of the forward pass. "Before that," Callicrate remembers, "quite often they'd take the fullback by the seat of the pants and the back of the neck and throw him over the line with the ball." Callicrate notes that after the forward pass was legalized, of course Notre Dame made good use of it. The Fighting Irish threw the ball instead of the player.

"Notre Dame began using the pass immediately," Arch Ward points out in his book, *Frank Leahy and the Fighting Irish*. "At first it was either a shovel toss or an end-over-end one. Regardless of where the spiral pass originated elsewhere, the season of 1907 saw the Notre Dame backs getting the idea of using it from watching a substitute center who was practicing passing the ball back spirally. By the time the 1908 season

32

rolled around, the spiral, as used for forward passes, was fully developed. Notre Dame's fullback, Robert E. (Pete) Vaughan, for many years Wabash College's coach, became especially adept and could throw a 50-yard pass like a baseball. Red Miller developed accuracy with a low pass at 40 yards, and Don Hamilton, quarterback of those years, was one of the best short passers in the Middle West, even though his fingers were too small to grasp the ball and he had to throw it while it lay loosely in his upraised palm."

The new rules opened up the game and sparked enthusiasm both on the field and in the stands, recalls Callicrate. "There was a lot of spirit. . .much enthusiasm." The game was no less rough than before, however. "Good night, we were tough. In other words, if we didn't play the full game, we weren't a good player. You had to go through the full game if you wanted to get any spirit."

Callicrate played for two coaches, Henry McGlew in 1905 and Thomas Barry in 1906 and 1907. Barry was the more successful of the two, losing only one game in his two years. "Barry was a good coach. . .very good," says Callicrate, "and a very fine man." McGlew was apparently not as polished as Harvard graduate Barry. "McGlew was a real rough and tumble guy," notes Callicrate.

An insight into Barry's character is supplied by John Weibler, writing in the *Notre Dame Alumnus*:

"(The season of) 1906 introduced a stranger to the West, but a man who became a very successful coach at Notre Dame, Thomas Barry. Barry was graduated from Harvard in June of 1906. Previous to this he had taken a college course at Brown, where he played football for four years. In 1902 he was chosen as the All-American halfback. The material that Barry had to deal with in 1906 was green, but he so whipped it into shape that it finished second in the Indiana Championship competition. Barry had a good system of coaching. He believed in leading his men, never in pushing them, and in giving every man a fair trial, playing no favorites. He showed a great deal of reserve power but it never became necessary for him to call upon this. A proof of Barry's football knowledge came forward in 1907. The material was terrible and things looked mighty gloomy. He knew his men, however, and so in the middle of the season, he took (Red) Miller, a man who

33

played nothing but the backfield, and placed him at center. At the end of the season, Miller was picked by nearly every critic as the All-Indiana center. Also in 1907, the team was tied for the championship honors."

It was this same Red Miller who started a family dynasty at Notre Dame. After his seasons in the sun from 1906 through 1909, he was followed by four other brothers who played football at Notre Dame—one of the obscure "records" in school history. Red Miller's brother Ray was a substitute end behind the fabled Knute Rockne on the 1913 team. Walter, third of the Miller brothers, played fullback with the marvelous teams of 1919 and 1920. And from 1922 through 1924, Notre Dame rosters listed two more Millers—Gerald and Don. Gerald was injured early in his career and served mostly as an understudy at right halfback. Don, of course, was a member of that legendary quartet, The Four Horsemen.

The success of eastern football in the early 1900s no doubt encouraged Notre Dame to bring in Easterners as coaches. Barry was an obvious example. And after he left, Notre Dame authorities reached out to the East again to get Victor Place, formerly of Dartmouth. Place guided Notre Dame to an 8-1 record in 1908, and the Fighting Irish proved that they could hold their own with some of the country's best teams. The only loss that season was a 12-6 decision to powerful Michigan, and the Fight-

The 1909 team, directed by Shorty Longman (first row, left), played to the tune of the Notre Dame Victory March.

ing Irish continued to beat traditional opponents like Indiana and Wabash. Marquette appeared on the schedule for the first time. One year later, when Frank Longman took over for Place, Notre Dame added Pittsburgh and Miami of Ohio to the list of new opponents. Not incidentally, the Fighting Irish beat both in 1909 and also scored a startling 11-3 victory over Michigan, their first in history over the mighty Wolverines. This conquest over the famous "Point-a-Minute" team ranked undefeated Notre Dame as champion of the West but also led to one of the most storied feuds in college football history.

After the victory, probably Notre Dame's most significant at that point in history, Michigan coach Fielding Yost raised some questions about the eligibility of several Notre Dame players. A controversy flared for some time and was aired in the national press, but Notre Dame was eventually given a clean bill of health by the journalistic society. The Fighting Irish later appeared to be officially exonerated when Michigan signed a contract for a return match in 1910. However, 24 hours before the game was to be played—in fact, while the Notre Dame team was en route to Ann Arbor—the Wolverines canceled it. Michigan was subjected to severe criticism in the press after that, but Yost shrugged it off with the comment that the contest with Notre Dame would have been no more than a "practice game." And, Michigan authorities said, "it was to have been dropped anyhow."

George Philbrook and Ralph Dimmick were the Notre Dame players who started all the fuss. But if they had had college football experience before coming to Notre Dame, as Yost claimed, then Michigan was not above reproach, either. It was well known that some of Yost's players had played three years of football at other schools before joining the Wolverines.

This event created bitter feelings between the midwestern neighbors. Once on the friendliest of terms, Michigan and Notre Dame broke off athletic relations for more than 30 years, and it was not before 1942 that they played football again. They met once more in 1943. Many believe that the feud with Yost also resulted in blackballing Notre Dame from the Big Ten (then the Western Conference). Notes one writer: "The Conference, without taking formal action, agreed back in 1910 that life would be simpler, on and off the field, without the pushy Irish." Yost, of course, was a patriarchal figure in the conference and greatly influenced many of its decisions.

35

That Yost had a healthy fear of Notre Dame's emerging football strength and wished to shut out the Fighting Irish in the Midwest was no secret. His feelings were well founded, for Notre Dame had become a palpable force in the region. The Fighting Irish had lost only two games over four seasons, and the undefeated 1909 team reflected their growing power. Notre Dame, still known in the press as "Notre Dame, Indiana," and "the Catholics," won seven straight games and finished the season with a scoreless tie against Marquette. Only two of their opponents scored on the Fighting Irish and they held a cumulative point advantage of 236-14 against the opposition. Notre Dame drew national attention from the grand victory over Michigan. Typical of the applause in the press was this comment in the *Chicago Inter-Ocean* on November 7, 1909:

"Michigan was the stepladder by which Notre Dame today mounted the dizziest heights in its football history, the Catholics downing the Wolverines by a score of 11 to 3. The game by which Notre Dame won its right to claim to have one of the best elevens in the country was won by its team by hard, fast, clean play. Luck had nothing to do with either of the two touchdowns which Notre Dame made."

The Notre Dame lineup that day carried the team through the year and included: fullback Robert E. (Pete) Vaughan; halfbacks Billy Ryan and Harry "Red" Miller; quarterback Donald M. Hamilton; ends Joseph Collins, James Maloney, and Robert L. Mathews; tackles Ralph Dimmick and Howard Edwards; guards Samuel M. Dolan and George Philbrook; and center Edwin J. Lynch. Miller and Dolan were towers of strength for Notre Dame not only in the 1909 season, but in a significant four-year period starting in 1906. During that time the Fighting Irish compiled a record of 27-2-2—outscoring opponents 806-66—and created great impact on the midwestern football world.

Assessing these extraordinary talents, one writer in a 1935 article singled out Dolan and Miller for the Notre Dame success in this period: "Dolan played for four years at Notre Dame in a guard position and still holds the record for the Irish's most durable performer at that or any other position. In those four years he played every minute of every game, never was hurt and was one of the team's greatest stars. 'Red' Miller was left halfback and is still ranked by many Notre Dame veterans as the greatest all-around halfback ever to wear the Blue and Gold, including the immortal George Gipp."

If these players needed spiritual uplifting, they had some of the best background music in the world. The "Notre Dame Victory March," probably the most famous of all college fight songs, was composed by a brother team, Michael and John Shea, in 1909. The two had traveled to Indianapolis and Ann Arbor during the 1908 football season to see Notre Dame's games with Indiana and Michigan but were disappointed because the Fighting Irish lacked an original fight song. A few days later on a piano at Sorin Hall, Mike played a "tune that had been running through my head," and John wrote the lyrics to it overnight. The next day they returned to Sorin Hall to test their work on the piano but found the place too noisy. They instead retired to the Sacred Heart Church, the student church at Notre Dame, and there for the first time sang the "Victory March" to the strains of an organ:

"Cheer, cheer, for old Notre Dame,
"Wake up the echoes cheering her name,
"Send a volley cheer on high,
"Shake down the thunder from the sky.
"What though the odds be great or small?
"Old Notre Dame will win over all,
"While her loyal sons are marching
"Onward to victory."

A Boy's Education

When he first saw it, the Notre Dame campus held terror for Knute Rockne. "I felt the strangeness of being a lone Norse Protestant invader of a Catholic stronghold," he remembered.

His adjustment to college life came as soon as he was installed in the Brownson Dormitory, one of six student halls on campus in 1910, and someone handed him a football.

"There were 400 undergraduates, physical training was compulsory, and a fellow wasn't thought much of unless he went out to try and make his hall team for football," Rockne said.

Rockne did more than that—he made the Notre Dame varsity. His period of adjustment and his trials as a player paint an invaluable and interesting picture of the Fighting Irish from 1910 through 1912.

In 1910 Frank "Shorty" Longman, an end on Michigan's famous "Point-a-Minute" team, was the Notre Dame coach—the first college coach that Rockne ever knew. And Rockne remembered him as "a snappy, belligerent figure" who effected a shock of hair after an actor of the day whose last name was McCullough.

"Freshmen were played in those days," Rockne recalled, "and with a small enrollment, we needed them. Longman sent me out with the scrubs in a test game with the regulars. He made me fullback. They should have changed my position to drawback. Never on any football field was there so dismal a flop. Trying to spear my first punt I had frozen fingers and the ball rolled everywhere it wasn't wanted. Longman kept me in that agonizing game. Finally, I tried a punt. Nothing happened.

As soon as he could play football, Knute Rockne found the adjustment to college life easy.

I might have been a statue of a player trying to punt. Nothing was coordinated. I was half paralyzed. A 200-pound tackle smashed into me. My 145 pounds went back for a 15-yard loss. Longman yanked me out of the scrubs and sent me back to Brownson Hall. I was a washout, not even good enough for the scrubs."

But if Rockne appeared to be all thumbs in his freshman year, he could still run with as much dynamism as anyone. This quality earned him a berth on the varsity track team and eventually another crack at football. Meanwhile Rockne was getting an education that could not be found in books. He found it enlightening—and shocking.

"I had sat at the feet of a learned tramp athlete whose name then was Foley, although he had played for many schools under many aliases. He was typical of young men who roamed the country, overflowing with college spirit, regardless of the college. His tongue teemed with professional jargon. He opened my eyes to a state of affairs in college football which has since been reformed—of the journeymen players who'd leave new names behind them wherever they went and live to a ripe, old age, from foot to mouth, so to speak, taking loyalty and sometimes talent with them to whichever Alma Mater would give them the best break."

Notre Dame's opponents in those days were far from simon-pure, Rockne found out.

"We played teams whose purity of enrollment was not quite 99 per cent. The Indian schools were careless in that respect, several Indian players changing legal names to Indian names as they switched from one Indian school to another. The famous back, Emil Hauser of Haskell, became Chief Waseka at Carlisle; another lad I knew named Dietz blossomed into Chief Long Star."

Rockne's initial reaction to Longman was one of awe. But this waned with time, owing to the coach's propensity to talk too much. Rockne pointed out, "Longman knew much about football, but he talked much more. His method was that of the old-fashioned oratorical coach. Before a game he would enter the dressing room dramatically, toss back his shock of hair and burst into rhetoric. One oration a season is quite enough for any football squad. Action brings reaction, and if the coach talks too much, his words lose weight."

Rockne remembered the first time he heard Longman

speak. This was before Rockne's first game.

Exploding into the room, Longman exclaimed: "Boys, today is the day. The honor of the old school is at stake. Now or never, we must fight the battle of our lives. I don't want any man with a streak of yellow to move from this room. You've all got to be heroes—HEROES, or I never want to see you again. Go out and conquer. It's the crisis of your lives."

It moved the younger players. The veterans could hardly stay awake.

"The team went out and all but pushed the opposing team—Olivet—over the fence," Rockne remembered.

The next Saturday, as the Fighting Irish lay resting in the dressing room, Coach Longman entered again with a burst.

"Boys," he announced. "Today is the day of days. The honor of the old school is at stake. The eyes of the world are on you. Go out and bleed for the old school, and if anybody has a yellow streak in him. . . ."

"By this time I was awe-stricken," said Rockne. "Then I saw (Gus) Dorais and (Dutch) Bergman, two veterans, yawn."

"What do you think of the act today?" asked Bergman.

"Not so good," Dorais answered. "I thought he was better last week."

John Marks, the Dartmouth back, was Notre Dame's next coach. He stayed for two years, 1911 and 1912. "He made us over from a green, aggressive squad into a slashing, driving outfit," Rockne said. "Marks was always a quiet mentor but he liked to pile up scores."

There was one time, however, when Marks showed some mercy on the enemy, and Rockne recalled a humorous story attached to it.

"Once we led Adrian by 81-0, and the Adrian coach said he'd used up all his substitutes and would we agree to let him send men back who had already played. Marks agreed. He returned to the sidelines. Some time later he saw a strange player on our bench.

"'You're on the wrong bench,' Marks said.

"'I know it,' said the lad. 'I've been in that scrap four times already, and they're not going to send me back if I can help it. I've had enough.'"

Under Marks, Notre Dame went through two prosperous seasons without a loss. The Fighting Irish were tied twice in 14 games and outscored their opponents by a composite total of

61-1 to 36. The team was high on accomplishment, and Rockne was floating on individual achievement.

"The team stepped out under Marks' leadership so that gradually we came to be noticed a little beyond the midwest. I won a regular berth as end under Marks, and had the pleasant surprise of seeing myself discussed as an All-America possibility toward the end of the 1912 season. Almost imperceptibly, it seemed to me, I was established in football. One year, practically abandoning the idea of continuing the game; the next, being talked of—never mind by whom—as an All-America prospect."

Another All-American prospect discussed that year at Notre Dame was Gus Dorais, a quarterback of several dimensions. Dorais will always be remembered as the player who established passing as an effective football weapon, but his talents extended equally to running and kicking.

"Dorais was a tremendous football player," said Fred Gushurst, a teammate who caught many of his passes. "He was the finest quarterback that ever stepped on a football field. He not only developed the forward pass, but he was as good an open field runner as football ever had and he could punt with the best."

Mal Elward, another of Dorais' teammates, remembered that he was "a great triple threat man and ran and passed a lot from punt formation. He was also one of the best drop kickers of all time and an excellent punter."

The combination of Dorais-to-Rockne would later demonstrate the effectiveness of air power in football, but the quarterback at first had to convince his coach that he could throw the ball at all. Dorais was a baseball pitcher, and when he went out for football at Notre Dame and began throwing the ball, he instinctively grasped it at the end, much like holding a baseball; he threw the football overhand with the same motion that he used to throw a baseball. In 1910 there were two accepted methods of throwing the forward pass. One was to lay the ball flat and sail it with an underhand motion, giving it a spin; the other was to hook the hand over the end of the ball and give it a discus hurl through the air, wobbling it endwise.

When Dorais turned out for football in his freshman year in 1910, it was the custom of the players to warm up for practice by kicking the ball back and forth. But Dorais was the exception to the rule. He threw the ball instead, and this caught

42

the attention of Coach Shorty Longman. The coach approached Dorais and tried to give him some advice:

"You throw the ball pretty well, but you don't hold it

One of Jesse Harper's prize players, Mal Elward.

right. You'd never be able to handle a wet ball like that. It'll slip out of your hand."

But the cocky Dorais thought that Longman was wrong.

"Sure I can," Dorais insisted. "Soak one in the water bucket, and I'll show you."

The ball was soaked in water, and Dorais made good on his claim. It was this confidence that made him an exquisite field leader. Rockne agreed. "Without his encouragement and execution, I would never have been able to carry out the forward pass idea." Rockne had great admiration for Dorais, perhaps because the two players were very much alike in style and temperament. "Like myself," Rockne explained, "Gus had to fight for everything he got. Neither of us was very big, and the fellow with the small build has to be so much more clever to hold his own against the bigger boys. He has to know all the tricks. He can't depend on brute strength, but must be foxy and a will-o'-the-wisp. And after a while these mental manuevers become second nature to him."

While Dorais' superb passing exhibition in the Army game of 1913 made him a universal figure and Notre Dame a national team, there were other golden days for the five-foot-seven, 145-pound quarterback. Like the time he set a Notre Dame record for field goals. Dorais, as good a storyteller as he was a quarterback, remembered it as an "accident":

"In the books you'll find that I kicked five field goals in one game (actually the Notre Dame football guide says that Dorais tried seven field goals and made three). That more or less was an accident and I'll tell you why.

"We were in Austin, Texas, to play the University of Texas and found that the game was to be played on a field devoid of grass. It was dusty and the alkali almost choked you. We went to work and piled up a commanding lead. The fellows were all complaining about burned throats and claimed they could hardly breathe. Finally, Texas punted to us and I launched another drive, using running plays that saw much of the dust kicked up.

"I called (Ray) Eichenlaub's signal and he yelled 'check,' meaning that he didn't want to carry the ball. I called (Joe) Pliska's number and he yelled 'check.' (Charles) Finegan, our other halfback, did the same thing. Fortunately, we had an end-around play for special occasions so I called Rock's number and he went for 12 yards. Then I called Gushurst around the other end and he made a nice gain. But when I tried to repeat Rockne and Gushurst, both hollered 'check' and I had nobody to carry the ball.

"In desperation, I called the team back into a huddle. 'Whatinhell is the matter?' I asked. 'None of you fellows want to carry the ball.'

"'The alkali is killing us,' they answered. 'Why don't you kick it?'

"That's what I did, and I did it four more times before the game was over. It's a record in the books and it was made only because I was the quarterback who couldn't get anyone to carry the ball."

Dorais and Rockne worked together and roomed together through 1911 and 1912, and it was this experience that helped them establish a rapport for the 1913 season, one of the most historic at Notre Dame. Ironically, Rockne almost quit school after 1912 because of family difficulties and was talked into going back. Otherwise, the course of Notre Dame football history certainly would have been changed.

"The end of my football and college career impended," thought Rockne after his father died. "It seemed imperative that I quit school, although it's on the record that I passed my special subject, chemistry, cum laude."

A wise sister interceded, however.

"If you quit," she told Rockne, "all right. You may earn a living, but it will be as a mail dispatcher."

Rockne did not have to think too long about that.

"So I went back and I had hardly got off the train at South Bend that autumn when I was greeted by a cordial voice."

It was the voice of Jesse Harper, the new Notre Dame football coach.

"You're Rockne?" Harper asked.

"Yes."

"Well, I'm grabbing you football men off the trains as fast as I can. We've got to work our head and legs off."

"What's the excitement?"

"They're letting us play in the East," Harper told Rockne. "The Army has agreed to play Notre Dame."

Air Power

"That summer of 1913 at Cedar Point, Rock and I practiced more than we had ever practiced before. Rock perfected his method of catching passes without tenseness in his fingers, wrists or arms, and with the hands giving with the ball, just as a baseball should be caught."—Gus Dorais.

The Army football team needed an easy game on the schedule in 1913, and Notre Dame was supposed to be the sacrificial lamb. But the lamb turned into a tiger that bleak, chilly, November day and not only shocked the Cadets but the entire football world. Harnessing air power, the likes of which had never before been seen in the East, the Fighting Irish overcame Army's bulk and reputation and handed the Cadets a sound beating, 35-13. It was probably the most significant victory in the history of Notre Dame football.

Heretofore unacclaimed outside of the Midwest, Notre Dame by virtue of its stunning victory over Army became recognized universally. The Army game was the starting point toward a national schedule and a predestined meeting with fate.

Ironically, the Big Ten Conference had done Notre Dame a favor a few years before when it blackballed the Fighting Irish. Shut off from natural rivalries like Michigan, Michigan State, Indiana, and Purdue, Notre Dame faced a critical decision—should it play smaller schools in the Midwest or look for bigger game elsewhere? Jesse Harper answered that question for the Fighting Irish when he took over as coach of Notre Dame football in the 1913 season. Harper's first year brought a national schedule to Notre Dame, flavored with such teams as Army,

Penn State, and Texas. "I was just looking for games," he said, "so I sat down and wrote a few letters."

Harper knew it was going to be a tough year, so before his players went away for their summer vacation, he gave a football to his quarterback Gus Dorais and end Knute Rockne and told them to throw it around in their leisure time. It turned out to be the best bit of strategy that Harper employed all year. Dorais and Rockne practiced the forward pass all summer at a beach resort in Cedar Point, Ohio.

"Perfection of the forward pass came to us only through daily, tedious practice," Rockne once said. "I'd run along the beach, Dorais would throw from all angles. People who didn't know we were two college seniors making painstaking preparations for our final season probably thought we were crazy. Once a bearded old gentleman took off his shoes to get in the fun, seizing the ball and kicking it merrily, with bare feet, too, until

Coach Jesse Harper (last row, far right) and captain Knute Rockne (second row, center) sprang the forward pass on unsuspecting Army in 1913 and started a football revolution.

a friendly keeper came along to take him back where he belonged."

Dorais invented a better way to throw the ball that summer, and Rockne developed a better way to catch it. "Rockne continued to develop his deceptive, stop-and-go style of going down the field for a pass, a style used by nearly all good pass receivers," Dorais said. "I worked hard to increase the accuracy and length of my passes. A rule change that would become effective that fall had removed all restrictions on the length of a legal forward pass."

Some of the stratagems developed by Dorais and Rockne that summer turned out to be quite helpful in the fall. Recalls a writer: "Not fast enough to outrun his opponents for scores, Rockne hit upon an idea for getting by that defense. For example, he would go down on a pass, and slip and fall flat on his face; then when the defensive player had counted him out of the picture, he would jump up and go for his pass. This was one of the earliest variations of the so-called 'button-hook' play. Rockne was also one of the first to develop the system of ends running in lanes. All of these tricks of the trade were tried out and perfected by Rockne and Dorais that summer."

The result of the summer's work was evidenced in the fall when Notre Dame utilized its powerful, new air weapon to pile up 169 points against 7 on its first three opponents. Although the Fighting Irish were not known in the East, it was obvious that they would not be a soft touch for Army. In the three years prior to 1913, Notre Dame had lost only one game. And Rockne and Dorais had played on two straight undefeated teams under John L. Marks, the coach before Harper. A football guide in 1912 had rated Notre Dame even with Wisconsin, the Big Ten champions. Still, powerful Army appeared to consider the Notre Dame game as a mere workout for its forces.

The mood in the Army camp was reflected by Willet J. Baird, who later became a high-ranking officer but at the time was the team mascot. "I was in the Cadet locker room on a Thursday afternoon following practice when I first heard of the Indiana institution called Notre Dame," said Baird. "The players, as usual, were asking questions about this Indiana team and no one present seemed to know a great deal about it. Everyone, however, was convinced that Saturday would bring a 'breather' and, while Notre Dame was unofficially reported to have a squad of big men, no great amount of trouble was expected. (Actually, this 'unofficial' report was wrong. Notre Dame's squad, far smaller than Army's, was outweighed 15 pounds to the man.) Johnny McEwan, a westerner from Minnesota, playing his first year with the Military Academy, seemed to be the only one who predicted a rather tough contest. McEwan told the players that as far as he was concerned Notre Dame would be plenty hard to stop, but he himself never expected that which actually happened the following Saturday."

Rockne, who later became Notre Dame's most famous athletic figure and perhaps the best-known name in college football lore, was just one of the troops that day when the Fighting Irish embarked on a tiresome journey for West Point. The great Rock once recalled for posterity: "The morning we left for West Point the entire student body of the university got up long before breakfast to see us to the day coach that carried the squad to Buffalo—a dreary, all-day trip. From Buffalo we enjoyed the luxury of sleeping-car accommodations—regulars in lowers, substitutes in uppers. There was no pampering in those days. We wanted none of it."

Notre Dame got $1,000 expenses from Army to transport a crew of 18 players and one coach. But apparently it was not enough to ship them in style. The team was only able to round up 14 pairs of cleats. Most of the players had dual-purpose shoes and stuck the cleats on them if they were required to play. In keeping with the spartan mood, the players all had sandwiches for their meals. These were packed by the school refectory. Each man carried his own equipment, too.

"We were permitted few luxuries on this trip from Indiana," Harper said. "The boys carried their uniforms in satchels—some wearing their jerseys under their coats to conserve space. Our only extra equipment was a roll of tape, a jug of liniment and a bottle of iodine. To cut expenses, we traveled by coach as far as Buffalo before changing to sleepers."

Baird, the wide-eyed Army mascot, was on the train platform when the Fighting Irish arrived. Like others, he had come out of curiosity to see what a midwestern football team looked like.

"They presented the usual appearance of a small college team which considered itself lucky to have so many players. They were a sterling group of men, dressed as the college men of the day—few wearing hats and some dressed

49

in sweaters of various shades, practically all carried a suit-case in which was contained articles of playing equipment. They had a small trunk with some equipment and the men seemed to carry the rest. They came without the usual large trunks of baggage which were carried in those days by many leading eastern teams. They were more impressed at having arrived at West Point and more concerned with the appearance of the academy than they were with the game that would take place.

"Jesse Harper was their guiding light and all arrangements were left to him. The players themselves were particularly concerned with the size of the institution, the buildings of the academy, and, above all, could not wait to take a look at the football field. Most of the players visiting the playing field expressed no end of amazement and joy over the fact that the field itself was very smooth, well marked, and resembled the appearance of a well-kept lawn. This to them was most remarkable. I remember being asked by many of the players, who were in the process of dressing before the game, if they could obtain some ankle wraps, knee guards, supporters, extra shoe strings, several pairs of shoes and two extra pairs of football pants. A man by the name of Blanchard, who was the storekeeper at that time, was able to supply them with everything needed and his kindness was most appreciated."

Before the game Rockne, the Notre Dame captain, was busy attending to last-minute details. Remembered Baird:

"It was in the dressing room that I first became acquainted with Knute Rockne. After bringing several articles of equipment to other players, Rock asked me if I could obtain some adhesive tape and handed me a dime in order to purchase it. I told Rock that the dime was not necessary; that he could have all he wanted, and proceeded to get him a large roll which was readily used not only by Rock but by a group of players nearby. After giving Rock the adhesive tape, I asked him if there was anything else; he replied, 'You may get a few extra pads for (Ray) Eichenlaub, he'll need them.' When I saw Eichenlaub, Rock's remark registered."

Then the Notre Dame players came out onto Cullum Hall Field for that historic game on November 1. A crowd of about 3,000, who got in free, had filled the bleachers.

"As they walked onto the field they presented a rather unusual sight," recalled Baird. "A small group varying in stature, impressed with the idea that they were going to play a football game which would last for four quarters. What the result of this game would be did not seem to concern them. Jesse Harper's chief worry seemed to be the football that was going to be used. The number of footballs that Jesse brought along from Notre Dame and their appearance would certainly not make a hit with the team of today. And when Jesse saw the football used at the academy he was bothered no end. After playing the game, Jesse could stand it no longer and requested that the Army show him and some of the Notre Dame boys how to lace a football; for, as Jesse said, they could not do a good job of this at Notre Dame."

The team captains—Benny Hoge of Army and Rockne—shook hands at midfield. The referee flipped the coin, and Notre Dame won the toss, electing to receive. The ball was set up on a mud tee on the Army 40 yard line, and McEwan signaled to the referees that he was ready to kick off.

The opening series of plays appeared to portend trouble for Notre Dame as Dorais fumbled and Army recovered on the Fighting Irish 27 yard line. But the Cadets' high-scoring team was unable to punch out more than a yard on three tries and got an idea of what they were in for that afternoon. The rest of the day belonged to the Fighting Irish after they started throwing passes. Rockne reflected on the euphorious moment in Notre Dame history:

"After we had stood terrific pounding by the Army line, and a trio of backs that charged in like locomotives, we held them on downs. Dorais, in a huddle said, 'Let's open up.' It was amusing to see the Army boys huddle after a first, snappy 11-yard pass had been completed for a first down. Their guards and tackles went tumbling into us to stop line bucks and plunges. Instead, Dorias stepped neatly back and flicked the ball to an uncovered end or halfback. This we did twice in a march up the field, gaining three first downs in almost as many minutes.

"Our attack had been well rehearsed. After one fierce scrimmage I emerged limping as if hurt. On the next three plays Dorais threw three successful passes in a row to (Joe) Pliska, our right halfback, for short gains. On each of these three plays I limped down the field acting as if the farthest

51

thing from my mind was to receive a forward pass. After the third play the Army halfback covering me figured I wasn't worth watching. Even as a decoy he figured I was harmless. Finally Dorais called my number, meaning that he was to throw a long forward pass to me as I ran down the field and out toward the sidelines. I started limping down the field, and the Army halfback covering me almost yawned in my face, he was that bored.

"Suddenly, I put on full speed and left him standing there flat-footed. I raced across the Army goal line as Dorais whipped the ball and the grandstands roared at the completion of the 40-yard pass. Everybody seemed astonished. There had been no hurdling, no tackling, no plunging, no crushing of fiber and sinew. Just a long distance touchdown by rapid transit. At the moment when I touched the ball, life for me was complete. We proceeded to make it more than complete."

For a while the Army resisted. The Cadets, though bewildered by Notre Dame's revolutionary passing game, managed to stay within a point at the half, 14-13. Despite the closeness of the game in the first half, the Fighting Irish appeared free of tension. Rockne at one point even went so far as to joke with the serious Cadets. After Army's Lou Merillat shouted, "Let's lick these Hoosiers!" Rockne took time out to pull his leg.

"I asked him, in a lull, if he knew how the word Hoosier originated," Rockne said. "'We started it at South Bend,' I informed him, John Markoe and what others of the Army team would listen. 'After every game the coach goes over the field, picks up what he finds and asks his team: "Whose ear is there?" Hence, Hoosier.' The gag didn't work so well."

The Notre Dame offense worked better. In the second half Army attempted to adjust to Notre Dame's passing game by sending its defenders wide. But Dorais cleverly took care of this Army maneuver by shooting Eichenlaub, his bruising, 215-pound fullback, inside for a pair of touchdowns. When Army closed in to stop Notre Dame's running game in the last period, Dorais went to the air again. Ends and halfbacks were always at the end of the quarterback's passes—Dorais to Rockne, Dorais to Pliska, Dorais to Fred Gushurst, Dorais to Charles Finegan. The Cadets were completely baffled, entirely helpless.

"The feature of the game that most amazed the sports fans

in the East was the length of Dorais' passes," pointed out Jim Beach and Daniel Moore in their book, *Army vs. Notre Dame, The Big Game.* "Some of the spiral throws traveled 35 to 40 yards to the receiver, an unheard-of distance in those days."

Dorais also threw an unheard-of volume of passes in those days—17. He completed 14 and compiled 243 yards through the air in the process. The accomplishment not only brought notice to Notre Dame but to the passing game in football. Bill Roper, the former head coach at Princeton who was one of the officials at the game, said that he knew such play was possible under the new existing rules but that he had never seen the forward pass developed to such a state of perfection. Football men and the eastern press marveled at such a concept. "The Westerners flashed the most sensational football ever seen in the East," the *New York Times* reported the next day. Actually, the forward pass had been used since 1906, when it was legalized under revolutionary, new football rules. Notre Dame was not its inventor but rather its vehicle toward national attention.

"The press and football public hailed this new game, and Notre Dame received credit as the originator of a style of play that we had simply systematized," remarked Rockne.

Along with Rockne at left end, Dorais at quarterback, and Eichenlaub at fullback, the rest of the Notre Dame team from that day is worth remembering: right half, Charles Finegan; left half, Joe Pliska; right end, Fred Gushurst; right tackle, Ralph Lathrop; right guard, Freeman Fitzgerald; center, Al Feeney; left guard, Emmett Keefe; and left tackle, Keith Jones.

Harper used only one substitute that day, but only because of a freak accident. When Finegan broke his shoelace in the last few minutes, Harper ordered Art "Bunny" Larkin to take off his shoes and give them to Finegan. But Larkin refused. He had decided that he had not come nearly 1,000 miles merely to sit on the bench. So Harper had no choice but to put Larkin into the game at right halfback. On the Army bench sat a substitute who never did get into the game—none other than Dwight Eisenhower, who was to become the 34th president of the United States. While Eisenhower sat on the bench, Army coach Charley Daly paced in front of it. "Daly paraded up and down the sidelines nervously as he watched the depressing spectacle," said a newspaper. But Daly learned from it. Later in the year Army used the forward pass almost exclusively while winning its big game from Navy, 22-9.

There is some misconception that Harper and his players stayed over at West Point for several days to give Army's team pointers on use of the forward pass. This never happened according to Rockne: "Hell, no. We were out of there the same night. South Bend would have barred us for life if we hadn't hustled home right away. We were heroes—and they wanted us to know it."

What a heroes' welcome awaited the Fighting Irish in South Bend! Remembered Dorais:

"When we got out of our day coach at the South Bend railroad station, we found most of the town waiting for us. There was a parade with several bands and plenty of red fire, and, of course, captain Knute Rockne was called on for a speech. He made one, but he was so nervous and embarrassed that he twisted most of the buttons off his coat while he was doing it; and no one in the audience could understand a word of what he said. . ."

That particular welcome home was one of Rockne's fondest memories, even if he was a bit nervous. Writes Arch Ward in his book, *Frank Leahy and the Fighting Irish*: "The entire populace of South Bend turned out to greet the boys who had upheld Western football against the East. There were brass bands and a torchlight parade and speeches. The players themselves had the most enjoyable trip of their lives." An incident before their arrival in South Bend put the giddy Notre Dame players in an even giddier mood. "Upon alighting from their Pullman in Buffalo on the return ride, they were greeted by a railroad agent who asked them if they were the football team. Upon discovering that they were, he told them breakfast was ready in the station. As they boarded their day coach for South Bend they noticed another husky bunch of young men singing the blues about the breakfast they did not eat. It turned out they were the Syracuse University eleven, who had just come from a 43 to 7 trouncing at the hands of Michigan. The bountiful repast which Notre Dame's boys had devoured had been intended for Syracuse."

The 1913 season marked an important transitional period in Notre Dame football. The forward pass was not the only new thing to come to South Bend. Perhaps of equal note was the evolution of the famed Notre Dame Shift, a backfield formation that started with Coach John Marks in 1911 and 1912, continued with Jesse Harper, and was eventually refined to sublime perfection by Rockne when he took over in 1918. Dorais prospered with the dramatic change in Fighting Irish style.

"In 1910," he said, "Shorty Longman of Michigan was my first coach, and we used a T Formation (with the quarterback, about a yard back of center, getting the ball on a toss from center) and a good deal of tackle-around-tackle offensive plays. Our T was devised more as a power attack than the deceptive, brush-blocking attack of today. In 1911 Jack Marks of Dartmouth became our coach. He played at Dartmouth under Major Frank Cavanaugh and he changed our formation to a box (right or left), and to my mind that was the beginning of the Notre Dame style—and it came from Dartmouth. Jesse Harper of Chicago was coach (in 1913) and under (Amos Alonzo) Stagg he had been taught a shifting style of offense. So he put the shift on from the T to the box either way, and as there was no rule on stopping after the shift, we went to town in good shape. Later Rockne incorporated the ends shifting in unison with the backs, and that was it."

And so it had begun. Notre Dame's impact was starting to be visibly felt on the football world. Before 1913 teams like St. Viator, Adrian, and Morris Harvey filled the Notre Dame schedule. But by 1914 Notre Dame had graduated to a whole, new level. The little college from Indiana was now taking on the likes of Syracuse, Carlisle, Army, and Yale—and enjoying every minute of it.

Cattle, Oil Wells, And Football

"Dad never knocked another man. He always believed one thing and that was, never say anything about a man unless you can say something good. And his whole religion was geared around the Golden Rule."—James Harper, son of Notre Dame football coach and athletic director Jesse Harper.

On Jesse Harper's ranch near Sitka, Kansas, the oil wells ran deep and the cattle ranged wide. In 1931 Harper was forced to leave this cowboy paradise in order to help an old friend, Notre Dame. After the tragic death of Knute Rockne in a plane crash, Harper grudgingly became athletic director of the school he had started on the road to fame.

"I was sort of a part-time employee," he once remembered. "I still ran the ranch and tried to take care of both jobs. I was happy to get back to Kansas to stay."

Harper had lost touch with football. When he had quit at the end of the 1917 season, he had done a complete job of it. He was up to his ears in cattle and oil wells when the call from Notre Dame came in time of crisis. And when it did, Harper answered it with characteristic loyalty. In three years he helped organize the athletic department and left it in sparkling shape for Elmer Layden. Then he retired to his farm again. It was this organizational and executive ability which distinguished Harper among his peers and helped establish Notre Dame as a national power in earlier years.

"There's no question about his business acumen," says Chet Grant, who played for Harper in 1916 and later became a well-known Notre Dame historian. "He was a great executive."

Just as he had developed Notre Dame in the 1913-17 period, Harper masterminded the athletic department from 1931 through 1933, although some were less than enchanted with his pinch-penny ways. Not long after Harper came back to Notre Dame, he cut the scholarship total for practical reasons.

"When dad came back as director of athletics, it seems to me they had 36 complete scholarships that they gave away every year," recalls Harper's son, James. "They cut it to 16 partial scholarships in 1933 and (coach) Hunk Anderson never forgave him because he felt he had taken away everything Rockne had and after all, he should have the same things Rockne had. But dad just felt Notre Dame took too many boys and actually was not able to utilize them all. There's no sense having guys that could play first-string for someone else sitting on your bench."

Harper's hand had been felt at Notre Dame for some time. He is perhaps best known as the coach who piloted the Fighting Irish to national prominence on the wings of the forward pass in the 1913 Army game. But his role in the development of Notre Dame athletics reached higher than that. Harper's accomplishments were somewhat dwarfed by the superhuman deeds of the great Rockne, but it was this gentle Kansas farmer who started Notre Dame on the glory road. It was Harper who developed Rockne into the superstar he was, helped save him when he faltered, and picked up the pieces after his death. And it was Harper who sowed the seeds for what is commonly known as the renowned "Notre Dame system."

"Dad was extremely fond of Rockne," notes Harper's son. "See, there wasn't a lot of difference in their ages. They were extremely close. Dad was instrumental in an awful lot of Rockne's decisions. And he was influential as far as the school was concerned because they were going to let Rockne go in 1928 when he lost four or five games. But dad talked the school into keeping him and he had a national championship the next year. Dad did an awful lot behind the scenes that you never heard of."

Jesse Harper, born in 1883 in Pawpaw, Illinois, learned his football under Amos Alonzo Stagg, the acclaimed Chicago University coach. Harper's meeting with football's grand old man seemed preordained.

"We lived in Iowa at the time," Jesse Harper once recalled,

"and my father was in the cattle business. I could always get a free ride into Chicago on a cattle train. For that reason, I went to Morgan Park Academy, a Chicago prep school, and then went on to the University."

Harper played for Stagg in 1902, sat out 1903 and 1904 with injuries, and played again in 1905, the year that Chicago was undefeated and won the "Western Championship" of football.

"I played halfback and quarterback on that club," Harper said. "And I didn't play too much at quarterback because I had a pretty good man ahead of me. You may have heard of Walter Eckersall." (Eckersall, Chicago's first All-American player, is remembered as one of the game's all-time greats.)

Stagg was a true father figure to the players and did not hesitate to spank them when they needed it, Harper remembered.

"The old man was always awfully strict. He was a wonderful man, and a great coach who had that knack of getting men to outdo themselves for him. But, boy, he was strict, particularly when it came to the conduct and training of players. And he was death on smoking or drinking. He was always a reasonable man, but the thing you remember most about him is how stern and strict he was."

The esteem in which Stagg was held by his players was never more evident than at the 50th reunion of the 1905 Chicago team. Most of the squad members were there in 1955, and Harper pointed out at the time, "some of those men still won't smoke or take a drink in front of Mr. Stagg."

When Harper graduated in 1905, Stagg helped him get a job as head coach at Alma College in Michigan. Harper was only 22 but obviously ahead of his time. In three seasons at Alma, Harper's teams only lost four games, and he moved onto Wabash College in Indiana. In four seasons at Wabash, Harper's teams produced a 15-9-2 record. He had a perfect season in 1910, when the opposition was held scoreless in four games. More games were scheduled for that season but were canceled when a Wabash player was killed in a contest with St. Louis.

Ironically, it was one of the losses that attracted Notre Dame to this efficient young coach. The Fighting Irish took notice of Harper after they were forced to pull out a 6-3 decision in the last five minutes over the 1911 Wabash team. The next year Wabash had a 5-2 record, and Harper had a job at

Jesse Harper, Notre Dame's great air strategist.

Notre Dame, as coach and athletic director.

"And nobody helped me get that job," Harper emphasized. "I was good enough at Alma that I got the Wabash job. And I was good enough at Wabash that I got the Notre Dame job."

Actually, Harper's coaching ability was taken into account at Notre Dame. But perhaps even more enticing to the school was his administrative ability and business sense. Recalls his son:

"While at Wabash, my father was talking to an attorney who was a Notre Dame graduate. And he made the comment that football should be made to pay for itself. In those days, none of the sports paid for themselves. This attorney conveyed that comment to the president of Notre Dame and the president said, 'I want to see that man.' That's how dad got hired from Wabash to Notre Dame."

Harper brought some of Stagg's concepts to Notre Dame. The most important one was the forward pass, which rocketed the Fighting Irish into the football heavens. But while developing this new offensive weapon to a high degree of efficacy, Harper also installed other interesting innovations at South Bend. His 1913 Fighting Irish not only used the pass to gain fame, but were also known for a balanced line and shifting ends (the backfield shift from the T-formation into a box). The Notre Dame Shift eventually became world famous under Rockne, but it was Harper who introduced it.

"I do not think anyone knows who first used the shift in one form or another," Harper noted in Allison Danzig's book, *Oh, How They Played the Game.* "Minnesota used the shift about 1903 or 1904. They shifted the entire line as well as the backfield. I started the shift at Notre Dame in 1913. Notre Dame was the first team to have a complete offense using a balanced line and shifting only the backfield. In 1914, we started shifting the ends."

On the forward pass, Harper recalled: "I used the forward pass a great deal at Wabash before going to Notre Dame. In fact, Wabash was the first team to use intentional grounding, also throwing the ball out of bounds instead of punting. At that time the ball thrown out of bounds went to the other team at the point it went out of bounds. There was no penalty for intentional grounding a forward pass. It was the same as an incomplete pass."

But with all of Harper's innovations, it is quite possible that Notre Dame would never have gained its present euphorious status without the 1913 Army game. Without a doubt, getting the Cadets on the Notre Dame schedule was Harper's most strategic move. And beating them was his greatest triumph.

"When he went to Notre Dame he found it difficult to get games with teams in the midwest because the Fighting Irish had an excellent team and people were afraid to play them," recalls his son. "He was literally forced to turn to intersectional games. Dad was a modest guy. He never wanted to take credit for getting Notre Dame started as a national power. I remember he told me once: 'Well, Lord, I was forced to get a national schedule. No one else would play us around Notre Dame. I had to go someplace where I could get some ballgames.'"

Harper sent out letters to several colleges across America and got positive responses in 1913 from Army, Penn State, Texas, South Dakota, Ohio Northern, Christian Brothers of St. Louis, and his former school, Alma. About the Army game, Harper supplied this insight: "The Army game was arranged in a very simple manner. I wrote the Army to see if they had an opening on their schedule, and if so would they give us a game. No outside person knew anything about it until the game was arranged and contracts signed."

The forward pass had been legalized seven years before but was slighted by the nation's football powers. In one historic afternoon at West Point, Harper and Notre Dame changed everybody's thinking. And soon after watching Notre Dame bomb Army with an aerial attack heretofore unseen in football, everybody was doing it. Harper's team not only enhanced its own image but opened new vistas in American football.

"We had Army on the schedule, and everybody figured they were way out of our class," Harper noted. "We had to do something, and we figured a lot of passing. The pass was nothing new. It had been in the rules for seven years. The thing was, no team that I know of had ever used it very much.

"We played a helluva game. At the half, we were ahead by 14 to 13, but I was afraid it couldn't last. We had only thrown a couple of passes and they weren't worth much. I told Gus (Dorais) to start throwing and keep throwing. We figured it was the best chance we had. Gus could throw the football as well as any man who ever lived, and I think he proved it in that game. He went out in the second half and completed 13 straight passes, most of them to Rockne. Army had its usual great team, but the passes demoralized them completely. By the time it ended, we could do anything we pleased, running or passing. They didn't know what to expect, or what to think about it. We just kicked hell [out] of 'em and beat 'em 35-13."

As with many games of such nature, dozens of anecdotes and sidelights are attached to it. Harper loved to tell the story about his meeting with a navy officer 30 years after the significant event.

"I was out on the West Coast and was introduced to a Naval submarine commander. As soon as he heard my name, he started cussing. 'You —!' he yelled. 'I've been looking for you for a long time. I'm Babe Brown, and I was captain of the 1913 Navy team that lost to Army. And it was your fault, because you're the one who showed 'em how to use those passes.'" Army, it seemed, had taken all the pass plays out of the Notre Dame book to upset Navy later that year.

The 1913 Notre Dame team had a gorgeous 7-0 record, the second such perfect season in a row, and the Fighting Irish were on their way toward a meeting with destiny. They were hurried along when Harper made another intelligent move—hiring Rockne as his assistant coach in 1914. The combination of Harper and Rockne proved irresistible.

Harper guided Rockne with loving paternal care. Rockne learned quickly and matured even faster. He was at first put to work developing a new pair of ends, and a Harper story connected with that incident reflected Rockne's maturing process as a coach.

"Rock was a very intense man. He was a tireless worker who lost himself in any job. He went to work on those ends like it was life and death. He pleaded, threatened, and did about everything trying to improve those guys in a hurry. A few days later we had a scrimmage, and the ends were terrible. Riding home after practice, Rock talked about it, and said he'd have to work even harder with them. I had a different idea. I told him to forget the ends for a while and work with the guards and the tackles.

"A week later, we had another scrimmage, and the ends looked pretty good. Rock commented on it right away, so I laughed and told him, 'Yeah, and if you'll leave 'em alone for another week, we might have a pretty fair pair of ends.' Rock was pretty upset by that, so I explained what I was getting at. I told him that his mistake was trying to teach those ends all he knew in a hurry. He thought he could make 'em as good as he was overnight. It's just as bad, you see, to over-coach a boy as it is to under-coach him. In later years, Rock often said it was one of the most valuable lessons he ever learned. He told the story many times."

Harper and Rockne worked together with extraordinary precision, a fact that was reflected by Notre Dame's excellent record during their time. Harper's teams won 34 games, lost but five, and tied one in five glorious seasons. Only once, in 1914, did the Fighting Irish lose as many as two games. During this period Harper was the cool manipulator and Rockne the fiery spirit. When Rockne needed fatherly advice, he turned to Harper. When Harper needed a Pied Piper, he turned to Rockne.

"Harper recognized his own limitations," points out Grant, who played for both. "When an emotional appeal to the players was indicated, he delegated that chore to his assistant, Rockne. And Rockne didn't take it on himself. He didn't take it away from him. It was just understood that if there was to be some exhortation, Rock was to be the exhorter. So they were a very good team and they remained very close."

Distinctly different in personality and makeup—"Harper was the more practical man," according to Grant—the two developed an exquisite relationship. It was more like a Mutual Admiration Society. When Harper left Notre Dame after the 1917 season, he was instrumental in having Rockne installed as the Fighting Irish coach in 1918. Harper stuck by his side despite the misgivings of some faculty members who considered Rockne too unstable and inexperienced. Finally Harper was asked why he insisted purely on Rockne and rejected all other candidates for the Notre Dame job. "Because I promised him the job," Harper insisted. Rockne returned Harper's adoration with respect of his own. Years after, when he became famous, Rockne always gave Harper credit for laying the foundation to the "Notre Dame system."

Harper's hand was evident in Notre Dame's far-reaching intersectional schedule. Army remained a fixture during his time, and new teams continually bobbed up each year, such as Yale, Carlisle, Syracuse, Nebraska, Creighton, Rice, and Washington & Jefferson. The second game with Army was almost as important as the first, for it fanned a rivalry which became a flaming passion in later seasons. Rather than dropping the Fighting Irish from their schedule, which some thought possible because of the humiliating loss in 1913, the Cadets scheduled a return match for 1914. It was obvious that Army wanted revenge, and its serious intentions were pointed up when a Cadet scout appeared in South Bend one day. A Lieutenant Hammond looked over the Notre Dame team and made this report back to headquarters:

"I arrived at the school and seeing some men throwing a

football about in a nearby field, inquired of them where the Notre Dame football team could be found. 'You are on the field now, fellow, and this is the Notre Dame team.' The playing field looked more like a cow pasture than a football field and as far as information is concerned, I haven't much to report."

Obviously a scouting report was not needed anyway because Army defeated Notre Dame that year, 20-7. Press coverage for this one was relatively quiet compared to 1913. The most startling headline of the day read: "Notre Dame which had defeated Army last year was defeated in turn in a game played at West Point on Saturday—West Point winning by a score of 20 to 7 in a well-fought game." A writer pointed out: "This game was most outstanding, for the large crowd of 5,500 fans yelled themselves hoarse and displayed unusual enthusiasm, while numerous fans, fillies and functionaries looked on with interest."

Willet J. Baird, the Army mascot at the time, gave an interesting look at the Notre Dame players after that game: "After the game I walked to the mess hall with three Notre Dame players who said: It was a shame that John McEwan, the big Army center, was not playing on the Notre Dame team, for they would hate to have to contend with him for another afternoon, or even another season. To me that was a mark of great respect, for in the 1916 game with Notre Dame this same McEwan, then an All-American center, gave an account of himself never again equalled by a linesman of either squad. In that particular game McEwan featured in stopping 18 out of the first 20 plays executed by the Irish squad."

Football fever continued to climb at Notre Dame, and it was apparent that the series with Army was one of the main reasons. Before the 1915 game at West Point, a special telegraph wire had been run into the field house on the Notre Dame campus so that Fighting Irish fanatics could get the report. Students had chipped in nickels and dimes to provide the setup. In downtown South Bend another wire was run into Jimmy and Goat's Pool Room, and proprietor Goat Anderson would lean out a second-story window and bellow a play-by-play account to passers-by.

A spirit of brotherhood and solemn respect prevailed among the players even as they sat in the West Point dining hall sizing each other up for the punishment to come. When the Notre Dame team arrived at West Point for the 1915 game, the

Cadets serenaded the Fighting Irish with Notre Dame songs. The yell leader mounted a table in the mess hall and directed a noisy welcome for the visitors. On the Friday before the game, coaches from both sides gathered in the officers' club for a mellow evening. The good humor even carried through the morning and afternoon of the game.

A few hours before kickoff of the November 6 contest, Rockne and some of the Notre Dame players visited Cullum Hall Field to inspect conditions after a storm the night before. The Notre Dame aggregation encountered Marty Maher, a soldier who was a fixture at West Point. Maher was directing a detail of men who were clearing the field of hay that had been spread to absorb the rain. Rockne inquired about Elmer Oliphant, one of the Army stars.

"Wan o' th' finest," Maher answered in his deep Irish brogue. "That lad is dynamite."

Rockne thought for a minute and turned to his players.

"What did I tell you?" he said with a wink. "I only hope he blows up before the game; I don't want any of you getting killed."

The brazen Oliphant later appeared to be as good as Maher had said. Once, standing on his own goal line on fourth down, he announced to the Notre Dame players that he was coming around end—and he did, for 30 yards. With the same braggadocio, Oliphant answered a challenge from Notre Dame late in the fourth period. The Army player had made a fair catch of a punt on the Notre Dame 46 yard line when one of the Fighting Irish players said, "Why don't you place kick it?" To which Oliphant remarked: "I will kick one that you have never seen before—one that will split the bar."

The game was a scoreless tie up until that point, and Oliphant's kick would have given the Cadets three points. He gauged the wind, looked at the goalposts, spit on his hands, and kicked the ball long and true. But it struck the middle of the bar, bounced five feet in the air, and dropped back onto the playing field for no score. Notre Dame won the game 7-0 in the last three minutes on a touchdown pass from Stan Cofall to "Little Dutch" Bergman, and later in the dressing room Fighting Irish players gathered around Oliphant and said: "Oli, you sure can call your shots, but what we can't understand is why you did not want to clear the bar instead of splitting it in half?"

The charisma of the Army-Notre Dame series was begin-

Stan Cofall: His touchdown pass helped Notre Dame beat Army 7-0 in 1915.

ning to hold the public in its spell. As the years went on, the passions became more fierce, and the crowds became larger. An observer at the 1915 game remembered: "People were standing around the field, due to a lack of seating capacity. Ladies were seated on bales of hay which had previously been removed from the gridiron and placed in the far corners. Many people brought along small chairs on which to stand and some even climbed trees which overlooked the field."

It was no secret that Harper loved to beat Army as much as any team on the schedule. In his five years he held a 3-2 edge over the Cadets and counted among his most cherished memories at Notre Dame a 7-2 upset in 1917, his last year.

"It was during the war and Army had a great team, while nobody else had much of anything for a squad," Harper once remembered. "We had George Gipp, but he was just a freshman. We had Slip Madigan, the old St. Mary's coach, who weighed 160, and our right halfback was Joe Brandy, who weighed only 140. Army had big Biff Jones at one tackle and Elmer Oliphant, an All-American, backing up the line behind him. So we told our boys to run the other way all day. Before you knew it, we were down to their seven-yard line, and I think it was third down with goal to go.

"I knew we'd never get that close again. I was wondering what we could do when Gipp first showed me what kind of a head he had. All during his career, you know, he had a habit of making up plays to fit the situation. He did it this time. He told our quarterback to fake a play the way we'd been going, and let Brandy run right at Jones. It worked. The Army was so surprised by the maneuver that Brandy ran right past them and scored a touchdown. We won the game; nothing else ever gave me quite as big a kick."

Frank Rydzewski, an All-American center for Notre Dame in 1917, recalls that the Army game that year "was the biggest game we had...I don't think that Harper or Rockne anticipated winning the game, but we won it." Rydzewski, revered by Harper as one of the best players he ever had, was almost a goat in the 1917 Army game. Rydzewski played with a bandaged forehead because of a bad gash received in the South Dakota game the week before. Blood spouted from the wound throughout the Army contest, continuously blinding him. This resulted in a bad pass from center by Rydzewski that led to an Army safety in the first quarter. A bit of clever fakery by Notre

Dame's Tex Allison saved it from being an Army touchdown.

Rydzewski's bad pass in a punting situation gave kicker George Gipp little time to set himself, and the Cadets charged through to block the ball. An observer from the Army bench picks up the sequence: "(Johnny) Stokes of Army blocks a Notre Dame punt, the ball bounding beyond the goal post and over the fence. As Allison starts up the fence he yells to Stokes that he will get the ball for him and as Stokes hesitates a moment, Allison puts on a full burst of speed. All other members of both teams, as well as the spectators, seem to enjoy the race and Allison, finding a hole in the fence, goes through it, steals the ball, the game and the show." Had the Cadets recovered instead of the Fighting Irish, they would have had a touchdown, and the game would have ended in a tie.

If Rydzewski committed a costly error, Harper could forgive him. The big center gave Notre Dame many shining moments as he helped the Fighting Irish compile a lofty 21-3-1 record from 1915 through 1917. Rydzewski was so respected by Notre Dame coaches that Rockne himself bandaged his injuries, instead of using the normal procedure by trainers. "I had weak knees and weak ankles and Rock bandaged my legs before every game," Rydzewski remembers. "He'd do things like that for the benefit of the team, even though he was the assistant coach. I don't like to praise myself, but evidentally I meant something to the team—so Rockne himself bandaged me with a couple of tapes. He was an expert on that."

Harper had "a good relationship with his players," according to Rydzewski, but it was Rockne who did most of the talking for the Notre Dame coaching staff. "In the classrooms, where we met often, Rockne had the blackboard and he got the team ready to play on Saturdays. He'd show us the strengths of the other players and their most successful plays, so that we could prepare against them. He also went over the rules so that the fellows would know what's what." Harper held practices every day after school for about an hour and a half, continually preparing for the opposition's strengths. There were no days off. "Oh, you just accepted it," Rydzewski says, "and you played."

Eventually, family ties proved stronger than ties to Notre Dame, and Harper resigned his all-purpose job as director of athletics and coach of football, basketball, and baseball to join his father-in-law as partner of a cattle ranch in Kansas. Financial trouble on the ranch had brought Harper home at the time, but he later confided to his son that he was close to leaving the Notre Dame job anyway. The pressures of big-time football were starting to weigh heavily on his shoulders, recalls James Harper:

"Years later when I told my father that I'd like to be a coach myself, he said: 'Sit down right now and we're going to have a man-to-man talk, and I'm going to tell you why I left Notre Dame. It wasn't because of the school or anything else; I had a marvelous relationship, but I could see the handwriting on the wall. I could see the pressure by the alumni to do nothing but win, win, win, regardless of what you did to the boys, the school or anything else. Football is to build men and to build good sportsmanship. That's why I left. You do not have any easy games. Every team that plays you is up. Every team that beats Notre Dame has a successful season. It's just a crazy, marvelous sport, the finest sport we have. It does more to develop character in men for future life than any sport we have. But I had to leave Notre Dame because winning was getting too important there.'"

Harper returned to more peaceful surroundings in Kansas and developed a ranching empire. "I've got the most successful breeding secret ever known on the ranch," he kidded once. "I've crossed Hereford cows with oil wells, and you can't beat that."

Besides supporting some 1,300 head of cattle, the 30,000-acre ranch was the scene of large-scale oil development and at one time produced 25 wells, all spouting black gold. Oil wells, in fact, became so commonplace on the Harper spread that after a while he revealed: "I'm getting blase as hell about the oil wells. I used to get all excited and be right there the minute they started drilling. Now I don't even bother to go watch 'em bring 'em in."

The business of running a ranch appealed to Harper more than the business of running a football team. "There's a certain glamour to coaching and athletic directing," he said at the time, "but I'm satisfied. There's something about being in business for yourself that gives you a sense of security. You're building for the future, and you can tell everybody to jump in the lake if they don't like your methods. I'd travel a thousand miles to see a game, but I have no desire to be a part of it."

However, the death of Rockne changed the course of his plans. By a strange twist of fate, Rockne died in a plane crash within 100 miles of Harper's ranch on March 31, 1931. Not long after that, Harper was back on the Notre Dame payroll, directing the athletic program with his old-time brilliance. Harper helped straighten out an athletic jumble left by Rockne's sudden death. He toured the country, renewed old contracts, and made some new ones. He not only strengthened relationships from coast to coast, but kept Notre Dame strong internally. Harper stayed just long enough to see Notre Dame through a tenuous period, then went back to ranching in 1934 when Elmer Layden was named the school's athletic director and coach.

In later years Harper suffered from a heart ailment and high blood pressure but was still active in his ranch and followed football closely. He usually visited Notre Dame at least once a year and at the 1958 Army game was honored with a plaque observing his selection to the Helms Hall of Fame. Harper's last visit to South Bend was in 1960 for the Purdue game. He had planned a visit for the Northwestern game of 1961, but died that summer of a heart attack at the age of 77.

Moose Krause, the present Notre Dame athletic director, delivered the eulogy at Harper's funeral in Ashland, Kansas. "It was heart-rending to see that big man standing there with tears just streaming down his face," remembers Harper's son. "They were very, very close. Dad had some tremendous friends at Notre Dame."

Although he was dwarfed by the monumental shadow of Rockne, Harper's place in Notre Dame history was nevertheless towering in its own right. And Krause and dozens of others were at his funeral site that day to see that it was not permanently laid to rest.

The Pied Piper

"We're going inside of them, we're going outside of them; inside of them, outside of them—and when we get them on the run once, we're going to keep them on the run—and we're not going to pass unless their secondary comes up too close. But don't forget, men, we're going to get them on the run; and we're going to go, go, go, go; and we aren't going to stop until we go over that goal line—and don't forget, men: today is the day we're going to win. They can't lick us, and that's how it goes. The first-platoon men go in there and fight, fight, fight, fight, fight!!! What do you say men!"—Knute Rockne.

One spring day Harold Lyle went back to the spot where it happened. He climbed through some barbed wire and walked across the hills. It was warm, and Lyle took off his jacket and wiped his brow.

"It was over there," he said. "That's where the plane crashed. That's where Knute Rockne died. It was pretty bad. The bodies were in bad shape. It was rainy and muddy and cold. It was pretty bad."

Lyle scanned the rolling Flint Hills of Kansas where a plane crash took the life of Rockne and seven others on March 31, 1931. The crash site was marked by a simple limestone and granite monument, carrying the names of the victims. The tragedy of the event was still seared in Lyle's mind. He was one of the witnesses to a death spectacle, in the role of a newspaper photographer. Lyle photographed the wreckage and took away with him a bizarre picture that stayed forever in his haunted memory.

71

This was what Lyle saw: a plane's wing a half mile from the wreckage; riders on horseback; a booted cowboy talking to a helmeted aviator; old black cars gathered at the scene along with airplanes; swirling tracks in the snow; tortured metal—and bodies.

Lyle had come to work early that day at the *Wichita Eagle*, he remembered. He noted reading a story on the teletype about Rockne leaving Kansas City on a Transcontinental & Western Air, Inc., plane for Wichita. From there the passengers were supposed to take a train to Albuquerque, New Mexico, for the final leg of the flight to Los Angeles. Rockne had business there.

"Then the bulletin bell on the machine started ringing, and there was a story about a plane going down in Chase County, Kansas," Lyle recalled, "and, of course, we all thought. . ."

Their worst expectations came true, after a long hunt. Lyle and the *Eagle*'s sports editor, Bill Cunningham, went to the airport and chartered a plane to search for the downed aircraft.

"We couldn't find the wreck once we got up in Chase County. But finally we saw the ground, and there was a cowboy on a horse waving a red bandana toward the southeast, and we followed this sign. In a couple of minutes, we saw the plane. I knew then, by the size of the airplane, it was the Transcontinental & Western. I knew Rockne was dead. I took the aerial photographs then. I hated to. But it was my job."

The plane that Lyle and Cunningham were in almost crashed itself, and after a wobbly landing, the photographer jumped out and continued to take pictures of the wreckage and peripheral drama. By midafternoon, the temperature had plunged to 28 degrees. More planes arrived at the scene, and hundreds of other persons had arrived through the muddy fields, either by horseback, high-axled black cars, or by walking. Lyle recalled that the wreckage of the plane was stripped by some of those who came.

The trimotor Fokker plane, made leaden by heavy ice on the wings and facing a sky "full of dust and smoke with an awful wind" (according to weathermen), had cartwheeled out of the air and crashed into a pasture near Bazaar, Kansas. Dead along with the 43-year-old Rockne were Spencer Goldthwaite, Waldo R. Miller, H. J. Christen, John Happer, C. A. Robrecht, Herman J. Mathias, and the pilot, Robert Fry. Federal investigators said the crash was caused by icing on the monoplane's

A coach for all seasons, Knute Rockne.

wings that made its controls inoperative. A wooden wing was snapped off in the process of its death dance through the sky.

"Every time I come back to the hills," Lyle said, "I don't know what it all means, but I just think back to that miserable day."

Like many others Lyle had been touched by Rockne in his lifetime. It was not easy to forget the man or the legend, and everybody, it seemed, had a Rockne story to tell. Lyle especially remembered his kindness. Once he was assigned to get a photograph of Rockne and his team when they stopped in Newton, Kansas, one day for breakfast. The weather was terribly cold, and the rookie photographer finally got up enough courage to ask Rockne and his players to step outside.

Rockne smiled at Lyle. "Sure, son, my boys are eating too much anyway, and we can all stand a breath of cold air."

"Then," Lyle said, "he rousted them all out of there, and I got my pictures, and I thought to myself that he was a fine man to take time to help an inexperienced and frozen kid like me."

Lyle was just one of Rockne's fans, of course. There were many others. And not just football people, either. There were scientists, truck drivers, and nuns who became Notre Dame followers simply because of Rockne.

That Rockne belonged to all types and all ages, there was no doubt. To the world he was a football demigod of vast dimensions. He was a national hero sainted by the press in his own lifetime. Perhaps more than that, he was a symbol—the personification of the American dream. To the millions who never met Rockne but read every word about him, his image reached larger than life.

To those who knew him, this highly complex man was less than a saint. He was all too human and displayed in varying quantities magnetism, wit, tremendous warmth, and burning anger if needed. The football players called him their confessor, and, for all intents and purposes, he was their father image, too. When they were in trouble, they went to Rockne, and he smoothed it over. When they needed money, they got it from Rockne. If there was a question of any kind, at any hour, Rockne was there to answer it. They always sought him out first.

To athletes of other sports at Notre Dame, Rockne was a champion of their causes, the ideal director of athletics. To other students at Notre Dame, he was equally a champion. He stirred their inner depths and set campus feeling afire with his magnetic words. On the field he was familiar to all—directing the Notre Dame attack from the sidelines like a flamboyant Napoleon. His quips at football luncheons or on the practice field were told and retold in campus dormitories—and made legend. He not only reached peoples' hearts and minds but their imagination as well.

One writer who knew him made this quite clear: "Leader

that he was, he had a way of looking pathetic at times that made every man in the school want to go out and fight for him, to die if necessary, even though there were nothing to fight for. Any attack on him in the papers brought a storm of indignation in the recreation hour after dinner at night."

Athletic romanticism flourished at Notre Dame because of Rockne. "Sneer at rah-rahism if you please; such primitive emotionalism is the kind of soil on which football success flowers," noted George Trevor in the *New York Sun* at the height of Rockne's glory. "The Brills, Metzgers and Carideos are heroes to their fellows, and football carries an appeal similar to that which the jousting lists used to hold for King Arthur's knights."

What few critics Rockne had, he could dispatch with a phrase or two. His derogatory comments carried as much wallop as his praise and could damage egos with ease.

To South Bend's citizens, Rockne became the exalted fellow who won fame for them with his football teams. With the fame came crowds and money and the loss of a small-town image. To neighbors, Rockne was a family man, a companion to his four children and devoted wife. He was the man revered by every small boy in town, as well as most every adult everywhere. Parents raised their children in Rockne's staggering shadow.

"The problem of a father was nullified if the child became unruly," noted an observer. "He could merely threaten to mention the misbehavior to Rockne, and all would become serene. He could tell the boy to eat spinach if he wanted to play for Rockne, and the boy would eat twice as much as he was supposed to."

Industrial leaders in South Bend found Rockne to be a colleague of imposing stature. Rockne's slick management of sales promotion with the Studebaker automobile company alone would have justified his position as a community leader, even without football. He also managed a branch office of a large brokerage firm and was able to quote stocks without end off the top of his head.

As a speaker Rockne was the continual guest of local luncheon clubs and was sought everywhere else for his spellbinding oratory. It is probable that he could have made a living in show business or as a statesman.

Rockne brought the populace to his feet during his euphorious reign at Notre Dame from 1918 until his death in 1931. Coming home from conquests on foreign soil, Rockne's triumphal processions made South Bend a town gone berserk. They turned out at the station and lined the curbs of Michigan Street, South Bend's main artery, as Rockne and his forces went through to the tune of band music, shouts, and ringing cheers. These were the same people who could not believe the catastrophic news of his death. Rockne was too vitally alive, too energetic, to be dead, they thought.

He had left a legacy of decency, honor, and sportsmanship that would be handed down through generations. Some of his words kept alive the spirit of the man. "To be a good player, a man must have brains, guts, speed, self-restraint, motor coordination, that something known as fire of nervous energy, and, to a lesser degree, physique and an unselfish point of view of sacrifice for the team. Sportsmanship means fair play. It means a real application of the Golden Rule. Bragging and gloating or any form of dishonesty have no place in it." Long before the sports world was embattled in a war of race and color lines in the late 1940s, Rockne had established a blueprint for fairness. When a wealthy alumnus of Notre Dame demanded that his son be placed on the varsity football eleven, Rockne replied:

"I care only about the team. We have no fraternities here. We play no favorites. My eleven best men will make up my first eleven, regardless of nationalities, creed, financial status or social prominence. Whatever man of whatever birth comes to this university and can play football—he is my man, a part of my team. We are just Notre Dame men here!"

Rockne not only made his presence felt to people, but to the national structure of football. It was the man's personality that made the legend and his innovative contributions that made the legend glow. Francis Wallace, a Notre Dame historian and one of the closest men to Rockne, remembers:

"Rockne was associated in the public mind with offense, but his defense was always sound. Because, in the upset of Army in 1913, he was the prime receiver in the first spectacular demonstration of the forward pass in a major game, he was considered an exponent of the pass. But as a coach he used it as an effective complement of a strong basic running game. On offense, he played percentage but never hesitated to use a daring play he thought most likely to succeed under the conditions of the moment. As a scientist (which he also was), he

76

accepted the best thinking and proven practices of the masters who had preceded him, and added his ideas. He was an innovator rather than an inventor, an adaptor who might pick up a new wrinkle from an opponent and use it to defeat that opponent the following year. He adapted his system to his personnel.

"He inherited the backfield shift from Jesse Harper. It operated from a balanced line, lined up in a basic T, shifted into the single wing. His refinement of the shift gave his lighter, faster backs such a jump on opponents that they actually went to the Rules Committee for relief. When his shift was slowed by the one-second stop, he went to heavier men and gave them a spinner to replace the last deception. This is why his 1924 Four Horsemen backfield of Stuhldreher, Crowley, Layden and Don Miller averaged 164 pounds; and his 1930 quartet of Frank Carideo, Marchy Schwartz, Marty Brill and Joe Savoldi averaged 186. As early as 1921 his Shock Troop system, which started the second eleven to absorb the initial shock of the opposing first eleven, was two-platoon football, with the players going on both offense and defense. When a game was well in hand, he sent in his sophomores. And this usually gave him a nucleus of experienced men with which to start each season. As early as 1922, he had his quarterback dropping back to pass after faking plays into the line. His runners and passers were also blockers; his offensive stars used their speed on defense. His best all-around players were always in the game or available. There was little leakage in Rockne football. He played what may have been the first spring game in 1922. He pioneered intersectional football and introduced the 'suicide schedule' by playing a major game every week, discarding the several 'breathers' which previously had been included. He was usually so far ahead of his field that the appearance of a Rockne-coached eleven, featuring the flashy boxer (as opposed to slugger) type offense became a style show that drew crowds and fascinated analysts."

Rockne stories are legend, and many of them concern his famous half-time speeches that motivated his teams beyond their normal capacities. Rockne perhaps did more with less talent than any coach in the game.

Reflective of Rockne's ability to fire up his team is this story from Grantland Rice, the famous sportswriter:

"I was sitting one night with the Army coaching staff before an Army-Notre Dame game. Novack, the smart Army scout, offered this tip: 'Starting the second half, take the kick-off if you can. Don't give the ball to Notre Dame. Rock will have them steamed up by that time. Don't give Notre Dame the ball.' But Army kicked off to Notre Dame. On the next play Chris Flanagan of Notre Dame ran 60 or 70 yards to a touch-down. Every Army man was flat on his back. Notre Dame won, 7-0.''

Rockne's most famous half-time speech, of course, is the one where he urged his charges to "Win one for the Gipper." And indeed, Notre Dame did go out and beat Army that day in 1928 in memory of George Gipp. But there were other Rockne classics, although not as glamorized as the Gipp tale. One of Rockne's tricks was to ignore his team completely during the intermission. He would sit sullenly in a corner for the full time, then finally get up and say disgustedly, "All right, girls, let's go." On another occasion, when Notre Dame had played a poor first half, Rockne merely opened the door to the dressing room, peeked in, and said: "I beg your pardon. I thought this was the Notre Dame team." This usually worked the Fighting Irish into a fighting dither.

Rockne, a master psychologist, could wrench tears from his players or make them so blazing mad at themselves that they would literally tear through the door to get on the field and at the other team.

Joe Boland, who played tackle for Rockne, recalls such a time when Notre Dame was losing 10-0 to Northwestern at the half and appeared certain of having its 20-year nonlosing streak at home broken.

"I remember walking back to the locker room, up in the northwest corner of the old fieldhouse, and wondering what Rock would say. We flopped down in the room and waited for him. We kept looking at the door, but he didn't show. The three-minute warning came, and still no Rock. Finally he walked in. He was really mad. When he was that angry, the cords stood out in his neck, and he bit off the words so that every one of them hurt. 'The Fighting Irish,' he said in a voice that curled your shoulder pads. 'Well, you'll be able to tell your grandchildren you're the first Notre Dame team that ever quit.' He turned to his assistant, Hunk Anderson. 'You take 'em, Hunk. I'm through with 'em.' Then he walked out.

"I don't remember how we got through the door, but I remember that Rome Dugan was standing behind it, and he got

Knute Rockne and his faithful assistant, Hunk Anderson, caught up in the emotion of a game.

flattened against the wall. We went out there and took the kick-off and slammed our way 75 yards for a touchdown. Didn't use a pass or an end run. (Rex) Enright and (Christy) Flanagan just socked tackle and guard, and we went over. When they kicked to us again, we pounded our way another 78 yards for a score in the third period. We won, 13-10. Earlier, I had looked over at the bench, and Rock was nowhere in sight. But by the end of the game he was there, crouching on the sidelines, twiddling that cigar of his just as if nothing had happened."

Jim Crowley, one of Rockne's beloved "Four Horsemen," remembers a different kind of approach by the ingenious coach. This happened before a game instead of in the middle of one.

"We were playing Georgia Tech in 1922, and they had been undefeated on their home field for years. We had several sophomores in our lineup because our team had been decimated by graduation, and Rockne came into the dressing room with a great number of telegrams in his right hand. He said they were from prominent alumni. He probably sent them to himself, collect, and he had a long wire in his left hand. 'I have a wire here, boys, and it probably doesn't mean much to you—but it means a great deal to me. It's from my poor, sick, little boy Billy, who's critically ill in the hospital in South Bend.' And then he reads the wire, with teary eyes, a lump in his throat and his lips quivering. 'I want daddy's team to win.' So, God, we knocked him down, went through a pole at the door, and got on the field about 10 minutes before game time. We took a hell of a beating from this great Georgia Tech team because they had been out to beat us for years, but we won the game anyway for little Billy, 13-3. I mean we really took a physical beating.

"Well, when we got back to South Bend, there must have been about 20,000 people to greet us the next morning. And as we stepped down off the train racked in pain, the first face we saw was Rockne's kid. He was in the front line. There was 'poor, sick, little Billy' looking like an ad for Pet Milk, and we were all basket cases."

Another time, Rockne used a "little white lie" to motivate his players against Army. Crowley recalls:

"Before the game, Rockne came in and told us: 'I just heard that Army's going to kick you off the schedule.' Then he paused for effect. 'Well, they might be able to kick you off the schedule, but they can't kick you off the field.' He used that as his theme for that day, and we went out and won the game. The next day we picked up the *New York Times* and found out that he had signed a new five-year pact with West Point officials. We found out reading the story that he had signed it the Friday before the game—and he was telling us the night before the game that they were going to kick us off the schedule!"

Crowley adds with good humor, "They were all lies, blatant lies. The Jesuits would call it mental reservation, but he had it in abundance."

Like a good actor, Rockne read his lines with precision and feeling. Not all of his great performances were in a locker room between halves of a game, either. One of his most-remembered performances came off the field when Notre Dame was en route to Los Angeles for a game with Southern Cal. The Fighting Irish had stopped over for a practice session in Tuscon, Arizona, and Rockne thought he had discovered apathy in the team. Rockne threatened to quit the club and go back to South Bend rather than go on with a "squad that did not seem interested in the game ahead." The players pleaded with Rockne to stay with them and showed their coach that they cared by routing the proud Trojans, 27-0, in a spectacular upset.

Rockne turned every situation to his own advantage—even his illness. In 1929 Rockne suffered from phlebitis, and a serious blood-clot condition developed in one of his legs. Rockne constantly referred to his bad leg as his "spare tire," but it was not really a joking matter during the football season. Rockne was eventually reduced to sitting on the sidelines in a wheel chair, barking orders through a loudspeaker, while Tom Lieb and other assistants did much of the active coaching.

Rockne was on his back the week of the Carnegie Tech game but insisted on going with the team against doctor's orders. He was accompanied by his personal physician to Pittsburgh and was carried into the locker room by Lieb before the game. Then one of the most dramatic episodes in Rockne's career unfolded before the astonished eyes of his players. Rockne was placed on a table by Lieb, his back to the wall, and his bad leg laid in front of him. He wore black overshoes and a large coat, and he sat for a long time just looking at the players, saying nothing. His face looked pale, and Doctor Maurice Keady leaned over and whispered to a companion, "He has an even chance of not leaving this room alive. If that clot is loosened from the excitement, it could kill him."

Finally, Rockne spoke.

"There has been a lot of water under the bridge since I first came to Notre Dame—but I don't know when I've ever wanted to win a game as badly as this one. I don't care what happens after today. Why do you think I'm taking a chance like this? To see you lose? They'll be primed. They'll be tough. They think they have your number. Are you going to let it happen to you again? You can win if you want to."

He paused for effect and his voice rose.

"Go out there and hit 'em. Crack 'em! Crack 'em! Fight to live! Fight to win! Fight to win, win, win, *win*!"

The players, many of them in tears, barged through the door intent on beating Carnegie Tech. And they did, 7-0.

If Rockne was able to build his players to a pinnacle, he was also able to tear them down if they needed humility. He was superb at reducing swelled heads. Once when he felt his

Four Horsemen were developing oversized egos, he ran them behind a third-string line one day, and they did not look quite as good as before. "Show 'em your clippings, boys," Rockne snapped. "Show 'em your clippings."

When one of his teams developed overconfidence, Rockne pulled one of his marvelous ego-smashing tricks.

"This team lost a game it should have won," Rockne told a friend. "I knew what overconfidence meant, so before the start of their next game I simply distributed newspaper clippings to the bunch. 'Read these,' I said. 'These clippings say you're all All-America. But you couldn't beat a team last week that had no All-Americas. I want you to read these clippings before every play. Either you just aren't that good, or you're yellow.'"

When Notre Dame showed poorly in the first half against Princeton one day, Rockne leveled his players with cutting sarcasm: "Remember, kids, no rough stuff out there today. We are playing back here in the elegant Ivy League and are supposed to be just a bunch of hayseeds from the bush league. Only the Princeton boys can afford to get rough."

Rockne-watchers have tried to describe his magical skill, and one writer called it "inspirational salesmanship." Harry Mehre, who played for Rockne from 1919 through 1921, defined it more deeply: "He was the greatest salesman sports ever had. Not just football but all sports. Rock sold football to the man on the trolley, the elevated subway, the baker, the butcher, the pipe fitter who never went to college. He made it an American mania. He took it out of the thousand-dollar class and made it a million-dollar business."

Rockne's hold on his players was phenomenal, and probably one of the very real secrets of his great success was his personal touch. He could be stinging in his criticism but was always generous with his praise. "We never knew what the word 'sarcastic' meant until we played for Rock," one of his players said. But Rockne never held a grudge long, and he sent his players away from the practice field adoring him. Frank Leahy, Rockne's most famous successor, learned everything he knew as a player under the old master. "If you asked me what one thing Rock left with me, as a coach, I would say this: No matter how sarcastic or critical he was of a player in practice—and Rock could be very severe—he always made it a point to show there was nothing personal in his attitude. After practice, he'd walk up to the boy and say, 'How are your folks, Frank?' Or, 'Father

82

Crumley tells me you're picking up in English.' Or after a particular grueling session, he'd make sure he showered with the players, instead of using his own private shower. I don't remember talking to him about this, but it made a firm impression on me. . ."

Moose Krause, Notre Dame's present athletic director, also remembers Rockne's endearing style. "I was just one of dozens of guys trying to make it at tackle. I was awed by the sight of Rockne then. When my folks came down to see me, the first thing they asked was, would I introduce them to Rock. Well, I was a little worried by the suggestion. I had no idea how to go about it. We were walking across the campus that day, and who should come down the steps of the Main Building but Rock. I was wondering if I had the nerve to call to him when he walked right over and said, 'Moose, how are you getting along with the books?' You could have knocked me over. He even called me Moose! My folks were mighty impressed. So was I. I never forgot."

Howard Smith, who played under Rockne in the late 1920s, recalls uncommon noble qualities in the man.

"He treated everyone the same, and that's why all the players respected him. And if you did something good, he liked to praise you for it. He didn't like the wise guys. You know how sometimes varsity men like to push around the freshmen. Well, Rockne would grab them and admonish them for it. He'd tell them, 'Just do your job and don't worry about him.'

"Another thing. If you had something to say, he'd listen. His mind was never so set that he couldn't change it. He was very flexible. If a player was doing something that was a little bit different than the book said, and it worked, Rockne never interfered. He let him do his own thing.

"He was wonderful with the players. In the sense of equipment, he made sure that everybody got fitted right and they were happy with their uniforms. When we were freshmen, they'd hand us some old stuff in the locker room sometimes, and we'd go outside, and Rockne would see us with pants too big or something. And he'd come over—he'd call you by your name, or he'd have a nickname for you, like 'Blondie' or 'Toughie,' and he'd say 'Come over here, I want to look at you.' He'd look at you and say, 'Who gave you that?' Then he'd say, 'Go in there, and tell that guy to give you a good pair of pants!' And he'd send a student manager with you to see the equip-

Knute Rockne (second from left) huddles with some heavy-weights from the sports world of his day—(from left) Pop Warner, Babe Ruth, Christy Walsh, Tad Jones, and Fielding Yost.

ment manager.

"He'd go to bat for anybody. Rockne would go out of his way to help his players. I had a roommate who didn't want to wait on tables. That was supposed to be his job while he was playing football. He got into trouble over it and had to be out of school for a while. Rockne kept him at his house until he straightened everything out. When you got into trouble, he helped you. When you needed a job, he got you one.

"Rockne gave you respect in all departments. He never made bed checks. He'd watch you on the field and would know whether you broke training rules or not. Nobody broke too many rules, anyway. Listen, after you were through with him on the practice field, you just wanted to go to sleep. He'd run us a lot but not if we were hurt. He was very fair about that. He was a very thorough, wonderful man. I've done a lot of coaching around the country, and I know other Notre Dame players will tell you the same thing. I've never run across a man like him."

Rockne's hold on the student body at Notre Dame was just as magical. The story is told about how a group of Notre Dame students had crowded into one of South Bend's theaters to attend a stage show and created a mild disturbance that aroused the actors. The actors retaliated with some cutting remarks of their own from the stage, and the students gathered in the lobby after the performance, looking for a fight. The manager of the theater, hoping to avoid violence, called Rockne and told him of the impending battle. Rockne arrived on the scene in short order and told the students: "Hey, you fellows, go on home." The group dispersed immediately.

Rockne was no matinee idol in looks, especially after he started to lose his hair prematurely. He stood only five-foot-eight and weighed about 145 pounds and was an easy target for callous sportswriters. Westbrook Pegler, a journalist with an acid typewriter, was one of those who made fun of Rockne's less than heroic proportions. "He looks like a preliminary fighter who becomes door tender in a bar. His nose is smashed, and his skull is more nude than otherwise. And when he talks, it is like an old battered oil can giving champagne."

Rockne was a familiar figure on the Notre Dame sidelines. He usually sat in a camp chair at the end of the Notre Dame bench with his assistants and quarterbacks. He liked to have them all within hearing range so they could plot strategy. He talked in endless, staccato tones, twirling a cigar between forefinger and thumb. He always had the cigar, squeezing it, waving it, chewing it madly, but hardly ever lighting it. In front of the coach was the student manager, huddled on a blanket, his arms full of charts, hurriedly writing down Rockne's critique of the game. These he later went over with the players.

Rockne was thoroughly engrossed in the action on the field. Nothing diverted his attention.

"Savoldi was sucked in a little too much on that last outside play," he would say, nervously twirling that ever-present cigar. "Kosky got caught flatfooted on the same play. If those boys keep making mistakes like that, they'll beat us by four touchdowns. . ."

85

He continually shouted instructions from the sidelines. "Hey, Schwartz! Hey, Brill! Be sure to take out those ends coming down! We have to give Frank a little chance to bring the ball back! We don't want him killed!"

He baited the referees.

"What does that official think he's doing? You mean to tell me that's interference? Why, he was only trying to get the ball! Don't let the official get away with it, Conley. Some of these refs need glasses. I guess we'll have to show up on the field next week as a bunch of Venuses; then the boys can use their heads entirely. There won't be any mistake about their hands and arms!"

He praised his players.

"Atta boy, Frank! They're still wondering where that scoring play came from. Hey, Savoldi, you must have seen the Italian legion waiting in the end zone, the way you stepped out for it. And Brill, you did a fine job backing up that line. Great work, Schwartz. You kinda put a crimp in their favorite pass, didn't you?"

Notre Dame often executed so brilliantly and efficiently on the field that it was like magic to the casual observer. But anyone who understood football and understood Rockne knew that torturous work had gone into the final product. The Fighting Irish made it look easy only because Rockne made it hard for them in practice sessions. From the minute that Rockne walked onto the field with his familiar command, "Everybody up," everybody went to work. Noted a writer:

"Rockne's winning tradition was built around a program of countless hours of infinite grooming and pains, of almost unbelievable attention to detail, of sweat and blood, of hard, diligent bone-crushing work; in short, all those extras that Rockne, and Rockne alone, seemed to blend into the molding of a championship team."

"He was very thorough," remembers Howard Smith. "He wanted everybody to learn just right. And you had to know your job perfectly before he'd let you play. He didn't allow any mistakes. I remember we were working out once. I was a sophomore, and I took the opposing end out with a great block. But I wasn't supposed to do that. I was only supposed to brush him and hit the linebacker. And Rockne called me over and said, 'It's great to have that enthusiasm, but you've got to play above the shoulders, too.'"

Rockne's ingenious practice sessions were a marvel of efficiency. In spring practice he had a habit of dividing up his players into different teams, taking the guise of opponents on that fall's schedule. Then round robin competition would be held between, say, the "Army," "Navy," and "Wisconsin" teams. The best players would eventually wind up on the Notre Dame team and have the opportunity to play with Rockne.

"Everybody would scrimmage like hell because they wanted to get on his team," Smith says. "You're young, and you figure, 'I want to get on the Notre Dame team where the boss is coaching.' And you'd work harder. In the meantime, you're learning the systems of these various teams that we were going to play the next fall."

The lessons of Rockne resulted in an unmatched record. From 1918 to 1930 his teams won 105 games, lost 12, and tied 5, for a winning percentage of .897. Five of his teams had unbeaten, untied seasons, and three won national championships. In a recent nationwide poll by the Associated Press, he was named coach of the all-time All-American team. He built Notre Dame into the supreme football team and turned out players who later, as coaches, carried on the "Rockne system" with success elsewhere. Rockne was a good teacher, but his lessons went beyond the field. He was football's most ardent supporter and an eloquent defender of the game when it faced heavy public criticism. But, although football was his whole life, he never put it above the lives of others. In a time when his word might have been law on the Notre Dame campus, he bowed to democracy. Rockne, for all his stature as a demigod, recognized that there were higher authorities than he and more important things than his football team. Education, for instance. He once described his feelings in this area.

"From the beginning of my career as a coach, with whatever faults I brought to my profession, I at least had the intelligence enough to recognize that the faculty must run the institution. The school is their school, and the coach must bear in mind that his is an extracurricular activity, like glee clubs, debating societies, campus politics and publications. If a player flunks in class, he's no good to the coach or the school, and the coach who goes around trying to fix it for athletes to be scholastically eligible when mentally they're not is nothing but a plain, everyday fool."

There is only one instance on record where Rockne

allowed any intervention scholastically for one of his players. That was in the case of George Gipp, a player whom Rockne adored as one of his own sons. Gipp was to be expelled from school for cutting classes, but the townspeople went before the priests of Notre Dame and asked if the school authorities would allow Gipp to take an oral examination since there was not time for a week of written exams. They agreed, and the brilliant Gipp passed with flying colors. When he came out of the examination room, Rockne was lurking in the background. Gipp, in his strange, flippant way, acknowledged his coach on the way out. "I liked that oral examination, Rock," said Gipp, flipping his cap.

When Joe Savoldi, one of Rockne's greatest backs, announced his intention to leave school in 1930, he was persuaded to do otherwise by his coach. "Please come back next year and finish your education—never mind football—your education is important," Rockne told him.

There is perhaps some feeling that Rockne's legend was heightened by his tragic death, that it grew larger than life because he became a martyr in some eyes. Notre Dame people do not think so. John Cavanaugh, for one, had a vision of Rockne as Lincolnesque in character.

"Some will say his field of achievement was too trivial and limited to warrant his canonization among the immortals," said Cavanaugh, a professor at the university, "but this man was vastly more than a football coach—there was something of Lincoln in the little immigrant from Norway."

Knute Rockne—the first name was correctly pronounced "Kanute"—was born in Voss, Norway, on March 4, 1888. He came from a line of prominent landowners, but by the time he was born, the family had left the soil, and his father was a carriage maker by trade. It was Lars Rockne's work that eventually brought the family to America. He had entered one of his carriages in the Columbian Exposition in Chicago in 1893, and the exhibit won second prize. But Lars Rockne was more impressed with the free atmosphere of America than he was with the prize, so he sent for his family.

Little Knute Rockne was in such a hurry to get on the boat that he fell off the gangplank into the harbor at Bergen, Norway. While his mother and sisters looked on in horror, the scrappy 5-year-old boy was rescued by grappling hooks and deposited on deck. One clever sportswriter in later years described this incident as "the first completed forward pass in history." Rockne's mother took no chances after that. When they were ready to debark in New York, she had him and his sisters bound to her by strong ribbons.

To the adventurous Rockne, his first look at America was a total disappointment. On the train ride from New York to Chicago, he complained that he saw no Indians. But a few days later his disappointment turned to delight when he found a group of American Indians in a miniature reservation on the Exposition fairgrounds. He was so fascinated by them, he stole away from his family and joined them for the night. This caused a good deal of anxiety and excitement, and the police searched all night for the lost boy. An alert policeman finally discovered young Rockne the next morning. In the midst of black-haired Indian boys, he said, there was a little blond head "wearing a feather headdress, wielding a wooden tomahawk and yelling for scalps" in Norwegian.

Lars Rockne got a job as an engineer in a Chicago factory, and the family settled in the Logan Square district, a neighborhood inhabited mostly by Irish and Swedish people. Rockne played sandlot football, but a free-for-all fight one day temporarily halted his football career. His parents, who considered football uncivilized anyway, forbade him to play after that brawl and instead approved the "gentler" pursuit of baseball. Once again Rockne was in the thick of a battle and eventually wound up with a nose flattened by a bat. Practically blinded for the moment, he arrived home and announced: "You think football is a rough game? Look what I got from baseball!"

When he entered Northwest Division High School in Chicago at the age of 13, Rockne had the permission of his parents to play football. A 110-pounder, he started out with the scrubs, but before his high school career was finished, he was a regular on the first team. Rockne also won recognition at track and set an indoor record of 12 feet, 4 inches in the pole vault. It took four years before Rockne got to college. He worked as a mail dispatcher with the Chicago Post Office and in his leisure time kept his athletic ability honed at various athletic clubs. It was Rockne's ambition to save enough money to go to the University of Illinois, a school better known than Notre Dame at the time. Rockne admitted that he never considered going to South Bend until two friends changed his mind.

Johnny Plant and Johnny Devine, a pair of Rockne's track

buddies, convinced him that Notre Dame was cheaper than Illinois and good scholastically. So Rockne, at the age of 22, took the $1,000 he had saved and a battered old suitcase and headed for South Bend and a golden destiny. Upon Rockne's arrival at his dormitory, he was greeted by a friendly face.

"Looks like we're going to be roommates," said Gus Dorais. "Where do you want to put your trunk?"

"I haven't any trunk," Rockne replied.

"Neither have I," countered Dorais. "Let's shake on that. We're starting even."

It was the start of a gorgeous friendship, and these two became inseparable in their years at Notre Dame. The Dorais-to-Rockne forward pass combination won them fame, but their partnership extended beyond the chalk lines of a football field. Rockne and Dorais were just as good at business as they were at football. At first they took charge of the Corby Hall pool room for two years and beat fellow students out of their money. But Rockne figured after a while that this was small potatoes. So the ingenious Rock loosened the screen to his room and charged curfew-breakers a fee for using it as a passageway in and out of the dormitory at odd hours. It turned out to be a highly profitable business for Rockne-Dorais, Incorporated.

"Candy, food, and, it must be confessed, even *beer* passed through this window until the Reverend John Farley, rector of the hall, discovered what was up and put an end to this traffic," said Dorais.

It did not stop the brazen pair, though.

"We put in a tunnel," Dorais noted.

Dorais was as close to Rockne as any person could be but never suspected his greatness while the two were in college.

"To me he was human. As a speaker, for example, he was embarrassed, fumbling, halting, tense at the team dinner his senior year. A scarlet line moved up and down his neck as he talked. But later, Will Rogers, who should know about these things, said that Rock was the best after-dinner speaker in the country.

"He came to Detroit once after we graduated, called me for breakfast, and, when I asked what he was doing there, he said, 'I'm going to give a talk. . .to the Catholic Ladies' Study Guild.' In response to my startled look and query concerning his topic, he said, 'Oh, I don't know what I'll talk about, but it's all right. I was reading the *Atlantic Monthly* on the train.' As a matter of fact, he gave them a talk on football, and they loved it. I had a hard time getting him away afterwards.

"Rockne worked harder at one thing, though, than any other. He fought a desperate but losing battle against falling hair. Sometimes I suspect that he took chemistry just in order to save his hair. At any rate, he brewed one concoction after another, and the odor of our room was never constant. He even slept on newspapers and tried every suggestion he got. And frequently he'd ask me how it looked, if I couldn't see a little new fuzz starting to sprout. I'd say, 'Sure, Rock, I think there's a couple of new ones there today.'"

Haunted by insecurity of a poor childhood, Rockne at first dreamed of becoming a wealthy pharmacist. His athletic ambitions were not as lofty. He immediately registered for campus work to support himself and studied hard, taking athletics as they came but not too seriously. His performance on the track team during his early years exceeded his accomplishments at football, and Rockne at the same time showed a remarkable aptitude for chemistry, a major he had changed to in midstream. He seemed destined to follow this field all the way. Rockne's genius in chemistry was so apparent that Father Julius Niewland, Notre Dame's noted research chemist, appointed him as one of his assistants upon his graduation in 1914.

By this time, however, football also had gripped Rockne's imagination. He had developed so rapidly that in his last year he was elected captain of the 1913 team. Rockne was mentioned in some circles as an All-American candidate. His ability to catch passes on the run, a revolutionary method in those days, gained Rockne universal fame. He impressed everyone that year, it seemed, except his mother. Rockne invited her once to see him play against South Dakota, and he had a great day, making many spectacular pass catches and several long runs. He was sure that she would be bursting with parental pride, but she was not. "Who was that boy who turned the pinwheels?" she wanted to know. "He was wonderful." The boy Rockne's mother referred to was the cheerleader.

After graduation Rockne married his campus sweetheart, Bonnie Skiles, and went to work supporting her with two jobs—chemistry assistant and football assistant. In accepting the chemistry job with Father Niewland, he stipulated that he be allowed to assist Coach Jesse Harper in football. Father Niewland accepted the arrangement grudgingly. He suspected that

Rockne's first love was football, despite all his brilliance as a chemist. And he was right. Eventually, Rockne drifted away from the classroom toward the football field for good. When Harper retired after the 1917 season, Rockne took over as Notre Dame's head coach, and his place in history was established.

Rockne gave some inkling of his extraordinary powers even as a subordinate. Harper depended on Rockne for most everything, including his inspirational oratory. Rockne had to instruct every player on the field—backs as well as linemen. He doubled as a ticket-taker, trainer, and jack-of-all-trades. The players were drawn to Rockne and came to him with their problems. He was a friend, but he was also a disciplinarian. Once when a conceited lineman refused to follow Rockne's instruction, the coach showed characteristic strength.

"Go turn in your suit," Rockne told the strapping, talented player. "We'll get along somehow without you!"

The player looked hopefully at Harper but got no response from the head coach. He immediately apologized to Rockne and pleaded for another chance.

That established Rockne's position at Notre Dame and his reputation as a tough, fair leader.

"A reputation as a martinet," Rockne once said, "is invaluable to a coach—providing he doesn't work too hard at it."

At one point during Harper's administration, Rockne was tempted to leave football for the more lucrative field of commercial chemistry. He appeared to be on the verge of quitting when the head coaching offer came from Notre Dame. The salary was a substantial $8,500 a year, and at the age of 30, Rockne became the boss of the Fighting Irish.

It seemed at first that he might have made the wrong decision. There was little money to run a football team properly. Rockne was brokenhearted by the shabby equipment and lack of medical supplies. There actually was not enough tape on hand to bind all of the players' injuries. There were only two trunks available for the team's equipment, and these were only enough for the first eleven. The other players had to pack their own gear in suitcases and carry it with them. The uniforms were all hand-me-downs—and that even included shoes. Once when a player came off the field with his feet in agony because of cleats that had worn through the shoes, he saw Rockne's tortured look and limped back into the game. Rockne once said of this demoralizing period of Notre Dame history: "If the sportswriters had really known the poverty of our equipment, they would have made us All-American on gameness alone."

But the spirit of Rockne's teams endured, and that, along with love and respect for him, was what made them so great. Despite a ragged countenance, Rockne's teams were successful from the start. They lost but one game in 1918, and by 1919 and 1920 they went undefeated and untied with the help of an all-star athlete named George Gipp, Rockne's first and most glorified All-American. But as much as Rockne adored his fabulous halfback, he loved and respected each player—including the lowest.

"A football team is as good as its weakest player," Rockne noted.

And the players returned the respect and the love.

"They would come as a man from the first to the last to the Old Man's aid if he needed them," a writer of the day said. "They would beg, borrow, or steal to come from the ends of the earth if he called for them."

Along with the Gipper, Rockne's teams had other astounding talents. He not only produced one of football's most legendary players in George Gipp, but its most legendary backfield—the "Four Horsemen." Harry Stuhldreher, Don Miller, Jim Crowley, and Elmer Layden became household names while leading the Fighting Irish to their first national championship in the 1924 season. Their swift striking power against heavier opponents personified the situation of the boxer against the slugger. This was Rockne's style and the style of his teams—sleek, fast, precise, and clever. If Gipp became Rockne's favored player, the "Four Horsemen" became his favorite backfield.

Rockne carried on Harper's philosophies and developed innovations that included the sophisticated backfield shift that characterized the "Notre Dame system." There is some belief that Rockne got his inspiration for the shift from watching a beautifully trained chorus in action in a musical show in Chicago. While watching the dancers, so the story goes, Rockne became fascinated with the idea of a shift that would have the rhythm of a ballet with the precision of a military march. True or false, the Notre Dame shift did have its own special music, although Rockne himself claimed that it was nothing new—he had only enhanced what had been originated years before by the revolutionary Amos Alonzo Stagg.

Believing that speed and grace were far better attributes than bulk, Rockne streamlined his teams with light, silk pants and traded cumbersome protective pads for less weighty equipment.

"Speed and more speed—coupled with brains and more brains—was his creed," a writer pointed out.

Rockne hoped that his players would think for themselves. He wished them to be more than robots.

"I can't play the game from the bench," he told them. "Only the quarterback can discover the weakness of an opposing team. And even if I could do some hokey-pokey from the bench, it would be poor football. If you can't think out there, you can't play!"

As Rockne and his teams became more famous, Rockne became more than just a coach—he became a national institution. Along with the fame came a strenuous schedule, and life whirled at an unhealthy pace for the football monarch. Along with running Notre Dame athletics, an awesome task in itself, Rockne was a busy public speaker and a devoted worker in the national youth development movement. In his spare time he wrote newspaper and magazine articles and gave radio broadcasts. That he still had time to be a father of four children and a devoted husband was astounding. But he did, and his devoted wife kept a warm refuge for him in their modest house, which was always filled with visitors and good fellowship.

Some of the most revealing Rockne anecdotes come out of his home life. For all his worldly accomplishments and many outside activities, Rockne was a homebody and dedicated family man. He enjoyed the fun and games of his children as much as the more serious games of the football field. Christmas was Rockne's favorite festival, and he delighted in handing out educational and constructive toys to his children. As they got older, scooters and tricycles became the order of the day because, as Rockne said, "they help to build and exercise strong bodies." He expressed a special joy when some of his children showed a promise of athletic ability, but he did not necessarily push them in that direction.

"I do not see how any father could be nobler or kinder," said Bonnie Rockne, whose intimate stories about her husband revealed another dimension of the overall Rockne picture.

Mrs. Rockne remembered when her husband played a flute once to soothe the crying of one of the children, baby Billy. The baby listened to the music, then ceased to compete with it. There was another incident when Rockne had to chase Knute, Jr., two blocks before catching up with him for a spanking. Rockne came back laughing. "That boy is going to make a good track man!" When Mrs. Rockne was out of town, the man of the house made supper. His specialty was usually slanted toward the "simpler dishes," most notably ham and eggs. When they were finished with supper, Rockne would put his children to sleep while all five sang an appropriate lyric:

There is a boarding house far, far away,
Where they serve ham and eggs three times a day,
Woe, woe, the boarders yell,
When they hear the dinner bell,
For they know the eggs will smell far, far away.

Rockne held a special nursery hour with the children, constantly reciting poems and telling stories. His sharp wit never deserted him, even during the children's hour. He once seriously asked one of his sons how old he was. "Seven," the youngster replied. "Impossible," said Rockne in mock surprise. "No one could get that dirty in just seven years."

Rockne read books avidly and sometimes would become so immersed in what he was absorbing that it would be hard to pull him out of it, even if guests were in his house. "Why, dad, you're positively rude," his wife would say, and then Rockne would wake up to his company and dive into an animated discussion. He enjoyed reading history, psychology, and mystery books, but he never completely got away from football. While smoking an after-dinner cigar and reading an Edgar Wallace novel, Rockne was just apt to flip over to the cover and start diagramming a play in X's and O's.

An evening out might find the Rockne family at a musical comedy, a light opera, or a good movie. He had more than just a passing interest in music—he had studied the flute as a student. And he owned a discerning eye for fine art, too.

Rockne also spent some of his free moments in the garden—digging, planting, and perspiring over his flowers. Neighbors saw him there constantly in the spring, wearing his favorite sweater, a relic bearing the monogram he had won as a Notre Dame player.

Before he went out on a speaking engagement, he tried out

his speech on Mrs. Rockne. Her approval meant a great deal to him. She was always there when he made the speeches, and afterward he would ask for her judgment. "How did it sound? Do you think it went over all right? Did I make my points clear?"

Away from home Rockne was on a nonstop, merry-go-round, and the pace of the outside world became too frantic for him after a while. It began to take its toll, and in later years Rockne was striken with phlebitis, an inflammation of the veins of the leg, and he became seriously ill. During part of the 1929 season he did his field coaching from an automobile with the aid of a loud speaker. He directed some games from a wheelchair despite orders from his doctor that he was endangering his fragile health. He was carried to one game on a stretcher but nevertheless had enough energy left to inspire his team to victory. The season of 1929 would have tested the imagination of any fiction writer and the belief of any reader, but there it was—a coach winning a national championship from a death bed.

"The season of 1929 probably was the most strenuous Rockne ever experienced," says Arch Ward in his book, *Frank Leahy And The Fighting Irish*. "He was in no condition to handle his team, but he never let up. His worth as a leader never was more strikingly demonstrated than in 1929. For three months, he held the works together—smoothing out here, cajoling there, lifting a stern hand in another place, and making the boys win. It took a student of human nature as well as a great football mind to carry that 1929 eleven along to a national championship. He used his illness to inspire his boys to play all the harder."

The undefeated team of 1929 was a younger edition of the 1930 team, considered by most to be Rockne's strongest. Rockne himself thought so because he told a friend before the season, "It looks like the best team I've ever had." The Fighting Irish were every bit as good as Rockne and everyone else thought. They went through their second straight unbeaten season and won their second straight national championship. The golden year was capped with a resounding 27-0 victory over powerful Southern California in Los Angeles. It was here that Rockne played his last and most dramatic scene on a football field. As his seniors came off the field one by one in the closing minutes of the rout, Rockne jumped up from the bench, put his arms around each boy, and escorted him off the field. Many in the huge crowd of the Los Angeles Coliseum were moved to tears while watching these gestures of affection by the famous coach. And as each Notre Dame star left the field for the last time, cheers rocked the stadium.

It turned out that the fans were not only saying good-bye to Rockne's players, but to Rockne himself. It was Rockne's last game, too.

After the season was over, Rockne took a much-needed vacation with his family in Florida. A few weeks of sunshine and swimming had a therapeutic effect on his health, and he appeared ready to dive into his work again. Prospects for 1931 looked bright. Notre Dame's gorgeous new stadium, for which Rock had pushed so hard, was being readied for the season. Big money awaited the man who had made comparatively little for his fame in previous years. Notre Dame authorities raised Rockne's salary to $10,000. The Studebaker Corporation offered him more income as a sales manager. Hollywood beckoned with motion pictures. Radio awaited. An autobiography was to be published.

Then came the fatal day.

Before spring practice got underway at Notre Dame,

Knute Rockne (third from left) is flanked by two old friends, assistant Hunk Anderson and dapperly dressed Pop Warner, the Stanford coach.

Rockne had scheduled a plane trip to Los Angeles to confer with the directors of a series of movie shorts he was doing. Just before he left, he stopped in to see an old neighbor, Tom Hickey. "I remember his last night in town," Hickey said. "He got down on the floor and played with the kids, and we had a lot of laughs. It had been a long time since I had seen him so relaxed."

On his way to California, Rockne had stopped off in Kansas City to see his two sons in school and had wired his wife in Florida: "Leaving right now—Love and Kisses." When he boarded a westbound airline in Kansas City, a friend saw Rockne off. "Soft landings," he called to the coach. "You mean happy landing, don't you?" Rockne replied, then boarded the plane.

Rockne climbed aboard and took a seat in front to protect an ailing leg. The plane wheeled down the runway and lifted achingly into a sky bleak with rain and fog. The pilot asked the Kansas City airport for weather conditions over Wichita. But his voice seemed nervous. Then, suddenly he said: "I do not have time to talk."

A few minutes later a Kansas farmer plowing his field near the hilly town of Bazaar saw the plane in trouble. The engine stuttered. A roar followed. A silver wing fluttered out of the clouds. Then the plane plunged to earth, and the nation shared a common tragedy.

On the Notre Dame campus, students stood around in numbed clusters, disbelieving. Then they went to the university church and prayed. Men and women reacted with shock throughout the country. A good friend had been lost in Rockne. Rockne's death provoked numerous stories, and in Atlanta one authenticated tale revealed what seemed to be a universal mood. A newsboy stood on a corner waiting for his quota of papers on April 1. When they were delivered, he read the headlines proclaiming Rockne's death. Crying, he tore up the paper he was reading and shoved the rest into the gutter. "I can't deliver them," he said. "I don't want my customers to read about Rock." Even before some papers could get out their extras, word of the tragedy had been sent out. Phone lines to South Bend were overloaded. You could not get through to the *Chicago Tribune* newsroom by phone. The switchboard operator at the newspaper answered every ring with a flat statement: "Yes, it's true about Rockne."

With every store closed and every flag at half staff in South Bend, they brought Rockne's body home. Funeral services were held in Sacred Heart church on the Notre Dame campus, where school president Father Charles O'Donnell delivered a stirring eulogy. In part, he said: "In an age that has stamped itself as the era of the 'go-getter'—a horrible word for a ruthless thing—he was a 'go-giver.' He made use of all the proven machinery and legitimate methods of modern activity to be essentially not modern at all; to be elementary human and Christian, giving himself like water, not for himself but for others."

Bonnie Rockne added her own touching note.

"Even to friends who are moved by love and not at all by curiosity, it is hard to write intimately of one whose life and death stirred even strangers to tears."

The funeral was impressive. Every significant name in the sports world was there, as well as a few others. The king of Norway sent a personal representative. Mayor Jimmy Walker came from New York. Rockne's aged mother arrived in tortured silence. Along with the great and near-great were people of every design, overflowing the church, flooding the campus and the town. They had all come to pay their last respects to Rockne.

This is the way it was, according to the *Notre Dame Scholastic:*

"Noon found the crowd beginning to assemble for the funeral services. Students who had left on vacations returned; sorrowing admirers of Rockne lined the walks and spread over the quadrangle. Rockne's closest friends, his associates, filed into the church to be with him for the last time, while the great bell in the steeple tolled at short intervals. The balcony of the administration building was packed with clergymen, faculty members, newspapermen; and students strained eyes from the roof of the Sorin Hall porch. Just before three o'clock, the long funeral cortege appeared past the statue of Father Sorin and made its way over a hushed campus to the church, while the crowd on the quadrangle edged closer to the ropes that formed the roadway. The long cortege came to a stop at the church door, and the casket was lifted out and borne into the church by six of Rockne's 1930 football stars, bowed now in grief at the death of their leader. They were Larry Mullins, Marty Brill, Marchmont Schwartz, Tom Yarr, Frank

Carideo and Tom Conley, captain last season. They were weeping grimly as they consigned the casket to Father O'Hara.

"Inside the church Rockne's friends listened to Father O'Donnell's splendid eulogy of his beloved friend, while out on the campus the crowd pressed around the loud speakers which carried to them the message and the solemn chanting of the funeral dirges by the Moreau choir. Heads were bared, and some knelt on the grass in prayer. The service over, the funeral cortege wound slowly out of the grounds and through the city towards Highland Cemetery, on the western outskirts of the city, where Rockne was to be interred. Streets along the route of the procession were packed, and all traffic was suspended while the crowds stood silent to honor Notre Dame's coach. At the cemetery police fought the crowds which attempted to get a last glimpse of the casket. Men and women pressed around the grave where relatives and close friends of the great man stood in mourning. Father O'Donnell conducted the simple and touching burial services, and the casket, with its monogram blanket for mantle, was lowered into the grave by those six teammates who played their best for their coach. Rockne was buried as he lived, simply and earnestly, with his men and his friends gathered around him."

Free Spirit

"George Gipp was the greatest football player Notre Dame ever produced. He was unequaled in any game by anybody save, perhaps, by Jim Thorpe. Gipp was Nature's pet, and, as with many of her pets, Nature also punished him. Gipp had everything to make a man great—splendid physique, balanced temperament, a brilliant mind. He became great at the art he loved most—football. If his untimely death held a touch of tragedy, it was not because of any lack of mental or moral assets on his part, [but] because Nature, that had given to him so generously, denied him at the very peak of his career when he was to be crowned the outstanding All-American halfback."—Knute Rockne.

One early autumn afternoon in 1916, the practice field at Notre Dame was practically deserted except for a tall boy in street clothes kicking a football to a player in uniform. The workout was no more than a casual duet of punts, but the style of the tall boy intrigued Knute Rockne.

"He picked up the ball, poised his body with natural grace, slid the ball to the ground and drop-kicked with perfect ease—50 yards," Rockne recalled. "For about 10 minutes I watched. His kicks were far and placed evidently where he wanted them to go to give the other player catching practice. Here, I thought, was somebody worth examining. When he strolled from the field as if bored, I stopped him."

Rockne asked his name, but the boy seemed indifferent.

"Gipp," he said, "George Gipp. I come from Michigan."

"Played high school football?" Rockne asked.

"No," Gipp said. "Don't particularly care for football. Baseball's my dish."

"What led you to come to Notre Dame?"

"Friends of mine are here."

"Put on a football suit tomorrow," Rockne said, "and come out with the freshman scrubs. I think you'll make a football player."

This casual exchange led to one of the most exciting relationships in college football lore and to one of its most colorful stories. Gipp's swaggering character matched his sublime talents, and he became Rockne's most glorified player and easily his most eccentric figure. Gipp was equally filled with enough staggering bravado and flaky nonchalance on a football field to make him one of the most exciting—and enigmatic—characters in the history of the sport.

His first game on the freshman team was characteristic. Notre Dame and Western Normal had struggled through a scoreless tie with three minutes left. When the Fighting Irish went into a huddle, Gipp insisted he be allowed to try a dropkick for three points. But he was overruled by the quarterback, who preferred to play it safe with a punt that would get the ball out of Notre Dame territory and insure a probable draw. But Gipp refused to bow to orders and did what he wanted anyway. He took the ball back at the Notre Dame 38 yard line and dropkicked a 62-yard field goal that won the game.

"This Frank Merriwell finish was so poetically right, that I thought Gipp too good to be true," said Rockne, at the time Notre Dame's assistant coach. "He himself seemed to have no thought on the matter. Where another boy would be flushed in triumph, this youngster took congratulations calmly."

The cocky Gipp later smashed egos on the hardened Notre Dame varsity when, posing as an Army back during a practice session, he ripped 80 yards through the dazed veterans. Despite his startling talents, Rockne brought him along slowly, even though Gipp was champing at the bit.

"In his first year of gridiron play (1917) we held him under the leash," Rockne pointed out. "We had plenty of stars, and as he was only 20, and the war was on, it was my policy to save him for the 1918 season. At that time it looked as if all our first-string men would join the service. That's exactly what happened. After a brief season that did not officially count as a scholastic year in 1918, Gipp, while having an opportunity to show that his greatness was growing, was not given too many chances to shine. My first year as head coach was 1918, and I made it an undeviating rule to handle the boys without the least putting anybody in a spot where I might be suspected of favoritism."

Gipp broke out of the leash and ran free in 1919 and 1920, accounting for most of his career offensive total of 4,110 yards. His running, passing, kicking, and brazen generalship lifted Notre Dame to two straight undefeated seasons. His flamboyance matched his feats and made him the most colorful college player of his time. Notre Dame's "wild horse" was wild in every sense of the word, and it is said that the "Gipper" was the only player that the great Rockne could not tame.

Once against Indiana, the Fighting Irish were losing 10-0, and it seemed inevitable that their 15-game winning streak was at an end. There were only a few minutes left in the game when Gipp, sitting on the bench with a dislocated shoulder, threw off his blanket and announced to Rockne: "I'm going in."

"Not today," Rockne snapped back.

But Notre Dame's blithe spirit ignored Rockne's order and trotted onto the field to the tune of hysterical crowd roars. Carrying tacklers on his back and driving straight downfield, the Notre Dame star went 60 yards in seven plays and scored a touchdown, tearing his shoulder from the socket as he went

Knute Rockne's 1919 Notre Dame team was declared "Western" champion after a perfect season.

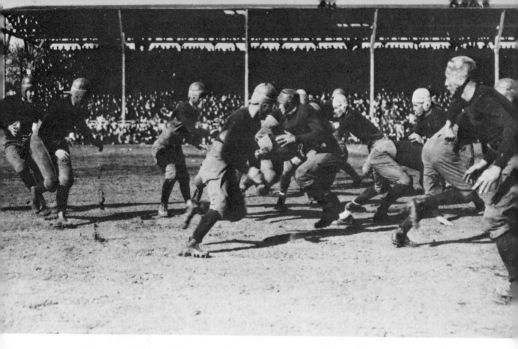

George Gipp (far left) carries the ball for a big gain. Notre Dame's free spirit was a hard man to pin down.

over the massed Indiana bodies into the end zone. The drive inspired the Fighting Irish, and they pulled out a 13-10 victory.

Gipp was perennially involved in dramatic finishes like that, scenarios keeping in character with his dashing personality.

In the 1920 Purdue game, Gipp loafed through much of the action until an opposing player sneered at him. The enraged Gipp returned a punt 92 yards for a touchdown, then knocked out his tormentor on another long touchdown run. Against Army in 1919, Gipp came alive only after the Cadets had built a 9-0 lead. With three tacklers clinging to his pants, he went 22 yards on one play. The next time he rushed for 15. Then, with the Army defense sucked in, Gipp completed six straight passes to the Army 10 yard line. He personally completed the drive with a smash into the end zone, and Notre Dame eventually won, 12-9. Against Nebraska one year, Gipp literally carried a teammate over the goal line in an unbelievable show of gall. When an unsung third-stringer failed to move the ball on two tries, Gipp told him: "Grab onto my belt—and don't let go." The lethal Gipp smacked in from the 10 yard line carrying his cargo. The touchdown was disallowed by a referee, who fined Notre Dame a 15-yard penalty. But Gipp had had his fun, and his teammate had had the pleasure of crossing the Cornhuskers' goal line even if it was illegal.

The most riotous Gipp story, and one which Rockne would retell to banquet audiences for years to come, involved a game in 1919 where Gipp had three long touchdown runs called back on penalties. After the third, the pained player could not help but bark to the referee: "Let's get together on this to save time. From now on, give me one whistle to stop—and two to keep going."

But while Gipp could be wildly exciting to watch, he could also be laconic on a football field. The whimsical player often loafed when Notre Dame had a big lead or he felt there was no danger of losing the game. The story is told about an Army game where Gipp was playing safety and let a Cadet runner take the ball in for a touchdown without making a move to get him. "The hell with him," Gipp said nonchalantly. "Let him go. We'll get it back and plenty more." Later in the same game, Gipp showed more of that unabashed ego that simply floored opponents. When Gipp's beautiful 45-yard pass from his own end zone was dropped by Roger Kiley, Gipp consoled his receiver with these words: "Don't worry about it, Rog. We'll call it again and stand them on their ear."

Gipp was so sure of his gorgeous talents that he backed his ability with money. Rockne's "Golden Boy" carried an appropriate sobriquet, for he was the team bookie and in charge of laying down bets for Notre Dame's games. This, some say, might have inspired him to greater heights. An amusing anecdote is attached to this side of the Gipp portrait.

Between halves of Gipp's last game with Army, with Notre Dame trailing 17-14, Rockne gave one of his most fiery speeches. When he finished talking, the coach looked around to note the effect and found every player fighting mad with the exception of Gipp, who was lounging against a door with a look of boredom.

Rockne gave Gipp a menacing look.

"I don't suppose you have the slightest interest in this game," the coach said.

"You're wrong there," Gipp said. "I've got five hundred bet on this game, Rock, and I don't intend to blow it."

Gipp then ran a punt back 30 yards, threw a 40-yard touchdown pass and kicked the extra point, then returned another punt 55 yards. He gained 236 yards on the ground and

96 in the air, for a total of 332—more than the entire Army team. And Notre Dame won, 27-17.

After Gipp's brilliant show, perhaps his best game at Notre Dame, Army coach John McEwan remarked: "He isn't a football player—he's a racehorse."

Gipp's showmanship was so revered by football audiences that they sometimes sat in silent awe when he left a field. Remembers Buck Shaw, a teammate of the Gipper: "They felt that any demonstration would be a kind of sacrilege. It was eerie. I've never known another who got people that way."

But despite his role as an All-American, he was far from the general concept of the All-American boy. Too sophisticated for schoolboy pleasures and rarely a social mixer with teammates, Gipp searched for the conventional vices and found companionship among gamblers, pool sharks, and other unsavory, honky-tonk types. He readily admitted, "I'm the finest freelance gambler ever to attend Notre Dame" and put his money where his mouth was time and again. Whether it was shooting pool, playing cards, or playing football, Gipp went for big stakes. It was not unusual for him to bet $100 on the flip of a coin or $500 on Notre Dame's ability to beat the point spread. He usually succeeded, too.

"He was gifted in all areas," says Shaw. "He was an expert in pool playing, billiards, any kind of cards, craps, poker. . .anything. He was just a natural."

Gipp found a second home at a South Bend hangout called Hullie and Mike's. His expertise at money games there helped finance his way through Notre Dame and, in fact, helped pay the freight for a few of his friends. After a while Gipp became a handful for the Notre Dame faculty, and Rockne had to work hard to keep him in school. Gipp's academic major was law, but he was more interested in the law of averages on a dice flip.

Gipp's erratic behavior was sometimes an embarrassment and a headache to Rockne. One writer recalls: "He was a pool shark of the first order, who once was expelled from Notre Dame and took his talent up to Ann Arbor to offer it to Michigan's Fielding Yost—quitting after two weeks when he decided he couldn't play for the Point-A-Minute Man. On another occasion he spent the summer playing semi-pro baseball under an assumed name, jeopardizing his amateur eligibility until Rockne heard about it and retrieved him. And just before he came down with the strep throat and pneumonia which took his life at 25, he left the team to go on a three-day bender in Chicago." Another writer pointed out that Gipp "avoided all the football practice he could to sharpen his skills in other areas."

Dutch Bergman, a roommate of Gipp's, once gave a revealing portrait of his "human side."

"Gipp is a Notre Dame legend now, rightly revered for his lovable qualities, but he was quite a problem for Rockne. Discipline irked the Gipper. Practice bored him stiff, and he never really trained during his meteoric career. A headstrong individualist, George scoffed at curfew hours, shunned drills whenever he could, loved his liquor, smoked cigarettes during the season and sat up many a night playing pool, craps or poker. He averaged three or four hours of sleep a night. Gipp was a born gambler—on the gridiron and off. He had a genius at cards as well as athletics. Nobody around South Bend could beat him at faro, shooting craps, pool, billiards, poker or bridge. He studied the percentage in dice-rolling and could fade those bones in a way that had the professionals dizzy. At three-pocket pool, he was the terror of the South Bend parlors.

"George was the soul of generosity, always sacrificing himself for down-and-outers. Though he came from a poor family, money meant nothing to Gipp. I've seen him win $500 in a crap game and then spend his winnings buying meals for destitute families. No wonder he was idolized by the South Bend townies. But some men just aren't born to conform with copy book rules. Gipp chafed under training restrictions. He reported for practice only three days a week despite Rockne's protests, but on Saturdays Gipp played like a man possessed. A shrewd student of human nature, Rockne gave Gipp free rein and winked at his capers. Nobody but Gipp ever got away with what he did under Rock. 'Hello, Gipper, got the asthma today?' Rockne would say when the prodigal son came out for a scrimmage drill. We players made a private rule that anybody caught snitching a cigarette would get a kick in the pants. Gipp never waited to be caught; he'd come and tell us: 'Kick me hard, boys, I just had a smoke.' We did.

"Some blue-nosed Puritans will tell you that Gipp would have been an even greater player if he had trained. But personally I think a genius like Gipp would have burned up if he hadn't let off steam. His amazing gift of relaxation between plays probably sprang from his lack of repressions. That is a dangerous doctrine for the average kid. George was the excep-

107

Good Luck from Gipp

George Gipp: A coach's nightmare during the week and a coach's dream during the game.

tion that proves the rule. A coach's headache during the week, Gipp was a coach's dream on the field."

Gipp's dominating personality was sometimes an annoyance to teammates, though. "Joe Brandy was our quarterback," says Shaw, who played tackle from 1919 through 1921, "and he was supposed to call the signals. But Gipp would sense things, and as we lined up he would call the signals on and off through the game on his own. And pretty soon, the other team would start saying, 'Well, who the hell's the quarterback? Is it Brandy or isn't it?' They didn't get into a fight or anything, but Brandy didn't like it worth a nickel. Gipp had a tendency to do that in ballgames."

Chet Grant, another quarterback of that era, also had problems with the forceful Gipp, even if he only spent a total of five minutes on the field with him.

"It was the last five minutes of our 16-7 victory over Nebraska (in 1920)," Grant remembers. "I was sent in to play it safe. Gipp said, 'Give me the ball.' So I gave it to him up the middle. On the next play Gipp said, 'give it to me again.' I wouldn't be told what to do. I called a fake crossbuck evolving into a pass. But Gipp doublecrossed me. He called his own signals—backs could do that in those days—and everything went awry. It was terribly embarrassing. We got the ball back, and again Gipp asked for it. It seems we were not winning the game by as much as we were favored. Gipp said he had some friends in South Bend who had bet the point spread. The whole matter displeased me greatly, but I let Gipp throw one long to Eddie Anderson. It just went over Anderson's fingertips. Gipp pleaded for the ball again. I looked straight at him and said flatly, 'George, that's all.' He said okay, and that was it."

But if Grant was not particularly enamored of his personality at times, he respected his talents.

"As all-around halfback, Gipp obviously still stands peerless in my well-worn book. As my strategist and tactician he towers above the whole procession of pre-eminent Irish pilots dating back to 1909, before Rockne and Gipp had been heard of. Call this another man's opinion if you like, but it may make a little difference to know that my conclusion is conditioned by over half a century of intermittently viewing, reviewing, reporting, playing, coaching or scouting Notre Dame football."

Grantland Rice, the noted sportswriter, was inclined to agree with that conclusion while selecting Gipp for his All-American team in 1920: "If one were to select an all-star array from the country, he should undoubtedly begin with George Gipp of Notre Dame. He is the best back in the country, a back

Chet Grant: Five minutes was enough with the Gipper.

who can punt, drop-kick, pass, break a line, or run an end. There has been a scarcity this season of triple threat backs. Gipp alone was worth two or three specialists for Notre Dame, for when he dropped back, the defense had no idea whether he intended to pass, kick, slide off tackle, or run an end. And he could do all four jobs better than any one of the specialists."

If Gipp was peerless as a football player, his baseball talents created excitement, too, and at the time of his senior year, the Chicago White Sox were negotiating for his services. The world was a ball in the palm of his hand in 1920, but Gipp was not around long enough to enjoy his euphoric circumstances.

In the Northwestern game of 1920, the next-to-last game on the schedule, a shoulder injury kept Gipp on the bench for most of the afternoon until the crowd sent out a steady roar: "Gipp! Gipp! Gipp!" Nobody in the stands knew that he had come from a sickbed to the stadium. And, after Rockne reluctantly sent him into the game, nobody could have guessed while watching the irrepressible Gipp operate. Recalls Norman Barry, a teammate:

"He had suffered a shoulder separation a week before

110

against Indiana, and since we had a big lead, Rockne didn't want to play him. But the people wanted to see the Great Gipp. They were calling for him from the stands. It was real acclaim, and finally, in the last few seconds, Rockne sent him in. He had this great big pad on his left shoulder, but he threw with the other arm. We ran from punt formation so that Gipp could drop back from his tailback position. We wanted to give him as much protection as possible for that shoulder. I was playing right half. The ball was snapped to Gipp, and he threw a pass to me that traveled 55 yards in the air. I caught it and ran 15 more yards for the touchdown to make the final score, 33-7. Rockne took Gipp right out after that. I think he was in only for that one play. The 70-yard gain was the longest pass on the books at the time."

Barry long remembered that pass from George Gipp, for more than one reason. Not only was it his biggest thrill in football, but it was also Gipp's last play. During a team banquet a little while later, Buck Shaw saw Gipp get up and leave quietly before the after-dinner speeches. Shaw followed him out into the lobby of the Hotel Oliver.

"I remember stopping at the desk where the telephones were, and from there you could see the manager's office," Shaw recollects. "I saw Gipp sitting in there. I said, 'What's the trouble.' He said, 'Geez, I have a terrible throat. It's giving me a lot of trouble.' That was the last time I saw him and the last time I talked to him. He went to the hospital the next day and never came out."

Gipp had what was commonly known as a strep throat. In today's world he could have been saved with miracle drugs. During his time it was fatal. The strep throat worsened and developed into pneumonia. Transfusions from his teammates prolonged his life, but Gipp continued to sink. He finally succumbed on December 14, 1920, at the age of 25.

His premature death came as South Bend, almost to a man, prayed for his recovery. As Gipp was on his deathbed, students were seen kneeling in the snow on campus, deep in prayer. Then bells tolled.

"It was pretty silent around Notre Dame, I'll tell you," Shaw recalls. "Of course they had a running account of the thing in the newspapers every day. And when the story was out that Gipp was dying, everyone was pretty somber around the place."

Connected with Gipp's death is the granddaddy of all sports stories. While his mother, his brother, his sister, and Rockne maintained a vigil at his bedside, Gipp made a memorable request in his last hour.

"I've got to go, Rock," he is quoted as saying. "It's all right. Sometime, Rock, when the team is up against it, when things are going wrong and the breaks are beating the boys—tell them to go in there with all they've got and win just one for the Gipper. I don't know where I'll be then, Rock. But I'll know about it, and I'll be happy."

Rockne of course made this famous by using it during a half-time speech in the Army game of 1928. The "win one for the Gipper" appeal helped win a game against overwhelming odds and established an incomparable legend that was dramatized in movies and glorified in prose for years afterward.

The stoic Gipp also had a brief repartee with Rockne in his final minutes, according to reports. When the coach said somberly, "It's pretty tough to go," Gipp answered with characteristic flippancy, "What's so tough about it?"

The "win one for the Gipper" request is almost too perfect

Shortly before his death, George Gipp (last row, center) posed for this picture with Notre Dame's Western champions of 1920.

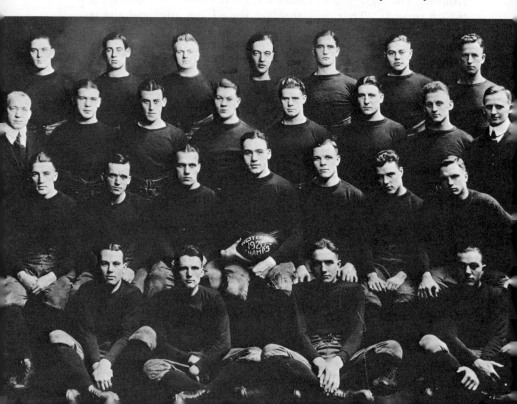

to be true and almost too corny to be real—points which have strained the logical thinking of sophisticated people. Some have had a hard time swallowing it, but Rockne himself put the stamp of authenticity on Gipp's melodramatic speech. In his autobiography the coach insisted it was for real. A priest who was in the room said he heard him say it. Hunk Anderson, Gipp's teammate, points out that Rockne told him about it minutes after Gipp died. And Notre Dame people, to a man, swear by it.

However, one sportswriter felt that Rockne should have bitten his tongue.

"Generations of movie goers and late, late show television night owls unmistakably have heard Ronald Reagan tell Pat O'Brien those famous words," says the disbelieving writer. "Not only have millions of 'Rockne of Notre Dame' audiences heard that speech, but also Rockne's football teams. Rockne should have at least mentioned it when he passed a confessional. The thing about what has become football's most quoted half-time speech is that it would have been out of character for Gipp to make such a request. It would have been much more like him to ask Rock to put down a bet for him some day when the Irish were a sure thing. On the night Gipp passed into mythology, the students on the campus weren't the only ones concerned about his condition. Shortly after he died, the lights at the Oliver Hotel in downtown South Bend were dimmed and then flicked off and on as a signal to the regulars at the nightly dice, poker and rummy session that Gipp was gone."

Gipp's death signaled a day of mourning at Notre Dame and a flow of eulogies from coast to coast in the newspapers. Telegrams and letters of condolences poured in from around the country. Classes at the university were suspended while the student body escorted Gipp's remains to the South Bend railroad station.

The *Notre Dame Scholastic* marked the occasion with this melodramatic report:

"There came the solemn message of his death just as the country was acknowledging his peerless quality as an athlete; there was the funeral cortege which took his body to the station and adorned it with a tribute which some of the Caesars have not received, and they took what remained of a happy boy to his home and laid him under the deep and solemn snow. Everything which we could do

113

for him was done with a spontaneity that is so natural that one cannot mention it without a vestige of pride. We noticed that there was a heartache in the aspect of the rugged field and that life was gray. . .''

Anderson and Fred Larson, Notre Dame teammates who had been classmates of Gipp in Calumet High School, accompanied the body back to his home town of Laurium, Michigan. On December 18, Gipp was buried in Lakeview Cemetery, on a hill overlooking Lake Superior.

"Snow, whipped in by a zero gale, swirled around the coffin, which had been brought to the cemetery by a horse-drawn sled that had to fight its way through drifts eight feet high," noted an observer.

Gipp's golden presence was so electric during his time at Notre Dame that he dwarfed the accomplishments of other excellent players. Notre Dame's game was a team game, and Gipp was the crowning jewel in Rockne's collection of gems. His brilliance enhanced the strength of a juggernaut that swept over 18 opponents in 1919 and 1920 and won recognition as western champions. Rockne himself classified his backfield of that era as the best in his early regime.

"The greatest backfield I ever coached was the 1918-19-20 layout," Rockne once insisted in the mid-1920s. "(Joe) Brandy

Notre Dame's All-American end of 1921—Eddie Anderson.

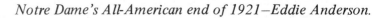

at quarterback, Gipp and (Johnny) Mohardt at halves, and (Chet) Wynne at fullback. They could do everything the Four Horsemen could do. They were equally as fast and heavier, and hence, there was more power."

Others deserving mention from that period include: Charles "Dutch" Bergman, Heartly "Hunk" Anderson, Lawrence "Buck" Shaw, Eddie Anderson, Roger Kiley, George Trafton, Slip Madigan, Frank Coughlin, James Dooley, Fred Slackford, Grover Malone, Clipper Smith, Walter Miller, and Leonard Bahan. Kiley, an end, was eventually picked along with Gipp on an all-time Notre Dame team that boasted top players from 1919 through the 1950s.

Gipp was the heart, soul, and fighting spirit of this fine group of talent and was so acknowledged by many distinguished observers. Particularly touching, and as close to the truth as any, was this observation from the *Chicago Herald* shortly after his death:

"George Gipp is dead.

"It is possible, even probable, that the death of not another young man of 25 in this country would attract so widespread attention.

"George Gipp, a senior at Notre Dame University, was in popular estimation the best football player in the country. It is a great thing to do well in whatever field of action one may have chosen. To do better than anyone else is given to few. Gipp reached that level.

"And at the summit of his achievement in the field he made his own, he dies. For him, no going on to yet greater things, as might have happened; but yet for him, on the other hand, no gradual sinking into obscurity. He passes in fullest brilliance.

"At Notre Dame and elsewhere, Gipp will become a legend. He cannot be forgotten. Circumstances have allied themselves with his own prowess to assure this fact. There will be a kind of consolation in this fact to those who knew him best; to whom he was not George Gipp, all-western, and All-American football player, but George Gipp, the boy.

"Peace to his marvelous activity. He brought honor to himself, honor to his college. He lived as many a man dreamed of living—for accomplishment; he dies as many a man would be willing to die—in the flush of fame."

Famine, Pestilence, Destruction, And Death

"Outlined against a blue-gray October sky, the Four Horsemen rode again. In dramatic lore they are known as Famine, Pestilence, Destruction and Death. These are only aliases. Their real names are Stuhldreher, Miller, Crowley and Layden. They formed the crest of the South Bend cyclone before which another fighting Army football team was swept over the precipice at the Polo Grounds yesterday afternoon, as 55,000 spectators peered down on the bewildering panorama spread on the green plain below. A cyclone can't be snared. It may be surrounded, but somewhere it breaks through to keep going. When the cyclone starts from South Bend, where the candle lights still gleam through the Indiana sycamores, those in the way must take to storm cellars at top speed. Yesterday the cyclone struck again, as Notre Dame beat the Army, 13 to 7, with a set of backfield stars that ripped and crashed through a strong Army defense with more speed and power than the warring cadets could meet."—Grantland Rice.

If ever a group of players belonged to an age, it was the Four Horsemen. Harry Stuhldreher, Don Miller, Jim Crowley, and Elmer Layden were suited to the rhythm of the golden 1920s and danced to its rollicking tune in perfect steps.

Romance was in high gear and so was good, old-fashioned corn. And sportswriters fed plenty of each to the hungry masses.

On October 19, 1924, sports fans picked up newspapers and read for the first time about the "Four Horsemen" outlined against Grantland Rice's "blue-gray October sky." That imagi-

116

Notre Dame's first national championship team of 1924 featured two of Knute Rockne's favorite combinations, the "Four Horsemen" and the "Seven Mules."

native piece of writing was all that was needed to capture the public's fancy. Stuhldreher, Miller, Crowley, and Layden did the rest, wearing their new title with style and elegance. After taking care of Army in New York, the Four Horsemen rode back to South Bend, a smart publicity man put them on horses for a picture, and a legend was made as quick as you could snap a camera shutter.

Rice's story in the *New York Herald Tribune*, the classic photograph, and Knute Rockne's brilliant coaching combined to thrust the Four Horsemen to the top of the field. They became the most famous backfield in the history of college football and played on one of the sport's most colorful teams.

Other groups such as the "Seven Blocks of Granite," the "Four Furies," the "Dream Backfield," and the "Vow Boys" would fill a book of nicknames about football legends. But all of these enjoyed just contemporary fame, while the "Horsemen" luxuriate in immortality.

It is unlikely that the Four Horsemen would have gotten a second glance from modern college scouts. Layden, the irrepressible fullback with a slashing running style, weighed all of 162 pounds—and he was the heaviest of the group. Stuhldreher, the quarterback who was adept both at passing and blocking, had only 156 pounds on his steely frame. Jim Crowley and Don Miller, the halfbacks with blazing speed, were no more than 160 each. They were one of the lightest starting backfields in college football history. But they had abilities which distinguished them from the ordinary.

"What they lacked in poundage, they more than made up for in speed, spirit, smartness and driving force," pointed out Rice one time. "They worked with a rhythm that was unbelievably beautiful to watch, whether or not football happens to be your favorite game.

"Notre Dame's Four Horsemen might not have been the best backfield that football has ever seen. They lacked the offensive power and crash of Rockne's 1930 squad that knew Carideo, Savoldi, Schwartz and Marty Brill. They may not have been as good as Notre Dame's 1943 outfit with Creighton Miller, a nephew of Don Miller's, Bob Kelly, Bertelli and several others—or the fast, powerful Army delegation of 1944 with Blanchard, Davis, Hall, Kenna and a few more. Not to overlook an old Carlisle avalanche that carried Thorpe, Calac and Guyon. But certainly, pound for pound, they stand alone. They had no need for any sheer power. If you consider such assets as speed, brains, heart, alertness and rhythm important, they had no equal."

The gorgeous timing of the quartet, coupled with speed, allowed the Four Horsemen to keep pace with their romantic press clippings.

The "Four Horsemen" did not ride alone—here they are accompanied by their great line, the "Seven Mules."

Noble Kizer (facing camera, hands on hips) and his Notre Dame teammates get ready for action in the roaring 1920s. Gene Oberst is the player wearing No. 3, and No. 41 is Jim Crowley, one of the "Four Horsemen."

"Layden could shade ten seconds for 100 yards, bursting away like a sprinter and rocketing through so low and with such impact that 200-pound linemen could not halt him," sportswriter Arthur Daley once noted. "Crowley and Miller were almost as fast. Stuhldreher and a 185-pound line could move right with them. Rockne used the single-man blocking in those days, predicating his attack on timing of such satanic preciseness that every play came perilously close to being a perfect play. The beauty of this backfield was that one was always exploding with a super-sensational day. This was Rock's favorite team."

Of the precision employed by the Four Horsemen, Miller recalls: "The fact that we played as a unit for more than two years really helped us. We got into a rhythm and timing that we all were aware of. We became very accustomed to each other's timing. The passes from Crowley and from Stuhldreher were right in your hands. . .you only had to turn around. The timing was excellent, just marvelous. Yes, Rock always built his whole team on timing and deception."

The Four Horsemen not only played together as a backfield, but played with a marvelous group of swift linemen called the "Seven Mules." The fame of the "Mules" was dwarfed by Rockne's notorious backfield, but their contribution to the national championship team of 1924 was evident to purists. The Seven Mules, many of them watch-charm size like the "Horsemen" but a celebration of courage and spirit, included center Adam Walsh, guards Noble Kizer and John Weibel, tackles Edward "Rip" Miller and Joe Bach, and ends Ed Huntzinger and Chuck Collins.

Before the "Horsemen" and the "Mules" ran roughshod over opponents in their mature years, many of them were just a bunch of nameless freshmen in 1921. Actually, the fact that the Four Horsemen ever got together was really an accident of fate. Crowley had been a high school sensation in Green Bay, Wisconsin, and had been steered to Notre Dame by Green Bay's Curly Lambeau. One of Rockne's top scouts was a coach at Davenport (Iowa) High School, and he pushed Layden in the direction of South Bend. Stuhldreher arrived at Notre Dame from Massillon, Ohio, at that time one of America's football capitals. Defiance, Ohio, produced a whole family of Millers for Notre Dame football teams, including the irresistible Don Miller. Even Rockne did not suspect their greatness as a unit at first sight. Writing about them years afterward, Rockne said he was not especially impressed with them as freshmen:

"The football epic of the Four Horsemen is the story of an accident. The four did not play as a backfield in their freshmen year—remember, I had seen them in practice and survived the experience. . .Stuhldreher, of the lot, had the most promise. He sounded like a leader on the field. He was a good and fearless blocker, and as he gained in football knowledge, he showed signs of smartness in emergencies. Layden had speed— he could run a 100-yard dash in under ten seconds at a track meet. But speed and some kicking ability seemed to be all his football wares. Jimmy Crowley was only less humorous in play than appearance. He looked dull and always resembled a lad about to get in or out of bed. He showed very little as a freshman—certainly none of the nimble wit that made him as cele-

Don Miller: "The passes from Crowley and Stuhldreher were right in your hands."

Harry Stuhldreher, the "most dangerous" of the "Four Horsemen," according to an Army scout.

brated for repartee as for broken-field running. Don Miller traveled that first year on the reputation and recommendation of his brother, Red Miller, the great Notre Dame halfback who made such havoc when his team beat Michigan in 1909. Don, an also-ran in his freshman year, (later) surprised me when he came out for spring practice and, with his fleetness and daring, sized up as a halfback to cheer the heart of any coach."

Layden, Miller, Crowley, and Stuhldreher took their places with the many other football aspirants. There were so many players, in fact, that there weren't enough full uniforms to go around, and Miller was finally stuck with a makeshift garment that made him look like anything but a football player. It provided amusement for the rest of the freshmen players and an unending string of razzing for the Miller boy.

The 1921 freshmen backfield at first had Layden at quarterback, Crowley at left half, Jerry Miller and Ward Connell at right half, and Rex Enright and Bill Cerney at fullback. Toward the end of the season, Crowley and Layden were alternating at left half, Don Miller was at quarterback, and Enright and Cerney were playing fullback. The "Horsemen" did not even play as a unit in their freshman season.

While the "Horsemen" were struggling for recognition on the freshman team, Rockne was in the process of developing the Notre Dame Shift on the varsity. The coach did not know it at the time, of course, but the Four Horsemen would later prosper under this exquisite system.

Rockne's unique idea met a storm of protest from coaches, particularly those whom had fallen to the Fighting Irish. As Rockne used the shift in 1921, the backs merely jumped into position and then kept going. The advantage was that it gave the runners considerable momentum. It was within the existing rules, but the success of Rockne's teams obviously galled enough people to have the system declared illegal. The football rules committee amended Rule 9, Section 5, in 1922 to outlaw backs in motion on the offensive team. But Rockne outsmarted the rules makers with a similar formation that gave him the same tactical advantage. A writer explains, "Rockne met this situation by having the backs shift in two counts. After the quarterback called the primary signals describing the play, and at the shift signal 'hip,' the backs moved into a box in two counts, both feet stationary on the ground on the count of two. The ball was snapped on the 'two,' and the backs were on their way. Although there was a momentary pause on the count of 'two,' the bodies were yet in momentum, and the effect of the shift was preserved."

The power of the shift drove Notre Dame through 10 opponents in 1921. The Fighting Irish lost only once that season, a 10-7 decision to Iowa in a game that perhaps they should have won. Apathy might have killed Notre Dame that gloomy October afternoon, recalls tackle Buck Shaw:

"I had lived in Iowa, and I knew what Iowa had—this was a hangover from a team that had been together for four years. They were a great football team. Heck, they won the Big Ten that year. But this was their second game, and our scouts came back from watching them play their first game against some small college and didn't seem too disturbed. 'If you play the ball you're capable of,' the scouts said, 'you won't have much trouble.' I think all of my teammates took it lightly, and I tried to tell them I knew what was coming. Hell, that's going to be a great football team, I told them. I knew it. Anyway, we carried

A heartbreaking loss to Iowa in 1921 prevented Notre Dame from having a third straight perfect season and possibly cost the Irish the national championship.

the ball over 400 yards that afternoon and were inside their 10-yard line, as I recall, four times. But we scored only once. We got mixed up badly on one play near the goal line with our quarterback, Chet Grant. It was a little rough. We had a chance to score a field goal from about the 40-yard line. Paul Castner, a good drop kicker, took the chance in the last few minutes of play, and he didn't quite get it through. He had the length, all right, as I recall, but it wasn't quite through the bars. So we lost 10-7. If we had beaten them, we would have been in a great position."

If they had won, the Fighting Irish would have had their third straight undefeated team and a shot at a national title. The end of the bittersweet season left Rockne with memories of what might have been and plenty of holes to fill for 1922. The finish of 1921 heralded the departure of a virtual era with the loss of Shaw, Chet Wynne, Hunk Anderson, Eddie Anderson, Roger Kiley, Fred "Ojay" Larson, and Johnny Mohardt. And Rockne had to build a new team.

Stuhldreher, Miller, Layden, and Crowley figured in his plans but not as a unit. Rockne at first alternated Layden and Crowley at left halfback, used Miller at right halfback, Paul Castner at fullback, and Frank Thomas as the quarterback. Stuhldreher was Thomas' understudy. The sophomore "Horsemen" shone individually through the early season and had a hand in a significant 13-3 victory over Georgia Tech, even though Stuhldreher made what Rockne called "the biggest mistake of his career" in this game. With the ball on the Georgia Tech five yard line, the Notre Dame quarterback threw an incomplete pass over the goal line. And in those days, that meant a touchback, with Georgia Tech getting the ball on the 20. It was a lesson well learned for the young Stuhldreher. "Never again did Stuhldreher make a tactical error," Rockne said.

It was during this time that Crowley emerged as the team entertainer. He was as quick with a quip as he was with a forward pass. He formed a comical act with Mickey Kane, a reserve halfback. Prohibition was one of the big issues of the day, and wherever the Notre Dame train stopped on its myriad journeys, Crowley could be seen making temperance speeches from the rear platform, while Kane, his "campaign manager," kept the crowd stirred up. Stuhldreher was almost in Crowley's league as a wit, if one can judge by one of his off-the-cuff remarks.

Elusive Harry Stuhldreher is chased in a 1924 game. Few opponents caught him.

Because Notre Dame traveled a lot, the Fighting Irish backs get "shifty from getting in and out of upper berths," Stuhldreher once told an opponent.

After beating Georgia Tech, the Fighting Irish continued on with victories over Indiana, Army, and Butler, and it was this last game that precipitated the birth of the Four Horsemen as a unit.

"We were playing Butler at Indianapolis, and Castner got his hip broken," remembers Miller. "And that weekend, all the football players were wondering who Rock would put in at that fullback position to take Castner's place. So the following Monday, he shifted Layden over to fullback, and that left Crowley at left halfback. And by that time, Stuhldreher had beaten out Thomas for quarterback, and I was playing the right halfback position. And then we played Carnegie Tech the next Saturday, and we played Nebraska the following Saturday. So in 1922, the Four Horsemen started to play as a unit. . ."

At first Layden was skeptical about his new position.

"I can't play fullback," he told Rockne, "I'm not heavy enough."

But Rockne, the supreme salesman, convinced him.

"That's where we're going to fool them, Elmer. Everyone is accustomed to the big lumbering line plunger who packs a lot of power. But in you we're bringing a new type to the game. You are very fast, and we're going to make you into a slicing and quick-opening fullback."

Layden made the change from halfback to fullback with such ease that even Rockne did not expect results that sudden. After watching a 19-0 victory over Carnegie Tech, the coach commented: "These boys surprised the football fans of Pittsburgh with their perfect timing as they functioned for the first time as a unit backfield. Layden amazed me by his terrific speed as fullback. He adopted a straight line drive that made him one of the most unusual fullbacks in football. He pierced a line through sheer speed—cutting it like a knife, although each man in the opposing line outweighed him by 20 pounds."

The *Chicago Tribune* acknowledged Notre Dame's newest royalty: "Don Miller, Crowley, Layden, and Stuhldreher, the flashy sophomore backfield, starred equally in the Notre Dame attack. Miller and Crowley ran the ends for big gains, and Stuhldreher revealed unusual smartness in directing the attack and in passing."

Rockne knew he had something golden in these four players, even though the Fighting Irish were beaten 14-6 by Nebraska on the last day of the 1922 season. Rather than sulk in defeat, Rockne found a certain consolation and a "thrill" in the loss to one of the nation's biggest and best teams.

"The Cornhuskers had one of the heaviest teams in their history—and they were known for very active heft. They pushed the relatively little Four Horsemen all over the field. At the half the score was 14-0, and it would have been another touchdown if the lightweight boys from South Bend hadn't held the Nebraska heavies on their one-yard line for four straight downs. They emerged from that battering a sadly crumpled team. But they came out fighting mad for the second half, whacked across a touchdown in the third quarter, and carried the ball to Nebraska's one-yard line toward the end of the final period. Stuhldreher called for a pass, and Layden spurted ahead to a corner of the field, where he was all set to receive and down the ball for six more points. But Stuhldreher, ever alert, this time was not alert enough. Weller, the huge 250-pound Nebraska tackle, crashed through the line and smeared the 150-pound Notre Dame quarterback."

The Four Horsemen did not have many disappointments after that. Rockne recognized their greatness and worked to make the unit even better. Because Stuhldreher and Crowley were a little bit slower than Layden and Miller, Rockne gave them lighter shoes, thigh pads, and stockings. Eventually Stuhldreher dropped the thigh pads entirely. In time the backfield became so fast that Rockne had to move their lining-up positions farther back from the line of scrimmage. Stuhldreher threw the passes, and his primary targets were the other backs—a concept dreamed up by Rockne. Rockne had just improved on an old weapon—until he came on the scene, passes were thrown exclusively to ends.

Feeling secure with his backfield, Rockne turned his attention toward the line for the 1923 season. With the help of Hunk Anderson, the former Notre Dame player who was now Rockne's right-hand man, the "Seven Mules" were born. One of Anderson's significant moves in this direction was making a tackle out of Joe Bach, a onetime substitute guard. Bach became one of the best at his position and helped galvanize the players up front.

The Fighting Irish opened the 1923 season with a bang, crushing Kalamazoo 74-0 as their backs ran wild. They next beat Lombard and then set their caps for Army. Grantland Rice, the nationally known sportswriter, attended this game at Ebbets Field in Brooklyn and was greatly impressed by the Notre Dame backfield. After the game, won 13-0 by the Fighting Irish, Rice recalled how the idea of the "Four Horsemen" was planted:

"I took my friend Brink Thorne, one of Yale's greatest football stars from the era of Frank Hinkey, across the bridge to see Army and Notre Dame meet in Brooklyn at Ebbets Field. Brink and I had sideline passes where we could follow the play at close range up and down the field. It was in this game that the name, 'the Four Horsemen,' received its subconscious birth, to find life a year later. Brink and I were crouched along the sidelines around midfield when, on a certain play, Notre Dame's four flying backs came sweeping from the Rockne shift around Army's left end. The interference was headed by Harry Stuhldreher at quarter. Elmer Layden and Don Miller were part of the speedy compact attack, with Jimmy Crowley carrying the ball. They had picked up twelve yards on the play before Crowley was finally forced out of bounds. But he was still moving at such high speed that he had to hurdle both Thorne and myself to keep from trampling us underfoot.

"'We'd better move back,' I said to Brink. 'They are worse than a flock of wild horses on a stampede.' This thought was in my mind as I saw them swing into action against another strong Army team at the Polo Grounds a year later. I know I felt much safer up in the press box than I had felt along the sidelines in Brooklyn where the back of my neck was almost impaled on Crowley's cleats."

It was also in this game that Crowley's zany antics began spreading heaping portions of Notre Dame color around the nation. At one tense point, Notre Dame had the ball in its territory in a third-down-and-ten situation. While the large crowd waited expectantly to see what the Fighting Irish would do, Crowley called time out, paced the yardage to the first-down marker, and yelled back to his teammates: "It's only ten yards. A truck horse could run that far." Crowley made the ten yards.

Everyone, from game officials to teammates to Rockne himself, was fair game for Crowley's sharp tongue.

After one contest which Notre Dame won despite prejudicial calls by one official, Crowley was accosted by the unjust referee.

"You guys were lucky to win," he told Crowley.

"Yes, Cyclops," said the player. "Considering the one-sided, one-eyed way you officiated, we were very lucky to win."

There was a game against Wisconsin at Madison, and Notre Dame was en route to an easy 38-3 victory. Stuhldreher had stressed the ground-gaining abilities of Layden and Miller for most of the afternoon, giving little attention to Crowley. This got Crowley mad, and during a time out, he had a little discussion with the quarterback.

"You know where I come from?" Crowley asked.

"Green Bay," said Stuhldreher, "and I don't blame you."

"Green Bay is in Wisconsin," Crowley snapped. "There's lots of people here from my town. Don't you think they want to see Crowley do something else besides kick points after touchdowns for Layden and Miller?"

On another occasion, Rockne was unhappy with Crowley's repeated mistakes at practice. Finally, the coach got so mad, he blew his top.

"Can you name anyone dumber than a dumb Irishman?" he roared at Crowley.

"Yes, coach," Crowley fired back without skipping a beat,

129

"a smart Swede."

He referred, of course, to Rockne, who had been known as the "Swede" even though his birthplace was Norway.

Crowley could take it as well as he could dish it out, a trait which marked him in Rockne's book as a class person.

"His style of thought and good-humored balance of character was of the sterling stuff that wears better in adversity than in success," the coach once said.

Once in a game against Princeton, Crowley appeared to be on his way for a long gain when he was tripped up from behind by a player named Slagle. When confronted by Rockne in the locker room at the half, Crowley was deeply apologetic for not breaking free.

"I made a mistake," he told Rockne. "I didn't know Slagle was that fast. I should have cut back."

"That wasn't the mistake you made," Rockne said.

"Yes, it was," Crowley shot back. "I admit it. A mistake."

"No," answered Rockne. "Slagle didn't know who you were. If you had shown him those New York press clippings you've been saving, telling how good you were, he wouldn't have dared come near you."

Later Rockne recalled: "Crowley laughed louder than any-

Princeton's Ivy Leaguers get a taste of Notre Dame punishment in the early 1920s. The Irish made lambs out of the Tigers.

body at this. Perhaps he knew what all the team knew, that the Four Horsemen—great though they were—received a measure of praise that they should have shared with the stalwart linemen, the Seven Mules."

The "Mules" were no less colorful than the "Horsemen," and they added whimsical stories to the growing Fighting Irish legend. The first-string line was taking a rest during one portion of the game against Lombard. While they watched from the sidelines, the Four Horsemen had trouble getting started behind the second-stringers. So Rockne sent in his Seven Mules.

"What seems to be the matter, boys?" center Adam Walsh said as he prepared to snap the ball back for the first scrimmage. "It seems you need a little help."

Rockne occasionally fretted that his famous backfield was getting too much attention and that not enough of the spotlight was given to his line. So one time he made a game effort to give his "Mules" equal billing.

"Rockne worried that the linemen might resent all the attention showered on us so he had the team vote on which was the more important, the backfield or the line," Stuhldreher once recalled. "The line won 7-4."

The Four Horsemen acted in concert not only as runners, but as kidders. They kept up a steady banter during games, often unnerving opponents with their matchless breezy style. Once forewarned about Army's great center, Ed Garbisch, the Horsemen found a way to irritate him. Whenever Garbisch was smeared on a play, one of the Horsemen would politely inquire of the other so that the Army center could hear:

"Is that the great Mr. Garbisch?"

To which another would reply with solemnity: "Yes, that's the great Mr. Garbisch."

"It didn't help Garbisch's game much," Rockne recalled.

For the second time in two years, Notre Dame had an unbeaten season spoiled by Nebraska. After winning six straight games in 1923, the Fighting Irish lost a 14-7 decision to the burly Cornhuskers. That was the second—and last—time that the Four Horsemen, used as a unit, would ever lose a game. There was no letdown the rest of the season as the Four Horsemen led victories over Butler, Carnegie Tech, and St. Louis and raced toward their meeting with destiny. It came in the third game of the 1924 season against Army, after easy opening victories against Lombard and Wabash.

There was tremendous interest in the East over the 1924 Army-Notre Dame game. The Polo Grounds in New York held about 60,000, but it did not seem large enough for this intriguing battle. Both Army and Notre Dame were at the height of their power. The Cadets had the extra advantage of using players who had already graduated from other schools, and it was not uncommon at this time to find several ex-All-Americans in their lineup. Still, Army seemed more concerned about Notre Dame than vice versa. Especially about Notre Dame's Four Horsemen. Pat Mahoney, the Army team captain, was sent to scout the Notre Dame-Wabash game the week before and came back with this report to Cadet coach John McEwan:

"Now, that Crowley, he's like lightning. Better put two men on him! And that Layden makes yardage every time. Put two men on him! Then there is Miller. I don't have to tell you that I advise putting two men on him! Stuhldreher, the quarterback, is the most dangerous of them all. He can think! Have three men on him!"

Of course if McEwan would have followed Mahoney's advice to the letter, he would hardly have had anyone else to play the rest of the Notre Dame team.

McEwan put his players through quick preliminary warm-ups before game time, then hustled them back into the locker room for a pep talk. Rockne, on the other hand, staged an extravagant show for the large Polo Ground audience before the game.

"He sent out his entire squad—six full teams—in waves that rolled the length of the field," Jim Beach and Daniel Moore wrote in their book, *Army Vs. Notre Dame, The Big Game.* "In dummy signal drill the linemen and backs charged in perfect formation, pulled up after 10 yards, got set and on the signal charged again. Punts crossed in mid-air, and ends leapt for passes on the sideline."

Before the game Rockne moaned about the Army powerhouse. He told reporters that Notre Dame was too weak to stop the Cadets, even though the Fighting Irish had lost but three games since 1918 and none to Army since 1916. Rockne did have some problems, it was true. Captain Adam Walsh, the center and tower of strength of the Seven Mules, had a broken right hand. Stuhldreher, the brilliant, little play-caller, was having trouble with his throwing arm. Both played, Walsh with his hand in a cast and Stuhldreher after trainers had spread some

Army's Bill Wood plunges through left tackle for a four-yard gain and a first down in the first quarter of the 1922 game with Notre Dame. The Irish and Cadets struggled to a 0-0 tie that day.

"magic" liniment on his shoulder. And both did their usual great jobs. Walsh broke a bone in his other hand but still was able to open up holes for the Notre Dame runners. And Stuhldreher sent them through with dazzling aplomb.

Up in the press box, Grantland Rice began structuring in his mind the most-remembered sports story in journalism history. These were his feelings at the time:

"It was the start of the second period, with the score 0-0, Army dominating the earlier play, that Stuhldreher, Miller, Crowley and Layden came rushing out from the Notre Dame bench. There they were again—a backfield that ranged in weight from 155 to 163 pounds, an average displacement of 161 pounds, by many pounds the lightest in the starring ranks of football history. It was at the start of the second period, or just after the start, that the Four Horsemen earned their name. (And at the risk of explaining the obvious, perhaps I should add that the name was derived from Vicente Blasco Ibanez's *The Four Horsemen of the Apocalypse*, who, in turn, got his idea from the Revelation of St. John the Divine. The four horsemen were known as Famine, Pestilence, War, and Death. These were the component ingredients of Notre Dame's famous backfield.)

"After (Bill) Wood's kick (for Army), Notre Dame had the ball on her twenty-yard line with Army goal eighty yards away. It was here that the swift, striking stampede started. Crowley picked up fifteen yards on the first play. Layden and Miller added sixteen more. A pass from Stuhldreher to Crowley gathered twelve just before Don Miller's twenty-yard sprint carried him to Army's ten-yard line. Over cracked Layden for the first touchdown—eighty yards in just seven plays. It should be noted here that 'The Seven Mules' who made up Notre Dame's forward wall, headed by such stars as Adam Walsh and Rip Miller, deserved far greater credit than they received while playing brilliantly in the shadow of their famous backfield. . .these South Bend linemen, while not bulky in any way, were also smart, fast and alert, matching one of the best lines in the Army annals."

Notre Dame won the game 13-7, and as the gun went off a telegrapher began punching out Rice's stirring report: "Outlined against a blue-gray October sky, the Four Horsemen rode again..." At the time, of course, no one dreamed that this story would add epic proportions to the Notre Dame legend.

"When we read the story the next day, we felt that people would forget about it in another month, and that would be the end of it," Miller says today. "But, gee, it kept on going and going. . . ."

Crowley agrees: "I didn't realize the impact it would have. At the time I thought it was just another well-written story. But the thing just kind of mushroomed because after that splurge in the newspapers, the sports fans of the nation got interested in us, along with other sportswriters. I think if we had lost a couple of games after that Army game, it would have been just a temporary thing. But because our record was so good, it helped a lot. I think if we would have lost a game or two after that splurge by Granny Rice, I don't think we would have been remembered. . . ."

While Rice got the ball rolling for the Four Horsemen with his magnificent story, Notre Dame publicity man George Strickler kept it in midflight with a classic public relations gimmick.

"When we came back from New York after Grantland Rice's article, that next Monday Strickler got four horses, brought them out on the field and took a picture of us on top of them," recalls Miller. "And then he copyrighted that picture and really sold a lot of them throughout the United States."

It made some money for Strickler and a lot of fame for the

Four Horsemen. The nation's attention now focused on the colorful Fighting Irish, and they lived up to their publicity with six more victories, to close out the regular season with a 9-0 record. Included in that string was a sweet-revenge 34-6 triumph over powerful Nebraska, the only school to beat the Four Horsemen teams.

The perfect record resulted in Notre Dame's first invitation to a bowl game. Rockne had been angling for a bid to the Rose Bowl for some time and finally got his wish in 1924. But as badly as Rockne wanted to go to California, he almost turned his back on Pasadena when he found out about the contract arrangements made by Notre Dame officials. For economic reasons the Notre Dame administration had accepted an arrangement whereby only 22 players and the head coach would go to California. Rockne was incensed about this arrangement, pointing out that at least 35 men had made every Notre Dame trip for the previous three years, along with assistant coaches, trainers, and managers. Rockne wanted them all rewarded with a trip west.

"The terms are wholly unacceptable," Rockne said.

Then he turned to a student who was working as a publicist. "Get Pop Warner on the phone, and call off everything."

It did not occur to Rockne that it was 5:30 a.m. in Palo Alto when the student called the Stanford coach. The call rocked Warner out of a sound sleep, and the student had a hard time communicating with him. Finally, Rockne had to get on the phone.

"Pop," Rockne barked. "You can play anyone you want and call them anything you want; but I won't be there, and my boys won't be there."

Rockne had made his point. By the next day, the Rose Bowl arrangements were changed, and Rockne began preparing a traveling squad that included 35 players, plus assistant coaches, managers, and trainers.

Another problem cropped up before they left, however, and Rockne again threatened cancellation. This had to do with tickets. Notre Dame was to receive 2,000 tickets priced at $1.50 each, but a friend of Rockne's on the West Coast informed him that these were of the student admission variety and in a bad location behind the goalpost. Rockne fired off a wire:

"I have no contract. We will get the same ticket arrangement as Stanford, or no game. Show this wire to Henry (Leslie

B. Henry, Tournament of Roses chairman), and tell him I am tired of no word on anything. We are no hick college, and I insist on equality." Notre Dame got it.

Climate was one of Rockne's chief concerns, and because he felt that his players had to be acclimated to California's warm weather, he mapped out an extensive tour of the South en route to the Golden West. Before he left, however, he had no control over the weather. A bad storm hit northern Indiana and encased the Notre Dame campus in ice. Temperatures plunged to zero and made outdoor practice impossible.

Notre Dame got to California by way of New Orleans, Houston, and Tucson, but by the time Rockne arrived, he was not too happy he had made the trip that way. At every stop the Fighting Irish were dined so sumptuously that they were not in the greatest condition to play football. Rockne got nervous, and a couple of the players almost got sent back to South Bend after missing curfew one night. Arriving in Arizona for the last practice session before California, Rockne acknowledged with evident strain: "Nobody on my squad is in shape to play a hard game. I will be satisfied with 3-0." But after a good practice session in Tucson, Rockne changed his tune a bit: "The men are in better shape than I thought. If the change in climate isn't too great, we may be able to cope with Stanford's attack."

The Fighting Irish were well aware that they merited the mythical national championship, and just about everyone except Stanford was ready to give it to them. The Indians with fabulous Ernie Nevers, the best-known individual football player in the country at the time, refused to concede an inch to the Fighting Irish.

When it came to the day of the game, however, they did concede plenty of yards. Nevers, despite playing with pained ankles wrapped in tape, had a fine day for Stanford. But Layden had a better day. Nevers ripped Notre Dame's line to pieces, but when it counted at the goal line, he could not punch through the Seven Mules. Twice, Layden set Stanford back on its ear with booming, 80-yard punts. Twice, he intercepted passes and ran for touchdowns of 80 and 70 yards. Layden scored three times and averaged 50 yards from scrimmage on his punts. Rockne had his team play smart football. He knew that Notre Dame's lighter team could not match the Stanford power. So the Fighting Irish played a kicking game until the Indians ran out of steam. When Stanford got tired of running and went to

Elmer Layden kicks one for Notre Dame. He put in a lot of hours on kicking drills.

the air, Layden was there to make key interceptions. Notre Dame won 27-10, and nobody then denied them the title of national champion.

Nevers remembered that game with some chagrin: "The difference between the Stanford team and Notre Dame that day was that Stanford featured power up the middle and through the tackles—Notre Dame featured knife-like thrusts through the line and speedy end runs. I was very impressed with the perfect precision of the ballet-like shift of the Four Horsemen. The two plays that can never be erased from my memory were the two accurate passes I threw to Layden. One good for 80 yards and a touchdown and the other, 70 yards for a touchdown. A total of 150 yards in two tries, and two touchdowns makes the passing combination of Layden of Notre Dame and Nevers of Stanford the best in Rose Bowl history."

A goal-line stand by the stubborn Mules and a dazzling kick by Layden in one sequence gave the Fighting Irish their winning impetus. Reflecting on that key series of plays, Stuhldreher said:

"We were leading by 14 to 10 when that Nevers started grinding us down on a long march. He kept punching us back, four and five yards at a time, until finally there we were with our own goal line showing under our linemen's feet. One way or another we stopped 'em there. I must admit there is some difference of opinion on the Coast over whether or not we really did stop Nevers short of a touchdown, Officially, we did. . . because they gave us the ball on downs. It was about a foot from our goal line. Right there, I got my greatest lesson in the value of practice. All that year, right up to our last practice at home before heading West, Elmer Layden had put in an hour of kicking drill. He would go out early, before the regular practice, and work on his kicking. Well, it paid off when we got the ball on the one-foot line. Layden backed up to the end of the end zone and kicked. The ball hopped out of bounds on the Stanford 18-yard line. . .82 yards away. And that was our ball-game."

Notre Dame eventually scored two more touchdowns, and another of Layden's kicks was responsible for one of them.

"It was one of his regular kicks," remembered Stuhldreher, "with tremendous height. He always got great height on his kicks. The Stanford safety man must have thought it was never coming down. Our ends, Chuck Collins and Ed Huntzinger, were flanking the safety man long before the ball came down. He must have felt awfully uncomfortable. Finally, it hit him, and he fumbled. Collins drove him away from the ball with a body block, and Huntzinger scooped up the ball and ran on over for a touchdown."

The score might have been even more lopsided, Crowley points out, if Stuhldreher had not been injured.

"It was always my opinion that we'd have really whipped them worse if it hadn't been that Stuhulie hurt his ankle," Crowley says. "They scored their only touchdown on a pass to (Ted) Shipkey over Harry. He couldn't move. At the time, we thought it was a sprain, but it turned out the ankle was broken, but he played all the way. But it bothered us on offense, too. You see, Harry was the blocking back, and he led the blocking on our sweeps. He couldn't move out like he did in other games."

Notre Dame's victory over Pop Warner's team in its first bowl game not only certified the Fighting Irish as national champions, but clearly established them as a power at the gate as well. A crowd of 53,000 had attended the Rose Bowl game in Pasadena, California, and, coupled with the regular season attendance, gave Notre Dame an audience figure of 318,425 for 1924, highest in the school's history. It was obvious that Notre Dame now was Public Friend No. 1. Eyeing the possibility of a lucrative intersectional rivalry, Southern California invited

Notre Dame back to the West Coast in 1926 and started one of football's grandest traditions.

"Rockne and the 1924 team pioneered modern football," pointed out a writer. "When it became clear that Notre Dame drew crowds all over the country, the backyard neighbors who'd been ducking the Irish came calling on them. The attitude now was, 'We have everything to gain—especially money—and little to lose.' There were no cries of 'break up Notre Dame.' Instead, the other schools fought to reach the Notre Dame level. This led to better competition and improved the quality of football. Until this time football had been a game followed by college men. It had also been a fairly dull game, featuring 'four-yards-and-a-cloud-of-dust' offenses. The appearance of Rockne's national champions with their great speed and daring passing game brought a new excitement to football."

In three years the Four Horsemen teams won 27 games, lost only two, and tied one. Famine, pestilence, destruction, and death were pretty hard to beat all at once.

Famine, Pestilence, Destruction, and Death.

One For The Gipper

"There was no one in the room that wasn't crying, including Rockne and me. There was a moment of silence, and then all of a sudden those players ran out of the dressing room and almost tore the hinges off the door. They were all ready to kill someone."—Ed Healey.

Knute Rockne called his 1928 team the "Minutemen." "They'll be in the game one minute," he said, "and the other team will score."

Rockne could do little else but laugh at his situation that year. It was his poorest season by far. The four losses represented one-third of the number of games that Rock lost in his entire career. Some said he was washed up, that he had lost his magic. More to the truth, the old master had lost a lot of his players. An unlikely string of injuries had hit the Fighting Irish and sent them spinning.

By early November the punch-drunk Fighting Irish had already lost two games, and a third loss seemed a certainty when they faced all-powerful Army in Yankee Stadium. As usual there was great interest in the game, but no one gave the Fighting Irish a fighting chance. No one, that is, except Rockne himself. "We'll take Army on Saturday," he told a neighbor. He seemed to have something up his sleeve.

The Cadets had spectacular Chris Cagle in their backfield, a host of All-Americans, and a record of six straight victories. Notre Dame had no one to match Cagle in the backfield and, in fact, almost did not have a backfield. Freddie Collins, who had broken an arm in the first game of the year, was forced to play the game at fullback with the arm in a cast because Rockne had no one else. Jack Chevigny, the right halfback, was the only whole man back there.

"Now no coach could be very optimistic with that sort of a setup," remembers Ed Healey, the Notre Dame line coach that year, "but yet Rock was very optimistic the day before the game."

A spirited pep rally had sent the Cadets off toward New York, and on the Friday before the game they staged a short workout at the New York Athletic Club Field on Travers Island. Then they went into seclusion in a midtown hotel to await Saturday's battle. Notre Dame stayed at a country club in nearby Westchester and motored to Yankee Stadium that November 12. They arrived about 11:30 a.m. for their pregame taping session, Healey remembers.

"The stadium was jammed, and it was not too inviting for Notre Dame. It was cold and clammy and kind of scary. Rockne let the boys go out on the field to warm up prior to the game. They were out there about 15 minutes, and then he pulled them in and he told 'em to all lay down on the floor. He had 'em lay down on these olive-drab blankets that came out of World War I. He wanted them to lay on those blankets instead of on that oily, clammy floor that the Yankee ballclub used to use. Silence prevailed for a while."

Then Rockne broke the silence with the most dramatic locker room speech in the history of college football. This game called for a command performance, and Rockne, indeed, was ready to give it.

"Rock was terribly disturbed on the day of the game," Healey recalls. "About five minutes before game time, he spoke to the team. He prefaced his remarks on the terrific Army team. Finally, he recalled standing beside the death bed of George Gipp and told of reaching out his hand and listening to the dying athlete say, 'Coach, when the going gets rough, especially against Army, win one for me.' And of course, he repeated the word, 'Gipper.' And he went on to emphasize not only how important it was to them, the boys, themselves, but likewise to answer the prayer of the Gipper, who was a convert to Catholicism on his death bed. So you see there was a touch of the spiritual motivation about it all. And I'm telling you, there wasn't a dry eye in the house. We were all crying, I don't give a damn who it was..."

Notre Dame's Fred Collins catches a pass in the final quarter of the 1928 game with Army at Yankee Stadium. The Fighting Irish, inspired by Knute Rockne's locker room speech, went on to win this one for the Gipper, 12-6.

Rockne's impassioned speech about the famous Notre Dame football player who had died prematurely eight years before had an electric effect on all those in the room. That included not only the players but also Mayor Jimmy Walker of New York and two policemen who wept unashamedly.

It was the piece de resistance as only Rockne could deliver it. In a low, emotion-choked voice, Rockne said that Gipp had asked for just one game and that, "This is the game."

There was no stopping the Notre Dame players after that. The inspired Fighting Irish won the game 12-6 with two touchdowns in the second half. Chevigny, who was just about the whole Notre Dame running attack, blasted over from the one yard line in the third period to tie the score at 6-6. When the emotional Chevigny picked himself up in the end zone, he was supposed to have said, "That's one for the Gipper."

Chevigny also led Notre Dame's winning touchdown march in the last quarter, although he was not there at the end to see its conclusion. The talented halfback hurt himself, and Rockne had to remove him just when the Fighting Irish were nearing the Army goal line. Fate had reserved the hero's role for "One-Play" O'Brien.

With the ball on the Army 32, Rockne substituted reserve Johnny O'Brien for Johnny Colrick at left end and Bill Dew for the injured Chevigny. O'Brien was a fine hurdler on the Notre Dame track team but was too slight and willowy for steady action in football. On the first play quarterback Pat Brady called O'Brien's number. Butch Niemiec backpedaled and fired a long pass in O'Brien's direction. The ball arched over the head of Army's defensive left halfback and hit O'Brien's hands on the 10 yard line. The receiver juggled the ball as he staggered toward the Army goal line. Finally, he clutched it firmly as he dived over the line, missing the straining grasps of two Army defenders.

"That's one for the Gipper, too," Chevigny muttered on the sidelines as O'Brien hit the end zone. Chevigny was crying.

After the play O'Brien returned to the Notre Dame bench to the tune of Notre Dame cheers. Rockne was so affected by the play that he came out to meet the big end as he came off the field. The coach shook his hand and personally draped the boy's blanket around him. That lone appearance marked the gangling end as "One-Play" O'Brien.

Frank Carideo, who played in that significant game, recalls

Frank Carideo races around Penn State's end for a substantial gain in the 1928 game won 9-0 by Notre Dame.

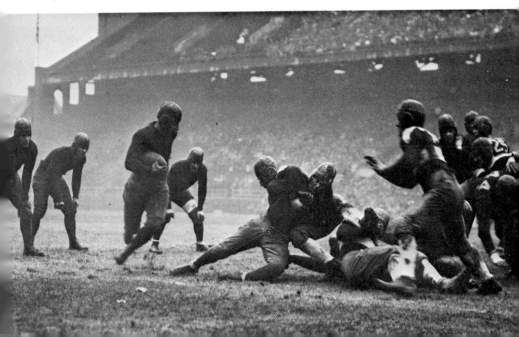

precisely how the winning play evolved:

"There were no huddles in those days. We signaled outright by numbers. During the week we worked very hard on strategy. Each man had a play that he was outstanding in, and that particular week, we worked on a pattern with O'Brien. He could run with the ease of any of them, and it was obvious that he would be sent in at a given time when a series of downs called for at least one passing play. And of course O'Brien came in; he went down the left side, across to the right, then down the field slightly. Then Niemiec threw the pass for the touchdown."

Rockne's immediate reaction to the touchdown play burns in Carideo's mind.

"You could see a great, big smile on his face. He was happy when things created during the week were used to perfection in the ballgame."

The game was not salted away at this point, however. Army still had one last chance with less than two minutes remaining. Cagle took the kickoff for the Cadets and traveled 55 yards to Notre Dame's 35. Eddie Collins, the last man between the great Army back and the goal line, made a saving tackle for the Fighting Irish. The Cadets continued to roll, with the irrepressible Cagle leading the attack. Cagle later dragged the

The Notre Dame team leaves for the 1928 Navy game at Soldier Field in Chicago. A monster crowd of 120,000 turned out to watch the Irish win 7-0.

Jack Chevigny makes a 10-yard gain against Navy in the 1928 game at Soldier Field in Chicago. A crowd of 120,000 watched Notre Dame beat the Midshipmen 7-0.

ball to the Notre Dame 10, before he was felled by exhaustion and had to be taken out of the game.

Dick Hutchinson moved Army to the four yard line with a pass to Charlie Allan. Army lined up quickly, and Hutchinson catapulted to the one, but that was the last play of the game. As Army center Bill Hall put his hands on the ball to pass it back, the final gun went off, punctuating the end of one of the most exciting Army-Notre Dame games in history. Rockne called this Notre Dame team his "greatest—for that afternoon."

It might have been all of that. Notre Dame's crippled team scored one of the biggest upsets of the 1928 season, or any other season for that matter. Notre Dame's limited power was exposed in the last two games of the year when the Fighting Irish were beaten soundly. A 27-7 thrashing by Carnegie Tech, the first home loss for Notre Dame since 1905, and a 27-14 defeat by Southern Cal made the victory over Army more dramatic and more illogical.

Despite Rockne's worst season on the field, Notre Dame had its best year at the gate. A total of 419,705 saw the Fighting Irish play in 1928, including 120,000 at Chicago's Soldier Field in the Navy game. The crowds got bigger and the record got better in 1929.

Undefeated, Untied, And Unbelievable

"There's no fun in losing, and the only thing worthwhile in life is to win because that's the American spirit. Regardless of what you play or where you play, this is something that has to be a part of you. It wasn't win at any cost in my time. It was win on an honest basis. But win."—Frank Carideo.

The year of the Great Depression was a tough one all around. The stock market crash hit bottom with a shot heard 'round the country. People were either sitting in the poor house or throwing themselves out of it. Everything was down. Everything, that is, except Notre Dame football.

While the nation's fortunes went spinning, Notre Dame's football fortunes were spiraling. Knute Rockne had promised at the end of the disastrous 1928 season that things would get better at South Bend in 1929. And they did.

Rockne added some great new plays—and some great new players—to his deadly formations. He stressed offense more than ever before, introducing slick spinners and single reverse plays. Of course he continued to insist on high-caliber blocking and tackling as the backbone for his Notre Dame system, and this was never better.

The new offensive plays were meant to take advantage of the talents of his dazzling backfield players, who included "Jumpin' Joe" Savoldi, Frank Carideo, Jack Elder, Marty Brill, Marchy Schwartz, and Moon Mullins. The linemen include two of the best in Notre Dame history—tackle Ted Twomey and guard Jack Cannon—and one of the best-known figures, Frank Leahy. Leahy, Notre Dame's famous coach of the 1940s and

1950s, won a tackle spot but later came down with a spate of injuries that hampered his playing career. Cannon, who played hatless while everyone else was wearing helmets, is listed on Notre Dame's all-time team. He joined with Twomey to give the Fighting Irish an irresistible force and immovable object on that rugged 1929 line.

This group of players, probably the best collection of talent Rockne had up until that time, went on to win the national championship with nine straight victories. That they went through 1929 undefeated is not amazing; what is, is just how they did it. Because a new stadium was being built at South Bend, the Fighting Irish had no home field in 1929 and as a result had to play all their games on the road. The Fighting Irish did it with a sometime coach, too. Rockne was stricken with phlebitis and was advised to give up football by his doctors. But he managed to struggle through the 1929 season with his bad legs, coaching one dramatic victory after another from either a hospital bed (by telephone) or in a wheel chair from the sidelines. One time while giving an impassioned speech at the Southern Cal game, the blood clot broke loose, passed through his heart, and lodged safely in his other leg. Medical men gave Rockne a 50-50 chance of living if he coached football that year. But Rockne lived through it, and the Notre Dame team

The 1929 Fighting Irish had no home, but the most famous vagabonds in college football managed to win a national championship anyway.

got healthier with each passing game.

"He was a very emotional fellow," remembers Carideo, "but in those years he had to be more or less quiet because of the phlebitis. He was very calm for the most part. I don't remember him being upset on the sidelines. But he was emotional at halftime. He brought fire to the game to get you ready. . ."

About 300 players turned out for spring practice in 1929, and Rockne's discerning eye trimmed this figure down to less than a hundred by the time the fall came.

"He was very selective," Carideo recalls. "He would bring back 75 or 80 in the fall and then make out a traveling squad of 36 to 40."

When Rockne assembled his players that fall, everyone knew he was looking for a kicker to replace Johnny Niemiec. Three members of the strong backfield were all given a chance to win this job—Elder, the fleet runner from Kentucky; Schwartz, destined to become one of Rockne's greatest players; and Carideo, a stocky New Yorker of innumerable skills. Rockne eventually gave the job to Carideo and was never sorry for it. Carideo became a master at punting and delivering extra points and a genius at running the team from his quarterback position. He might have been Rockne's most valuable player in that time, for he was a star on defense and could block extremely well, too.

Carideo was worth his weight in gold footballs to Notre Dame in kicking ability alone. His exquisite kicks continually brought opponents to their knees. Newspapermen recognized this magical quality in Carideo, and George Trevor was one of many who pointed it out. In an article in the *New York Sun* after Notre Dame beat Army 7-0 in 1929, Trevor said: "Not enough praise had been accorded Carideo for his remarkable 'corner kicking.' He strangled Army throughout the second half with his angled punts, aiming for coffin corner. These oblique kicks had height as well as uncanny direction. It seemed that he could place the ball on a dime. . .Carideo's geometric precision was an optical treat. . .an adept corner kicker must have skill, nerve, and poise under pressure. Carideo has 'em all."

Frank Carideo flanked by two pretty good running mates— Knute Rockne and Mayor Jimmy Walker of New York.

Another writer felt that Carideo might have been in a class by himself. "In the matter of the greatest quarterbacks who ever lived, I still like to think of Carideo," Warren Brown wrote in the *Chicago American* in 1969. "Carideo was as brilliant and as accurate a kicker as I have ever seen, with the possible exception of Don Nisbet, who functioned for Andy Smith's Californians in the 20s. Carideo could pass. He could run. He could think. There wasn't anything he couldn't do, or that he didn't do."

Only twice in his career were Carideo's booming punts blocked. Both times came against Army, and both times his own teammates, not the opposition, got in the way of the ball.

"One time in 1929 I kicked Marty Brill, our right halfback, in the pants with the ball, and in the 1930 game I kicked Larry Mullins, our fullback, in the same spot. It was a funny thing,

Notre Dame rushers blitz an Army passer in this 1929 game at Yankee Stadium. The Irish endured 7-0 and completed an undefeated season.

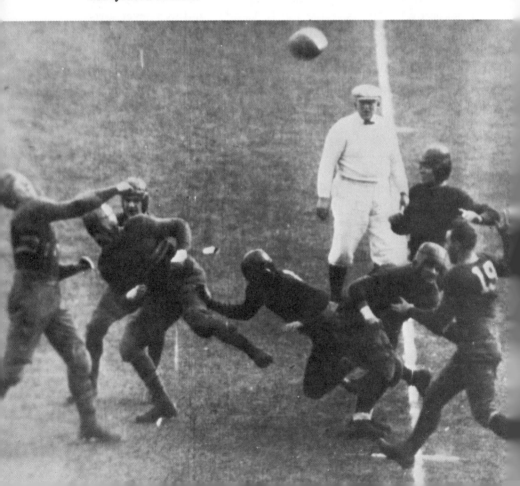

Marchy Schwartz follows his interference for a gain on an off-tackle play against Army in 1930. A duplicate of this play later in the game enabled Schwartz to run 54 yards for a touchdown which helped Notre Dame beat the Cadets 7-6.

but both these games were played on bad fields. In '29 in New York, the field was frozen and covered with snow and ice in spots. I went back to punt—and I think those teams gave me as much protection as any kicker ever had—if not more. But the Army man who came through and was blocked by Brill was moving so hard that Brill, who couldn't get set on the frozen turf, just slid right back in the way of the ball. In '30, in the mud at Soldier Field in Chicago, the same thing happened to Mullins. He couldn't keep his footing. Marty and Moon both put on good blocks on the rushers and kept 'em on, but they just skidded right back into the kicking area."

Rockne and his players entered the 1929 season with high spirits, but for a while it seemed that they would not get it off the ground. When they arrived at Indiana's stadium prior to their opening game on October 5, they were blocked by a persistent student manager who refused to let them in without tickets. He told Rockne at the head of the party: "You'll have to see Mr. Page (Indiana coach Pat Page) if you haven't got a ticket."

"What's the matter," the quick-thinking Rockne retorted, "wasn't he expecting us?"

The Notre Dame team finally got into the stadium after some hassle, but the Hoosiers probably wished they had stayed

Notre Dame and Navy players follow the bouncing ball in their 1929 game. The Irish got most of the bounces and eventually won the game 14-7.

out after all. Elder scored two touchdowns, and the Fighting Irish defense did the rest. Final: Notre Dame 14, Indiana 0.

It was at this point that Rockne developed his leg problems, and the announcement that he would not accompany the team to Baltimore for the Navy game concerned Notre Dame fans throughout the country. They were as much concerned over Rockne's health as they were over the fact that he would not be at the game to spin his special magic. But, typically, Rockne found a solution to the problem. He turned over the coaching duties to Tom Lieb, a Notre Dame player of the early 1920s who was regarded as one of the best line instructors in the country. Dismissing doctor's orders that he stay in bed, Rockne drove to Cartier Field each day for practice. His car was equipped with a loud speaker through which Rockne could guide the sessions.

It was after the team left that Rockne dropped his psychological bomb. On the morning of the game Lieb hustled the players most likely to see service to a telephone booth. While they lined up, the phone rang, and Lieb picked it up. In a minute he stepped out and told the players, "Fellows, Rock wants a few words with all of you. Just take your time and listen. Don't try to break in, because he's a pretty sick man."

One by one the players talked to Rockne and emerged from the booth, some with moist eyes and others with buoyed spirits. The message to Frank Leahy was typical of what Rockne told the players:

"This is an important game, Frank. Remember, I'm depending on you and the rest of those juniors. Go on out there and fight!"

Notre Dame did—and won, 14-7. Schwartz and Mullins alternated in line thrusts which finally produced the winning touchdown.

By the time the Fighting Irish beat Wisconsin 19-0 before 90,000 appreciative fans at Soldier Field in Chicago, they were recognized as one of the nation's best teams. In this one Savoldi was widely acclaimed after making touchdown runs of 71 and 40 yards. In his next game, a 7-0 decision over Carnegie Tech, Savoldi earned the colorful sobriquet of "Jumpin' Joe" and earned even more points for Notre Dame's image. The Irish, fighting to avenge an embarrassing defeat by Carnegie Tech the year before at home, struggled throughout most of the after-

Notre Dame pushes over a touchdown through a web of tangled bodies in the 1929 Carnegie Tech game. It was a happy ending for the Fighting Irish, 7-0.

Jack Elder crosses the goal line to complete a 95-yard run after intercepting an Army pass. It was the only score of the 1929 game as Notre Dame won 7-0.

noon until Elder shook loose for 38 yards. With the ball on the Carnegie Tech eight yard line, Carideo whispered in Savoldi's ear: "Look, we can't go through them or around them. You'll have to go over them."

Savoldi leapfrogged over the Carnegie Tech defense and made it over the goal line in his third shot for the only score of the game.

After victories over Georgia Tech and Drake, Notre Dame had its hands full with Southern Cal. In the best tradition of the exciting series, the fiercely fought game was tied 6-6 at half time, and the tired Notre Dame players trudged into their locker room in need of mental inspiration a la Rockne. But the ailing coach was nowhere in sight when they tumbled down at their locker spaces.

Paul Castner, a Notre Dame running star from an earlier era, stepped into the center of the room to take Rockne's place as orator.

"Fellows, who do you go to when you're in trouble? It's Rock, isn't it? Who do you regard as your best friend at Notre Dame? It's Rock again. Who is. . ."

At this point Castner was interrupted by the opening of the locker room door. It was Rockne this time, in the flesh. Two managers wheeled the sick coach into the room. He was obviously in pain, and the strain of making the trip from Notre Dame to Chicago for the game in Soldier Field and the further strain of watching that first half apparently did his health no good. But he had enough strength to speak. After looking around the room solemnly for a few minutes, Rockne told his players:

"Boys, I want you to get out there and play them hard in the first five minutes. They aren't going to like it, but you just play them hard! Rock will be watching you. Go ahead now, play them hard!"

It only took a few words from the beloved Rockne to get them going again. They played them hard, as Rockne had suggested, and finally beat them down, 13-12. It was probably the most important victory of the season, and Rockne knew it. Otherwise, he would not have gotten out of a sick bed for it.

Two traditional foes remained for Notre Dame that season, and the Fighting Irish beat both Northwestern and Army to complete a clean sweep of nine games. Notre Dame not only was recognized as the top team in the country on the field, but also at the box office. Notre Dame's magic pulling power at the gate was reflected in the crowds for 1929 when 551,112 fans watched the national champions on the road. The Notre Dame-Southern Cal game was becoming a natural crowd-pleaser. Soldier Field bulged with 112,912 on November 16. And 90,000 saw Notre Dame play Wisconsin earlier in the same stadium.

As early as 1924, the need for a new stadium on the Notre Dame campus was recognized, but it did not become a reality until the summer of 1929, when the Osborne Engineering Company began excavation work. Throughout the roaring 1920s, the Fighting Irish played at Cartier Field, whose outmoded wooden stands could accommodate, at the most, 30,000 people. More than twice that number would have paid to see the Fighting Irish in action as they barged through their golden era.

On October 4, 1930, the Fighting Irish opened their season in the imposing new stadium—an impressive $800,000 amphitheatre of dull red brick trimmed with limestone, measuring 670 feet by 480 feet. The arena seated over 50,000, and more important, just about every seat in the place was a good one. There were no posts or girders to obscure the view of the fans. The original sod of Cartier Field, where Notre Dame had been so successful, was transplanted on the field of Notre Dame Stadium, and it was on this earth that the Fighting Irish christened the 1930 season with a 20-14 victory over Southern Methodist University. The next week, the stadium was officially dedicated, and Notre Dame made it a happy occasion all around on the South Bend campus by beating Navy 26-2.

The 1930 team was living up to expectations. Rockne himself said before the season that it was his strongest ever. Carideo, Schwartz, Brill, and Savoldi, the latter-day version of the Four Horsemen, all made All-American teams that year. The Fighting Irish were not only stocked with explosive running backs but also had an exquisite collection of linemen. Center Tommy Yarr, guards Nordy Hoffman and Bert Metzger, tackles Joe Kurth and Al Culver, and end Tom Conley all made All-American teams either that season or the following.

This club was considered by many football purists to be Rockne's strongest, and yet ironically Rockne was not given the credit for developing it. Hunk Anderson was. Anderson, Rockne's line coach, took charge of the team while the head coach was recuperating from his illness in Florida during the spring of 1930.

Anderson and Rockne had a difference of opinion about the team when Rockne finally returned to South Bend—and it was one of the rare times in his career that Rockne was wrong.

"Jack Chevigny and I took over spring practice for six weeks, and we did a real good job," recalls Anderson. "Then Rockne came back and saw the spring practice, the final game, and he didn't like the looks of what we had. We had a good backfield, but he didn't think the line was worth a damn. But I did, because I had six weeks with them, and I knew those players. He wouldn't start Bert Metzger at all for the first couple of ballgames because he said, hell, he's only 155 pounds."

Of course Rockne had misjudged the talents of the watch-charm guard. He became a great lineman after Rockne consented to use him in the third game of the season, against Carnegie Tech.

"It started out to be a bad day," Anderson says. "They took the ball and just rammed through us for two easy downs. I went over to Rock and said, 'You'd better put the little guy in.' And Rock thought for a moment and finally said, 'Okay, go ahead and tell him what to do!' Metzger went in there, and we stopped them. From that day on, the kid developed better and better, and Rock got to liking him and played him all over."

The 21-6 triumph over Carnegie Tech, during which Metzger and another little guard, Tom Kassis, came into their own, was a significant building step for Notre Dame that season. Recalls Carideo: "The game that made our club in 1930 was that Carnegie Tech game. That was the first real tough one. Carnegie had a big club, and we were still finding out if our little guards could make us go all right against big opposition. We found out."

Savoldi, a brute of a runner who often knocked his own men down as well as others in his path, found Metzger a worthy bodyguard. "That Metzger was little. But he could really get out and go. Anybody who ran behind him could gain ground with no trouble."

The scores got bigger as the season went on. Notre Dame beat Pitt 35-19 but had a 35-0 lead at the half and probably could have beaten the Panthers by a larger score had not Rockne put a rein on his charges in the second half. "Rock could have beaten me 100-0 that day," acknowledged Pittsburgh coach Jock Sutherland.

A bit of negative reaction from the Pittsburgh fans inspired

Marchy Schwartz goes 65 yards for a touchdown on Notre Dame's first play against Pitt in 1930. It was all downhill after that, with the Irish winding up an easy 35-19 victor.

Notre Dame to its first touchdown and sent the Irish on their merry way. It still lingers in Carideo's mind.

"There we were, 60 yards away from the Pitt goal, and we went into a huddle. I called for a shift play, and as we were going up to the line of scrimmage, one of our players called 'Signals' to check the play. As we stopped and went back to huddle again, a roar went up from the Pitt side of the field. One of the jibes that came clearly to our ears was 'What's the matter—don't you guys know your signals?' I called the same play again, and as the ball was snapped, the booing was still going on. It did something to our gang. We leaped into action and were on our way. Pitt was caught flat-footed and failed to meet our shift. The next thing I knew I was shoulder-blocking a player out of the way and breaking into the clear in the Pitt secondary. I went on to take out Eddie Baker, the Pitt safety man, and we both went down. As I got up I looked back to see what had happened to Schwartz. He wasn't to be seen. So I turned around and looked in the other direction, and there he was, just going over the goal line."

Rockne had a ton of superlative talent in 1930 and got every pound of flesh out of it. The character of Rockne's squad

Notre Dame's 1930 team, believed to be Knute Rockne's strongest, gave the old master his third and last national championship.

was no more apparent than in the Penn game when Brill was switched from blocker to ballcarrier and ran wild with three touchdowns. Legend persisted long after that 60-20 Notre Dame romp that Brill's father had offered him $100 for every touchdown he scored against Penn that day. Brill was a Philadelphia boy who had failed to make the Penn varsity a few years before. But the player continually disclaimed the story. "My dad didn't have that kind of money," Brill said.

Brill had plenty of assistance that afternoon. Carideo, Schwartz, and Savoldi each scored at least one touchdown in the massacre, as well as Larry "Moon" Mullins and Bucky O'Connor.

"Rockne never wanted to run up a score, but that day, gosh, everything Penn did was wrong, and everything we did was right," Schwartz says. "There wasn't anything you could do about it. There was no way you could hold the score down."

The victory over Penn followed a 27-0 rout of Indiana and extended the Notre Dame winning streak to 15 over two years. Triumphs over Drake, Northwestern, and Army followed, but they turned out to be just small gems compared to the crowning achievement of the 1930 season.

En route to Los Angeles to play Southern Cal in the last game of the year, the Irish team stopped off in Tucson, Arizona, to work out. Despite its 18-game winning streak, though, the situation did not look too bright for Rockne's gang. Savoldi, Notre Dame's great fullback, had been thrown out of school after the Penn game when it was learned that he was married. This was against university rules. In addition, Mullins had injured his knee in the previous week's tough 7-6 victory over Army and could not play against the Trojans. Southern Cal, on the other hand, had one of its strongest and healthiest teams. The Trojans' high-powered machine had outscored nine opponents by 382 points to 39 and had the advantage of the home field. Odds-makers pointed out that Notre Dame had struggled to beat Army while Southern Cal was rolling in high gear at the time and thus made the Trojans 5-3 favorites.

Rockne, never short on psychological ploys, pulled a beauty before the game. The coach held secret practices in Tucson but finally permitted a group of California newspapermen to attend the final warm-up session. What they saw was Dan Hanley playing Joe Savoldi's old fullback position—at least that is what they thought they saw. They wrote stories that Hanley would start for Notre Dame at fullback, but actually it was really Bucky O'Connor in that spot. Hanley, a third-string fullback, lacked the experience to start against the strong Tro-

Bucky O'Connor at the start of an 80-yard touchdown run against Southern Cal in 1930. O'Connor became a storybook hero for Notre Dame that day, leading a stunning 27-0 victory over the Trojans.

jans, so Rockne decided to use the quick O'Connor, normally a halfback, at fullback. He had O'Connor switch jerseys with Hanley during practices, and before the eyes of the California newspapermen, O'Connor dutifully ran short bucks as a fullback would and avoided the outside running at which he excelled. At one point O'Connor even went through an interview as Hanley with a Los Angeles columnist.

During the game, however, there was no reason for disguise. O'Connor played fullback with his proper number and ran like the halfback he was. He became a storybook hero that day, scoring two touchdowns, one on a spectacular, 80-yard dash that simply stunned the crowd of 73,967 at the Los Angeles Coliseum. The Fighting Irish pushed the Trojans all over the field, and little Bucky O'Connor, a dramatic late substitute, was the man of the hour in the 27-0 victory that certified Notre Dame's second straight national championship.

Howard Jones, the Southern Cal coach, said aloud perhaps what everyone else thought: "That was the greatest Notre Dame team I've ever seen."

That Southern Cal game was Rockne's last in the record books, but it actually was not his last appearance on a field. After beating the Trojans, he was invited to gather an all-star Notre Dame team to play the professional New York Giants for charity in the Polo Grounds. Doctors warned Rockne not to go through with it, but he dismissed their advice. Rockne always had a weak spot for charity affairs, and this game would raise $100,000 for New York's unemployed during the Depression. The players, dating back from before the Four Horsemen, came from all over the nation to practice for a few days before the big affair. Most of them were out of condition, but they had not lost their spirit. They had gone through a few days of practice at Notre Dame under Adam Walsh when Rockne made an appearance at Cartier Field. Rockne was obviously tickled to see his former stars, even if they were long on weight and short of breath.

"How long have they been working?" he asked Walsh.

"Only a couple of days, Rock," Walsh replied.

"Send them in; they look overtrained," Rockne ordered with a grin.

The overmatched Fighting Irish were beaten easily by the pros, but it was a game that Rockne could not lose. He won money for the poor people and respect everywhere as a sports-

Notre Dame's national champions of 1930 get a hero's welcome in Chicago.

Marchy Schwartz gets perfect interference for a run against Penn in 1930. It went that way most of the day for Notre Dame as the Irish routed the Quakers 60-20.

man who never backed away from any challenge.

The charity game was a fitting curtain to Rockne's fabulous career. The following summer he was dead in a plane crash that shook the civilized world and climaxed the most significant era at Notre Dame and possibly any other university in America.

Hunk Anderson, who would step into Rockne's giant shoes, was notified of his death by a phone call.

"I was selling cars at the time during the off-season," Anderson remembers, "and my wife called me. She said Rock got killed in an airplane accident. I called the school right away, and they wanted me to go out and get Rock's body. So Jack Chevigny and I got on a train and went out and picked up the body and brought it back. . .the funeral was the saddest thing that ever happened. . .you never saw such an awful thing as that."

But there was not too much time for remorse. Anderson and the rest of the Notre Dame people had to pick up the pieces in a hurry. Everybody pitched in to keep the Fighting Irish on their feet, and Notre Dame did indeed continue to run in the right direction.

Just Plain Hunk

"If all the Notre Dame men who are now coaching college football were lined up before me to make a choice, I would pick Hunk Anderson. That's right from the heart."—Jesse Harper.

As a player, Hunk Anderson had to share the spotlight with George Gipp. As a coach, he was forced to live in Knute Rockne's shadow. But he came out of both situations looking pretty good. While Anderson's accomplishments were dwarfed by two towering legends, they were not entirely invisible.

Heartly "Hunk" Anderson had been one of the best guards turned out at Notre Dame during his playing days from 1918 through 1921, a rough-hewn lineman who opened holes for the irrepressible Gipp to run through. His body seemed as hard and compact as the iron in his native hills, the copper-mining country of Calumet, Michigan. Here was toughness personified, a small brute capable of unleashing terrifying power. This was reflected in the Purdue game of 1921 when an enraged Anderson, set off the week before by a three-point loss to Iowa, blocked two punts and scored two touchdowns within three minutes. At five-foot-ten and 170 pounds, he was one of the most beloved of Rockne's "watch-charm" guards. And he soon became one of Rockne's closest confidants and top assistants.

When Anderson graduated in 1922, Rockne hired him as his line coach. And from that day on, Rockne never failed to show his appreciation for Anderson. In later years Rockne called him the best line coach in the country and went so far as crediting him with the complete development of the 1930 national championship team. Other loyalties took Anderson's

165

Hunk Anderson had the toughest act in the world to follow—Knute Rockne.

attention for a while, but he kept returning to Rockne. He played with the Chicago Bears and served as head coach of the St. Louis University football team but was a faithful Tonto to Rockne for the better part of a decade.

Like Rockne, Anderson literally had come up through the school of hard knocks and scrapped for every step toward the top. After Rockne died, he believed, justifiably so, that he could move into the head coaching job with no trouble. But there were assumptions that no man could follow in those giant footsteps, and thus Notre Dame's hierarchy actually appointed three men to do the job. Anderson was appointed "senior" coach and Jack Chevigny "junior" coach. By that unique arrangement, Anderson would continue to coach the line and Chevigny the backfield, while it was understood that Hunk would be the boss of sorts. Meanwhile, Jesse Harper, the former Notre Dame coach and athletic director, was brought back to give the football program general direction. It was probably the first time in the history of college football that a "committee" had been formed to coach a team, and Anderson was not especially happy with the situation.

"The only time I was the boss," Anderson recalls, "was when I was behind the green fence coaching. So that made it kind of tough."

Harper, though, insisted at the time that he would have a general "hands-off" policy as the Notre Dame athletic director.

"I'll be out there looking on, but the coaching of the team will be in Anderson's hands," he said. "I may have a suggestion to make now and then, and he can take it or leave it as he sees fit. Anderson doesn't need my help to teach football. He is the best line coach in America, bar none, and his knowledge of backfield play will be established before the season is far along."

Chevigny was as unhappy as Anderson with the setup, and this led to his departure after the 1931 season. It was then that Anderson had the top job to himself, no strings attached.

If Anderson was not completely in command, as Rockne was before him, he certainly took the full credit—or the blame—for Notre Dame's victories and defeats of 1931. It began as a glorious year and ended on a sour note, but still the music of Rockne was with the team.

After a resounding 25-0 decision over Indiana that opened the season and continued Notre Dame's winning streak to 20 games, a Des Moines newspaperman said: "I could pay Anderson no greater compliment than to say that while watching his Notre Dame team play at Indiana I forgot for the moment that Rockne was gone—so much did Anderson's team resemble Rockne's."

However, Anderson did eventually find it difficult to fill Rockne's place—but not for obvious reasons. The pressure never bothered him, but the lack of support from the Notre Dame administration did. When Harper came in, he went on an economy kick and cut the athletic scholarships practically in half.

"The coaching part was easy," Anderson says. "That part of it never bothered me, because I had learned a lot from the Great Guy. But when you go from 36 scholarships down to 20, and you lose at least five more of these in the general process of things, then you have practically nobody left. And you have no money to spend to go out and look boys over, either."

Anderson lacked Rockne's electric character, but there

were few better as a pure coach.

"During the three years he was head coach at Notre Dame, there is only one instance on record where the opposing team used a play he had not anticipated and provided a defense for," pointed out an observer. "This was in the Army game of 1933 which Notre Dame won, 13 to 12, with a great fourth quarter rally. Army worked a lateral pass off a fake line buck for a touchdown. The players say, however, that they can recall no other play which he did not anticipate, whether or not it showed in the scouting reports."

Anderson streamlined Rockne's system, making several progressive changes in the offense. He used the man in motion extremely well to beat Army 21-0 in 1932 and introduced the split tackle on one side of the line in 1933. His inventive genius concocted several new plays from these formations and from the standard formations already in the Notre Dame playbook. Coaches flocked annually to the Army game to see Anderson's newest twist.

Since Anderson followed on Rockne's heels, comparisons were inevitable. Anderson's team resembled the old master's, observers soon found out, except for the size of the guards. While Rockne picked his guards for speed rather than for weight, it was just the opposite with Anderson. The new coach selected his guards for power and strength and structured one of the strongest lines that Notre Dame had until that point in time.

Marchy Schwartz pounds off tackle in the 1931 Pitt game. The Irish won this one 25-12 for their new coach, Hunk Anderson.

Chuck Jaskwhich, one of Hunk Anderson's star pupils, carries the ball for Notre Dame on a punt return.

For the better part of the 1931 season, Anderson had Rockne-like success with it. During the first seven games, only one team scored on the Fighting Irish, and nobody beat them. Anderson's team picked up where Rockne's left off and expanded the Notre Dame unbeaten streak to 26 games. The only blemish on Notre Dame's record was a scoreless tie with Northwestern. But that was dismissed as a fluke by some, because the game was played in mud. Pittsburgh, in the fourth game of the year, was looked upon as a significant test for Notre Dame, but the Fighting Irish beat the Panthers 25-12 with little apparent trouble. Carnegie, an old nemesis, was shut out, as were Penn and Navy, and Anderson was seen as the second coming of Rockne by a few observers.

"I gained a wholesome respect for the judgment of the new leader of the Fighting Irish," wrote Bert McGrane in the *Des Moines Register.* "He was no nervous, excitable young coach, rushing pell mell into action. Rather, Anderson directed his men like a man seasoned for years under heavy firing on major battlefronts. I saw him on the bench when (Chuck) Jaskwhich fumbled a punt in one game, only a moment after the same player had sent a bad Notre Dame punt out of bounds less than 10 yards from its starting point. Anderson did not pace the sideline excitedly and rush in a new quarterback. He knew Jaskwhich. He knew he might need a play or two to settle himself, so he left him in the game, sat tight on the bench and studied the game in progress."

Two of the toughest games remained on the schedule—Southern Cal and Army—but Anderson had already accomplished more than was expected of him. Before his death, Rockne himself predicted that Notre Dame would probably lose two or three games in 1931. His pessimistic feelings were predicated on the loss of several players, including Frank Carideo, Marty Brill, Joe Savoldi, Moon Mullins, and Bucky O' Connor from that all-star backfield. In addition, the Irish lost the services of two brilliant ends, Tom Conley and Johnny O'Brien, and two other linemen. With only Marchy Schwartz left from the regulars, Anderson was forced to rebuild a new backfield. Anderson also faced a typical rugged schedule built up by the ultrasuccessful Rockne.

The situation had led Harper to comment at the beginning of the year: "Two or three defeats this season will not change my opinion of Anderson's ability. Nobody expects him to go through the schedule he faces undefeated. I doubt if there is any other coach who could. If Notre Dame wins seven of its nine games, I'll call the season a grand success."

Anderson was riding tall in the coaching saddle before being ambushed by Southern Cal. It was one of the most dramatic—and bizarre—losses in the history of Notre Dame foot-

Guard Jim Harris, one of the strong links on Hunk Anderson's powerful lines of the early 1930s.

ball. At first it looked like Notre Dame would have a field day with the Trojans. Their backs were running untamed, and the Fighting Irish held a 14-0 lead in the third period and were driving for a third touchdown. The game was so one-sided, in fact, that Anderson put in his second team. It was, however, at this point that the flow of the contest changed in favor of Southern Cal. The Trojans checked the Notre Dame offense, took over the ball, and relentlessly drove down the field against the helpless Irish. Notre Dame had a 14-0 lead when the third quarter ended, but the Trojans had gained the momentum and had the Notre Dame fans buzzing.

Early in the fourth period, the Trojans went in for a score behind the inspired play of Orv Mohler. Later in the period, a pass interference call gave Southern Cal the ball on the Notre Dame 24. Gus Shaver and Mohler sliced through, moving the ball to the Notre Dame 9. Then Mohler lateraled to Shaver, and his backfield mate raced around left end for a touchdown. The Trojans, who missed the extra point try the first time, made it on the second try and trailed 14-13 with eight minutes remaining.

"The fury of Troy's attack astounded everybody," wrote Los Angeles newspaperman Braven Dyer. "Mohler's choice of plays was almost perfect, and the way the 162-pound Orv rammed into the Irish line inspired his mates immensely."

Smelling Irish blood, the Trojans went to the air for their winning drive. They moved the ball into field goal position. Johnny Baker kicked it through the goalposts with one minute left for a 16-14 Southern Cal victory, perhaps the most golden in the Trojans' history and, no doubt, one of the most bitter in Irish lore. Francis Wallace, the Notre Dame historian, was prepared for the inevitable when Baker lined up to kick the ball from the 23 yard line. "When Baker prepared to kick the winning field goal, I knew it would be right down the middle and plenty long. It was. He could have kicked that one from the 50-yard line," Wallace said.

Attached to that grim Notre Dame loss that stopped the cherished 26-game unbeaten streak is the story of Anderson's classic fumble.

"Notre Dame wound up with many of its regulars, especially in the backfield, on the bench and unable to get back into the game," explained Wallace. "The rules prevented a man from entering the lineup more than once in each period. When the

A Fighting Irishman, Nick Lukats, battles for yardage. Notre Dame had a hard time in the early 1930s matching the great records of Knute Rockne.

Irish did get the ball, the enfeebled offense couldn't move it. Notre Dame would have to punt, and Mohler would put the Trojans in commanding field position with a strong runback."

Schwartz, one of the few regulars to play the whole game, acknowledges, "It was a tough one to lose. . .I always questioned the fact that Anderson took most of our linemen out after one or two minutes of the fourth quarter. They couldn't go back in after that. When he put in his second string, that's when Southern Cal started going. And there wasn't a damn thing he could do about putting his regulars back in. We had a 14-point lead, and in those days, that was a big lead. I guess he thought the regulars were tired, you know, and that the substitutes would play better. It didn't work out that way."

The game was marked by the first capacity crowd at Notre Dame Stadium—50,731—and if the Fighting Irish had lost a tough one, there was at least some financial gratification from the affair. This lofty crowd figure would be indicative of future

Southern Cal-Notre Dame games, intersectional warfare that eventually grew to command national acclaim.

That bitter loss to Southern Cal took the spirit out of Notre Dame, and then Army kicked the Fighting Irish when they were down, 12-0, to finish the season on a downbeat note for Anderson's charges.

A writer observed: "This time there was no fighting-fury comeback (a Rockne trademark) after a defeat. The Rockne era, unparalleled in the history of football, had ended."

Those last two weeks of 1931 were a strange mixture of pleasure and pain for the Notre Dame players. Schwartz remembers that it was almost a relief to have the pressure of the unbeaten streak taken off their shoulders, and yet still a nightmarish experience.

"The first defeat in three seasons was a shock. . .I guess because we seemed to have the game under control, and it was taken right away from us. Perhaps that feeling that the game was won had a lot to do with losing it. After it was all over, it seemed as if a weight had been lifted from us. But we found, a week later, that the weight was still upon us; there was no stopping Army in that game."

Notre Dame started out the 1932 season as if it meant to obliterate the disappointing finish of the year before. The Fighting Irish scored resounding shutouts over Haskell, Drake, and Carnegie Tech and were being hailed as football's newest "point-a-minute" squad. A 12-0 defeat at the hands of Pitt stopped that talk, but the Fighting Irish picked up again with victories over Kansas, Northwestern, Navy, and Army, before an unceremonious comedown at Southern Cal, 13-0. The loss to the Trojans was the fourth for Anderson in two years, and the continual comparisons with Rockne cropped up. A 13-4-1 record for two years was good enough at most schools, but Anderson had to be no less than perfect to follow Rockne.

"He suffered of course because he was stepping into the shoes of a giant," notes Schwartz. "When you played for Rockne you played for the best—and I don't care who succeeded him there, comparisons would be made. No matter the degree of the abilities of any newcomer, compared to Rockne he's bound to have a lot of shortcomings. Anderson did as good a job as anyone could do under the circumstances. He was a tough, rugged individual and a good coach. But along with the Rockne thing, he also had the problem of few good people

A straight arm of an Indiana player, and Notre Dame's Nick Lukats is away.

returning. There were quite a few new faces in 1931. That was a handicap. A new quarterback was taking the place of Carideo. Carideo was pretty hard to replace. We had a new halfback, a new fullback, and quite a few linemen were changed. So it was a rebuilding thing, really."

As early as 1932, and despite a solid season of 7-2, Anderson was open season for the coach-baiters. And there were plenty. But Anderson also had his defenders. Included among these were Jim Armstrong, Notre Dame's alumni secretary, who took editorial notice of the situation: "The bay of the hunch-hounds is heard from dawn to dark. The concrete niche where Rockne was enshrined was impossible to fill. Had there been a man able enough, Rockne would have not been Rockne, unique and unsurpassed. No alumnus has expressed an adverse criticism of Anderson's coaching to the alumni office."

Anderson came under heavier fire in 1933 when his team slumped to a 3-5-1 record, Notre Dame's first losing mark since 1888. This time Notre Dame's administrators did not wait for the "hunch-hounds" to bark. They simply threw Anderson to the wolves themselves.

Steve Banas carries against Carnegie Tech in 1932. Notre Dame was hailed as the newest "point-a-minute" squad after this resounding 42-0 triumph.

Notre Dame's Norb Rascher, hugging the ball to his chest, is pursued by a Carnegie Tech player in this 1932 game.

Thus, one of Notre Dame's ancient heroes was let go with no ceremony. Anderson did leave on a heroic note, though—a 13-12 victory over Army despite overwhelming odds.

It was announced that both Anderson and Harper had "resigned" their posts, and Elmer Layden, one of the original "Four Horsemen," would become both head football coach and athletic director at Notre Dame. The "Horseman" took the reins with a strong grip.

Return Of The Horseman

"Following a genius in anything is a trying role to play. I can testify, from firsthand knowledge, that in football it is sometimes heartbreaking, and most of the time backbreaking."
—Elmer Layden.

One drab autumn day in 1921, Knute Rockne was in the process of bawling out a halfback during practice when he was cut short by a tap on his shoulder.

"He's gone again," said Walter Hollis, one of Rockne's scouts who had run excitedly on the field.

"Who's gone again?" Rockne asked.

"The kid from Davenport," Hollis said. "You know, the one I recommended."

"This is the third time he's pulled that," said Rockne, "but he'll be back for dinner, like he was before."

Rockne resumed chewing out his player when Hollis tapped him on the shoulder again.

"But this time he's packed up, and he's down at the station waiting for the train. The kid's so homesick and lovesick he'll swim back to Davenport if he can't make it any other way."

Rockne's attitude changed.

"Hop in a car and get down to the station as fast as you can," the coach told Hollis, his voice rising. "Get him if you have to drag him off the train."

Hollis was on his way almost before Rockne got the last word out and roared into high gear toward the South Bend station. He glanced at his watch and noted that it was 4:12, just

178

the time for the Illinois Central to be pulling out of the station. Hollis drove faster but really had no expectation of catching the runaway player. He is probably gone by now, Hollis thought.

Exceeding the speed limit, Hollis made the station in record time and was relieved to find the wandering boy on the platform, waiting for the train. The Illinois Central was late.

"Get in here," Hollis commanded, opening the door of his car as a whistle signaled the approach of the tardy train.

Sheepishly, the boy obeyed. And that is how Elmer Layden stayed and played at Notre Dame.

If Layden had made that train, he would never have brightened the pages of football history as a member of Rockne's masterpiece, the Four Horsemen. And he certainly never would have brightened the pages of Notre Dame history as coach and athletic director of the Fighting Irish in the 1930s.

Painfully shy and sensitive when he first came to Notre Dame, Layden lost his shyness after a few years in Rockne's school of hard knocks. But Layden never lost his sensitivity— and this, perhaps better than anything, made him a marvelous leader of men, and one of the most adored figures at Notre Dame.

Anyone who saw Layden as a player had to wonder how this hunk of lean meat could play halfback. But his 160-pound weight served more as a credit than a debit against the larger players of his day. Layden was a novelty at his position—a sleek arrow rather than a battering ram—and used his speed for dazzling, quick-opening plays. He was not afraid to mix it up with the big boys, though, and could also be seen firing his wafer-thin form into a mass of bodies. His propensity for winding up at the bottom of pileups inspired a sort of battle cry from teammates: "Where's Elmer?" Actually, Elmer could be seen here, there, and everywhere, running like the proverbial gazelle through the football meadows. He was perhaps the heart and soul of the Four Horsemen and gave Rockne a wonderful going-away present in his last year, a one-man performance that rocked Stanford 27-10 in the 1925 Rose Bowl.

Layden, the lovesick, homesick boy as a freshman, hardly would have been recognized in his senior year. After passing his final exams and while waiting around on campus for his diploma, the new, outgoing Layden got himself into a big jam because of a campus prank. And he almost left school prematurely for a second time because of it. After a night of celebrating in South Bend in June, 1925, Layden and his friends started back toward the campus. Having nothing to do on the way, they decided to collect every milk bottle at every front door they saw and eventually lined up hundreds of bottles on the Notre Dame campus like a regiment of soldiers. Meanwhile, most husbands in South Bend that morning had to drink their coffee black. For a while it looked as if Layden's diploma would be withheld, but he finally got it and went on to more respectable things.

In the fall of 1925 Layden succeeded Eddie Anderson as coach of little Columbia College in Dubuque, Iowa, and produced two winning teams there. At the same time he passed the Iowa bar examination, joined a Dubuque law firm, and was married. However, he only flirted with law. Layden's real love remained with football, and when the right offer came, he embraced it. Aware of Layden's success at Columbia, Duquesne University offered him the head coach's job, and Layden made his choice away from the law profession in 1927. Duquesne needed help, and Layden really gave it to the Pittsburgh school. The Duquesne team in 1926 had lost every game and had won only eight out of 31 in the previous four years. In his first season there, Layden produced a 4-4-1 record, the best mark for any Duquesne team up to that time, and during his seven years Layden lost only 16 games of 70 while playing stiffer schedules each season. His 1933 team won 10 of 11 games, losing only a 7-0 decision to a superb Pittsburgh squad. Pitt, along with Carnegie Tech, ruled the territory while Layden was there, and the onetime "Horseman" had a hard time gaining recognition in that setting. But once when his best team beat Jock Sutherland's Panthers, he received national attention. Notre Dame, of course, looked in Layden's direction and thought of him as a possible successor to Hunk Anderson after the 1933 season. But his eventual selection was not all that simple. There were other candidates for the job, including Jim Crowley, another of that golden Four Horsemen unit. Crowley was at Fordham when the Notre Dame vacancy occurred.

The intimate story of Layden's selection is told by Francis Wallace in his book, *Notre Dame, From Rockne to Parseghian*. Wallace, the noted Notre Dame historian, was as close to the situation as anyone could be, as he explains:

Elmer Layden: Nearly a runaway from Notre Dame.

"I was one of a number invited to suggest five names from the coaching field during the 1933 season. I talked to Crowley, who suggested that I clear the matter with his athletic director. This was done favorably, and the next week, on campus for the Southern Cal game, I submitted my five names to Father (later Cardinal) John O'Hara, with a rundown on each and my reasons for placing Crowley at the head of the list. I felt he had proven himself as a big-time coach, was popular among other coaches and athletic directors, the Notre Dame fraternity would accept him warmly, and while coming closer than any of the rest to the Rockne image as a wit and personality, he would be himself and not try to be a carbon copy of Rockne. My other four nominees were well known to Father O'Hara, but I thought Layden's name brought the sharpest reaction. I emphasized the Rockne-type job he had done in the Pittsburgh situation, and answered a few questions. Layden's schedule had been completed. I suggested he come to New York for the Army game that weekend. I told him I thought he was being seriously considered as successor to Hunk and that it would do no harm to be where the action was. This was the game where Army was upset. The alumni were happy at their dinner for the squad and the brass that night. The response to Layden's introduction was surprisingly hearty. It could have been the final evidence the selection committee needed. Later I was told that, while Layden was nobody's first choice, he was on everybody's list. He was a consensus man, a good middle-of-the-road man; and that's the kind of coach and director he became."

When Layden came to Notre Dame, he restored confidence and reestablished tradition. In seven years his teams won 78 percent of their games, with a 47-13-3 record. The Layden squads displayed the classic hallmark of Notre Dame football: they seldom beat themselves either on the field or on the bench. Layden never worried whether he was another Rockne; he just concentrated on being Layden, and that was good enough for the Notre Dame camp. His painstaking attention to detail was one of his trademarks, as was his ability to keep a step or two ahead of opponents.

"He's the smartest head coach and athletic director Notre Dame ever turned out," Illinois' Bob Zuppke said once of the Notre Dame thin man. "At a meeting or in a conference his mind runs right to the point. He doesn't mix things up."

Layden's success at Notre Dame is regarded with special

esteem, considering the situation he was faced with. When he first arrived at South Bend, he was confronted with two problems—putting together the scattered remains of the Anderson regime and surviving a de-emphasized athletic program. Following a national trend to clean up the so-called professional atmosphere in college athletics, Notre Dame tightened up eligibility rules for players and toned down recruiting practices. As a result, Layden had less talent to choose from than in Rockne's golden era. It did not stop him from turning Notre Dame into a continuous winner from his first year on, including an excellent 8-1 season in 1938 when the Fighting Irish played one of their most treacherous schedules. A 13-0 loss to Southern Cal on the last day of the season probably cost Layden a national championship. Another highlight of the Layden years was a spectacular 18-13 victory over Ohio State in 1935, classified in anthologies as the most exciting game in college football history. During his seven-year reign at South Bend, Layden was as well liked by the opposition as by his own side and sealed innumerable friendships for Notre Dame.

"Elmer was a sharp person and very diplomatic," recalls Milt Piepul, Layden's captain in 1940, his last year. "I thought he was an excellent teacher, and one of the greatest assets to Notre Dame was the fact that he was a very fine link between the university and other schools. He enjoyed excellent rapport with other college coaches and did a great deal to establish relationships. When he beat them, they didn't feel too badly."

Layden's genius as an athletic director usually rivaled his genius on the field. In his first six years he played against, or scheduled for the future, every member of the Big Ten Conference (then the Western Conference), including three schools which had been off the Notre Dame schedule for many years—Illinois, Michigan, and Iowa. Layden assuaged bad feelings between Notre Dame and Michigan when he invited Michigan's old athletic director, Fielding Yost, to the South Bend campus to watch a game with Purdue. "Yost hadn't set foot on the Notre Dame campus in nearly 30 years," points out a writer. "A week later he was still commenting on the Layden hospitality—a morning tour of the campus, luncheon, a couple of hours at Layden's home after the game. His remarks tended toward the conclusion that such relaxed hospitality on the part of a football coach on a Saturday in autumn is something of a rarity."

The Notre Dame-Army series was becoming lopsided in

favor of the Fighting Irish but continued to flourish with some cultivation from the affable Layden. In 1939 Layden brought the entire squads from West Point and Notre Dame together for luncheon the day before the game.

Layden's relationship with his own players was more remarkable. He served as a friend as well as a teacher, regarding his charges paternally. His players never heard public criticism from their leader, although they heard plenty from Layden in private. It was Layden's family style. Once when one of his quarterbacks made a bonehead play in a game, Layden's response to reporters was typically noble: "Our quarterback is always right." Because he himself was a sensitive man, Layden concerned himself with his players' sensitivities. Once when he was leaving Chicago for Los Angeles and the Southern Cal game, in which his team was to risk an unbeaten record, Layden's main worry was two players he had to leave behind because of university rules limiting the size of the traveling squad. Layden's warmth and sincerity touched the lowliest freshman to the loftiest All-American.

"Buster," Layden would say as he wrapped his arm around a player, "you're my kind of guy."

Actually, everybody was Layden's kind of guy. And Layden was everybody's kind, too.

"He was a majestic man," remembers a friend. "He'd walk away from a dirty story or gossip. Elmer's loyalty and integrity never bent with the wind. He kept a low profile. He didn't want the headlines or fame. Once he told me: 'Buster, don't ever jump too deep in the pool, 'cause the water's pretty cold.'"

Don Elser carried the ball for both Hunk Anderson and Elmer Layden as Notre Dame moved forward in the 1930s.

Layden was basically a low-key coach who prepared his teams with detailed planning rather than fire-breathing oratory. Yet he could rise to the occasion when a Rockne-type speech was called for. "He could send his team out for the second half ready to die a dozen deaths apiece for Notre Dame," recalled an old New York newspaper friend, Dan Parker.

While his team played, Layden himself died a dozen deaths on the sidelines. The combat of football continually jabbed at his nerves. Layden nervously chain-smoked through every game, and it was not an uncommon picture to see the coach squatting on the sidelines surrounded by piles of cigarette butts. The pre-game ceremony was usually unbearable for him.

"I don't think people realized what he went through before a ballgame," says Piepul. "I happened to see him by accident in the locker room all by himself, and he was really nerved up. I knew it was taking an awful lot out of him, but it really surprised me because this was the first time I had seen anything like this behind the scenes. He began to vomit. And I said, 'What's the matter?'

"He said, 'It's those oranges.'

"I said, 'Oranges don't make you sick.'

"And he said, 'They sure as hell do when you eat the rind.' He was so nervous that he had eaten the whole orange, peels and all."

But as nervous as Layden was, he rarely made the wrong moves on the field. Against Ohio State in 1935, he used five quarterbacks for five plays in the closing minutes. His substitutions all worked, and his plays produced one of the most remarkable victories in college football history.

"When Layden went to calling plays," pointed out an observer, "he didn't seem to miss many. He shook off three or four field goal ideas through 1937 and 1938 and always won some other way. Late in '38 Notre Dame won from Northwestern on a field goal, and in 1939 defeated both Purdue and Georgia Tech by the same device. Combined with a '35 kick against Pittsburgh, those four field goals represent more than Notre Dame had made, or even tried, in the preceding twelve years. The four were made by four different players who neither before nor since scored from the field by kicking."

A situation against Navy on a snowy day in 1937 was typical of Layden's strategic thinking. The teams were tied 7-7 with about 100 seconds left in the game, and the ball was on the

Navy two yard line, squarely between the goalposts. It was fourth down, and the Notre Dame quarterback decided to try for a field goal. When he sent word to the bench for a towel to dry the kicker's shoe, word was sent back that there was no towel available. The quarterback, knowing full well that there were plenty of towels on the Notre Dame bench, judged this to be a veto from Layden on his field goal idea. He called another running play and failed to get the touchdown. But on the next play the Navy punter, trying to get the ball out of the end zone, fumbled and was thrown for a safety, and Notre Dame won 9-7.

"It was the better percentage," said Layden, explaining why he called off the field goal try. "The ball was wet and hard to handle for a place kick. Also it was hard to control even if we got the kick away. If we missed the kick, Navy got the ball on the 20-yard line, and our chance was gone. If they blocked the kick, they might have run it for a touchdown, and we'd have lost. But on the running play we had a bigger margin: We might have made a touchdown. If not, we still had Navy pinned near the goal line. Then the danger of the wet ball was in our favor, not against us. We might block their punt, or our quarterback, who had just returned one 50 yards, might run the kick back for a touchdown or close enough for a scoring play. Or, they might fumble, as they did, and we'd score."

Not all of Layden's maneuvering worked out, of course. In his first game against Texas, he played every man on his squad because he wanted to see what all his players could do under fire. He lost, 7-6. In a game against Iowa in 1939, he admitted that he used substitutions badly. He lost again, 7-6. Against Southern California once, Layden also booted one, he conceded.

"I had a play in mind, and I sent a substitute in to call it. When the first quarterback came out, I asked what he'd been planning to call. Just to get a line on how he was thinking. He told me, and I knew I'd kicked it. His play would have worked, I'm sure. Mine didn't. And I had never thought of the one he wanted."

That inauspicious debut against Jack Chevigny's Texas team was not in the least bit disappointing for Layden. He explained later: "That was probably the best thing that could have happened to us. If we'd won that game, the public—and the boys—would have felt: 'Notre Dame is in the van again.' But I knew that, while the team would come along, it was pretty green. The opening licking prepared the boys for a hard-fighting season—that it did not shake their confidence was proved later."

Layden, perhaps not the supreme psychologist that Rockne was, still was pretty clever in his mental approach to football.

"At our first meeting, I told the players we were in the same boat—we were all starting from scratch. The idea that I believed everyone was equal, and on the same footing, produced new enthusiasm. Each boy on that first squad who had a low rating as a player prospect tried his best to show that he should be rated at the top. Those at the top worked harder than ever to prove they belonged there."

Layden's unique approach discovered talent at the lower echelon of Notre Dame squads that perhaps others would not have found. Such was the case of Nevin "Bunny" McCormick, who became a member of Layden's "pony backfield" of the 1937 team.

"Early in 1936 one of the varsity men, working with the B squad, told me about a fellow who hit hard enough and had spirit enough to knock down brick walls—only he wasn't big enough to do it," remembered Layden. "I looked him over and moved him to the A squad at once. He had been so far down on the list that his name did not even appear on the programs of home games. Yet he started the Army game and became a regular right halfback. After the Army game, Bunny McCormick told me that he still couldn't believe he was a first-stringer. He had thought I was kidding him when I moved him up from the B team. Bunny remained skeptical when he was picked up to make the New York trip to Army, and was the last man on the train at South Bend, waiting for his name to be 'recalled.'"

"I thought you were fooling me!" McCormick confessed to Layden after the Army game.

"I wasn't fooling you," Layden replied. "But you fooled me plenty when you set up that fake for Bob Wilke!"

McCormick had so convincingly faked a reverse that he set up Notre Dame's first touchdown in that game and later pulled another one to give the Fighting Irish another score. Notre Dame won, 20-6.

As Layden's first season unfolded at South Bend, it became increasingly apparent that Notre Dame had made the right choice in a coach. After the Texas loss, victories followed over Purdue, Carnegie Tech, and Wisconsin. Losses to Pittsburgh and Navy could not shake the faith, even though Layden himself admitted, "We looked very bad in both these games."

The Northwestern game the next weekend seemed to turn the season around, Layden recalled.

"We were losing 7-6 at the half. Just before we went back into action, Jack Robinson suddenly stood up and yelled: 'They had a lot of fun at their turn at bat! Now it's our turn to knock a few home runs!' The team laughed, the tension relaxed. The boys went back in and won, 20-7, in the second half."

Notre Dame finished out the 1934 season with victories over Army and Southern California, the last one fashioned by the touchdown running of Mike Layden, the coach's younger brother. Until that point, the younger Layden had not figured too prominently in brother Elmer's plans, causing embarrassing family difficulties. Once at a family dinner with all present, someone asked the father of the Layden clan how his son Mike was doing, and he replied while glaring at Elmer: "*He* won't give him a chance."

Actually, Mike Layden later said, his father was very understanding of the situation. Mike said he always told Elmer: "Don't listen to anybody. Always play your ten best men—and your brother."

Hello, Columbus...
Good-bye, Ohio State

"I'm sure glad I caught that ball. I'd hate to be remembered as the guy that dropped it. That's for sure."—Wayne Millner.

"I've thought a lot about the pass. But I wake up nights dreaming about the one before it—the one the Ohio State guy had in his hands and dropped. If he'd held it, Wayne and I both would have been bums."—Bill Shakespeare.

The first half ended, and Elmer Layden walked off the field glancing in dismay at the scoreboard which read: Ohio State 13, Notre Dame 0.

"Here, indeed, is the spot for the magical touch of Rockne," he thought. "What would the Old Master do under these circumstances?"

If anyone was prepared for fireworks in the Notre Dame locker room, he was disappointed. Layden gave quiet encouragement to his players as they rested—no more—and then announced that he was calling off the starting team for the second half. "Gaul's team will start," he said, referring to the second team under quarterback Frank Gaul.

"I took pains to tell the first team that they had played good football, but had not smashed in hard enough to stop the multiple handling of the ball featuring the Ohio State attack," Layden revealed later.

Actually, there was not much difference between the first and second team, especially in the line. It was a masterful move by Layden. The second team had played little in the first half and was fresher, and perhaps more eager to prove something.

189

During his half-time talk, Layden dissected the game in a subdued, clinical manner. There was no need to fire up his team. The importance of the game itself did that.

"He was analytical," recalled Mike Layden, the coach's younger brother who had been a goat in the first half. "We didn't need to be roused up. That had been our trouble. He had calmed us down."

Just before the players were let out of the room for the second half, Layden gave them the proper send-off: "They won the first half. Now it's your turn. Go out and win this half for yourselves."

That is precisely what Notre Dame did—and wound up with an 18-13 victory over Ohio State in 1935, in one of the most electrifying games ever played in college football. During the sport's centennial celebration in 1969, this fabulous game received recognition from a distinguished panel of sportswriters and sportscasters as the greatest college football game ever played. Fewer games, certainly, lived up to their advance billing than this one.

People started scrambling for tickets almost as soon as the game was announced, three years before. By game time on November 2, 1935, more than 81,000 people were in the stands at Ohio Stadium, and newspapermen at the time estimated that 200,000 tickets could be sold. Officials for both universities, harassed by ticket-seekers, went into hiding. One Columbus sportswriter, reflecting the mad situation, had his telephone disconnected so he could escape the barrage of calls for tickets. The setting could not have been more perfect. Both Notre Dame and Ohio State were undefeated, and both eyed the national championship. A carnival spirit prevailed, although most of the cheering was naturally for Ohio State as the Notre Dame boys rolled into Columbus. It did not lessen the Notre Dame spirit, however.

"The '35 Irish team was one that believed in itself to an extraordinary extent," Layden pointed out. "It was fired emotionally because death walked with it in every game. The team's captain, Joseph Sullivan, had died during the winter before. The boys decided against the selection of another captain—dedicating every game they played to Joe. We worked carefully to bring the squad to its peak for Ohio State. Observers noted that against Pittsburgh and Navy we were abandoning the seven-man line, that weak-side plays were appearing, and that flankers were

In a pregame pep rally of the 1930s, they cheered for old Notre Dame.

interspersed with spinners in the attack. The local papers were filled with predictions of what was to happen to us. The same dire forecasts came from the lips of everyone we encountered. (One newspaperman predicted that Ohio State would win by 40 points.)

"We ran the squad through a limbering drill the day before the game. Without instructions, Andy Pilney went out with a kicker and practiced taking punts on the dead run. This is a very dangerous stunt, because inevitably a fumble means the loss of the ball. And Andy had suffered from 'fumbilitis' for three years! Andy had many disappointments before that Ohio State game. He had not lived up to what some critics had expected from him. And here he was, a day before the peak game of the season, practicing taking punts on the run! I admired the boy for his inherent confidence in himself. I felt even better about him when, the next morning, he told Chet Grant, one of our coaches: 'I feel like going today!' Andy, we all felt, wouldn't say a thing like that unless he really felt like going."

Pilney was extremely nervous before the game, although he tried not to let it show.

"I was pretty fidgety," he remembers. "But I thought that

we were about as well prepared as you could be for a game. We got a tremendous scouting report from our assistants on Ohio State, and I read the scouting report on the train all the way from South Bend until I fell asleep. See, the problem that I was concerned about was playing defensive left halfback. Ohio State had about 11 different formations, and they were quite razzle-dazzle, and they hid the ball quite well. So I was concerned about getting sucked out and have them come around my end with some of those double reverses. . .so the scouting report meant a great deal to me."

When Pilney arrived in Ohio, his nervous system was no less quieted by the hordes of antagonistic Buckeye fans.

"On the Friday before a game, normally we work out on the field where we are going to play. But for this particular game, Coach Layden felt that if we went to the Ohio Stadium, there would be probably 10,000 students or more raising heck. So he decided that he was going to go to this little seminary just outside of Columbus to work out. Well, I'll never forget that Friday afternoon. We went by buses, and when we got off, there must have been 15,000 people there. That's how big a secret we had. And of course, they were yelling, 'Catholics, go home.' It didn't shock me, but it kind of made me feel tense and tight."

That "tight" feeling seemed to be a team disease carried over to the first half of the game on Saturday. The Fighting Irish made some bad mistakes and found themselves in an immediate hole. Mike Layden hurriedly fired a pass, and the ball was intercepted and run back for a Buckeye touchdown. Later, Bill Shakespeare was trapped trying to get off a kick. He had gotten a bad pass from center. The ball hit Ohio State center Gomer Jones in the chest, giving the Buckeyes good field position. Their flamboyant attack went into motion and gave them another touchdown and a 13-0 lead at the half.

"I had never seen a Notre Dame offense so completely stopped," says writer Francis Wallace. "When the Irish passed, the ball was intercepted and converted into a touchdown. It was difficult to get a running play started against the hard-charging Ohio State line. It was even hard to get a punt away."

When Layden sent in his second team to start the second half, his orders were clear: Stop the Buckeye offense, and start generating one of your own. Both missions were eventually accomplished. The Notre Dame ends began crashing into the

Ohio State backfield and stopped the Buckeyes' dazzling multiple offense.

Toward the end of the third quarter, Pilney was overheard saying from the bench: "If they'll put me in there now, I'll win this game for them."

"Knowing Andy, I knew that meant something," Layden said later. "We sent him in. He played one of the greatest games of football in that last quarter that I have ever seen in my life, as player or coach."

When the third period ended, Ohio State still had a 13-0 lead, but Notre Dame had a first down at the Buckeye 12 yard line and had the momentum as well.

"Our second ballclub came in there full of zip and vinegar and with the advantage of some very good information from the press box," Pilney remembers. "We went in there with a series of plays that Wally Fromhart called. . .some short passes over the middle. We usually didn't throw much to Fromhart, a blocking back, but he slipped through the middle there, and I was hitting him over the middle. I was also throwing to Mike Layden. We hit him over the middle three or four times. I think I threw seven passes in a row at one point to bring us down in there for one of our touchdowns. . .and I think that kind of rejuvenated us, and we started getting back in the huddle with a lot more zip and a lot more pep. We were talking so much in the huddle, we were so keyed up that Wally Fromhart had to quiet us down. I got bumped around quite a bit, but I was so high I didn't notice my bruises and scrapes. I know I walked in a huddle on one play, and Wally looked down at my shin, and he said, 'Hey, look at your leg.' I had a contusion on my shin bone, about six inches long and about three inches high, and I didn't even know it. That's really how high and tense we were."

Pilney was the hot one. He passed to Francis Gaul on the Ohio State two yard line. Seconds later Steve Miller took the ball across for a touchdown. The goal was missed, and now the scoreboard read: Ohio State 13, Notre Dame 6.

"It was heartbreaking," Millner recalls, "when Ken Stilley's placement for the extra point hit the cross bar, squarely between the uprights, and bounced back on to the field. All the ball needed was a few more inches."

What happened next was more heartbreaking for Notre Dame. The Fighting Irish later took possession of the ball and appeared headed for a certain touchdown with Pilney, the wild man, driving them inexorably down the field. Miller bucked over again, but this time he fumbled, and Ohio State recovered. It just was not Notre Dame's day, it seemed. The reprieved Buckeyes worked the ball downfield until they were checked and had to punt. That gave the Fighting Irish possession on their 20 yard line with three minutes to go. It looked safe for Ohio State. Then Layden sent in his first team to aid Pilney. The halfback passed to Fromhart on the Ohio State 33, and before the crowd had a chance to recover its breath, Pilney threw a touchdown pass to Mike Layden.

"But we still couldn't kick that extra point," notes Millner. "When Fromhart missed the tying point from placement, with less than two minutes to play, it appeared again that this was not Notre Dame's day."

Losing 13-12, Layden ordered an onside kick, hoping that Notre Dame could recover a fumble. But Ohio State had been expecting it and recovered the short kick. Then followed some of the most frantic moments ever seen in a football game. Dick Beltz drove off right tackle for a good Ohio State gain but was hit hard by Larry Danbom and Pilney (who had come up from the deep secondary like a pile driver). Pilney's final blow shook the ball loose, and it bounced toward the sidelines. Henry Pojman, the Notre Dame center, recovered, and the Fighting Irish miraculously had the ball on the Ohio State 49 yard line with the last seconds ticking away.

The crowd was hysterical. A mass audience swarmed near the sidelines, crowding the Notre Dame bench. Layden was in front of the bench, squatting on his heels, chain-smoking and running the show. Up in the press box, assistant coach Joe Boland was calling plays down to the bench, but the noise was so loud he was not sure that Chet Grant heard him. Layden sent a quarterback in with a play. "Go in. Call 57." The ball went to Pilney, and he rumbled through the Ohio State defense with the most dazzling run of the day.

"It was the climax play of the game," recalls Millner. "He faked a pass, raced through a hole at center, dodged eight separate Ohio State men, and was finally pinned on the 19-yard line by three Buckeyes, after a run of 30 yards which included every trick of ball-carrying, perfectly executed."

The great play cost Pilney plenty, though. He tore a cartilage in his left knee and had to be carried from the field on a stretcher. Layden sent in Bill Shakespeare as a replacement, and most everybody in the stadium knew that he was going to pass. He did—right to Dick Beltz. But the Ohio State back could not hold onto the ball, thus costing the Buckeyes the game. Shakespeare passed again and this time hit Millner with a beauty in the end zone with 32 seconds left. The extra point was missed again, but this time it did not matter. Notre Dame had the game won, 18-13.

Layden had been using so many substitutes in the last five minutes that he had practically run out of men to send into the game with plays. Ironically, the one who brought the winning play in was a scrub who did not even travel with the team to Columbus, rather paying his own way with the student body.

"Jim McKenna had come down on his own and worked out with us at practice and all that," Millner recalls. "So Layden told him to put a suit on and sit with us on the bench. There was no free substitution in those days. A player could not return in the same quarter, so when Layden ran out of players, he sent in McKenna. It was a pretty simple play, too. We shot

Notre Dame's "Thin Man," Elmer Layden, in the middle of a Fighting Irish huddle.

to the left, the ball went to the fullback. . .he gave it to old Shakespeare coming around on a reverse, and the ends crossed, and he had to throw it to one of the ends. And I was there, and I caught it. . .and that was the ballgame. Nothing special happened in the huddle. They just called the play and we ran it and that was it. It just so happened that everything clicked. Of course nowadays you tell everybody that you went 80 feet in the air for it with 9,000 guys around you. . ."

Pilney, the hero of the day, was being carried to the dressing room at the time of the dramatic touchdown play and was not able to see it. But he felt it, literally.

"As they were carrying me off the field," he remembers, "our trainer was at my head, and I had a manager at my feet, and of course my foot was twisted and doubled up and kind of hanging over the stretcher. And of course, the trainer and the manager were more interested in the damn ballgame than they were in Andy Pilney. While they were carrying me toward the dressing room door, I was trying to turn my head, even though I was in intense pain, to see what was happening. And as we were going into the door at the end of the stadium there, why the trainer and manager were still looking at the field, and as a result they caught my foot on the end of the door. And of course that kind of thing made me yip a little. Then they stopped, not because of me, but because they wanted to watch the end of the game. Then I heard the crowd. And the trainer says to me, 'Andy, it's over. We won. Millner caught the pass.' That was the last thing I remember. Then I went out."

When Pilney woke up, he was in the middle of a berserk dressing room.

"The place was a bedlam. And there was Elmer Layden standing near me, and a doctor was trying to set my leg. They had given me a shot. As I was coming to, Layden patted my head and said, 'Andy, here's a man right behind you that wants to say something.' And I kinda looked back over my head, and there was a fellow standing there with a gray stetson hat on, and he patted me on the shoulder. And he said, 'Andy, I'm Grantland Rice. I just want you to know that I've been writing and watching football for over 40 years, and that was the greatest single performance that I've ever seen.' And I said, 'Well, thank you very much, sir.' And then Grantland went away. I'll never forget that scene."

Chuck Sweeney, an All-American end in later years but

just a bench-rider that day, remembers the locker room as "absolute pandemonium. People knelt to pray; everyone was so crazy, we were almost delirious. Everyone was patting Layden on the back. He was so emotional at the time, he was crying. It was the greatest moment in my life, the greatest elevation I've ever been raised to, even though I didn't play. We stayed overnight at Columbus, and Columbus at midnight was just like New York on New Year's Eve. There was a tremendous outpouring of people. Most of them were Notre Dame fans, of course. The Ohio State fans stayed away. There was a tremendous reception when we came home by train, and the whole student body came down to the railroad station to see us. I think they got a day off from classes when we got back. The kids went downtown in waves, broke into theaters. I think it was the Palace Theater that they just took over. It went on for three days like that before things simmered down. When Notre Dame men get together to talk about a game, that's the game we talk about."

The large crowd was so affected by Notre Dame's stunning comeback that it took hours before the stadium was cleared of people. Either from elation or shock, most of the audience could not leave the arena. Recalls Pilney:

Bill Shakespeare threw the biggest pass of the 1935 season for Notre Dame, the one that beat Ohio State in the famous "game of the century."

"I think it was at least a good hour before the ambulance took me to the hospital, and when I finally came out of the dressing room, one of the managers said to me: 'Good God, there's still about 40,000 people in the stands.' And it was getting dark. I think they were both Ohio State people disappointed and Notre Dame people so elated they couldn't stand up, I guess."

Innumerable stories spun off from this game, in keeping with its wholly eccentric character.

The press box, almost always a haven of tranquility, was a crazy house after the final gun went off. Damon Runyon, the noted writer, was said to have thrown his camel coat out over the crowd. Francis Wallace, the Notre Dame historian, lost his hat and found himself dancing with Bill Cunningham, the Boston columnist and former Dartmouth center.

Years later, while they were reliving old times, Wallace prodded Cunningham: "Me, I could understand, but why were you so excited about Notre Dame winning?"

"Notre Dame?" Cunningham said. "I had just got word over my wire that Dartmouth had beaten Yale in the Yale Bowl for the first time in 33 years."

Millner says that Ted Husing, who was doing the game on radio, was so excited at the finish that he did not even know who caught the ball for Notre Dame's winning touchdown.

"They also tell me that one of the newspapers in Ohio thought the game was over before it actually was, and they had the score that Ohio State beat us 13-12. Then they had to retract it because we won."

Another story had a drunk just arriving at the end of the contest and asking: "How's the game?"

The response, presumably from an Ohio State fan: "First half great—don't stay for the second, it's lousy."

Many years after The Game, Pilney found himself in Columbus on a recruiting mission for Tulane and checked into a hotel. There were no rooms readily available, so the room clerk told Pilney to wait in the lobby for a while. Finally, after a long wait, a bell boy told Pilney that the room clerk would see him.

"I was able to find a room for you, sir; it's not much, but it has a bed," said the clerk. "Would you sign in please?"

When Pilney signed the register, the clerk looked at the name, his eyes widened, and he started cursing.

"Andy Pilney! You little son of a gun! You cost me $100

in 1935!"

Pilney got the room anyway and later found a bowl of fruit on his dresser with a nice note from the management.

The Fighting Irish were conceded a good chance to win the national title after that big victory over Ohio State, and perhaps they were still thinking about how good they were when they met Northwestern the following week at home. They certainly did not appear to be thinking about Northwestern, for they lost a 14-7 decision to the Wildcats.

"We had two touchdowns called back, otherwise we would have won," surmises Millner.

But Layden thought otherwise. He felt that his team had a tremendous letdown after beating the mighty Buckeyes.

"The Ohio State game put the spirits of the team up pretty

Wayne Millner: He caught the pass that beat Ohio State in the greatest cliff-hanger of them all.

high. The boys got pretty cocky during the next week. Then came one of those upsets to put the team's feet solidly back on the ground before heads got too big for helmets."

The following week Notre Dame had to rally in the last minute to tie Army 6-6, then closed out the season with a 20-13 victory over Southern California. In both these games Notre Dame used the passing game effectively—a hallmark of Layden's 1935 team. Passing was the Irish specialty, and Shakespeare was the specialist in this department, a quality which earned him All-American recognition that year. Shakespeare could also kick and made one of the greatest punts under pressure ever seen in a football game. Standing deep in his end zone and faced with a blitzing Pittsburgh line, Shakespeare punted 80 yards on the fly, 25 yards past a startled Panther safety man. The ball rolled dead on Pitt's 10 yard line—nearly 100 yards from the kicking point. The kick changed the complexion of the game and helped Notre Dame beat Pitt for the first time in four years. It was one of seven victories for the Irish in 1935.

"It was a fantastic season," Shakespeare said later, "and for some reason, everything seemed to come out at the last second. The Pitt game was tied 6-6 in the last seconds when Marty Peters kicked a field goal to win it for us. But it wasn't the usual end-over-end type of field goal. Marty kicked a spiral, and it curved over the crossbar. I never saw anything like it, but it won the game, and Marty won the Golden Shoe Award for it."

By 1936 Shakespeare and Notre Dame's other heroes of the 1935 game were gone. The Fighting Irish played with smaller squads and lesser talents, but still managed to win their share of games against an increasingly tough schedule. Although Layden himself believed that Notre Dame material had "fallen off" in the previous seven years, he still continued to schedule the toughest opposition in the country, "because we might as well lose to good teams, if we have to lose."

The new heroes were less than king-size but just as dynamic despite their lack of proportion. They included stocky Andy Puplis and little Bunny McCormick, who had worked his way up from the seventh to the first team by pure grit. The team was predicated on speed and precise execution, much like Knute Rockne's earlier squads, rather than size and power.

"Layden had ballclubs that were very quick and clever, and he threw the ball more than average in those days, and he followed Rock pretty close," acknowledges Pilney.

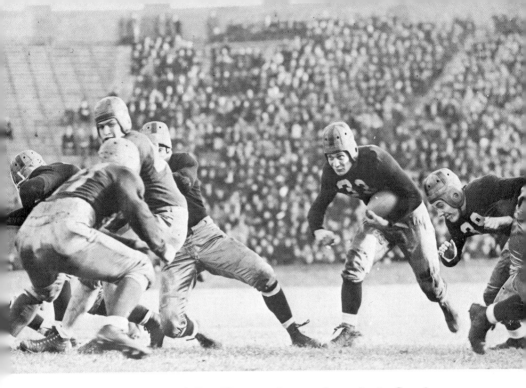

Notre Dame fullback Joe Thesing plunges through the Southern Cal line in this 1937 game. He got a few yards and the Irish got the victory, 13-6.

"A typical Layden squad was taut, tough and starless and always determined," points out another observer.

In both 1936 and 1937, Layden's teams had 6-2-1 records. The Fighting Irish lost each year to Pitt, and this understandably bothered Layden immeasurably. Jock Sutherland's squad had been a bitter rival when Layden had been at Duquesne, and the Panthers were probably the team that the Notre Dame coach most wanted to beat. By 1938 Notre Dame was without a celebrated hero but still managed an eight-game winning streak. The only loss for the Fighting Irish that year, Layden's best, was a 13-0 decision to Southern Cal in the last game of the year.

Seemingly following Layden's predictable conservatism, the 1939 and 1940 seasons fell into patterns, too. In each season he won the first six games and lost two of the last three, finishing with 7-2 records.

Milt Piepul, one of the Notre Dame All-Americans produced in this period, gave Layden possibly the best fullbacking he had in his seven years at South Bend. At 210 pounds and six-foot-one, Piepul was one of the biggest players on Layden's

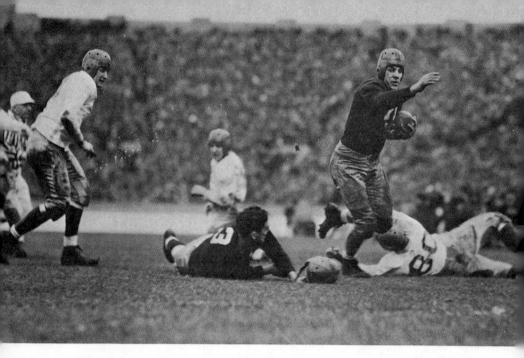

Milt Piepul crashes across for the first Notre Dame touchdown against Southern Cal in 1939. The Trojans did most of the scoring that day, however, and won 20-12.

mini squads. Piepul himself remembers how he would tower over some teammates.

"We had fellows like Benny Sheridan, who was all of 145 pounds," notes Piepul. "We were never a very big team."

Piepul at first had a hard time convincing Layden that he should play fullback. During Piepul's freshman year, Layden called him into his office and decided that he was too slow to be a fullback, and perhaps he should try out at tackle.

"I must have been in there for about five minutes, and all I could say was, 'No, sir. No, sir. I don't think so,'" says Piepul. "Elmer just said, 'Well, we'll find out this spring 'cause I don't think you're fast enough.' As a result, he let me play, and I guess I wound up one of the top fullbacks. . ."

Piepul was practically indestructible, nearly mistake-proof, and usually fearless. In his senior year he played with a sore leg against Georgia Tech. The injury was not disclosed until after the game so his presence as a decoy would make other stuff work. He was kicked by an Illinois player, and he spent four to six hours a day in the training room trying to mend a torn side muscle and hip bruise for the Army game. He played a tremendous defensive game against the Cadets, although he was hurt one time when he carried the ball and had to be removed from the field. He came back against Navy, at the risk of reinjuring himself, and made crucial tackles and yardage to help the Fighting Irish win their sixth straight game of 1940. In three years Piepul only fumbled the ball twice, perhaps his most amazing statistic.

Piepul was one of five All-Americans produced by Layden from 1938 through 1940, but he was the only one that made it in both 1939 and 1940. The others: tackle Joe Beinor, ends Earl Brown and Bud Kerr, and guard Jim McGoldrick.

Although Layden's fine records did not show it, times were not especially easy for Notre Dame's coach-athletic director, called "The Thin Man" after Dashiell Hammett's popular detective character. Not only was Layden thin, but so were his teams, by Notre Dame comparison. "It was probably a shade below the Notre Dame level," said a writer close to the scene. Layden lost games he should have won, like defeats by Iowa in 1939 and 1940, and the main complaint against his teams was that they lacked offensive punch and played football too conservatively.

"Gradually, the disaffection developed into disenchantment until graceful resignation was the pleasant solution," said Francis Wallace, a close Layden associate.

Larry Danbom on the loose against Carnegie Tech in 1936. Notre Dame won this season opener, 21-7.

Notre Dame beat Georgia Tech 17-14 in 1939 with the help of this 14-yard run by Lou Zontini.

Notre Dame beat Georgia Tech 26-20 in 1940, and Milt Piepul (No. 71) led the way, as usual.

These rugged looking specimens turned out for Elmer Layden's last spring practice in 1940—(from left) Norm Berry, Jr.,

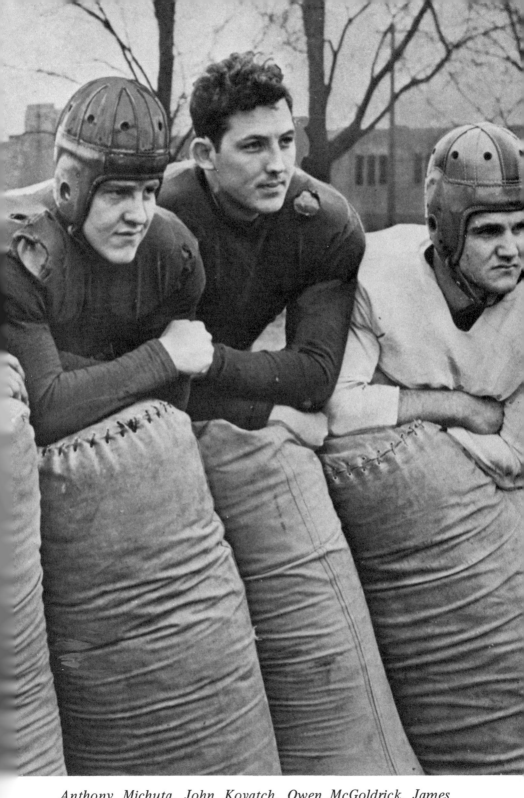

Anthony Michuta, John Kovatch, Owen McGoldrick, James Brock, and Ed Sullivan.

In the spring of 1940 a young man's fancy turned toward football at Notre Dame.

So although Layden resigned without warning on February 4, 1941, to take a job as commissioner of the National Football League, it was not completely unexpected. If there was any pain from cutting ties with Notre Dame, this was somewhat assuaged by the security of the new job. Layden got a five-year contract at $20,000 annually.

Frank Leahy, an old Notre Dame man, was hired to be the new Notre Dame coach, and no one suspected to what euphoric heights he would take the Fighting Irish.

A Notre Dame Man

Frank Leahy: Now lads, if we expect to beat Oklahoma come next September, we're going to have to put more time into practice. In order to do this, we're going to have to practice on Sundays. Any lads that don't want to beat Oklahoma next September, raise your hands.

A player: Well, coach, isn't it against the Commandments to work on Sundays?

Leahy: Football isn't work.

A fractured elbow kept Frank Leahy out of several of Notre Dame's games in 1929. But he was determined to start against Southern California that year, and he told Coach Knute Rockne that the elbow was healed.

"That's not the doctor's story," Rockne said. "Let's have a look."

Leahy rolled up his sleeve, extended his left arm and flexed it easily, showing no apparent pain. Rockne was sold and gave his intense tackle the okay to start.

Leahy played against the Trojans despite terrible pain. Because he wanted to see action so badly, he had fooled Rockne. The fractured elbow was the *right* one, not the left.

The preceding story, often told by Notre Dame men, points up the grim determination that marked Leahy's life—an unyielding tenacity that took him from the prairies of Dakota to the mountains of coaching fame. It explains his extravagant successes of the 1940s, when Notre Dame swaggered through an unmatched era in the history of college football.

Before Leahy's glory years ended with still another golden

209

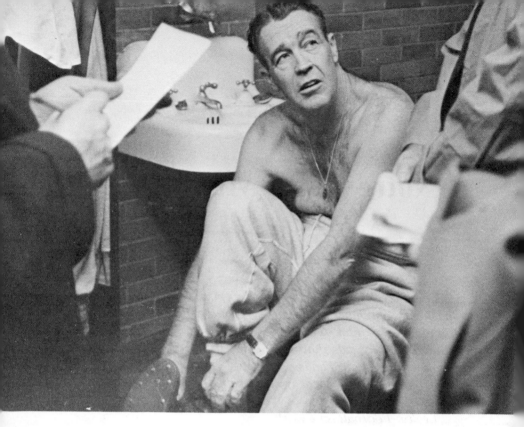

Frank Leahy: "No football teams were ever better prepared physically or mentally than our squads at Notre Dame."

season in 1953, these were his accomplishments at Notre Dame: four national championships, six undefeated seasons, a streak of 39 games without a loss, and a record of 87-11-9, a winning mark of nearly 89 percent. (Included in this record is one spectacular seven-year period of 60 victories, only 3 losses, and 5 ties.)

That Leahy accomplished all this and still did not reach all his goals is another illuminating insight into the man's character. At one point in his career, Leahy turned down a blank-check offer to coach the professional Cleveland Browns in favor of a 10-year contract as coach and athletic director of Notre Dame. His reasons were simple enough, he said.

"My goal was to go through 10 seasons without a loss," Leahy pointed out.

"And you know," he added, "I still think we would have done it if our scholarships hadn't been cut down in 1948."

The minute Francis William Leahy stepped on the football

field at Notre Dame in 1941, he was the boss. He was the czar of football at South Bend, and everybody knew it.

"To him there was only one way to play football," sportswriter Edgar Hayes once wrote. "The Frank Leahy way. His system was simple: You won."

How did Leahy win? He won with superb conditioning and intense preparation.

Being prepared, like the proverbial Boy Scout, was Leahy's motto. Unpreparedness was a capital sin, he thought. Once trying to explain his great success, Leahy said, "In my opinion, no football teams were ever better prepared physically or mentally than our squads at Notre Dame."

His players would agree with that.

"He taught us to be successful through hard work," says George Connor, one of Leahy's prize pupils. "He taught us to know what your opponent is doing. We knew every play our opponents had used, and were contemplating using." Notes Johnny Lujack, "He said there was no shortcut. I think he meant you have to give it 100 per cent. You're not an automatic success. You have to work at it. One of his favorite expressions was, 'You've got to be willing to pay the price.'

"I was coaching for him in '52 and '53. He was a great fundamentalist. We were running this off-tackle play, and he didn't feel the right guard was pulling out properly to hit the end, so he'd say, 'Let's run that play over again,' and he'd tell the guard how to do it. They went over that play about six or seven times. In the meantime, this halfback was getting killed on every play. I knew this halfback, and I felt it was getting so rough in there that soon he would fake an injury. And he sure enough did on the fourth or fifth play. He didn't think that Leahy noticed it, but Leahy said, 'Ah, lad, I know that you're not wounded. And if I were to permit you to become disassociated with this scrimmage, I'd be doing you a grave injustice because later on in life when you have a family decision or a big business decision I think you may want to fake an injury then. So, lad, we're going to run this play over until that right guard blocks that end properly. So let's get in there.' Someone might say that's cruel, but I figure it taught that kid something, because he wasn't hurt, and we knew he wasn't hurt, and he turned out to be a dandy halfback."

Another classic story about Leahy's militant philosophy comes from another practice, when the coach approached one of his players and asked him how he felt.

When the player answered, "a little tired," Leahy replied, "You're out of condition. . .you'd better do 20 laps."

The next day Leahy had the same question for the same player. But this time the player was ready for him. He told Leahy, "I feel fine, coach."

"Then you didn't work hard enough," Leahy said. "You'd better do 20 laps."

Leon Hart was one of Leahy's biggest stars but was not spared any of the coach's harsh treatment. Leahy believed in equal sweat for all. When Hart missed an assignment during one practice, Leahy had him run 25 laps around the field. When he did not run the 25 laps to Leahy's high-stepping specifications, the coach had him do 25 more.

After the 50 laps, Hart complained: "I wonder what the hell the old man will want next?" But Leahy heard it—and Hart paid for it.

"A little more respect, lad," Leahy told the All-American end. "Do 25 laps more."

Zygmont Czarobski, an All-American tackle, was another who all too frequently heard Leahy's familiar order to run laps. It seemed that the colorful Ziggy was always running laps whenever his father was visiting Notre Dame. One time Czarobski's father complained to Leahy: "Ziggy came here to play football. How come you got him on the track team?"

Leahy was just as willing to sacrifice himself to get things done, Lujack remembers.

"Many times we'd come from late classes at night, and we'd go by the film room in his office, and there would be the light burning 10, 11 o'clock at night. Leahy even had a bed in there, and he'd call his wife and just tell her that he would sleep there. He covered all the angles of football, never left a stone unturned. And again, it all boiled down to one thing, are you willing to pay the price? If you are willing to pay the price of success, then we'll have success."

George Ratterman, a fine quarterback and one of the legions of professional players that Leahy produced, remembers him as kind of a personable Captain Bligh.

"He was kind of a slave driver guy, but you won and appreciated him for that. People who played for him are unanimous now when they're not playing for him—he probably had more of a favorable influence on their lives than anyone else.

But like anyone that works you very hard, there are usually a lot of complaints at the time, and a lot of unhappy people."

Neil Worden, one of the best fullbacks produced by Leahy or any other coach at Notre Dame, "liked and respected" him and understood his passionate attachment to football. "He played for keeps. He played to win. If you have to do something, you do it the best you can. That was his philosophy. I enjoyed playing for him. We practiced, we played hard. . .and we looked at defeat pretty badly."

"He couldn't stand the thought of losing," agreed Angelo Bertelli, the Heisman Trophy-winning quarterback of 1943. "Everytime he'd lose a game, he'd end up in the Mayo Clinic."

Because Leahy put so much importance on leadership, he gave his quarterbacks special stature. Players understood this caste system and lived with it.

"He always put us quarterbacks up on a pedestal," explains Frank Tripucka. "His theory was that the quarterback was the guy that had to be looked up to. If you made a mistake, he would never chew you out in front of everybody. He would always call you aside and say something like, 'Oh, Francis, how could you miss that receiver? How could you miss Leon? He was out there all by himself.' He'd give you that stuff. 'The Lady on the Golden Dome doesn't like you to miss those passes. . .' That quarterback had to be the master, had to be the kingpin. He didn't want you to be looked down upon by other members of the team. The other people, he didn't care how he embarrassed them. I remember once, Leon Hart made a helluva catch of a pass in a crowd. There were six guys hanging on him, but he comes down with the ball. But Leahy didn't bother to congratulate him about that great catch. He only said to Hart: 'Oh, Leon, at Notre Dame, we not only catch the ball, but we run with it after we catch it.'"

"He tried to spend a great deal of time with his quarterbacks," notes Ralph Guglielmi, a star of the 1950s. "Every day, every night, he just did a lot with his quarterbacks, and by Saturday they would be calling the kind of game that Leahy wanted."

Leahy instilled tremendous confidence in all his quarterbacks, a fact which brings up this story from Lujack:

"In 1943, Angelo Bertelli went into the service after the Navy game, and it was up to me to follow in his footsteps and take over as No. 1 quarterback. And it was pretty much conceded at the time that whoever won the Army game would eventually become national champions, so it was a big game for us. To show you the psychologist Leahy was, the night before the game, he started talking about me before the team, but at the time I didn't know who he was talking about. He starts telling the team how blessed we are to have such a 'great' passer, this man who is going to lead us today. . .such a great runner, great defensive man. The accolades were so great, I got up to look around to see if he had brought in a ringer to start at quarterback. But what he was trying to do was convince the team that even though it was a kid coming in, he could really handle the job. We did win that game 26-0 and the national championship."

Leahy, however, was just as adept at cutting down players as building them up. More than one felt his wrath, which was often quiet but as sharp and deft as a surgeon's blade. During the first half of a game once, he was troubled because he felt that quarterback Ralph Guglielmi was neglecting fullback Neil Worden in the plays. During the half-time break in the locker room, Leahy went to pains to dramatize and correct the situation. While the whole squad looked on, he formally "introduced" the two. "Oh, Ralph, perhaps you don't know this man," said Leahy, "he's in the same backfield as you." Guglielmi got the point, and Worden got the ball after that.

Once during a practice session, Leahy felt that one particular player was not giving his all.

"Coach McArdle," Leahy said to line coach Joe McArdle, "did the block that lad at right guard just make truly represent his desire to play for Notre Dame? I sincerely trust not." The player blocked better the next time.

When Zygmont Czarobski reported overweight one year, Leahy only had to mention it to a reporter, and the tackle quickly trimmed off some poundage. All Leahy said was, "If Zygmont is not willing to make the necessary sacrifices, it may become necessary for him to disassociate himself from our operation."

Czarobski, the team clown, took a lot of jabs from the stern coach but nevertheless was able to supply the stone-visaged Leahy with a laugh or two along the way. Leahy was all business but could appreciate some fun at the right time. Remembers Connor, the All-American tackle:

"In 1947 we got back for fall training, and the first day,

Leahy had us scrimmaging, but plays weren't going so well. So he stopped practice and said, 'Lads, you have a terrible football team, and you couldn't beat the girls at St. Mary's across the way.' He asked for a football. He said, 'Lads, this is a football!' He said he was going to start at the beginning, and Ziggy said, 'Wait a minute, coach—not so fast.' That broke Leahy up, and the whole meeting, and added some humor to our practice. . . .''

That Leahy was not totally without a sense of humor is further confirmed by Lujack.

"One of my favorite stories happened in 1943, right before the Iowa Pre-Flight game. It was wartime, and they were loaded with pro football stars, and I think Leahy had used every bit of psychology in the previous eight games to bring us around and win. So he tried something new—Knute Rockne's grave. He got a bus about three hours before the game, and we went out to the Notre Dame cemetery to visit. We had heard of George Gipp and things like that, so Leahy probably thought maybe we could win one for Rockne. I was 18 and very impressionable at the time. Well, we went out there, it was the first time I'd been there, and we knelt over Rockne's grave and said whatever message we thought to say. Creighton Miller and I were faster at prayers than the other players, and we got up quickly and started looking around at other grave sites. We saw the grave of George Keogon, the former basketball coach who had just died. We thought it would be nice to say a prayer for him, but when Leahy saw us kneeling at his grave, he shouted over: 'Ah, lads, come away from there. You can visit him during the basketball season.'"

Leahy, as far removed from Rockne in personality as one could be, still had a bit of the Old Master's con man in his soul. Lujack recalls one half-time talk that was pure Rockne, even though it came out of Leahy's mouth.

"It was a tough game, we were leading 6-0 at the half, and Leahy hadn't shown up on time. It was getting late, and we were wondering where he was. Finally it was just about time to get out on the field when Leahy walked in, and it looked like he had tears in his eyes. He said, 'Lads, I received a telegram from my wife saying that my son, Frank, would rather be dead than lose to this team today. And, lads, well, I love that boy. . .' Well, with that sort of thing we just sort of tore out of there. I don't remember the door being opened."

He not only conned his own players, but opposing coaches

215

as well. The night before he was to play Oklahoma in 1952, he thanked Sooner coach Bud Wilkinson a thousand times over for playing Notre Dame.

"It is most generous of you to bring your great ball club to South Bend to play us in a year when we are not too good," Leahy said. He went on like this for nearly a half hour before Wilkinson was able to pull away. The next day Notre Dame whipped Oklahoma 27-21 for one of Leahy's greatest triumphs. Wilkinson never believed Leahy much after that.

Because of Leahy's well-known locker room performances, most of the veteran players became callous to his act.

"The kind of ballplayer I was, I didn't need the stories," says Neil Worden. "I knew the job we had to do. Some people are affected that way. And Leahy was a great inspirer, he could tell stories. But being there for four years, you heard all the stories. You got to hide in the background and become lost because they became humorless. For people who first heard them, and needed that inspiration, it'll get you there. Like the first year I was there, you'd run through the wall. The second year, I'd heard this before. I was inspired by the situation, not the stories. If you didn't win, you'd scrimmage on Monday. . .so you had to go out there and do the job."

Once when Leahy had a pancreas attack during a game and was actually on the verge of death, some veterans who did not know any better just winked and said that it was another of Leahy's motivational tricks.

"It was the halftime of the Georgia Tech game," remembers Johnny Lattner, "and we were resting when there was a lot of commotion in the coach's room. The trainer ran back there, and then a priest ran back. A player went back, too, and about two minutes later, he ran up to me and my buddy, Bob Rigali, and said: 'Geez, the coach is dying.' Rigali gives me a nudge and says, 'Don't you believe the son-of-a-gun. He's pulling another Rockne.'"

Leahy strove for perfection and usually got it. Otherwise he wanted to know why. He was apt to stop a scrimmage to move a lineman's foot three inches to insure a better blocking angle. He did not believe in having punts blocked, not even in practice, and had his teams rerun plays over and over if that happened. During one session when a Notre Dame back made a sparkling touchdown run, Leahy even found a flaw in that. "Look at him," he said, his face a grimace, "he's carrying the ball in the wrong arm." Even Leahy's calisthenics were drills of fanatical intensity. He would stand in the middle of this strenuous gridiron circus and not miss a trick, so well were they organized. "I must have organization," he confessed, "or I get confused."

None of his players were misled by Leahy's lack of strong language. Although he never used expletives, his criticism stung nevertheless.

Leahy could make poised players squirm with such stock expressions as, "Maybe you are unwilling to make the necessary sacrifice to play for Notre Dame," or "Perhaps you lack the character to see the job through."

This velvet-glove approach won him respect. Players called him "sir" to his face and "the master" behind his back. There was no horseplay, loafing, or profanity when Leahy was around. Even the coaches could not smoke. Anyone violating the Leahy code was subject to memorable penalties. One of the few times that the straitlaced Leahy relaxed his code, so the story goes, was during the remembered scoreless tie with Army of 1946, when Bob Livingstone missed a tackle to allow an Army runner to make a good gain. An emotional Johnny Lujack, sitting on the bench, shouted, "Oh, Bob Livingstone, you son of a bit. . . ."

Leahy turned to Lujack and said menacingly, "Another sacrilegious outburst like that, Johnathan Lujack, and you will be disassociated with our fine Catholic university."

When Livingstone missed another tackle on the next play, Leahy turned to his bench and said, "Lads, Johnathan Lujack was right about Robert Livingstone."

Practice sessions under Leahy were not only tough, they were also spirited. There was constant chattering and a continual burst of encouragement. When a lowly reserve joined the first team for a scrimmage, he got a round of applause from his teammates. The players even led cheers, remembers George Connor.

"I guess it was kind of unusual to go on the field and hear the Notre Dame players leading cheers. But there it was every week. And every week, we had a different cheer. I remember in 1946, we were going to play Army in New York. They had beaten us 59-0 and 48-0 the two seasons before, and our cheer for that week was, '59, 48, Let's beat the Army and reciprocate.' Then every once in a while, when Leahy was at the other end of the field, we'd give a bugle sound, and we'd chant, 'We want to eat, We want to eat.' And as Leahy would come rushing up, we'd say, 'We want to eat the Army.' And he'd laugh."

It goes without saying that Leahy was never satisfied with practice sessions, being the supreme perfectionist he was. Even after the best scrimmage, Leahy would have an unbroken string of criticisms like: too many downfield blocks were missed; the backs were not running hard enough; the linemen were not charging fast enough. Before every game Leahy was the eternal pessimist, the all-time Gloomy Gus. Before one season started, Leahy moaned aloud that his team would never make a first down that year. Then the Fighting Irish went out and won every game and took home the national championship. Paul Neveille, the onetime sports editor of the *South Bend Tribune*, summed up the Leahy picture in two revealing sentences: "Nothing ever goes right during the week. That's why it goes perfectly on Saturdays."

During a typical day Leahy would rise about 6:45 a.m. and hold his first staff conference at 8 a.m. He spent the next hour or so looking at movies. At about 10 a.m. he was back at his office, checking the mail and taking care of correspondence. Every day at noon he followed a Rockne tradition by holding a meeting with his players. After that session Leahy took a fast time out for a sandwich, usually eaten at his desk and washed down with milk. At 3 p.m. he left for the locker room and got ready for a torturous practice that took at least two hours and sometimes longer. If he missed supper on occasion, his food was football. And he fed on it until the late hours of night, usually watching films or plotting strategy. If his charges worked, the persistent Leahy worked twice as hard. This year-round, man-killing schedule once put Leahy in the Mayo Clinic with a nervous breakdown but did not keep him off his feet for long.

Perhaps because of his overzealousness and no doubt because of his gorgeous successes, Leahy was not universally loved. The ultrasuccessful man always has critics, and this was the case with Leahy. Many of Leahy's fellow coaches were not completely enamored of the Notre Dame hero and expressed their dislike openly or covertly. Some of this feeling was attributed to jealousy, according to one professional coach of the time.

"Why don't they like Leahy? Hell, that's easy. He beats them too often," the coach said.

But, actually, some were as disgusted with his methods as his accomplishments. Leahy, it was pointed out by one Chicago newspaperman, wanted to win so badly that he did not always observe the letter of collegiate law. Lloyd Lewis, then sports editor of the *Chicago Daily News*, accused Leahy of holding an illegal practice one summer for his entire first-string backfield. The players—Angelo Bertelli, Harry Wright, Dippy Evans, and Steve Juzwik—all held down summer jobs at Notre Dame Stadium while practicing two hours a day from June on, Lewis reported. Leahy did not deny it. Leahy was also well aware of the shots of criticism fired at his warlike practice sessions.

"Frankly, we do work the players hard. . .awfully hard," he confessed one day. "We keep after them all the time on the practice field; we find fault with much that they do out there. We raise a lot of Cain with them."

But he never changed. Leahy drove his players to their endurance and sometimes beyond it. The story is told of how he once loomed over a crumpled player who had broken his leg and beseeched: "Lad, get to your feet! Resume the struggle for Our Lady!" The player tried to rise under Leahy's exhortations but fell back on the field in agonizing pain.

Leahy's grim philosophy made Notre Dame a winner on the football field but a loser in other areas, it was maintained. Some critics said that Leahy's personality caused several teams to freeze Notre Dame off their schedules. One Army man blamed Leahy for the cancellation of their series after 1947: "When Rockne was alive, Army seldom beat Notre Dame, but it was different. You didn't hate to lose. Rock would come up to the Point every spring, stay around two or three days with Biff Jones or whoever was coaching, and renew and strengthen relations. Losing to Leahy is just the same as losing to a concrete mixer."

Leahy might have been better loved by his rivals had he been less "concrete mixer" and just a good mixer. Leahy was so immersed in football that he had little time for small talk and pleasantries, and this could have cost him the esteem of some of his peers. Leahy was not the handshaking, backslapping type, though. Even his players say that he was tough to get near.

"He was very formal and not the happy-go-lucky type," recalls Angelo Bertelli. "You couldn't talk to him; he was not easy to know. You would run into him on campus, and he'd ask you the same question all the time. 'How are you, Angelo?

A frantic moment during an Army game gets Frank Leahy up on his feet.

What are you doing now? How's your mom and dad?' Things like that. But he didn't listen to the answers. It was his way of making conversation."

Discussing Leahy and Hugh Devore, who filled in for Leahy during a wartime season, Frank Tripucka says, "Hughie was a much friendlier type off the field. . .Leahy was a loner. If you wanted to see him, you had to make an appointment."

Leahy greeted each player with three stock questions: (1) How are you? (2) How is your mother? (3) How much do you weigh? This annual ceremony produced one of the most revealing anecdotes about the one-track Notre Dame coach. Once when he encountered Jim Mello, the impish player gave Leahy some well-designed answers, but all he got was a characteristic Leahy reaction.

On the first question, Mello answered, "Well, I had a serious operation, but I'm doing fine now." Leahy nodded and said, "Fine."

On the second question, Mello responded, "She passed away this summer." "That's fine," Leahy said again.

On the third, Mello's answer was, "214 pounds." Leahy looked the boy squarely in the eyes and told him, "You're four pounds overweight, James."

Along with the other criticisms, Leahy was also said to have taught "dirty football." One critic noted: "He's not satisfied with all that material. He's not even satisfied with his own talent for coaching. He can't bear to leave a single thing to chance, so he teaches the boys every dirty trick in the books. And, furthermore, he sees that they use them all." More than one opponent has accused Leahy's teams of playing that way. One Southern Cal player pointed out: "They'll give you the knee, they'll hold you, they'll clip you, and they'll belt you with an elbow every chance they get. Maybe Leahy doesn't tell them to do it, but he sure doesn't tell them not to do it."

Marchy Schwartz, an old teammate of Leahy's, was understandably distressed when Leahy's boys did a lot of fighting with his Stanford team in 1942, much of it off the record. "The boys on the Stanford bench were so infuriated that Schwartz had to restrain them from piling off the bench and turning the contest into a gang fight," said Ed Fitzgerald, writing in a national magazine. The game was supposed to be the first of a two-game series between the schools, but the second one was never played. "And it never will as long as Leahy is the Notre Dame coach," Fitzgerald concluded at the time.

Leahy, of course, denied that his teams used any underhanded tactics. But he was branded by some rivals as a "hypocrite" and a "phony." They felt that the end result did not justify his means for getting there. A few of his peers were so bitter about Leahy that they prevented his installation in college football's Hall of Fame until December, 1970. That was 17 years after he departed from Notre Dame, leaving a heritage that few coaches equaled in the whole of college football.

Leahy came from an appropriate place to make his niche in the world—Winner, South Dakota. He was actually born in O'Neill, Nebraska, in 1907, but his family moved to South Dakota when Frank was only a few months old, and that is where he grew up. Even as a babe in arms, Leahy was prepared for the hard life of the prairies. While he and his father and mother and seven brothers and sisters awaited the building of their home in Winner, they spent a long, bitter winter housed in a tent. Frank Leahy, Sr., worked as a freighter for a number of years and later went into the produce business. Young Frank worked as a farmhand when he was just six years old, making a dollar a day. Later he graduated to the "big time"—five dollars a day as a cattle herder and virtual cowhand. By the time he was 16, he had become an expert rider and roper, and once, with a friend, he shepherded 12 head of horses 150 miles across the South Dakota Badlands. While growing into manhood, Leahy built his muscles by carrying loads of grain and flour from his father's produce center out to the wagons on the street. He also worked at a soda fountain and as a clerk in the local trading post.

Like his broad-shouldered father, Frank, Jr., was an athlete with great coordination. The younger Leahy could box and wrestle well and was a regular winner at local boxing shows. At one time in his life, it is said, he wavered between a career in the ring and higher education.

Leahy's early interest in fighting was prompted by his father, who used to wrestle and engage in stick-pulling contests with Farmer Burns, then the world's champion wrestler. His early interest in football was prompted by his older brother, Gene, who was an All-American center at Creighton University. "When Gene came home to Winner wearing his sweater bearing a huge 'C,' the eight-year-old Frank determined he would be a football player—and a good one," said a friend.

Leahy starred in football as halfback and captain of the Winner High School team. The energetic Leahy also won letters in basketball and baseball. Even while a teenager in Winner, Leahy was being pointed toward Notre Dame. His football coach there was Earl Walsh, a Notre Dame monogram winner in 1920 and 1921, who encouraged young Frank to think about going to South Bend. This destiny was later shaped when the Leahy family moved to Omaha, Nebraska, and Frank—now an all-star athlete at Omaha Central High School—heard Knute Rockne on one of his speaking tours. After listening with reverence to Rockne's magnetic voice and actually shaking the hand of the Notre Dame coach, Leahy's mind was made up. "I'm going to Notre Dame," he told his coach, George Schmidt.

Although Leahy was a star in high school, he found that things were not going to be quite that easy for him at Notre Dame. When he came to South Bend in 1927, he was just one of hundreds of eager new faces shooting for the football team. His spirits were not helped any, either, when he lost his wallet containing $19, all the money he had with him. It turned out that Leahy was not to have any money until the Christmas holidays, when he and a friend got a job shoveling coal at the university for fifty cents an hour. Leahy, a small-town boy from the prairies at a big league school, had a growing inferiority complex until Rockne made him feel at home. Leahy's first encounter with the Notre Dame coach took place in a locker room. Leahy, already shy and in awe of Rockne, felt even more uncomfortable because he had most of his clothes off. Rockne, as was his habit, scrutinized the boy's physique and extended a hand.

"Leahy, eh? From South Dakota, aren't you? Earl Walsh wrote to me about you."

Sensing Leahy's bashfulness, Rockne took some extra time with him. After a while Leahy felt a part of the Notre Dame family.

"Feel a little lost here, do you, Frank? Well, we'll have you over that in a couple of days. Don't forget there are a lot of other fellows here in the same boat. Wait until we get you out on that practice field. Everything will be O.K., then, O.K."

All through the conversation Rockne had been appraising Leahy's body, and on the way out, he mentioned to his assistant, Tommy Mills, "A pretty good pair of football legs there, Tommy, uh?"

Leahy had played tackle at Omaha Central High School, and it was at this position that he attempted to make Notre Dame's freshman team. But Rockne finally decided that Leahy would be better utilized at center. Leahy's response pointed up the intense determination of his character. Never having played center, two hours of daily practice with the freshman team was not enough for him. Leahy borrowed a ball from the equipment room and during the evenings, with the help of classmates, practiced snapping the ball back in his freshman dormitory. This nightly application continued for a long time until Leahy put too much power behind one pass and broke a window. However, by this time Leahy was a polished center and did not have to do his homework near dormitory windows. He was good enough to win the Frank E. Hering Medal for proficiency in center-passing, one of the medals of accomplishment given out at Notre Dame's spring practice.

By the 1928 season Leahy was elevated to the varsity and

managed to see action in a few games, even if Rockne usually frowned on using sophomores in his lineup. By the fall of 1929 Leahy was shifted back to tackle and was important enough to rate a couple of lines in the preseason review: "Rockne seems to have filled his two line vacancies with Leahy and (Jack) Cannon."

Leahy did manage to hold the first-string job on Rockne's 1929 team, playing most of the season with injury as the Fighting Irish won the national championship. Then came 1930 and Leahy's most disappointing season as a player. On the last play of the preseason scrimmage before the home opener with Southern Methodist, Leahy tore a cartilage in his right knee while blocking the safety man and had to be carried from the field. That was the end of his playing career, even though his gallant spirit would not let it die easily. Everyone at Notre Dame knew Leahy was through, except perhaps Leahy himself. For three weeks he submitted impatiently to crutches, then threw them away and tried practicing, although in obvious agony.

While Leahy threw himself into the charging machines, Rockne would point out to writers: "That's Frank Leahy. He would have been our regular left tackle. The poor guy has torn a cartilage, and he's washed up. But he won't admit it. He still thinks he can get ready for the Army game. Look at him."

Finally, Rockne let Leahy learn the awful truth with a graphic lesson. Once when Leahy intercepted Rockne near the practice machines and announced, "My knee is O.K. now, Rock. I'm ready to go," Rockne gave him the green light. It soon turned into a red light for Leahy, though.

"Let's see you sprint 20 yards," Rockne said.

Leahy started to run, his knee sagged under him, and so did his heart. He staggered for a few yards and then tumbled over.

"You've got more guts than brains," Rockne muttered over his shoulder as he turned and walked away.

But even though Leahy knew then he was finished, it did not keep him away from the football field. "Hunched on crutches, he stood peering at signal drills, dummy scrimmages, group work in fundamentals," said an acquaintance. "He never missed."

Leahy absorbed everything from the coach's viewpoint, picking up clinical details that the active player misses. He got to know thoroughly the theory and fundamentals of each position and got to know Rockne even better. Impressed by Leahy's spirit and attitude, Rockne put him in charge of the B team for its games with Wisconsin's B's and Kalamazoo Normal. Rockne's undergraduate coach won both games and, in addition, won Rockne's heart.

As a reward for his service and loyalty, Rockne took Leahy along on the final trip of the season to Los Angeles for the Southern Cal game. There he reinjured his knee playing tiddlywinks, of all things. Leahy was limping badly, and Rockne decided that he had better do something to help the wounded boy.

"I'm going to the Mayo Clinic to get my leg looked after," Rockne told Leahy in December of 1930. "Why don't you come along, and we'll see if we can't get that leg of yours fixed up—in case you want to play tiddlywinks again."

Leahy accepted so fast that it made Rockne's head spin, and the two, who spent three years together on a football field, found themselves companions once more—but this time in a hospital room. An operation on Leahy's knee made it as good as new and gave him a sparkling, new outlook as well. Once looking back on his time at the clinic, Leahy remembered it as one of the most kindly acts in Rockne's entire career:

"Rock knew I was brooding about the leg injury, and he thought he could bolster my spirits by having some famous physicians see if something couldn't be done to repair the damage. He realized I was finished as a football player, but he wanted to put my mind at ease. I didn't realize what he was doing until several years later. At the clinic we had a big room with beds on either side of the window. Rockne did practically all the talking during the time we were there."

For two weeks Rockne talked about football, and Leahy listened and learned. Finally the pupil told the teacher that he would like to be a coach himself. "When I told Rock of my choice, he said, 'Frank, I think you're doing the right thing,'" Leahy said.

Rockne did more than just applaud Leahy for his choice—he got him a job. One day he tossed his morning mail over to Leahy and said, "Take your pick of these." All the letters that Rockne had given to Leahy were from coaching friends asking his aid in the selection of an assistant coach.

Leahy perused the letters and decided on Georgetown.

There he rejoined an old Notre Dame acquaintance—Tommy Mills, his onetime freshman coach. Leahy worked for one year as Mills' line coach and then began to shoot up the coaching ladder. Jim Crowley was so impressed by the job Leahy did with the Georgetown line, he brought him to Michigan State as an assistant in 1932. When Crowley went to Fordham in 1933, Leahy went with him and built one of the best-known lines of the Rams' glory years—"The Seven Blocks of Granite."

Success came not only in public life, but in private as well. Leahy met a Brooklyn girl named Florence Reilly, and they were married in 1935. Their wedding was a story in itself, and quite humorous at that. An old friend of the Reilly family almost broke up the affair when he confided to the bride's father: "Don't you let her marry that football coaching fellow. I happen to know he's already married and has a couple of youngsters." The trouble was quickly dissolved when it was discovered that the old man had confused Leahy with Elmer Layden, the old Notre Dame coach and onetime member of Rockne's "Four Horsemen" backfield.

Along with producing Fordham's most famous line in history, the once-bashful Leahy accomplished a more personal goal in his six years at Fordham. He made a study of talking properly and proper breathing and blossomed forth as an accomplished public speaker. During this prosperous time, Leahy was in great demand at coaching schools across the country, and he lectured in a big league of coaching notables. One of them, Carl Snavely of Cornell, helped Leahy land a job as head coach of Boston College in 1939, when Gil Dobie retired. Boston's reaction to the signing of Leahy was reflected in this newspaper headline: "B. C. Signs Unknown Leahy." For although Leahy was well known among his peers, he had not yet established a "name" big enough to suit the Boston press. But Leahy did not stay an unknown for long. After a month at the school, he had developed superlative relations with the press and later began developing superlative teams.

"I came to Boston College to succeed and not to fail," Leahy said, and then put his words into action.

In two seasons Leahy's Boston College teams lost only two games—by a total of 10 points. One of them was a bizarre 6-3 loss to Clemson in the Cotton Bowl during Leahy's first year. But that was the last time he lost at Boston College. In 1940 his squad won all 10 regular season games and claimed the eastern championship. Then the Eagles completed the glorious season by beating Tennessee 19-13 in the Sugar Bowl, Leahy's crowning achievement at B. C. Joe Zabilski, the right guard on that outstanding Boston College team, reflected the profound impression that Leahy made on his players: "He was a great defensive coach. . .but also an offensive innovator ahead of his time. His attention to detail, his preparation for every possible contingency were incredible."

Apparently Notre Dame felt so, too, because the Fighting Irish hired Leahy away from Boston College not long after the Sugar Bowl triumph. This time, there was no talk about an "unknown" on the campus. In fact, the coming of Leahy was hailed by some as the second coming of Rockne, and although the new coach stressed, "There'll never be another Rockne," Leahy came as close as was humanly possible. His record at Boston College and Notre Dame, in fact, was incredibly similar. In 13 years, Rockne's teams won 105, lost 12, and tied 3. In 13 years, Leahy's teams won 107, lost 13, and tied 9. Rockne's winning percentage was .897. Leahy's was .892. Rockne won three national championships and had five unbeaten seasons, as opposed to Leahy's four national championships and six unbeaten years.

Leahy broke off with Rockne tradition soon after his arrival at South Bend. In his second year, 1942, he scrapped the old Notre Dame "box formation" because he felt that it had outlived its usefulness. In its place Leahy installed the "T," a new, high-powered offensive setup used so effectively in the pros. Leahy at first got a lot of criticism from Notre Dame purists who had grown up with the old Rockne formation. But Leahy felt that Rockne himself would have condoned the change. "Rock's system of football didn't stand still," Leahy said in self-defense. "It changed and developed each year."

The shift in formation also brought about a dramatic shift in personnel changes at Notre Dame. Harry Wright, the 1941 quarterback, was moved from his glamorous job to guard, and Angelo Bertelli, the left halfback, was given the intricate T-quarterback job. Bertelli, and his understudy, Johnny Lujack, spent long hours in conference with the indefatigable Leahy. The Notre Dame coach worked so hard in his new role, usually from 14 to 18 hours a day, that his health eventually began to fail. After a while the tension and overwork forced Leahy into a hospital bed, and he never was able to see firsthand the first successful results of his handiwork. After opening the 1942 season with a tie with Wisconsin and a loss to Georgia Tech, the Fighting Irish finally used their new formation to perfection while beating Stanford. By that time Leahy was at the Mayo Clinic and had to hear a radio announcer describe Notre Dame's 27-0 victory.

The new system produced a 7-2-2 record in 1942 and led to more spectacular accomplishments in 1943, when Leahy's gang won the national championship. The only mar on the record came in the last game of the season, a 19-14 loss in the last 33 seconds to Great Lakes, a professional-like service team. In 1944 Leahy was commissioned into the Navy and missed two years of coaching. He found, though, while on duty in the South Pacific, that he felt as close to Notre Dame as ever. Once on an inspection tour of a little, out-of-the-way island, Leahy and his men ran into some friendly natives who insisted on serenading them. After several weird and lusty renditions of exotic songs, the native interpreter proudly announced to the Americans that the next number would be, "American song. . .learn from Victrola." The group then drew deep breaths and wheezed out, "Cheer, cheer for old Notre Dame. . ." Leahy was not surprised, nor were any of his men, that the Notre Dame Fight Song had reached out halfway across the world. But Leahy was extremely touched and made homesick by the off-key rendition. He could not wait to get back to his alma mater.

When he did, Leahy began a most extraordinary period that befitted the rich Notre Dame heritage. From 1946 through 1949 Leahy's teams were unbeaten and won three national championships in those four years (1946, 1947, and 1949). The other year the powerful Fighting Irish, boasting an awesome array of talent, finished No. 2 in the national wire service poll. Leahy's teams became more overwhelming, and his formations became more complicated and more unorthodox. As Terry Brennan once described it, "It was like the Marx Brothers playing leap frog." It certainly gave the defenses something to ponder. Leahy went from the T to the I-formation, where the quarterback lined up over center followed in single file directly behind by the other three backs. In this formation the quarterback received the ball and either handed off or faked to the other backs running past him to the right and left. Leahy also devised a play where he used two quarterbacks lined up side-by-side by center. As the ball was snapped, each quarterback would pivot in an opposite direction, thus confusing the opposition as to which way the play was going. Leahy also came up with something called the "Defensive I," a formation where the linebackers were in tandem and then shifted to the play just before or at the snap.

Another of Leahy's innovations included the "straight" huddle. Under this setup the three running backs and ends lined up in a straight line, with the tackles, guards, and center in front of them. The quarterback, with his back to the opposing team, faced them and barked signals.

"This way," explained an observer, "the signal only had to be called once; moreover, with the quarterback facing away from the opponents, there was no danger of detection of the play, so the team could stand closer to the line of scrimmage and consequently go into action quicker."

Leahy's unconventional huddle eventually became the vogue in college football.

Leahy favored a wide-open game with plenty of passing and an occasional trick play to give Notre Dame a psychological advantage. The opposition was ready for anything from a Leahy team but usually got something they did not expect.

"A team feels better if it believes it has something in reserve," said Leahy, who used an unorthodox alternating quarterback system one season to keep the enemy on its toes.

Leahy even went so far as to put an "injury play" in the Notre Dame repertoire. This he saved for crucial game situations when the Fighting Irish ran out of time outs. The player would feign injury, the referee would halt the game for the supposed injury, and Leahy would have time to plot strategy. He was able to use this "play" to good advantage in the 1953 Iowa game, when Notre Dame tied the Hawkeyes in the final six seconds and salvaged an unbeaten season. Leahy's maneuver created quite a flap in the football world, however, when it was discovered that the player was not really hurt.

Leahy's sense of humor, though usually hidden under a darkly serious countenance, bubbled to the surface every so often in the most unexpected times. In connection with the "injury play," Leahy once instructed a designated victim to run it through one practice session. Tackle Frank Varrichione knew what to do. After the usual collision of bodies, Varrichione clutched his leg, moaned and screamed like a man truly wounded, and fell to the ground in the best Hollywood tradition. But Leahy thought it had been a bit overdone. He rushed on the field and confronted his player.

"Frank," he said, "I think we'd better make it total unconsciousness."

The 1947 season marked the termination of the famed series with Army, and Leahy, not known for long pep talks, gave one of the shortest—and most devastating—on record before that game. He walked into the electrified atmosphere of the dressing room and said merely, "Army is waiting."

"He said that," a player recalled later, "and I was in such a hurry to get out there I felt like running through the wall."

Notre Dame won that game 27-7 and continued on toward its first unbeaten, untied season since the days of Knute Rockne.

When the Fighting Irish repeated another perfect season in 1949, with a 10-0 record, the Football Writers Association of America voted Leahy "Man of the Year." He also edged out New York Yankee manager Casey Stengel for the title of "Sports Man of the Year." And Leahy got "Coach of the Year" acclaim from several newspapers and football clubs, an honor he had also received in his three previous seasons.

In February of 1949 Leahy was relieved of his duties as athletic director by Ed "Moose" Krause, and there were persistent rumors of his premature departure from coaching, also. Leahy replied to these rumors: "I have no thought of quitting. . . but you never know when a man's health may go bad on him. I was sickly in 1942. If that condition comes back, I would ask for my release." As recently as 1947 Leahy was sidelined with a bad arthritic attack, which forced him to miss the season's finale against Southern California.

When the Fabulous Forties ended, so did Notre Dame's unbeaten streak. Leahy's mammoth string of 39 games without a loss broke in the second game of the 1950 season, when the Fighting Irish were beaten 28-14 by Purdue. It was not the only loss of the year, either. Leahy had his worst season ever with a 4-4-1 record. Rockne, the old Notre Dame demigod, also had one bad season in 1928 when he lost the same total of four games. Leahy, only 43 in 1950, looked older than his years. The dismal season had created a tremendous emotional strain on the man who was not used to losing. Leahy missed the season-ending game with Southern Cal that year, as he had in 1947.

"The surprising thing about this only non-winning year in

Leahy's career was that it could have been worse," points out Joe Doyle, the sports editor of the *South Bend Tribune*. "Those close to the team said, 'We could have lost all of them.' If it had not been for the brilliance of Bob Williams at quarterback, Jerry Groom at center and Jim Mutscheller at end, the season would not have been merely dismal. It would have been a disaster."

Leahy was not only sick physically, but he had suffered also from a bad case of nonsupport by the administration. In the late 1940s the Notre Dame administration had scaled down Leahy's recruiting efforts considerably, and this, along with the loss of superlative players and some injuries, had really hurt him in 1950.

By 1951 the Fighting Irish were back on their feet again by the sheer power of Leahy's determination and a new rule that allowed freshmen to play varsity ball. The predominately freshman-sophomore team had a successful 7-2-1 season, capped by a 19-12 thriller over Southern Cal, in the first football game ever televised from the West Coast to the rest of the country. In 1952 Notre Dame had a 7-2-1 record in what some consider Leahy's best coaching performance. The schedule was possibly the most difficult in Notre Dame history and perhaps could have been as difficult a season as any college football team ever encountered. As underdogs the Fighting Irish upset Texas, Purdue, Oklahoma, and Southern Cal—all of whom either won or tied for conference titles. Notre Dame also tied Penn, the Ivy League winner, and gave national champion Michigan State its toughest battle of the year. The Fighting Irish, out of sight in the national rankings the year before, finished No. 3 in the country in 1952.

In 1953, through sickness and emotional strain, Leahy led his team to an undefeated season and No. 2 ranking in the nation. Except for a tense 14-14 tie with Iowa, Notre Dame would have probably been national champion that year. It was after this game that Leahy showed the torture of his last season. During a postgame interview, the strung-out Leahy bent his head over, virtually between his knees. "There were few questions," said a newspaperman. "His friends didn't want to ask and others were too touched by sympathy for an almost-broken man." Leahy earlier collapsed during the Georgia Tech game and had to be taken to a hospital. He suffered more because he was not able to cope with his ailments. One of the first visitors to Leahy's bedside heard him say, "I've always told the boys never to quit in the second half, and now I've let them down."

It was at this point that Leahy knew he was finished at Notre Dame.

"I knew then I'd never coach another season," Leahy said. "The doctors only made it official when they told me any more coaching would bring on another attack of acute pancreatitis that might be fatal. All jobs have tensions. But coaching eats a man's insides. At Notre Dame, the pressure is worst. . ."

After the 1953 season Leahy still had two years to go on his contract but turned down an offer from the university to finish them out. "I told them that my health wouldn't permit it," Leahy said. "Then they tried to get me to stay the final two years and work with my successor at my side all the time. I told them that it wouldn't work because of morale problems with the other coaches."

Although everyone knew he had been sick, Leahy's resignation was a startling blow, with impact felt throughout the sports world. An American hero was fading away. Leahy's image of strength made him immortal in most eyes. "I just can't believe it," said Johnny Lujack, Leahy's backfield coach at the time. "I was convinced Frank would never leave Notre Dame."

Although a lot of people at South Bend were unhappy about his departure, Leahy was not.

"Weekends in the fall, I'll be able to eat something besides tomato soup," he said. "I'll see the team play every Saturday. But it will be different. All I'll have to worry about is arriving on time to replay it at a cocktail party. I suppose I'll even develop into a second guesser.

"Also, now I'll be able to work on my golf game. And I'll be able to see something of Floss and our eight kids. Floss had wanted me to quit for a long time."

In this regard, Leahy's wife received a telling message from Earl Blaik, the Army coach and one of Leahy's most bitter rivals during his career: "Congratulations. You have won a clean-cut victory over football, the mistress in Frank's life. Many happy years to you both. Red Blaik."

Although Leahy was retiring from Notre Dame, he was not planning to be inactive. "But now I'm only going to be a 10-hour-a-day man," he said with some truth.

Leahy resigned on January 21, 1954, and tried various business projects with indifferent success. There was speculation—and partial confirmation—at one point in his later years that he would return to football as head coach and athletic director at Texas A&M. But this never came to fruition because Leahy's doctors did not deem it advisable. He surfaced briefly as the first general manager of the San Diego Chargers, then in Los Angeles, but resigned before the 1960 season because of poor health. In the late 1960s Leahy had a TV program and did a newspaper column in Chicago, but that was his last fling at football. His health steadily worsened until it was revealed that he was being treated for leukemia in the 1970s. When Leahy finally made the collegiate Hall of Fame, he was in such terrible shape that he could not completely enjoy it. "He was moving pretty slow," says Charlie Callahan, the longtime Notre Dame publicity man. "Two friends supported his elbows as he walked about 10 feet from his chair to the microphone."

Along with his leukemia, Leahy also suffered from spinal arthritis, diabetes, and an infected bladder in his later years and spent much of his time in and out of hospitals. During this time he was ever thankful for small favors. Once when he returned to South Bend to see Notre Dame play football, he confided to a friend: "They gave me a sticker for my car and a parking stall at the stadium. I don't mind admitting that means a lot to me. It was a thrill."

Leahy died as he lived—putting up a great battle. On a hot summer morning he was whisked off to the Good Samaritan Hospital in Portland, Oregon. For a day he continued to fight for his life, putting up remarkable resistance against death. At one point of the morning of June 21, 1973, a doctor told the Leahy family: "He is an amazingly strong-willed man. Since four this morning, his heart has stopped beating five times. And still it starts again every time. Anyone else would have been dead years ago. He simply does not want to die. However, the chances for living are not good. You should know that."

A few hours later the life was squeezed out of Leahy's stubborn body. His death, though expected, still was an electric shock to those touched by him.

He was buried in Portland, but his soul belonged to Notre Dame. A touching story at the time of his retirement from football certifies this.

After a press conference to introduce Terry Brennan, Leahy's successor at Notre Dame, the old coach suggested to a friend that they take a walk into Notre Dame Stadium "just one more time." As Leahy walked toward the home team's bench, he spotted a dime atop the snow. Leahy stooped over and picked up the coin with this remark: "This will forever remain a token of my last bit of luck on this field, which I'll always call my home."

Then Leahy, his eyes moist, placed the dime in his billfold and walked on in silence.

Some Great Days
For The Irish

"We were down at Parris Island, and that particular Saturday, when we got beaten in the last second, we had all been in this clubhouse, listening to the game on the radio. And when we got beaten, we all left the place, tears in our eyes and crying. And it was at that particular time that a guy came and handed me a telegram, saying that I had won the Heisman Trophy. So from complete sadness, now I'm torn between happiness and sadness."—Angelo Bertelli.

Angelo Bertelli answered the call to Frank Leahy's office and no sooner got inside than the coach pulled out a memorandum pad.

"Bert," Leahy said, "you are the finest passer and the worst runner I've ever coached. We've got to do something about it."

Leahy diagrammed a pass play on his pad, then showed it to Bertelli.

"We were lucky to win last year, Bert. We didn't have any deception. Everybody knew when you were going to pass. You just took the ball from center, dropped back a few yards and threw. No deception, but they'll be laying for us next fall. Think you can play quarterback?"

"I guess so," Bertelli replied, a bit puzzled. "Why?"

"Because," said Leahy, sketching a new diagram, "here's what we're going to try out in spring practice. It's the T-formation. This is you, Bert. You'll play right behind center and handle the ball on every play. You'll feed it to the other backs, or you'll fake and drop back to pass—that's where we'll get the

235

Halfback Elmer Angsman, quarterback Frank Dancewicz, full-back Marty Wendell, and halfback Phil Colella (left to right) saw plenty of action for Notre Dame in the 1940s.

deception we lacked last fall. Of course, it means a lot of work for you. You'll have to memorize 50 or 60 new plays next month."

"Sounds good to me," Bertelli said. "I think I'll like this T-formation."

If ever a play was made for a player, this was it. Bertelli, once a halfback, thus became a T-formation quarterback at Notre Dame and gave the Fighting Irish a hot, new offensive threat in 1942. The new system, which took the place of Rockne's timeworn single wing, drew a few howls from some of the purists before it got untracked. But by the third game of the 1942 season, the T clicked, and Notre Dame clobbered Stanford 27-0. By 1943 the Fighting Irish had their first national championship under Leahy and their first Heisman Trophy winner in Bertelli.

Introduction of the newfangled T-formation at Notre Dame was a tip-off on Leahy's unquenchable desire for continual improvement. In his first year at Notre Dame, 1941, the Fighting Irish were unbeaten in nine games. But Leahy felt that the old Notre Dame single wing would eventually be left in the dust.

"The only blemish on our record in 1941 was a scoreless tie with Army in a torrential rain storm in Yankee Stadium, and we finished third in the nation that year. . .but Leahy wasn't satisfied," remembers Bertelli. "In spite of that undefeated season, Leahy had been watching the Chicago Bears every Sunday to see what they were doing, because they were great during those war years. So he decided to go with the same T-formation that the Bears were using. He brought in Bob Snyder, who was an understudy to Sid Luckman with the Bears, and Bob served as an assistant coach for Notre Dame before the 1942 season. There was no vacation from the end of the 1941 season right through to 1942. We started right in with learning the T-formation, spinning and faking. The T-formation at that time was strictly faking and passing, no running, and I fit right into the picture."

Despite the amount of work put into Leahy's pet formation, it obviously was not ready for opening day against Wisconsin. For that matter, neither was Bertelli. He boarded the wrong train in Chicago's Union Station and did not reach the dressing room until just before kickoff. Although he insisted that his tardiness did not unnerve him, he looked completely unglued when Notre Dame unveiled its new offense.

"That day I fumbled twice within the 20, had a couple of passes intercepted, and the alumni started hollering, 'Hey, let's go back to the single wing,'" Bertelli says, recalling that 7-7 tie with the Badgers.

In the second game Bertelli completed only 6 of 16 passes, and four of his throws were intercepted at crucial moments. Notre Dame also committed three expensive fumbles that day, and Georgia Tech, which had lost to these same Fighting Irish in 1941, beat them 13-6 in South Bend.

"Now the alumni really hollered," Bertelli recalls.

While they were screaming for Leahy's head, the beleaguered coach was also having serious problems with his back. Leahy was stricken by spinal arthritis at this point and forced into a hospital. There was some possibility that the disease could have been caused by an old diving accident, but doctors were more inclined to believe it was sparked by overwork and worry. Ed McKeever, Leahy's first lieutenant, took over, and the T looked letter-perfect for a change. The Fighting Irish walloped Stanford 27-0, and the players mailed the game ball, completely autographed, to their coach at the Mayo Clinic in Rochester, Minnesota. Leahy had a telephone installed at his bedside and ran up a terrific bill plotting strategy with McKeever for the game with the Iowa Seahawks, a strong team composed of prospective Navy airmen. So detailed were the preparations that Leahy even had movies of the Stanford game flown to Rochester and flashed in his room.

The Fighting Irish looked good in practice and better in the climate of a game. They trounced the Seahawks 28-0 as Bertelli appeared to have mastered the intricacies of the T. "The formation started to take hold," Bertelli says, "and we got more confident."

Leahy was beginning to feel better already, and by the time Notre Dame defeated Illinois 21-14, he was ready to return to work. The Fighting Irish played five more games that year and lost only one of them while completing a 7-2-2 season, highly respectable considering the evolution of a new system.

Leahy had picked on a good one when he nominated Bertelli to showcase his exciting T-formation. Bertelli was said to be the calmest player before, after, or during a game since Frank Carideo quarterbacked Notre Dame in 1930. An example of Bertelli's unflappable demeanor occurred in 1941. As a sophomore halfback, he completed 12 of 18 passes for 232 yards against Navy. He threw a touchdown pass and set up Notre Dame's two other scores with passes deep inside Navy territory to lead a 20-18 victory for the Fighting Irish. After the game a

The referee signals "touchdown" as Angelo Bertelli scores on a quarterback sneak against Navy in 1943. Bertelli is somewhere underneath that pile of tangled bodies.

reporter asked Bertelli, "What do you think about when you drop back to pass?"

After hitching a towel around his middle and thinking for a moment, Bertelli replied: "Not much of anything. You see, I know who the receiver is and where he should be before the play starts. Nine times out of ten, he's there. Then it's automatic. I throw the ball."

"Were you surprised at completing so many passes?" the reporter pressed Bertelli.

"Not surprised, exactly," said Bertelli, taking another hitch at his towel. "Every pass I completed this afternoon I've practiced a hundred times in practice. And it's a lot tougher completing passes in a scrimmage against our second and third teams because they are familiar with every pass I throw. Navy didn't have that advantage. I figure this way: If I can complete 25 percent of my passes in practice, I should complete 50 percent in a game."

(Actually Bertelli did better than that in his career at Notre Dame. The player known as the "Springfield Rifle" completed 169 of 324 passes for a percentage of .522.)

Amazed at Bertelli's stage presence, the reporter turned to Harry Wright, the quarterback of the 1941 team. "Doesn't that guy ever get excited, even on the field?" he said.

"That guy," said Wright, "has sherbet for blood. Remember when Navy intercepted Angelo's flat pass and ran it back for the tying touchdown in the third quarter? That was Bert's fault—he threw two yards behind (Bob) Dove, the end. Couple of minutes later we had the ball at midfield. Time for another flat pass, but I was afraid Bert might be a little shaky after throwing one away. I nudged Bert in the huddle. 'How do you feel?' I asked.

"Bert didn't change expression. 'I feel fine,' he said, 'How do you feel?'

"So I called the flat pass. Bert hit Dipper (Evans) right on the nose, and Dipper ran down to Navy's eight-yard line. Two plays later we had our winning touchdown."

Bertelli, the talk of New England prep schools when he starred in several sports at Cathedral High in West Springfield, Massachusetts, was a heavily recruited athlete. He was wanted by the Boston Bruins for his hockey play. He was wanted by both the St. Louis Cardinals and Detroit Tigers for baseball. And he was also wanted by colleges in the East, West, North, and South for his football playing abilities. When Leahy was at Boston College, he had heard of Bertelli's accomplishments and hoped to land him for the Eagles. He dispatched McKeever, his sweet-talking assistant, to West Springfield to corral the popular schoolboy star, but Leahy's recruiter came back empty-handed. Bertelli had already made his decision to go to Notre Dame because of Milt Piepul, the 1940 captain of the Fighting Irish who had preceded him at Cathedral. The story goes that before McKeever appeared at Bertelli's door, the youngster had slipped out and gone to a movie in order to avoid him.

When McKeever moved to Notre Dame with Leahy in 1941, Bertelli was in their possession, but when they finally saw him, they were not sure they wanted him. Tall and skinny, he was one of the most unlikely looking athletes they had ever seen. Only 168 pounds hung on his frail, six-foot-one frame.

"Discovering Bertelli's identity did not exactly uplift student morale," said William Cullen Fay in a magazine article. "He didn't look like much without his shoulder pads. There is a story of the freshman who got a good look at Angelo, then went out and canceled his two-dollar bet on a game."

Bertelli could punt, but not far. He could run, but not fast. "Actually, Angelo didn't really run," pointed out a writer. "He skated along, ankles close to the ground, no high knee action, a hangover from his hockey training."

Bertelli could throw a fast, accurate pass, though, and it was this ability that eventually raised him from the fourth to the first team and helped Notre Dame through an unbeaten season in 1941. The Fighting Irish flew down the field in a hurry on the wings of Bertelli's passes. Once they landed inside the 10 yard line, Owen "Dippy" Evans, Steve Juzwik, and Creighton Miller often carried the freight. Evans alone scored eight times from the seven yard line or closer that season. Miller was Leahy's prize thoroughbred, and the coach later called him one of the two best runners he ever had at Notre Dame. The other one, Leahy said, was Emil "Six Yards" Sitko, who played on his awesome teams of the late 1940s.

Miller, son of Harry "Red" Miller, the famed Notre Dame runner of the early 1900s, was as high-spirited and unpredictable as he was good. He loved golf almost as much as football and frequently would skip practice for a round on the Notre Dame course. Because he was not on a scholarship, Leahy had little control over the prodigal player. So the coach finally had to go to Creighton's father for help, and Harry Miller cut off his son's supply of money until he decided to play ball the Frank Leahy way. Later, the young Miller realized that it was all for the good, but at the time, he told his father, "Dad, you sold me down the river to that man."

Miller's behavior was often as wild as an untamed colt and sometimes as damaging. He once bet his roommate that he could remove the pennants that decorated the walls of their room without using his hands. This he proceeded to do by running up the walls and dislodging the tacks with his sneakers. While Miller was bringing down the last of the pennants with his dancing feet, the wall collapsed. For several days he and his roommate shared a "suite" with the boys in the next room.

Miller was more efficient at hitting holes than hitting walls, though, and it was this talent that earned Leahy's admiration. "Miller would belong on my All-Notre Dame team, if I picked one," Leahy once said.

Leahy also was enamored of Bernie Crimmins, the All-American guard of the 1941 team. Termed by Leahy "the greatest defensive player" he ever had at Notre Dame, Crimmins, like

Indiana was unable to stop Fred Evans or Notre Dame in 1941. The Irish conquered the Hoosiers 19-6 for rookie Coach Frank Leahy.

Bertelli, underwent a position change before he became a bona fide star. Under Elmer Layden in 1938 and 1939, Crimmins had been a fullback and a quarterback. Then he got a visit from Leahy before the start of the 1941 season.

"He came to see me in Louisville," Crimmins recalled, "and after the usual questions about the health of my mother and all the Crimmins' relatives, it was apparent that he had driven 300 miles from campus to impress me on the need of great guard play. After telling me that a great pulling guard was the most important member of the backfield, the truth suddenly dawned on me. Frank was trying to tell me that he wanted me to switch to guard. He was so convincing that I agreed, even though I wanted to be a quarterback and run the show."

Zygmont Czarobski, another of Leahy's favorites, surfaced in 1942. This eccentric tackle was possibly the most popular man on campus at the time, as well known for his colorful stunts as his excellent line play. The whimsical Czarobski produced the most appealing stories from the 1940s, one of the most laughable concerning a game with Southern Cal.

Aware that he would be facing a great tackle in the Trojans' John Ferraro, Czarobski started a psychological war against his adversary before the game. The zany Notre Dame player first sent his opponent a telegram informing him that he was leaving South Bend and that Ferraro should begin to get ready for him. At every train stop en route to Los Angeles, Czarobski found time to fire off a telegram to Ferraro, informing him that he was getting closer. On the morning of the game Czarobski was in a barbershop getting a manicure when a teammate walked in.

"Why are you getting a manicure on the morning of the game?" he asked Czarobski.

"That will be my final message to Ferraro," Czarobski replied. "On the first play of scrimmage, when I get down to my three-point stance, I will call his attention to my nails, have him notice how clean and polished they are, then I will tell him, 'When I stick these fingers in your eyes, you needn't worry about infection.'"

In the classroom the irrepressible "Ziggy" was no less unpredictable. One warm fall afternoon he burst into a speech class 10 minutes late wearing a thick bearskin overcoat. The teacher told Czarobski that he had to pay for his tardiness by

Bob Kelly played halfback for Notre Dame's fine teams of the early 1940s.

performing before the class. Czarobski was ordered to the front of the room and told to deliver a few chosen words from Hamlet's "Directions to the Players."

"And while you're at it, take off that Daniel Boone trapping," the teacher thundered.

Czarobski balked at first but then complied. Off came the coat, revealing only his red and white pajamas.

Czarobski's antics were just as valuable to the Notre Dame team as was his playing ability. Notre Dame's Good Humor Man provided invaluable comic relief as Leahy struggled to coordinate a highly complex group of players while facing one of his toughest schedules in 1943.

When Leahy called spring practice for that season, he invited everybody from the preceding team, even though he realized that many would not be available for the fall because of service duty. Some of the players, including the superlative Bertelli, would only be able to play part of the year before reporting to the armed forces. But Leahy still could count some blessings. He had an ace in the hole in Johnny Lujack, an 18-year-old flash who appeared ready to take over Bertelli's quarterback job. Leahy also had a strong line and in midsummer got more help in that area with such service transfers as John Perko and Vic Kulbitski of Minnesota and Julie Rykovich of Illinois. Because of the war, many college players shifted their allegiances in order to take military programs at certain schools. The future brightened even more considerably when Creighton Miller, already in the army, was given a medical discharge. Then Frank Szymanski, Jim Mello, and Herb Coleman, assumed to be lost, all passed a special Navy V-5 test during a South Bend volunteering campaign, and this gave them another year's eligibility. With all this good luck, Leahy must have thought he was dreaming when Bertelli announced that he would be able to play for more than half the season.

Considering the killer schedule, Leahy needed all the talent he could get. Included among the opponents were Michigan and Georgia Tech, who not only beat the Fighting Irish in 1942, but were bolstered by service adjustments. By the time Notre Dame met them, they were ranked, respectively, No. 1 and No. 2 in the country. Powerful Army, Navy, and Northwestern, also strengthened in 1943, and Iowa Pre-Flight, considered the top service team in the country, lay ahead as well. There was not too much notice when Notre Dame opened the season with a 41-0 rout of Pittsburgh, but people did sit up and pay attention when the Fighting Irish beat Georgia Tech 55-13. This was supposed to be one of the best Yellowjacket teams in years. There was more notice directed in Notre Dame's direction after a 35-12 success over Michigan, a game where Leahy's controver-

Notre Dame gained national attention after beating Georgia Tech 55-13 in 1943. Here, Jim Mello carries the ball against the highly regarded Yellowjackets.

sial T-formation worked to sublime perfection under Bertelli's expertise. Red Miller sat in the stands and watched his son, Creighton, score two of Notre Dame's touchdowns.

This game deserved an unusual place among many of Notre Dame's golden victories—and not only because a record crowd of 85,688 showed up at Ann Arbor or because the stadium's electric timing device collapsed in the third period, causing the session to run an actual 23 minutes. (By consent of both coaches, the final quarter lasted only seven minutes.) The game was a complete vindication of Leahy's judgment in adapting the T-formation to the Notre Dame attack. The impressive victory over one of the nation's foremost teams silenced the last critic.

"Never since its incorporation at Notre Dame had this offensive weapon worked with such consummate precision," says Arch Ward in his book, *Frank Leahy And The Fighting Irish*. "Best evidence of this was the all-around play of Angelo Bertelli, who had been the real basis of Leahy's choice of the T. In that Michigan game, Angelo directed the team perfectly from his quarterback position and indicated his passing genius by completing five out of eight pitches, two for touchdowns and one which led to a third score. Still another example of the finished perfection of the Notre Dame T-formation was the work of Creighton Miller, who averaged 16 yards per play."

Notre Dame then rolled past Wisconsin 50-0 and Illinois 47-0 and Bertelli remembers: "We were beating everybody so badly that Johnny Lujack was getting as much playing time as me. In anticipation of my leaving, Leahy was trying to give Lujack as much game experience as he could."

The next game, against Navy, was Bertelli's last, and he gave Notre Dame fans something to remember him by. The Irish beat one of Navy's best teams 33-6 as their fine quarterback threw three touchdown passes and scored the last one himself on a two-yard run.

With Bertelli gone, Lujack was given command of the team and a pep talk as well.

"Johnny, you've got a big job from here in," Leahy told his new quarterback the week before the big Army game. "You'll probably make some mistakes, but don't let them worry you. You've inherited one of the toughest assignments in Notre Dame football. Bert, as you know, was a big loss. A lot of people think he can't be replaced. I don't. I have confidence that you will be able to carry on for him."

Lujack answered quietly and confidently, "You're right, coach. Don't worry."

As it turned out, Leahy could have skipped that little chat of encouragement. While the football world watched, along with about 75,000 fans at Yankee Stadium, Lujack displayed remarkable poise. He was the perfect T-formation quarterback. Lujack threw two touchdown passes, scored another himself, and made several fine defensive plays while leading Notre Dame's 26-0 victory over the Cadets. Few players became as famous as quickly as Lujack did that day in New York. Lujack was not the only fledgling who made good for Notre Dame. Bob Kelly, another 18-year-old, filled in at right halfback for Julie Rykovich, who was sick, and shone offensively and defensively. Kelly also scored two touchdowns in the next game as Notre Dame beat Northwestern 25-6 for its eighth straight victory of the season. Fred Earley missed three extra-point tries in that game, but the diminutive Notre Dame halfback vowed to Leahy afterwards, "Don't worry, coach, I'll get them when they count." Leahy did not have to wait too long for Earley to fulfill his promise. The next week Earley was perfect on both his

John Yonakor stretches to gather in Johnny Lujack's 28-yard touchdown pass as Tom Lombardo (No. 10) and Glenn Davis (right) of Army try vainly to break it up. Notre Dame collected three more touchdowns and beat the Cadets 26-0 in this 1943 game.

placements as the Fighting Irish beat the undefeated Iowa Seahawks 14-13.

One more service team stood in the way of a perfect season for Notre Dame, and by this time, the Fighting Irish were already conceded the national championship. The game with Great Lakes originally was scheduled for Chicago's Comiskey Park, but a Navy directive prohibited the Bluejackets from playing on a neutral field. Notre Dame had the option of playing at home, but the school's administrators turned their back on the more than $50,000 revenue so that the sailors at the naval training center could see the game. The contest was moved to Ross Field at Great Lakes.

Frank Leahy's capable wartime replacement, Ed McKeever.

The Irish scored first but surprisingly found themselves trailing 12-7 in the fourth period. Paced by Jim Mello and Creighton Miller, Notre Dame marched 80 yards in 20 tough plays, making first downs by inches. Miller finally went over, and Notre Dame had a tight 14-12 lead with 1:05 to play.

Notre Dame kicked out of bounds. Steve Lach, who had starred at Duke, passed to Cecil Pirkey to move Great Lakes to Notre Dame's 46 yard line. There was still time for a desperation pass, and Lach took it. As the last seconds ticked away, Lach wheeled back and seemed trapped by a swarm of Notre Dame defenders. But he squirmed loose and threw a long pass toward the Irish goal line. The deep Irish defenders were caught flatfooted, and the ball sailed over their heads. Paul Anderson fielded Lach's pass at the six yard line and continued into the end zone unassailed, giving Great Lakes an electrifying 19-14 victory that spoiled Notre Dame's perfect record.

It was a heartbreaking loss for Leahy, and he needed to summon up all his courage to make the final locker room speech of the 1943 season. While the sailors were celebrating at the other end of the station, Leahy told his boys in the depressing silence of the Notre Dame dressing room:

"You're still champions to me, boys. You fought your hearts out every inch of the way in the greatest drive I've ever seen. I don't know how to show my appreciation to each one of you, but if the day ever comes when you need something, call on me. Then I'll try to show you what is in my heart toward the grandest bunch of boys who have gone through the toughest schedule any team ever has been called on to face. Nobody is to blame for that last Great Lakes touchdown. It was just a fine play, splendidly executed."

One of the Great Lakes stars had been Emil Sitko, who would eventually become one of Leahy's greatest runners. When Leahy went in to congratulate Sitko on his performance, the player naturally had mixed emotions because he had been recruited by Leahy for Notre Dame.

"How are you?" Sitko said, trying to make conventional conversation with Leahy.

"Not so well, Emil," the Notre Dame coach answered. "My school lost today."

"So did mine," said Sitko, hanging his head low.

The game was the last for several of the Notre Dame players and for Leahy as well. The navy commissioned Leahy as

Bob Kelly eludes an Illinois tackler in 1944. This run helped the Irish win 13-7.

a lieutenant, and he turned his coaching job over in 1944 to a loyal friend, Ed McKeever. McKeever guided Notre Dame to an 8-2 record and then relinquished command to Hugh Devore for the 1945 season. Devore's Irish won seven games, lost two, and tied one. But while both coaches had respectable records, they knew that they were only stopgap measures until Leahy returned.

While Leahy was away during the war years, he was plied with tempting offers for new jobs. When the new All-American Conference was formed, Leahy was promised a fat contract to lead the Cleveland Browns. There were then four little Leahys, and his officer's pay of $225 a month looked pale in comparison to what the Browns were offering. Not only would Leahy get a 10-year contract at the then fabulous salary of $25,000 a year, but his family would get $1,000 a month until he could take over the job. Leahy considered the offer seriously before turning it down.

"Only one other offer—by Southern California—was ever seriously considered by Frank," said Rev. John C. Cavanaugh, C.S.C., then chairman of Notre Dame's athletic board.

When the Second World War ended in 1945, Leahy itched to get back to his old Notre Dame job. He applied for immediate discharge, but his request was held in abeyance by the navy. Leahy could not understand why until a friend explained the obvious:

"So you asked the Admiral, did you? And where did the Admiral go to school? Oh, to Annapolis, of course. Well, you can bet your bottom dollar you won't get out until after the Navy game!"

And Leahy did not.

Shaking Down The Thunder

"There have been more spectacular teams. There have been teams with a more diverse attack. There may even have been teams with 11 better men. But there has never been a team with the enormous depth, with the deep-ranging quality, with the assurance that it could lose its first string, its second string, and perhaps even part of its third string—and still remain undefeated."—Bill Furlong, sportswriter.

The train moved through the near-dark of early morning, heavily loaded with passengers, including the Notre Dame football team. As the New York Central slowed down at a whistle stop, one of the players sat up and yelled, "Hey, look!"

"Well, look at that," another added softly.

Out on the station platform and along the side of the tracks were strung out groups of school children, ranging in age from 7 to 16. It was not yet 7 a.m. in the morning, and the weather was very cold for November.

The children held up signs to the Notre Dame players as they passed in view. "Beat Army," said one. "Victory For Notre Dame," said another. The crowd was waving and cheering wildly before the train picked up steam and soon rolled out of sight.

Sights like this were not uncommon for Notre Dame's teams of the late 1940s. In towns and villages from coast to coast, the Fighting Irish had become not only an American Dream, but America's team.

Notre Dame's success in the lush postwar period of 1946 to 1949 was so staggering, small wonder that the Fighting Irish

The 1946 Notre Dame team—a fortune of talent.

made fans everywhere. Frank Leahy's teams of this era, perhaps the most stunning array of talent ever gathered in one period, won national championships in 1946, 1947, and 1949 and finished No. 2 in the country in 1948. They never lost a game in this time and extended their fabulous unbeaten streak of 39 into the 1950s. The 1947 Notre Dame aggregation has been acknowledged by some as the most talent-laden of all college teams—42 players from that bunch went on to play professional football. There was a player who did not get into a game that year with Notre Dame, Vince Scott, yet he went on to play with the old All-American Conference and the Canadian Football League. Another one who did not get a letter, Zeke O'Connor, was named to the College All-Star team. And when you consider that some of the first-stringers, like Terry Brennan, did not even try to make the pros but went into coaching instead, the talent at Notre Dame in that period boggles the imagination.

"Charlie Callahan, the onetime Notre Dame sports information director, maintains that these teams were the best that ever played, including the Miami Dolphins in their Super Bowl-winning years," says George Ratterman, who was a backup quarterback to the celebrated Johnny Lujack during this time and went on to professional fame.

Along with the exquisite talent, the 1946 and 1947 Notre Dame squads also stood apart statistically. These teams were never behind at any point along the season. Except for two ties from 1946 through 1949, Leahy's masterpieces usually beat everybody with clinical ease, although these gorgeous Notre Dame teams rarely embarrassed an opponent. Leahy did not like to run up scores, even if he could with his clubs. "He felt that 35 points was a pretty decent lead," said a friend of the coach.

During these golden years the Fighting Irish were so destructive that they eventually destroyed some relationships with other schools. Perennial rivals, tired of getting beaten year in and year out, dropped off the schedule. Leahy remembered:

"In 1948, Father Cavanaugh (Notre Dame president at that time) told me that we were winning ourselves out of a schedule, that Army, Michigan, Illinois and Northwestern had already dropped us and that Navy and USC were about to. He pushed the panic button and cut scholarships from 33 to 18 and ruled that we couldn't make personal contact with prospects. I told him it wouldn't work."

256

The 1947 Notre Dame team gave Frank Leahy his second straight national championship and stocked the pros with plenty of good players.

Terry Brennan (No. 37) digs out yardage against Pittsburgh in 1946 while Cornie Clatt (far right) comes up to help.

And it did not work. In 1950 Notre Dame lost four games—Leahy teams lost only 13 games overall in 13 seasons.

"He saw the error of his ways," Leahy said, "and we got a break in 1951. Because of the Korean War, freshmen were declared eligible. Nineteen of our first 33 were freshmen, including 10 starters on defense."

The Fighting Irish went back to winning in the 1950s but could not duplicate their performance of the Fabulous Forties. The four national championship teams of that period were linked together by a common bond. The fortunes of the Second World War had a lot to do with Notre Dame's destiny and dealt Frank Leahy a superior hand.

When Leahy resumed his duties as Notre Dame's coach and athletic director in 1946, he came into a fortune of talent as a result of the war. A virtual black market existed after the war, with some of the nation's "name" players peddling their services to the highest bidders. But Notre Dame did not lose a major star and, in fact, gained some new players to go with the veterans of 1941, 1942, and 1943 and a flock of returning freshmen whose college careers had been interrupted by the war.

"We had plenty of guys coming back from the war, and I felt like a little baby among these men," says Frank Tripucka, one of the fine Notre Dame quarterbacks of that time. "There were five of us who were only 18-years-old at the time—myself, Terry Brennan, John Panelli, Bill Fischer and Bill Walsh. Most of the other guys were big, bruising veterans who had not only played football, but fought through Iwo Jima, Guadalcanal and the European Theater. As far as talent goes, the second team was every bit as good as the first. In fact our toughest ballgames used to be the scrimmages between the first and second teams. They used to end up 18-17, 21-20, 7-7. Any of our second-stringers would have started anywhere else. Because of the war, Notre Dame had concentrated five years of talent into a few years. It was unfortunate that they couldn't spread that talent out over more years."

Among this group of rich, deep, and confident material was Lujack, whom Leahy later called one of his greatest all-around players. Lujack was more than just an exceptional passer, an obvious skill for a quarterback. He could run like a halfback (and, in fact, averaged 11.1 yards per carry one year) and excelled at defense. In addition, he was poised and enormously self-confident. "John was the best all-around football player I've ever seen," recalls a contemporary.

Lujack had shown his poise when three years before, as an 18-year-old freshman, he took over for Angelo Bertelli in the seventh game of the season and performed astonishingly well against Army under enormous pressure. Lujack continued to display his feeling for the offensive tempo with a grand showing against Iowa Pre-Flight that season. He sent the Fighting Irish through 13 plays in less than five minutes, shooting a back at the service team every 20 seconds. In his first three games as Notre Dame's first-string quarterback, Lujack completed 18 of 39 passes for a total of 287 yards.

By 1946 Lujack was back directing the show with his usual flair—and a successful, long-running hit it was. Lujack was an inspirational play-caller who rarely did the obvious. Once against Pittsburgh, a penalty forced the Fighting Irish back to their one yard line. Lujack dropped back, ostensibly to kick, but fooled the Panthers with a long pass. It was completed, and later Lujack fired three more passes to give Notre Dame a touchdown. Lujack's skill as an offensive player sometimes overshadowed his ability as a defender. He made a number of crucial tackles, but the one most acclaimed was when he stopped Army's Doc Blanchard in the open field to save a scoreless tie and salvage an unbeaten season for Notre Dame in 1946.

*A combination of quarterbacks hard to beat—(left to right)
Johnny Lujack, Angelo Bertelli, and George Ratterman.*

All day long Blanchard had been trying to break through
the Notre Dame line and finally did late in the game. With the
ball on the Army 37, the big Army back broke around end and
headed for the sideline, completely in the clear. Lujack cut
across the field to meet him and roared down the sideline with
the cheers of 70,000 spectators ringing in his ears. Lujack closed
in, hit Blanchard right at the ankles, and both went down hard
at the Notre Dame 37. The spectacular play earned Lujack
uncommon praise but did not swell his head. Lujack, who never
got too big for his deeds, displayed characteristic humility after
the Army game. "They said Blanchard couldn't be stopped,
one-on-one, in the open field, yet I did it. I really can't understand all the fuss. I simply pinned him against the sideline and
dropped him with a routine tackle."

Lujack got the starting berth over Ratterman, a skillful ball
handler with a more powerful arm. Leahy gave the edge to
Lujack because he liked the way he called games—unspectac-
ular, balanced, well rehearsed, and usually brilliant. Ratterman's
talents drew Leahy's admiration, but his eccentricities appalled
him. "He was the kind of guy who might go into a game walking on his hands," notes one of his teammates. "You couldn't
tell what he was going to do." In one game Ratterman dropped
back to pass and tripped over his own feet purposely so he
could move the ball back a few yards. His reason? "I just

wanted you guys to get a load of that girl in the stands," Ratterman explained to his teammates. In the 1946 Navy game, Notre Dame was moving down the field, and the Midshipmen were praying for a time out to stop the Irish momentum. Ratterman obliged them, but not especially for that purpose. He called a time out and gathered his Notre Dame teammates around him. "Say, I forgot to mention this," he said, "but there's this party tonight, and I was wondering if any of you guys wanted to go."

"And that," said a contemporary of Ratterman's, "was why Lujack was Leahy's quarterback."

Although Ratterman did get to see plenty of action as a second-stringer (he led the team to 49 percent of its touchdowns in 1946), he was not entirely enchanted with his situation. He left Notre Dame prematurely and played the 1947 season with the Buffalo Bills of the All-American Conference. Tripucka, another quarterback of soaring talents, was a Lujack understudy for two years before finally getting his chance in 1948, when the Heisman-winning quarterback graduated.

The 1946 team boasted certified All-Americans in Lujack, tackle George Connor, guard John Mastrangelo, and center George Strohmeyer and plenty of other future All-Americans, including Bill Fischer, Leon Hart, Ziggy Czarobski, Emil Sitko, Jim Martin, and Marty Wendell. Freshmen were eligible in 1946, and it was common to see a superlative talent like Hart, only 17 years old, competing for an end position with 24-year-old Jack Zilly. Bill Walsh, a regular in 1945 but only 18 in 1946, was battling the 22-year-old Strohmeyer and 26-year-old Bill Vangen for center. Russell Ashbaugh, Corny Clatt, Bob McBride, George Tobin, John Creevey, Bob Livingstone, Gerry Cowhig, Luke Higgins, and Bill "Bucky" O'Connor returned from 1942. From the national champions of 1943 were Czarobski, Jim Mello, Fred Earley, Paul Limont, Zilly, Bernie Meter, Joe Signaigo, Bob Hanlon, and Lujack. "Leahy got a little thin when he reached down to the sixth and seventh string," joked a writer.

Notre Dame's depth was not funny to the opposition, though. Even though Leahy, the perennial pessimist, insisted before the 1946 season that "we could lose three or four games," hardly anyone believed him. And they believed him less after the tough Fighting Irish opened with resounding victories over Illinois, Pittsburgh, Purdue, Iowa, and Navy. That set the stage for the Army game, touted as the battle for the national championship. The Cadets, with their famous "Touchdown Twins," Doc Blanchard and Glenn Davis, had a 25-game winning streak and were shooting for their third straight national championship. Notre Dame was out to avenge two embarrassing losses to the Cadets during the war years—unprecedented scores of 59-0 in 1944 and 48-0 in 1945.

"Before the 1946 season had begun," said a writer, "it had been accepted that Army-Notre Dame would be *the* game of the year, a vengeful vendetta in which Leahy and his legions, who had listened to those games overseas, would demand repayment in kind for the humiliation."

Preparations for the Army game bordered on near-insanity at Notre Dame. Running through formations, the Irish would stop every so often and bellow:

"Fifty-nine and forty-eight

"This is the year we retaliate."

Army got hate mail from Notre Dame students. They sent daily postcards to Army coach Earl Blaik, signed "SPATNC." This was translated to mean "Society for the Prevention of Army's Third National Championship." The buildup toward the game at Yankee Stadium was incredible. Dozens of writers poured into South Bend to watch the intense Notre Dame practice sessions. Lujack suffered a mild sprain on his ankle, only adding to Leahy's already outlandish pessimism. "If it happened without the writers around, no one would have believed me," said Leahy, who rarely looked on the bright side of things.

The game that was supposed to decide everything decided nothing, except that here were two defensive giants. The Cadets and Fighting Irish put so much emphasis on defense that they failed to score, and the 0-0 tie turned out to be a monument to conservative football and a bloody bore for the 74,068 customers in the Stadium's yawning environs. Because of the tone of the game, Lujack's defensive play stood out conspicuously. Bill Leiser described it in the *San Francisco Chronicle* on November 10, 1946:

"New York, Nov. 9—Felix (Doc) Blanchard, Mister Football of 1946, broke around right flank, sped 15 yards down the sideline and headed for the touchdown that was to be the climax of all gridiron climaxes in this topsy-turvy football year. Johnny Lujack, the only man who could possibly have anything to say to the contrary, said no. The only man in position even to reach the flying 6-foot, 205-pound one-half of the touch-

262

down twins now on a rampage, Lujack didn't miss. Cutting in on an angle, he sliced the big West Pointer down in a dramatic and solid tackle 37 yards from the goal as an approximate 74,068 standing customers sat down again either vastly disappointed or greatly relieved, for this moment near the end of the third period prevented the last possible scoring chance of the costly afternoon.

"By the margin of Lujack's tackle, which cut the threatening 57-yard goal line blast off with a paltry 20 yards, Coach Earl Blaik's Army missed scoring its 26th consecutive victory in a battle in which the Cadets had displayed an undecisive but

Pete Ashbaugh (hand shading eyes), Coach Frank Leahy, and George Ratterman (adjusting helmet) watch as Notre Dame crushes Illinois and starts the march to the 1946 national championship.

One of the most famous and adored players ever produced at
Notre Dame, incomparable Johnny Lujack.

definite superiority throughout. The battle of the century, or the battle of all time, as some New York observers styled it, ended just where it started. For Notre Dame, no points at all, for Army just the same."

Lujack, who played the full 60 minutes of the torturous game, was the first in the locker room and appeared to be the most drained. Sitting before his locker with his head down, he whispered like a disappointed kid, "Gee—that was tough."

The rest of the Notre Dame players straggled in, anguish and disappointment written on their faces. They had stopped Army's great running attack but failed to win the game they wanted most that season. Leahy locked the door to the dressing room and faced his team.

"You played your hearts out, but you were not quite good enough today," Leahy said softly. "Remember one thing now— the test of a champion is how he reacts to adversity on the days when it is bound to come."

Years after digesting and replaying that famous game in his mind, Tripucka comes to the conclusion that Leahy himself blew it, not the players.

"I felt we should have won it," he says. "I felt that the whole responsibility of the tone of that game fell on Leahy's shoulders in the sense of one of the judgments he made. Up until that time, he had so many ballplayers that he had two full offensive teams. And he would always play them that way—the starting team played the first quarter, the second group played the second quarter, and he'd use them the same way in the third and fourth quarters. Finally in the fourth quarter, if we were far ahead, he'd clear the bench. But that particular Army game, he didn't use that method. It was the only game in the four-year span that he was undefeated that he didn't go with that system of his, and that day, as a matter of fact, he only used about 18 ballplayers. I felt, in retrospect, if he had stayed with that system of substitution, we would have worn them down. He even told us afterwards that he made a mistake by doing that."

It was the only tough game of 1946 for Notre Dame. The Fighting Irish either bludgeoned people to their knees or just frightened them to death. After the Fighting Irish walloped Tulane 41-0, in one of three season-ending victories, a player from the Green Wave told this story:

"We had heard an emotional pep talk. We had come on that field all roused up, ready to show Leahy and Notre Dame we were as good as they or better. And maybe we were. But there was this long wait. We nervously put in time. The fire built within us was cooling. Then we saw the Notre Dame eleven come out; but it was the sixth team. Then the other five teams came out. And we watched them. Finally, Leahy and the coaches and the terrier mascot appeared. And all the while there was that cheering from the stands. And the thought came, the depressing thought: This is Notre Dame. By the time the game began, we were ready to be plucked."

Notre Dame won the national championship in 1946 with an assist from Navy. The Midshipmen, who had been crushed earlier in the season by the Fighting Irish, fell only a few yards and a few seconds short of upsetting Army on the last day of the season. By comparative scores, Notre Dame was given the national title over the Cadets.

This Notre Dame triumph over Army in the national polls only seemed to drive a wedge deeper between the schools. There were some indications that Army wanted out of their renowned series because it was getting to be too lopsided in Notre Dame's favor. It was perhaps one of many reasons for the intersectional powers to temporarily call off the passionate rivalry after the 1947 season. Rumors of the impending rupture were certified by this statement from the schools on December 30, 1946:

"The football relationship between Army and Notre Dame will be temporarily interrupted after the 1947 game, according to a joint announcement made today by Major General Maxwell D. Taylor, Superintendent of the United States Military Academy, and the Reverend John J. Cavanaugh, C.S.C., President of the University of Notre Dame. Two reasons led to the decision. The first was the conviction of the authorities of both schools that the Army-Notre Dame game had grown to such proportions that it had come to be played under conditions escaping the control of the two colleges, some of which were not conducive to wholesome intercollegiate sport. The second reason was the desire of West Point as a national institution to achieve greater flexibility in the scheduling of inter-sectional opponents throughout the country."

On the surface the Army-Notre Dame series would seem to have had the greatest justification for continuation. It brought together two of the nation's most glamorous football teams at a

266

time of their highest prosperity. They filled New York's Yankee Stadium each year, guaranteeing a gate of at least a half-million dollars. And year after year, even despite Army's inability to win many games, the hot rivalry constantly intrigued new fans. Starting with the game of 1913, during which Notre Dame revolutionized the forward pass, the series had a strong influence on football technique.

Ironically, though, the very fact that it had gotten so large was probably just cause for its abandonment. The annual Notre Dame-Army game, attended in New York by as many Fighting Irish fans as those from nearby West Point, caused too many headaches because of its gargantuan proportions. Fair distribution of tickets was impossible. Avaricious ticket scalpers pounced on the situation, and seat prices shot sky-high. The game also drew a tawdry gambling element that further diminished the purity of the collegiate affair. With these professional gamblers on hand, it was estimated that something in the neighborhood of $5 million was wagered on the Army-Notre Dame contest each year.

The annual spectacle became a blood war each season—and not only on the field. Zealots who attached themselves to Notre Dame, called the "Subway Alumni," became a constant source of embarrassment to the Fighting Irish and a continual pain to the Cadets. Their taunts from the stands were extensively spiced with sheer venom and born of uncommon hatred. They helped turn the series into a war. The "Subway Alumni," as far removed from Notre Dame as the Cadets themselves, nevertheless became a very real enemy for the West Pointers and their fans.

It was the belief of Army coach Earl Blaik that because of Notre Dame's wild New York following, "we never made a friend out of that game." During the war the undisciplined "Subway Alumni" hit at the Army players' national pride. From the minute the Army team stepped on the field, jeers rolled down from the stands. "You draft-dodging sons of bitches" was the most common heard from the heated Notre Dame fanatics, who chided the Army players for not being in the war. The cries became more intense as the game became more intense.

Blaik was sharply conscious of this anti-Army feeling. "The game has provided a form of psychological hatred detrimental to the best interests of the Army," he said, "and it could

Terry Brennan: He broke Army's back and spirit with a 97-yard touchdown run.

hardly tolerate a condition that bred such ill will for the service and the Military Academy." Blaik pointed to, among other things, reams of daily "hate" mail that Army players got.

But even with the obvious distractions, it was thought that something more profound was involved in the split. Grantland Rice surmised: "The real reason goes deeper than the ones given. Under the rule of Frank Leahy, Notre Dame has grown entirely too powerful for what other coaches call even competition. . . .Leahy is a great coach but the prevailing opinion is that he is also too smart or too subtle a collector of winning football talent for other coaches to meet on even terms. . . .After a long absence from football duty, they point out, Leahy was able to collect the best college football team in the country on less than a year's notice. The Big Nine feels just as Army feels—that Notre Dame belongs in a class alone in the way of college football material. . . .Army undoubtably struck the first blow."

Although the announcement of the split was couched in friendly language, promising resumption of the series after a few years' cooling-off period, there were indications of great bitterness between the schools. "There are signs that it wasn't all sweetness and light," wrote Lewis Burton in the *New York Journal-American*. "Harsh criticisms of Notre Dame's recruiting measures openly expressed by Earl Blaik, Army coach, could not be described as 'cordial' by any stretch of the imagination. Joseph M. Byrne, Jr., commissioner of the New York Authority and Notre Dame's number one alumni representative in this section, told the writer last November 23 in Boston that Blaik wanted the series brought to an end."

The 1947 game was taken out of the big city and moved to the more prosaic surroundings of South Bend, "out of consideration for the cordial relationships which have always existed between West Point and Notre Dame," the announcement said.

The Fighting Irish, to a man, hoped that they would be the ones to end Army's unbeaten streak that year. If Army won or tied the games prior to the 1947 Notre Dame contest, the Cadets' streak would have been 34 by November 8. Notre Dame was to have the pleasure of beating Army in their last game before the split, but not the pleasure of stopping the Cadets' undefeated string. Columbia did that while the Fighting Irish were beating Iowa in the fourth game of the year. Army's shocking loss to Columbia was a visible annoyance to the Notre Dame players. When the score was announced over the loud-

269

speaker at Notre Dame Stadium, several of the Irish players were seen slamming their helmets down in disappointment.

While Army had been beaten, Notre Dame had not. The imperturbable Fighting Irish opened 1947 with easy triumphs over Pittsburgh, Purdue, Nebraska, Iowa, and Navy before the Army game. This was essentially the same national champion team of 1946. John Mastrangelo, the All-American guard, graduated, as did ends Jack Zilly and Paul Limont. Jim Mello was among the backs who left, along with Gerry Cowhig, Jim McGurk, John Agnone, and Emil Slovak. The line was depleted slightly by the departure of Luke Higgins, Bob McBride, Bernie Meter, Tom Potter, Fred Rovai, Vince Scott, and George Tobin.

Notre Dame still had enough talent to take Army and everyone else that season, and Earl Blaik knew it. His Cadets went into 1947 with hardly the exalted material of the year before and were decided underdogs to Notre Dame's superior forces. Leahy, however, displayed his usual lack of confidence on the eve of the game. "Earl," he told the Army coach, "I think your team is going to be very happy after this game."

Blaik felt that Leahy's renowned pessimism was getting the better of him, but he was not ready to completely count out his team.

"I'll tell you one thing—the Cadets will give you a battle," Blaik told Leahy.

Army came to play Saturday but did not come to play too hard, obviously. Notre Dame took the spirit out of the Cadets in the opening minutes when Terry Brennan ran back a kickoff 97 yards for a touchdown while a record crowd of 59,191 at Notre Dame Stadium went crazy. A little while later Lujack directed an irresistible ground attack that went 80 yards. Brennan dashed over for Notre Dame's second touchdown and a 14-0 lead. At half time the big crowd, which had supplied a record gate of $360,000 on that crisply ideal day, watched the Notre Dame band spell out "1913" and "GIPP" on the field. The Irish had enough points already to beat the inoffensive Cadets, but they were not through scoring. Lujack directed a quick touchdown march in the third period before Army came back with its only touchdown of the day. Then the Fighting Irish smashed 80 yards behind their great quarterback to make the final score 27-7. Blaik was not embarrassed by the outcome; he said, "They had beaten us only 13-7 in the last 51 minutes."

Notre Dame then had its only close game of the season, a

A Navy tackler gets his hands on Terry Brennan in 1947, but the Midshipmen had a hard time holding the Irish that day.

26-19 victory over Northwestern in the rain, and closed out the year impressively by shellacking Tulane 59-6 and Southern Cal 38-7. The perfect year brought Notre Dame another national championship and established the Fighting Irish as something more than earthly. A cartoonist drew a parallel to Notre Dame's status on the planet—showing a giant Irishman standing on the earth and shouting to the moon, "Anyone over there want to play football?"

Five players from the 1947 squad made All-American teams—guard Bill Fischer, tackles George Connor and Ziggy Czarobski, a 19-year-old sophomore end named Leon Hart, and Lujack. Lujack made All-American status for the second time and also won the Heisman Trophy that year. Connor, Lujack, and Czarobski all could have stretched their academic work out and played for another year but did not. Otherwise, Notre Dame probably would have never come down to earth in 1948.

*Frank Leahy and his boys on the sidelines during a dramatic
moment in the 1948 Southern Cal game. This was when Steve
Oracko kicked the extra point that enabled Notre Dame to salvage a 14-14 tie.*

As it was, the Fighting Irish went undefeated but had to struggle to beat Purdue and Northwestern and nearly lost to Southern Cal in the last game of the season. Only a touchdown in the
final seconds pulled out a 14-14 tie with the Trojans and salvaged Notre Dame's growing unbeaten streak. Tripucka, who

took over for Lujack as the first-string quarterback in 1948 and worked his own brand of magic, remembers that game as one of the most significant of his career for personal as well as other reasons. He broke his back.

"Here we were No. 1 in the AP poll for about seven weeks, and we were heavy favorites over Southern Cal," Tripucka recalls. "We jumped right off to a 7-0 lead. I had thrown Leon Hart a touchdown pass earlier in the quarter, and then I got hurt and broke my back on the last play of the half. Funny thing about that day. We never fumbled—yet on that day, a nice, clear, warm day in the Los Angeles Coliseum, we'd work the ball out to midfield, and then we'd fumble. Then Southern Cal would run three plays and punt, and their kicker would put the ball out of bounds inside our 5-yard line, and it would start all over again. This went on the whole first half. Guys like Terry Brennan, on quick opening plays, he's breaking open, and he's cutting across the field, and he's going one way, and the ball's going the other way. Terry never fumbled, but on that day he did."

Nursing a 7-0 lead, Tripucka played conservative football in the waning minutes of the first half, intending to take that slim advantage into the dressing room.

"There were only about 40 seconds on the clock," he remembers, "so I ran two quarterback sneaks in a row to kill the clock. And on the third one, a guy clobbered me and broke

George Connor, Notre Dame's All-American tackle of the fabulous 1940s.

a bone in my back. It seemed like the whole stadium hit me. I missed the entire second half, I was in the hospital. Bob Williams took over. Then Southern Cal scored to tie it 7-7. Then they scored another one with just a few minutes left to play in the game, and it looked like it was over for us. But Bill Gay ran the kickoff back deep into Southern Cal territory, and Sitko scored. We kicked the extra point and tied it, but, of course, it blew the national championship for us. We ended second that year."

Gay's exciting run at the end was preceded by a meaningful scenario on the field. Just after Southern Cal had taken a 14-7 lead on Bill Martin's four-yard touchdown run, the cocky Gay approached a referee.

"Mr. Referee," he said, "how much time is there left to play?"

"Two minutes and 35 seconds," replied the referee.

"That will be plenty of time, sir, if they will just kick it to me," said the swaggering football player.

Gay was as good as his word. He took the ball on his one yard line and followed blockers down the right sideline. He ran all the way to the Southern Cal 13 yard line before being dragged down by Don Doll. The game was quickly dying when Williams cracked through the middle for five yards. Williams missed two pass attempts, but a pass interference call on one of them put the ball on the two. Panelli carried the ball to the one, and from there, Sitko took it into the end zone. In a deadly silent stadium, Steve Oracko kicked the tying point for Notre Dame.

The tie was a tremendous moral success for Southern Cal, virtually the same team that had lost to Notre Dame by 31 points the year before. "That the Trojans had enough stuff to tie these babies speaks volumes for their fighting hearts. . .and their coaches," praised one writer. Others, looking at Notre Dame's All-American-studded lineup, called the tie "the biggest upset of the decade." Leahy conceded, "I've never seen a better coached team more ready mentally than the Trojans were against us."

Hart was one of the few Notre Dame players who looked as good as his press clippings. The brutish receiver bounced off at least half a dozen Trojan players en route to his first-half touchdown, leading one California writer to enthuse: "Of all the college ends I've seen since 1919, Hart is the greatest. He

274

Frank Tripucka: He had to wait for Johnny Lujack to graduate before getting his chance.

caught the ball, swung off to his left, and set sail. He went all the way, after several Trojans bounced him. Several times it seemed they had him cornered for sure, but big Leon's tremendous power helped him to break away. It is doubtful if any end in college football save Hart has the power to accomplish such a run—with the Trojans hitting as they were."

Hart's explosive 25-yard run was a yardstick of pure football power after that. Leahy later reviewed the movies of the bruising run about 20 times, each time with astonishment. "Eight Southern California lads had their arms around Leon at various times after he caught that short pass from Frank Tripucka, but Leon just ran over them and left them for dead. It was the most destructive run I had ever seen."

It was nothing new, of course, for the indestructible player called "The Monster" by his contemporaries for his formidable size—six-foot-four and 245 pounds. There was the story about Hart running over one of his own teammates that conjured up visions of his raw power. During a game against Illinois in 1946, Hart was an eager reserve thrust into battle by Leahy.

"Leon," Leahy said, patting the wide-eyed Hart on the back, "you're only a freshman—a seventeen-year-old freshman.

Leon Hart, the most irresistible force since Bronko Nagurski.

This is your first game, and I expect you to be nervous. You're up against older, more experienced opponents, but remember this: if I didn't have confidence in you, Leon, I wouldn't send you into the game. Now, get in there at right end for Zilly."

Leahy cracked a hand across the seat of Hart's pants and sent him supercharged into the game. The huge freshman spun away from Leahy—and crashed into halfback Bob Livingstone, who was returning to the bench for a rest. Down went Livingstone, and Hart ran over him, planting his size-13 shoe in the halfback's chest. When Livingstone regained consciousness and learned the name of his assailant, he noted hazily: "You know, that Hart's going to be all right. Nobody ever hit me that hard before."

"Yes," agreed the Notre Dame trainer while applying a bandage to Livingstone's chin, "but first he's got to learn that he's on our side."

It was not coincidental that Hart and the Notre Dame winning streak grew together through 1949. Pro scouts, drooling over the Fighting Irish's sublime end, were unanimously convinced that Hart was the most irresistible football force since Minnesota's Bronko Nagurski. Hunk Anderson, the former player and Notre Dame head coach, was line coach of the Chicago Bears at the time and had an eye for a well-turned football leg. "When Hart was a sophomore," said Anderson, "I thought he was the finest end in college football, but he was growing so fast I was sure he'd lose speed and be forced to shift to tackle or guard. But he hasn't slowed a bit. He's the niftiest, fastest big man in football, college or pro."

Hart threw as much fear into his own teammates as the opposition. A reserve halfback who had to face the Notre Dame Hercules in practice every day confided once, "Maybe I should have gone to Michigan State or Iowa—then I'd only have to play him once a year."

Hart was one of four Notre Dame All-Americans in 1949. The others included tackle Jim Martin, fullback Emil Sitko, and quarterback Bob Williams, a daring play-caller with no compunction about passing from deep in his own territory, even on fourth down. Williams was at his gambling best in the North Carolina game. The score was tied 6-6 in the second quarter, and Notre Dame had the ball on its own 19 yard line on fourth down. Probably any other quarterback would have called the logical play, a punt. But in the huddle, Williams told his teammates: "We ought to kick, but we're not going to. I'm going to throw one, and if it doesn't work, I'm heading for the nearest

Steve Oracko kicks an extra point against Michigan State in 1949. It was one of many scored by Notre Dame as the Irish walloped the Spartans 34-21.

Mike Swistowicz (No. 44) of Notre Dame looks for a way to elude Purdue tacklers as Bob Toneff (No. 75) comes up to help with the blocking in this 1949 game won by the Irish 25-12.

These players provided a happy ending for Notre Dame fans in 1949.

exit. I won't go anywhere near the bench." The play worked. The confident Williams threw an 18-yard pass to Larry Coutre, and the Fighting Irish got their first down. Later they got their ball game, 42-6. "Coach Leahy never told me I couldn't pass on last down," said Williams about the play that brought him national attention. Williams was soon recognized as the best signal-caller in the country.

The 1949 Fighting Irish edition was as strong as any of Leahy's previous teams. "The backfield of Williams, Sitko, Frank Spaniel and Larry Coutre was as devastating a crew as ever put on pads," said Joe Doyle, sports editor of the *South Bend Tribune*. The power of that wonderful offensive machine is reflected in Notre Dame's point total for the season—360, more than any other Leahy team. Such scores as that victory over North Carolina in the seventh game of the year were representative of the season. Notre Dame, in fact, pushed everyone all over the field with the exception of Southern Methodist, in the last game.

The tone of the season certainly gave no forewarning of stiff SMU resistance. Notre Dame had won all nine of its games and was conceded the national championship. SMU had already lost four games and was considered a decided underdog. Adding more negativism to the Mustangs' predicament was news that Doak Walker, their Heisman Trophy-winning back of the year before, would not play because of injury. The Notre Dame party, including not only players and coaches, but wives and friends, were given a tremendous send-off at a Chicago train station. Moose Krause, Notre Dame's athletic director, reflected the holiday mood by wearing a huge white Texas hat. Several of the players put it on and posed for pictures before leaving. At every stop the famous Notre Dame players were besieged by autograph-seekers and squealing females. In Dallas things were no different, for the Fighting Irish fame and stature had preceded them. When the Notre Dame players attended mass one morning, the cathedral was so crowded that people stood in the aisles. The players were served breakfast in the basement of the church while school children peered in through the window to see college football's supermen. Even before the game had started, Notre Dame had taken the play away from the home team.

The Notre Dame workouts were supposed to be held secretly in a high school stadium, but it seemed the whole world was there to watch Leahy's wonder team. Not only present were Notre Dame alumni from all over the Southwest, but Texans who came to see what an honest-to-goodness national champion looked like. "More people got by the security guards than attended the average high school game," a writer said. All the while, SMU students were going by the stadium, blowing horns, and ringing cowbells.

At the Friday press luncheon, SMU coach Matty Bell acknowledged his role as the lowly underdog with a little bit of humor. "The only reason my boys will show up," he said, "is because all the tickets have been sold."

Some impressions were that Notre Dame would beat SMU by 40-0, and it certainly looked that way at the beginning of

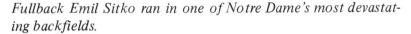

Fullback Emil Sitko ran in one of Notre Dame's most devastating backfields.

the game in the Cotton Bowl. Before a huge crowd of 75,428, the Fighting Irish dominated play in the first half. They led 14-0 and almost scored another touchdown. The start of the second half was all Notre Dame, too. The nation's top-ranked team had the ball most of the time and held a 20-7 advantage late in the third period. On two occasions Notre Dame fumbled away the ball deep inside SMU territory and possibly could have led by as much as 34-7.

The character of this SMU team was such, however, that the Mustangs were not especially awed by Notre Dame or particularly discouraged by the Notre Dame power show. Kyle Rote led a Mustang counterattack that left the Irish sucking wind and the big Texas crowd breathless. Running almost at will, Rote scored his second and third touchdowns of the drizzly day, and except for a missed point, the Mustangs would have led Notre Dame. But as it was, miracle of miracles, the game was tied 20-20 with about seven minutes left. And Notre Dame was not only fighting for its reputation, but its life.

"For the first time all fall," said Frank Leahy, "we had only a few minutes to prove we were really a championship team."

The Fighting Irish proved it in the face of tremendous pressure. Leahy later recalled it:

"I never saw more excitement in a game in my life. Before a fantastically partisan crowd and against a team that was truly superb, we had to take the kickoff and go on to score. Often a coach is given credit for giving a quarterback prudent information pertaining to how he should direct the team and win a game. At this moment the fans were going crazy, ringing cowbells, cheering. Bedlam was everywhere. Bob Williams, a wonderful quarterback and a terrific young man, brought the team over to me.

"'Coach,' he said, 'this is it. We're going out there now. Do you have any advice?'

"I looked at Williams and could see they were awfully tense. I wanted desperately to relax them. 'Yes,' I said. 'I have some very good advice to give. Don't ever enter the coaching profession.' They laughed and went out."

Frank Spaniel ran the SMU kickoff back to the Notre Dame 46. Emil Sitko and Bill Barrett took the ball to the SMU 26 in five plays. Leon Hart, moved to fullback, slammed to the 20. Barrett followed with a six-yard gain. Bill Gay got six more.

Notre Dame's Ernie Zalejski grabs a pass despite the defensive work of Navy's Vic Vine. The Irish sailed past the Midshipmen 40-0 en route to the national championship in 1949.

Then Barrett went for two. The SMU line was having trouble holding the Notre Dame running attack, and on the next play Barrett skirted around end and dashed over for a Notre Dame touchdown. The breathtaking drive had taken so little time that SMU still had a chance to score and pull out a tie. The Mustangs drove to the shadow of the Notre Dame goalposts but finally were stopped by Notre Dame's defenses. At the five yard line, Rote's fourth-down pass was grabbed by both Jerry Groom and Bob Lally, two fabulous linebackers for Notre Dame that day.

The conclusion of one of the most thrilling games in Notre Dame history had a unique aftereffect: both the winners and the losers were happy, remembers Terry Brennan.

"The Mustangs were most happy because they didn't lose by a big score as predicted, in fact came within an ace of possibly winning the game. The Notre Damers were happy because of winning, and doing it with a long march in the closing minutes to preserve their undefeated, untied record. Both the opposing team members and fans were shaking hands, clapping each other on the back after the game. The opposing coaches visited each others' dressing rooms, so did two or three of the players, and gave congratulatory talks to the respective squads. Bill Fox, sports editor of the *Indianapolis News*, who had been covering football for more than 35 years at the time, was present, and in describing the scene after the game, called it 'the greatest public relations game of all time.' Mr. Fox maintained that he had never seen the likes of it before. . .or since."

The fans who were lucky enough to see that thriller in the Cotton Bowl would never forget it. Nor would one particular radio listener who found it impossible to tear himself away from the drama. On the afternoon of the game, Bob Bowie, a sportswriter for the *Denver Post*, was to be married in Colorado Springs, Colorado. But the wedding was delayed an hour because Bowie and most of the members of the bridal party would not leave the radio until the game was over. Now, *that* is excitement.

The Fainting Irish

"Notre Dame's dressing room that had echoed with whoops and hollers the past four years was silent a little before five tonight. The few intruders in the equipment room talked in whispers. When Coach Frank Leahy walked in they seemed reticent about asking questions. The coach apparently understood for he spoke first. 'Gentlemen, we lost to a better team than we were today. But if we had to lose I am glad it was to a time-honored foe like Purdue. That Purdue team was great. They didn't make any mistakes. . .offensively, they were superb.'"—Notre Dame Scholastic, *October 7, 1950.*

Notre Dame's loyalists stood outside the locker room, waiting in a cold, drizzling rain, cheering and yelling for Frank Leahy. The door swung open, and the coach appeared. The cheers peaked.

"Men, a lot of people will be watching how we take this adversity," he said. "It's a real test of real men to be able to lose like champions."

The crowd roared in unison, "We're behind you, coach." Then they started chanting for the players. As each one came out of the locker room, he was raised aloft and carried part way back to the campus. The band was playing, and the students continued to cheer.

Thus did the Notre Dame camp react bravely to its first defeat in five years—a 28-14 whipping by Purdue in 1950 that ended an unbeaten streak of 39 games and an era as well.

"The personal sadness of our first loss in five seasons was indescribable," Leahy remembered later.

Using Johnny Lattner as the dynamite, Notre Dame blasts away at Purdue's middle. Lattner got five yards with this plunge, and the Irish went on to win the 1951 game, 30-9.

Leahy had seen it coming, though. Graduation had taken most of his gorgeous wartime talent and left him with precious little. After the last of the war veterans left, the stardust had turned to mere dust. Quarterback Bob Williams, center Jerry Groom, end Jim Mutscheller, and tackle Bob Toneff were the only players resembling the caliber of the 1946-49 dynasty. Leahy's seniors lacked seasoning, his juniors lacked experience, and the sophomore crop was sparse as the result of a university policy two years before to cut scholarships and temper recruiting practices.

There was some suspicion that this would be one of Leahy's weakest teams after Notre Dame opened with a tough 14-7 victory over North Carolina at home. The year before in Yankee Stadium, the Irish had routed the Tar Heels 42-6. Purdue then put an end to Notre Dame's glamorous streak. Dale Samuels, Purdue's sophomore quarterback, directed the downfall of the Irish. His passing produced three touchdowns in the first half, and the Boilermakers almost scored three more. The Fighting Irish stopped Purdue thrusts twice—once on the one yard line and another time on the seven. The Boilermakers also had a touchdown run called back. For a while it looked as if Notre Dame could produce some of its old resourcefulness. Williams passed to Mutscheller for a touchdown in the third period, and halfback John Petibon ran 10 yards for another score on the first play of the fourth, to cut Purdue's lead to 21-14. But the omnipresent Samuels crushed Notre Dame's comeback hopes with a 57-yard touchdown pass to halfback Mike Maccioli.

A visitor to the Notre Dame locker room after that loss heard only the sound of silence and saw a grim spectacle. Leahy walked down the locker room aisle, stopping to whisper condolences to each player as he went by. Chuck Feigel came up to the coach, tried to talk, then broke down and cried. The only noise was the hissing of showers. Players toweled themselves, their eyes red-rimmed. "You could see," said an observer, "they were more exhausted mentally than physically." Leahy, sensing that reporters were reticent to ask questions, offered the first words of the post-game interview. "We were outcoached," he said. When questioned about the "breaks," Leahy responded: "The breaks usually go to the team that is most alert. We have no alibis; we lost to a team that was better than ours." Later, Leahy was to reflect: "Where had I, as a coach, failed in our preparation for our time-honored friends?"

While Leahy expressed concern over the ineffectiveness of his complex preparations, Purdue coach Stu Holcomb revealed the shocking simplicity of his game plan: "In the past we had geared ourselves up with a high, emotional desire to win. This time, with a soph quarterback, I told the boys to go out and throw the ball and have fun."

Not only Purdue rejoiced in the victory. Notre Dame haters loved it, too. As one sportswriter pointed out: "A national holiday was declared for all of those who were anti-Notre Dame, for the same reason some people are anti-Yankee in baseball and anti-Dempsey in boxing. They get tired of extended success and want to see the champ knocked off."

Such people found the rest of the year quite enjoyable, for Notre Dame lost games to Indiana, Michigan State, and South-

Frantic action during one of the great rivalries in college football, Notre Dame vs. Michigan State. The Fighting Irish won a lot of the wars, but the Spartans won this 1950 battle, 36-33.

ern Cal and needed all the gallantry it possessed to tie Iowa and prevent a losing season. As it was, a 4-4-1 record was not anything to be proud of, especially at Notre Dame. It gave the administration something to think about, and soon the scholarship restrictions were lifted, and Leahy was given the green light on hard recruiting.

It all resulted in a crash program the likes of which have rarely been seen at any university. To say that Leahy did a great job in 1951 would be an understatement. Considerably aided by freshmen who were allowed to play because of the Korean War, Leahy's young squad produced a 7-2-1 record against some of the best teams in the country. The nucleus of the 1951 Notre Dame team was built around veterans like Mutscheller, Toneff, and Petibon, but the younger players added considerable skills to the attack. Among the newcomers that year were halfback Johnny Lattner, fullback Neil Worden, and quarterback Ralph Guglielmi, who eventually were to join forces in one of the best backfields ever at Notre Dame. The youthful aggregation had some embarrassing moments in 1951, like a 35-0 loss to Michigan State on national television, but that was laid to inexperience. The delicate age of the 1951 team was underscored in a story told by Leahy when he went through a "luggage" check. "Did you know, gentlemen, that we had to search through 23 pieces of luggage before we found a single razor,"

Leahy told reporters. "This has got to be a young team if it doesn't shave." A total of 25 freshmen were eligible that fall, and nine of them were on Leahy's defensive unit. Of the 35 players who earned monograms that year, 18 were teenage freshmen.

In the opening game of 1951, Worden showed promise of things to come by scoring four touchdowns in one period against Indiana. And the Fighting Irish showed signs of revitalization with a 48-6 rout of the Hoosiers. The third game was notable even though Notre Dame lost 27-20 to SMU. Guglielmi, who was to help lead the resurgence of Irish football, made his debut. Lattner, whom Leahy would eventually regard as one of his best all-around players, displayed his sublime talents to help Notre Dame beat Southern Cal 19-12 later in the year and put the football world on notice that the Fighting Irish were back.

As satisfying as the 1951 season was to Leahy, 1952 was even more fulfilling. Notre Dame's record was 7-2-1 again, but

Johnny Lattner intercepts a pass against Michigan State in 1951. He did everything but sell popcorn.

Leahy had the pleasure of beating four conference champions—Purdue, Texas, Southern California, and Oklahoma—and tying another—Penn. The master coach watched the development of one of his finest all-time backfields—Guglielmi, Worden, Lattner, and Joe Heap. Lattner was the glamour player in this distinguished group. A triple-threat halfback who played both ways in Leahy's two-platoon system, Lattner was on everybody's All-American team and won the Maxwell Trophy as the outstanding football player of 1952. Leahy, who was opposed to singling out any of his players for glory, relaxed the rule in Lattner's case. "He's our bread and butter ballcarrier," Leahy would tell newsmen. Lattner's power running, only one phase of his multitalents, was also assessed with great respect by backfield coach Bill Earley: "Some guys, when you get a hand on them, they go down. Not John."

Lattner, a rawboned brute of six-foot-two and 195 pounds, averaged five yards a carry every time he had the ball. But his ability to pass from a running play was a constant threat to the opposition, as well as his ability to kick high and far. Lattner's punts reached such dizzy heights that opponents rarely were able to run them back. One season the opposition could only average two yards a runback try. Lattner's abilities extended to defense as well. He was one of football's rare iron men in those two-platoon days, a 60-minute player who enjoyed a crunching tackle almost as much as a crushing run. Lattner was not truly great in any single phase of football, but he was exceptionally skilled in them all, a fact which led Leahy to comment one day:

"I think that if you would evaluate John's playing ability, you would find a lad on our squad who is a better runner, another lad who is a better blocker, another lad who is a better tackler, and another lad who is a better passer. However, you would find no one on our squad, or any other squad, who has the ability to do all of these things as well as John Lattner."

Lattner's individual statistics were not overwhelming in any single category—he did not rank among the nation's top twenty players in anything but rushing in 1952, with 732 yards. But his value was defined in consistency, explained tackle Joe Bush at the time: "John's greatness isn't that he's spectacular. It's that he's consistent. It isn't 'There goes John Lattner for 90 yards and a touchdown!' It's 'There's Lattner for five yards.' 'There's Lattner for seven yards.' 'There's Lattner falling on a

Johnny Lattner gets some of his 732 yards in 1952 here against Michigan State.

fumble.' 'There's Lattner intercepting a pass.'"

    Lattner's only failing, as far as Leahy and everyone else could see, was his sense of insecurity, which led to self-deprecating talk at times. When he was acclaimed for his heroic accomplishments, the introverted, almost shy Lattner would usually add something like, "Also I broke the school record for fumbles." The hard-driving back was known to give up the ball a lot, but that did not detract from the overall artistry of his performance. It did lead, however, to a massive inferiority complex. "John isn't worried about making the All-American team. . .he's still worried about making the Notre Dame team," Lattner's brother Bill said one summer. Lattner's penchant for dropping balls forced a self-imposed punishment one week. He carried the football with a handle taped to its skin around the campus for seven days. Leahy was hard-put trying to explain

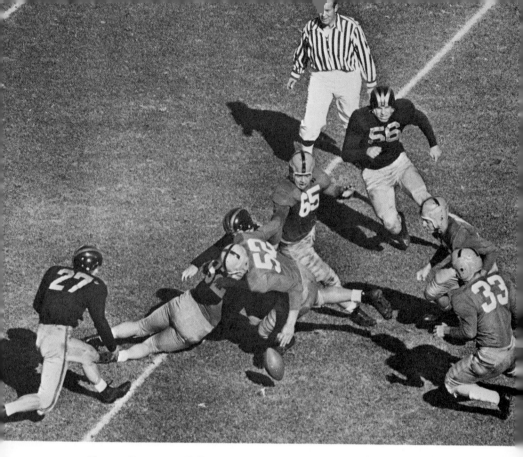

Notre Dame and Purdue players go after a loose ball in 1952. The bounces went to Notre Dame, and the Irish won, 26-14.

why Lattner fumbled so much, "unless it's because he becomes so intense and actually tries too hard."

Lattner, termed by one clever headline-writer as "the bashful terror of Notre Dame," played 422 minutes in 1952—more than any other Irish player. And it was a good thing, too. Here were some of his accomplishments: In a 7-7 tie with Penn's Ivy League champions, he dashed once for 21 yards and again for 22 to highlight an 89-yard march that climaxed when Lattner scored. When Notre Dame beat Southwest Conference champion Texas 14-3, Lattner took a pass from Guglielmi and then relayed the ball to Heap, who fell on the one yard line. Lattner ripped over for the touchdown. Lattner took a pass from Guglielmi to score on a 47-yard play, and Notre Dame beat Purdue, the Big Ten co-champion, 26-14. The Irish beat Pacific Coast Conference winner Southern Cal 9-0 as Lattner scored the game's only touchdown. Against Oklahoma, the Big Seven winner, Lattner set up one touchdown by intercepting an Eddie Crowder pass and carrying 20 yards to the Sooners' seven yard line; he highlighted another touchdown drive by taking a pass from Heap covering 36 yards; he raced 17 yards to the Oklahoma seven to set up the winning touchdown as Notre Dame took an exciting 27-21 decision.

His performance against the powerful Sooners, who finished No. 4 in the country that year, led Oklahoma coach Bud Wilkinson to remark: "Johnny was involved in more decisive plays against us than any other Notre Dame man. Before our game we knew that he was one of the finest all-around football players in America. His performance against us certainly lived up to every expectation."

Lattner remembers the 1952 Oklahoma game as perhaps the most significant of his day.

"They had a great team that year," Lattner says, "with Billy Vessels, Buddy Leake, Buck McPhail and Eddie Crowder. They had been averaging 44 points a game, which was a lot of points in those days. It was Bud Wilkinson's split-T offense, and they were an explosive type of football team. But we did an exceptional job that day. Probably if we had played them 10 times, they would have beaten us nine, but on that particular day we beat them."

The superiority of the Oklahoma team was not only reflected in statistics (the Sooners were unbeaten, and Notre Dame already had a loss), but in manpower. Lattner points to Oklahoma's pregame warmup, when the Sooners flexed their muscles at Notre Dame Stadium. "They occupied most of the field, they had such a big squad. And when we came out to warm up, we didn't have much room to work in. We had to do our calisthenics in a big circle. Oklahoma's warmup was very impressive. It aroused our inner feelings, for it was the first time I remember a visiting team taking over our home field more than we did."

The game had a massive publicity buildup and justified every superlative. While the crowd of 57,446 watched in the stadium and 15 million more on national television, Notre Dame came from behind three times to overtake Oklahoma, finally winning with the help of a jarring tackle by Dan Shannon.

"It was one of the big turning points," Lattner remembers. "It was the beginning of the fourth quarter, and we had just scored the tying touchdown to make it 21-21. We kicked off, Shannon went down under the kickoff and encountered Larry Grigg around the 30 or 35 yard line. They both were going forward full steam ahead, and Shannon hit Grigg real hard, and both of them were knocked out. Grigg fumbled the ball, we recovered and from there went on to score the winning touchdown."

Among the Notre Dame fans watching Shannon's crucial tackle was his mother. When Mrs. Shannon saw her son being carried off the field, she started thumbing through her rosary beads, in obvious prayer. Lattner recalls the story of this peripheral drama: "A lady sitting right above her made mention to a friend of hers, 'See, Mrs. Shannon's got her rosary beads out praying her son isn't hurt.' And Mrs. Shannon overheard that lady and said, 'Ah, I'm praying that he isn't hurt, all right, but I'm praying harder that he gets back into the game.'"

A tense moment has everyone on the Notre Dame bench on their feet.

Notre Dame finished No. 3 in the national polls in 1952, a dramatic climb for Leahy's forces since the disappointing season of 1950. In 1953 the Irish reached even higher with a team that Leahy called one of his all-time favorites. Notre Dame did not lose a game that year in 10 starts and tied one, a controversial 14-14 decision against Iowa that probably cost the Fighting Irish the national championship and subordinated them to No. 2 in the national rankings behind Maryland. Once again a victory over mighty Oklahoma set the tone of the season. The game at Norman on opening day was played in most unpleasant conditions, Lattner remembers.

"The temperature on the field was over 100 degrees. It was brutal. They were selling water in the stands because they had run out of soda. We only used about 19 players in that heat while Bud Wilkinson was using nearly twice that many for Oklahoma. He was throwing whole teams at us."

But the Fighting Irish had enough stamina—and desire—to beat Oklahoma 28-21 that day. Lattner explains how Leahy used a bit of psychology to turn the trick:

"They wouldn't let us stay in Oklahoma City for the game. We had to stay in Guthrie, a one-street place that had one hotel in the whole town. The hotel didn't have any air-conditioning, and it was awful. We worked out Friday afternoon and then had to go back to that hotel, and it was terribly hot. Well, we found out the next day why we had to stay there. Right before the game, Leahy walked into the dressing room and said: 'Now, gentlemen, we couldn't stay in Oklahoma City because of the fact that on our squad we have two colored ballplayers, and they wouldn't let us stay in any big hotels in Oklahoma City.' Leahy said they had forced us into this small, uncomfortable hotel in Guthrie. Well, you could imagine 35, 40 kids thinking this way. I don't know if it was true or not. Leahy was a psychologist, and he would tell an untruth if necessary to motivate you. Here we were in this dinky hotel, getting madder every day, and right before the game, he tells us this."

While Notre Dame was winning just about everything, so was Lattner. The honored player won the Maxwell Trophy for the second year in a row, an almost unheard-of feat, as well as the Heisman Trophy as the best back in the country. Lattner was joined on the All-American team by two teammates, tackle Art Hunter and end Don Penza. The 1953 opener against Oklahoma showed that the prize-winning halfback was only human,

Neil Worden started and finished fast at Notre Dame.

but also displayed Lattner's ability to bounce back from mistakes—a quality of resiliency that stamped him as a true champion. Leahy had misgivings about starting Lattner in that game because the star halfback had a painful Achilles tendon bruise and was hobbling a little.

But Bill Earley, Lattner's backfield coach, thought differently. "Coach, you've got to start him," he told Leahy. "He's an All-American."

"Okay," said Leahy, and Lattner lined up deep with Joe Heap to take the kickoff. The ball bounced toward Lattner, hit him on the knee, was kicked a couple of times, and squirted out of bounds at the Notre Dame four yard line.

The intense Leahy was visibly upset, screaming at Earley, "Coach Earley, *there* is your All-American!"

Earley hung his head in shame for the moment, but eventually Notre Dame took the lead over the Sooners with the help of Lattner. And finally, with the score 28-21 in Notre Dame's favor, Lattner helped save the day with some defensive heroics. Lattner smashed through a convoy of blockers and nailed an Oklahoma halfback with a stunning tackle, one of the biggest plays in the game. The play happened directly in front of the Notre Dame bench, and Earley could hardly contain himself.

"Coach, *there* is your All-American," he screamed at Leahy. Leahy laughed about that one for years afterward.

Lattner's extraordinary accomplishments were enhanced further by the extraordinary backfield accompanying him. The finely tuned quartet moved to the same rhythm, and Notre Dame's modest "Two-Way Johnny" himself acknowledged that he would not have climbed as high without the exquisite combination of Worden, Heap, and Guglielmi beside him. Worden, especially, was a favorite of Lattner's.

"Believe me, I'd never be an All-American without Worden," Lattner said at the time. "He's tops when it comes to blocking. He helped me a lot. Notre Dame really moved the ball when Worden was in there. Particularly on that optional play of ours in the Split-T. On that play the fullback puts on the key block. If he doesn't get the halfback on the side where the play goes, you're dead. You just don't gain. I tried to block just as hard for Neil as he did for me, but I wasn't as good."

Worden was more than just a blocker for Lattner, of course. During his three years at Notre Dame, he scored 29 touchdowns, perennially winding up as the team scoring leader. The most remarkable accomplishment by the fullback known as "The Bull" was a four-touchdown performance in six minutes against Indiana in 1951, his first game with the Irish. Worden made 676 yards in his sophomore season and carried the ball 181 times, establishing himself as the workhorse of the Notre Dame backfield for the next few years. When short yardage was needed, Worden always got the ball and always got the yards. Typical of his power running performances was the 1952 game with Oklahoma. The Fighting Irish were losing 21-14 and had the ball on the Sooners' 22 yard line in the third quarter. Worden got the ball seven straight times and eventually blasted into the end zone to tie the game. The Irish went on to win, 27-21.

Worden was discovered by Notre Dame in Milwaukee's Pulaski High School, where he was named all-state fullback after leading his school to the city championship. The powerfully built youngster received some flattering offers, but Notre Dame's was the one he wanted most. "When they came down to talk to me about Notre Dame," he says, "I was sold. I thought it was a privilege just for me to talk to them."

Worden did not impress Leahy right away. The head coach regarded him as a defensive linebacker only until he ran out of material and began to "scrape the barrel for offensive cogs," according to one writer. That Leahy had great confidence in Worden once he gave him the ball, there was no doubt. As a sophomore, Worden was the only back to run with the ball more than 100 times, and he became one of Notre Dame's best touchdown runners of all time, holding the No. 3 position behind Red Salmon (36) and Stan Cofall (30).

Guglielmi did not start his Notre Dame career as fast as Worden did. In fact he was a disappointment as a sophomore in 1952 and never reached his potential until his junior year. As a freshman, he had shown promise by directing a 19-12 victory over Southern Cal on the last day of the 1951 season. But even though Guglielmi did lead a 14-3 upset over Texas in 1952, it was the rare bright spot in an otherwise dull year for him.

"Let's be honest about it," Guglielmi says with some chagrin. "In 1952 I just didn't have it. For me it was a terrible season even though the team won seven games, lost two and tied two. When I went home (to Columbus, Ohio) for Christmas vacation, I was ashamed to accept congratulations from friends who would say, 'Nice season, Ralph.' I made up my mind 1953 would be different."

It was. It was an undefeated season, and Guglielmi was responsible for Notre Dame's climb to No. 2 in the national rankings. By 1954 Guglielmi had become an All-American and was conceded by most to be the top quarterback in the country. He was obviously one of the best passing quarterbacks in Notre Dame history. In his senior year he threw for 1,162 yards and received the Walter Camp Trophy as the nation's "outstanding back." Guglielmi's career total offense record of 3,285 yards ranked him second to George Gipp during his time. Both were eventually surpassed by Terry Hanratty and Joe Theismann, but that did not diminish Guglielmi's herculean accomplishments. Veteran observers rated Guglielmi on a par with other great Notre Dame quarterbacks of past years such as Frank Carideo, Angelo Bertelli, Johnny Lujack, and Bob Williams. A writer covering Notre Dame in the 1950s made this observation: "Guglielmi is a deadly clutch passer; he handles the difficult option play in Notre Dame's split-T flawlessly, and he's big enough (6 feet and 190 pounds) to meet the rugged defensive demands of one-platoon football."

One of the most impressive statistics of his career was Guglielmi's knack for steering clear of interceptions. He was only intercepted four times in 113 pass attempts in 1953, a Notre Dame record, and had only 24 of 436 passes picked off in four years. Guglielmi's play-calling was speedy and efficient, a factor which enabled Notre Dame to average 75.3 offensive plays in

Ralph Guglielmi: "A better passer than Angelo Bertelli, a better field general than Johnny Lujack, and more daring than Bob Williams."

1953, as opposed to 57.5 for the opposition. Once explaining his time clock on offense, Guglielmi said:

"I figure it takes us about three seconds to get back into the huddle, then I allow myself three seconds to size up the defense. The actual call of the play, plus instructions, may take three more seconds, and in two seconds we're at the line. This leaves me two seconds to check the defense and then five seconds to call the play or an alternate. I try to average 18 or 20 seconds for each play, and it usually works out that way."

Guglielmi was also a threat as a runner, a quality which added an extra dimension to the Notre Dame offense. In 1953 he was one of the few quarterbacks with a plus yardage figure on the ground and scored six of Notre Dame's touchdowns. Guglielmi carried the ball 60 times that season, only two less than Heap, Notre Dame's fine left halfback. Along with his net yardage figure, Guglielmi helped pile up countless more yards for Notre Dame on split-T option plays where he lateraled to halfbacks, sometimes after a sizeable gain. Opponents acclaimed Guglielmi's command of the team. He was often in the habit of changing plays at the line of scrimmage after reading defenses with his sharp eye. His all-around play drew extravagant praise such as, "a better passer than Angelo Bertelli, a better field general than Johnny Lujack and more daring than Bob Williams."

Ironically, the Fighting Irish almost did not get this wonder player. And when they did, they were not sure they could keep him. Guglielmi was an outstanding athlete at Grandview

Ralph Guglielmi's threat as a runner added another dimension to the Notre Dame offense.

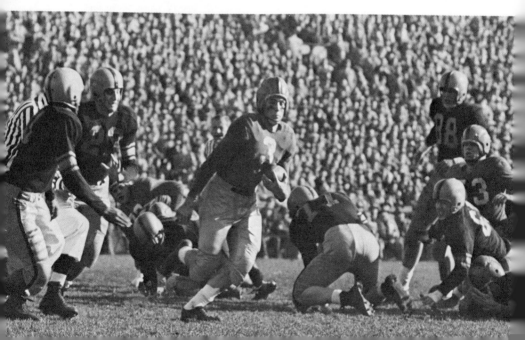

Heights High School in the suburbs of Columbus, Ohio, and was more attracted to Ohio State at first than he was to Notre Dame. He had just about made up his mind to go to the school in Columbus even though Leahy himself had come to recruit him.

"Naturally, I was quite flattered to meet coach Leahy, but I had every intention of attending Ohio State," Guglielmi recalls.

Then, for some unexplained reason, Guglielmi changed his intentions literally overnight.

"It happened one night in early June," he explains. "I don't know whether it was a dream or just my subconscious desire coming forth. When I went to bed this night, I was dead set on Ohio State. In the morning, I was just as convinced I should attend Notre Dame. Two days later, I enrolled for the summer session."

Guglielmi came to Notre Dame willingly, but there were two incidents which almost forced him to leave South Bend. The first one followed his great showing in the 1951 Southern Cal game. Guglielmi was still being romanced by Ohio State partisans, and one benefactor was alleged to have offered "everything but the moon" if he were to join the Buckeyes. A writer close to the Notre Dame situation discloses: "The story, denied officially by Ohio State and passed as a 'rumor' by Notre Dame, was apparently true. Roommates say Guglielmi had his bags packed, ready to go home." Guglielmi did not go but was somewhat sorry for his decision when he ran into campus trouble in his junior year. One day after the conclusion of the successful 1953 season, Guglielmi and Heap, his roommate, were suspended for the remainder of the semester for breaking midnight curfew imposed on Notre Dame students. The suspension denied the players credit for half a year and led to several emotional outbursts from Guglielmi. The bitter player threatened to quit school but thought better of it after a cooling-off period. "At first I thought, 'That's gratitude for you,'" Guglielmi says. "After a long, hard season, you'd think they would give us a little leeway. But then I realized the school was sincere in not making a football player something special."

Notre Dame's conquering heroes of 1953 would give Leahy some of his most cherished moments, yet he was characteristically gloomy before the season began. After a preseason practice one day he said to a friend, "Now tell me honestly, did you see a single running back out here today?" Another time he moaned, "I doubt if we'll even make a first down this year." Leahy, of course, was wrong on both counts. With Lattner, Worden, Heap, and Guglielmi running behind a great line, Notre Dame not only got a first down on the second play of the season, but ran through Oklahoma, Purdue, Pittsburgh, Georgia Tech, Navy, Penn, and North Carolina in the first seven games. The 27-14 victory over Georgia Tech was notable not only because Notre Dame stopped the Yellowjackets' 32-game unbeaten streak, but because of a dramatic scenario played out in the Irish locker room at half time. Leahy had trudged off the field at half time with heavy chest pains and made it as far as the equipment room. He began dictating notes for a talk to his players before he blacked out. One of the Notre Dame fathers thought he was dying and gave him the last rites of the church. Leahy was rushed to a hospital in the ambulance held at the ready for players. Before the players went out on the field for the second half, they prayed that Leahy would live.

It was obvious that something had gone wrong. From the press box someone pointed out that Leahy was not with the team. The Fighting Irish looked sluggish, in a state of shock. Their 7-0 half-time lead quickly disappeared as Georgia Tech stormed back. "Then the boys got mad," Lattner remembers. "They talked about the coach now and then, but they also began to play football for him."

"They survived penalties, came up with key plays in the pinches—including as fine a pass reception as I've ever seen, by Don Penza who went up with three Tech defenders to make a fingertip catch of Guglielmi's bullet pass," says writer Francis Wallace. "The second team, which had saved the day against Pitt, was most affected by the dressing room tragedy. Two fumbles in deep Irish territory, both recovered by Tech, put the game in severe jeopardy. The first team had to play 50 minutes, but it finished strong while Tech was faltering in the closing minutes of the game."

Notre Dame had a 20-14 lead near the end and the ball on the two yard line of Georgia Tech when the student body called the play. They sang "Happy Birthday" to Lattner, and everyone in the stadium, including Georgia Tech, knew who was going to carry the ball. Lattner went in standing up to celebrate his 21st birthday and cap the day's scoring.

The victory apparently had a therapeutic effect on Leahy

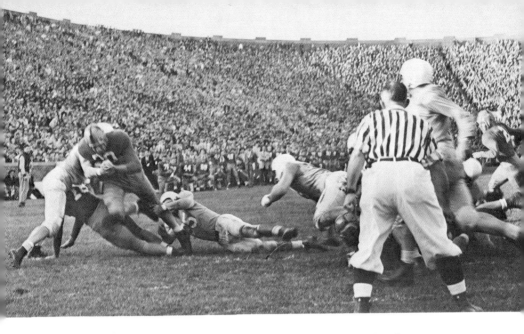

Notre Dame and North Carolina go to war before a big house at Notre Dame Stadium. The Irish won this 1952 battle, 34-14.

because he was back on his feet a few days later. Leahy had suffered a severe intestinal spasm and was forced to curtail some of his work. While Notre Dame was beating Navy 38-7, Penn 28-20, and North Carolina 34-14, Leahy was relegated to supervisory duties instead of his usual rigorous coaching routine. Finally, for the Iowa game, Leahy joined the team on the bench. But as it turned out, it was no place for a sick man.

Heavily favored over the Hawkeyes, the Irish came up with their worst game of the season and were forced to use an old ruse, the fake injury play, to pull out a tie. With one second left in the first half and Notre Dame losing 7-0, with no time outs left, Irish tackle Frank Varrichione stopped the clock with an "injury," although one observer noted later that the player was only injured "when struck by the thought that Iowa was ahead." Injured or not, it gave Notre Dame time to pull off one more play, and Guglielmi took advantage of it by firing a nine-yard scoring pass to Dan Shannon to tie the game 7-7. Guglielmi, contrary to some opinion, insists that Varrichione was "really hurt. . .he got taken out of the ballgame. . ."

However, it stretched the imagination somewhat when an identical situation existed late in the game. Notre Dame was losing 14-7 with only seconds remaining when the same Var-

Johnny Lattner returns a kickoff 86 yards for a touchdown against Purdue in 1953. It was a great day for the Irish, 37-7.

richione fell to the ground, appearing mortally wounded. This time Guglielmi concedes it was faked. Apparently everyone else knew it, too, but the officials, for they called time out. "Actually there were about five guys who hit the turf at the same time," Guglielmi recalls with a chuckle. "We had to go around kicking them in the ass and telling them to get up."

Given six seconds, the speedy quarterback took Notre

Dame in for the tying touchdown and triggered one of the biggest controversies of the 1953 season. The Iowa partisans were not the only ones who jumped up and down at the fake injury ruse. Leahy's enemies screamed bloody murder and started a national clamor. Finally, the National Collegiate Athletic Association stepped in and publicly slapped Leahy's wrists. The NCAA determined that the feigned injury play was "dishonest, unsportsmanlike and contrary to the rules," making the Notre Dame coach a villain in the piece.

Leahy protested.

"Feigned injuries have been a part of football since Walter Camp invented the first down. Consider only a couple of fairly recent examples I witnessed. At Dallas, in 1949, we skinned by Southern Methodist 27-20. Near the end, the Mustangs feigned injuries to gain time, play after play. In fact, their fans began booing us for dirty playing. With two seconds to go in our 27-21 victory over Oklahoma at Notre Dame in 1952, one of their players lay sprawled. This stopped the clock and gave them a chance to get off one more pass. It didn't click. But it might have. Earlier that year in Pittsburgh, a feigned injury near the end of the first half gave us time to throw a touchdown pass. Nobody said anything about it. We lost the game, 22-19. There may be a connection.

"'Be sure,' Rockne used to tell us, 'that the man who fakes the injury has the most capable replacement.' Other coaches have told their players the same thing. Just ask any coach or player you know, at the college, high school or even the grade school level. Yet, you probably never heard about a feigned injury until our Iowa game, and I'll tell you why. Usually, the extra seconds gained avail a team little or nothing. Against Iowa, we used the extra seconds to score two touchdowns, a tribute to Notre Dame's typical determination and poise. It seems to me that the feigned-injury controversy was caused not by what was done, but by who did it and how successfully."

The NCAA not only slapped Leahy's wrist, but the Rules Committee eventually slapped his face by legislating against feigned injuries. It was seen as a put-down of the Notre Dame coach. Leahy-haters rejoiced.

Notre Dame's image suffered a bit after that episode. Leahy's boys became known as the "Fainting Irish," and their bizarre escape from defeat also knocked them loose from the No. 1 ranking in the country. They were destined to remain No.

2 the rest of the way even though they closed out the season with routs of Southern Cal and Southern Methodist and even though national champion Maryland was beaten by Oklahoma (an Irish victim) in the Orange Bowl.

At season's end there was speculation that Leahy would retire because of his bad health. At one point near the end of the year, he gave some indication of this when he remarked to a reporter, "At times lately, I think that coaching the Notre Dame football team is a job for a younger man." Leahy was 45 at the time but his tortured body seemed much older. The retirement rumors seemed more plausible when Leahy closed himself up with his team for a half hour after the last game of the 1953 season. After emerging, he said to the press, "I have told these lads that they are the greatest I have ever coached." It appeared to be a good-bye speech to any discernible ear.

But a vacation with his wife appeared to buoy Leahy's spirits, and fresh rumors abounded that the "Master" would fulfill the obligations of his Notre Dame contract, which still had two years to run. Then one January afternoon he told an acquaintance that he was going to see Father Cavanaugh, one-time president of the school and Leahy's first boss as chairman of the athletic board. After a warm, heart-to-talk with his old friend, Leahy decided to quit. Actually he had no choice. The doctors told him to give up coaching, or he would die.

Terry Brennan, one of Leahy's "lads" who had coached the freshmen for only one year, was the surprising choice as his successor. There was skepticism about the selection. Brennan had never coached a college varsity and at 25 was thought by some to be too young to tackle the pressurized Notre Dame job. But Leahy himself endorsed him. "Terry has everything," the outgoing coach said.

Brennan arrived in a tumultuous, high-powered era. It was a legacy left by Leahy. Because of his enormous successes, the Fighting Irish were constantly treated as the greatest football show on earth. Wherever they played, they packed stadiums, as witnessed by their record attendance of 610,704 in 1953. Wherever they went, they were besieged by autograph hounds, "Subway Alumni," and reporters. Their moves were watched by a fair-size piece of the world population, thanks to national television and a 115-station radio hookup described as the "Irish Network" which reached out across the nation and into Alaska, Hawaii, and the Philippines. For the television audiences as well, there was a 13-theater chain showing the games on Saturday afternoons and a 45 to 60-station setup on Sunday nights. The growing hysteria made Notre Dame the only truly national team, and there was the young, untested Brennan in the middle of it all.

Cardiac Special

"I think it's better now that we've lost. The pressure the boys were building up within themselves will be relieved, and they'll settle down and, I hope, start another winning string. Notre Dame was better, and after all, it's not too bad to lose a ballgame to a school of Notre Dame's tradition."—Dr. George Cross, president of Oklahoma University, 1957.

When Notre Dame went south to play Oklahoma in 1957, it was hardly the Good Ship Lollipop.

"We stayed in a little town called Chickasha, with red dust in the road and an old, dumpy hotel," recalls Monte Stickles. "We didn't get treated very well."

There were other distractions. The place was brimming with hostility. "Rednecks, Go Home " were among some of the "welcoming" signs.

In the midst of this inhospitable aura, Stickles remembers the oppression of the Mexican-American children. That might have depressed Notre Dame players the most.

"There was an awful lot of animosity against Catholics in that state. At that time, the state was only three per cent Catholic. I remember we went to our game mass that Saturday morning, and there were these little Mexican kids just begging us to win so they wouldn't have to take all that crap for so long. If we beat Oklahoma, maybe that would make it easier on the Catholics in the state."

As if Notre Dame did not have enough motivation, here was more. Oklahoma boasted the longest winning streak in the history of college football—47 games. That, alone, would have

Notre Dame stops an opposing player here, but the Fighting Irish did not stop many in 1956. They had their worst season in history and were accused of losing their fight.

been enough to stir up the Fighting Irish. That Oklahoma had embarrassed them 40-0 the year before in South Bend was another electric factor. Add this to the fact that Notre Dame was playing the defending national champions in their home stadium and was branded as a 19-point underdog. Well, it was enough to shake down enough motivational thunder to drown out all of Oklahoma.

The Sooners were riding high in the national wire service polls while the Fighting Irish were nowhere in sight. Navy and Michigan State had beaten faltering Notre Dame with fury on two successive weekends, and one sportswriter labeled the November 16th game as a battle between the "haves" and "have-nots."

"Oklahoma has a tremendous repertoire of plays, hitting

Bob Williams, Notre Dame's quarterback of the late 1950s, runs for a touchdown against arch-rival Indiana.

with great speed," reported Lawrence Robinson in the *New York World-Telegram.* "Though mainly a Split-T outfit, it goes to flankers, single wing, uses well-executed traps and draw plays; even has a buck lateral in which the fullback overtakes and feeds the blocking back, who then fades back and throws to the right end."

Notre Dame's system was not as elaborate. But the Irish did show a proficiency at passing. Bob Williams was a better thrower than either of Oklahoma's best, Carl Dodd or Dave

Baker. Notre Dame relied on more mundane plays such as the "Tank 75"—a linebuck prepared especially for fullback Nick Pietrosante. "The play is simple," a writer pointed out. "The guard pulls out to block the end. The right tackle (Don Lawrence) blocks the rival tackle and is helped in a double-team block by the right half (Dick Lynch). The latter slides off to take the linebacker, if possible. Powerful Pietrosante slams into the hole or blasts his way if none is open."

Most of the pregame talk was about these offenses, but when the game was over, most everybody talked about the defenses. The goal-line stands in this herculean struggle in Norman were enough to last a season. In the first period the game was played mostly in Notre Dame territory. Oklahoma got as far as the Notre Dame 12 yard line and once more to the 13. A great punt by Pietrosante got the Fighting Irish out of the hole for a while. Notre Dame's second team went in and fumbled, and Oklahoma was back knocking on the Irish door again. The Sooners got the ball as far as the 24, but on fourth down Notre Dame tacklers broke through their line and hit their ballcarrier so hard that the ball bounced back to midfield.

Later the game was played in Oklahoma territory. With Williams passing often, the Irish moved once to the three and again to the six. But both times Oklahoma held, the last time stopping the drive with a pass interception in the end zone.

In the third period the game reverted to its original pattern: Oklahoma on the march, and Notre Dame with its back to the wall. Two times the pressing Sooners booted coffin-corner kicks that put the Fighting Irish in deep trouble. But both times they managed to squirm free.

"The amazing thing about that game was that it was still scoreless after three quarters, yet there was a lot of good offensive football played," Stickles says. "The thing was, both teams did so well on defense, stopping drives when they really counted. We had a fake field goal stopped. Our back was pulled down from behind once to save a touchdown. Dave Baker intercepted a pass in the end zone to stop another of our drives. It was really something."

It was not until late in the fourth quarter that either team was able to score—and this Notre Dame did with a beautiful 80-yard drive, labeled "true precision and team effort" by Oklahoma coach Bud Wilkinson. Using the aforementioned "Tank 75" play several times, Pietrosante cracked Oklahoma's stub-

311

born defense for crucial yardage. The scoring play from the three yard line on fourth down with 3:50 left in the game came off with professional perfection. Williams faked at the line, drew in the secondary, and pitched out to Lynch going wide around his right end for the three final yards. Stickles kicked the extra point, and that was the only scoring in the game.

"Nobody left the stadium, they were so stunned," Stickles recalls most about that 7-0 victory. "They couldn't believe that we came down there and finally ended it all. The Oklahoma fans didn't leave the stadium for some 20 minutes to a half hour after the game. And when we got home, I've never seen a reception like we got at the airport. They had parades through town, thousands of people, you know, the whole bit. . ."

The victory was easily the highlight of Terry Brennan's coaching career at Notre Dame. He called it later, "My biggest thrill in football."

"What I focused on was our defensive unit," Brennan notes, looking back on his greatest triumph. "We didn't have a whole lot of speed, and we tried to be as basic as possible. I knew that Wilkinson was a fine coach and would have a handful of plays, and he would run these from different formations to try to confuse things. So we just approached the game from the point of view where we were not going to confuse ourselves. We figured they could light up in all different kinds of formations or whatever they wanted to do, but there were only four or five basic plays—and if you stopped them you had a chance to win.

"We prepared in detail for them. The big thing was to stop their running game, which we did with some new defensive wrinkles. I got quite a bit of satisfaction out of this because I called 90 percent of our defenses from the sidelines. In short yardage situations, like third and one, when Oklahoma had the ball, I'd call for gap, slant or stunting defenses, and we stopped them every time. Those crucial situations came up close to a dozen times during the game, and our defense. . .fellows like Al Ecuyer and Frank Kuchta. . .was great."

It had to be to stop Oklahoma, a team which had averaged more than 300 yards rushing per game that year and had not been shut out for 123 games. The Sooners were held to a paltry 98 yards on the ground that day.

Two big gambles paid off for Brennan in that game. Because Oklahoma showed little ability as a passing team, Brennan installed a strong, tight defensive alignment which included

Pietrosante playing the left corner linebacking job like an end. The Sooners stuck to their usual ground attack, and Pietrosante ended up stopping everything which came near him, especially bottling up the feared deep reverses of Clendon Thomas. Secondly, Brennan left his second unit in more than half the time against Oklahoma's first team in the third period "so that our first unit would be fresh for the last period." In retrospect, of course, that turned out to be sheer genius as Notre Dame's first team ground out precious yardage against the tired Sooners at the end.

Notre Dame's conquering heroes got a welcome at home befitting the occasion. The team plane was met by 5,000 rooters, after students had snake danced several miles from the Notre Dame campus to downtown South Bend. Many more gathered on Notre Dame Avenue in front of the school for an impromptu celebration. The celebration continued over through Monday, when a campus-wide holiday was declared for the day.

"There were lots of happy people," says Brennan, "just having a lot of fun."

If this dramatic reaction to the victory over Oklahoma seemed a bit overdone, it could be explained in part by Notre Dame's recent fortunes in football. Used to being the best for so long, Notre Dame had been among the worst just one year prior to 1957. With a woeful 2-8 record in 1956, the Irish had their

The 1956 Notre Dame-Michigan State game featured a lot of scoring—mostly by Michigan State. The Spartans beat the hapless Irish 47-14.

first losing season since 1933 and their worst season ever since they started playing football on a regular basis. It was enough to bring cries for Brennan's head. The faculty board of athletics indeed wanted to fire the coach who had taken over for Frank Leahy, but Father Theodore Hesburgh, the Notre Dame president, vetoed the recommendation. Brennan's option was picked up for another year, and the troubled coach was vindicated somewhat by his stunning triumph over Oklahoma and a 7-3 record in 1957. A loss to Iowa the week after the Oklahoma game did not diminish the season's glow for Brennan or Notre Dame. The Irish were voted the Associated Press "Comeback Team of the Year," beating out the professional Cleveland Browns by an overwhelming margin, and Brennan took honors as the "Comeback Coach of 1957."

The triumphs of 1957 helped erase some of the frustrations of 1956, when Notre Dame had one of the most "injured" teams of modern football history. There were 33 of Brennan's top personnel sidelined at one time or another because of injuries, and three of the men he had counted on heavily were lost for the season. Brennan was forced to depend on an unusual amount of sophomores, and the inevitable resulted.

When Brennan first started as coach at Notre Dame in

Athletic Director Moose Krause, right, passes the ball to Terry Brennan as the young coach prepares to take charge of Notre Dame football in 1954.

1954, there were no such serious personnel problems. In fact, there were quite a few holdovers from Leahy's unbeaten team of the year before, and Notre Dame's football future seemed secure in the grip of the new wonder boy. Brennan, one of Leahy's fine running backs of the glamour teams of the 1940s, was given the head coaching job at the young age of 25 with Leahy's blessing. Brennan's poise and quick humor were apparent right away when, at the press conference announcing his new job, a reporter asked: "Aren't you nervous, Terry, becoming coach of Notre Dame at 25?"

Brennan broke into a grin and answered, "Oh, I don't know, I'll be 26 in a few months."

True, there was some criticism about Notre Dame appointing a coach that young to "the most difficult job in college sports." But as far as the Notre Dame hierarchy was concerned, Brennan became of age as soon as he became the freshman coach in 1953. There was suspicion even then that Brennan was being groomed for Leahy's job. And when Brennan was offered the head coaching job at Marquette in early January, 1954, he turned it down with the assurance he would not have to wait long for a promotion. Brennan was selected as much for his character and fiber as he was for his coaching ability. As one writer expressed it at the time, "Terry is a Notre Dame man, a remarkable embodiment of the qualities of high scholarship, strong character and athletic prowess, which the college likes to stress. As an undergraduate, 1945-49, he maintained a classroom average of 85. He majored in philosophy, an unlikely major for a football star. He was a member of the student council and, as an 18-year-old sophomore, was elected president of the class. Joe Doyle, the sports editor of the *South Bend Tribune*, was in a few classes with Terry and says he stood out not so much because he was a football player, but because he always had a mind of his own and always spoke up when he questioned or objected to a statement made by the instructor."

Age aside, Brennan did seem a logical choice for the school that preferred to promote its own kind. Brennan had been a "Notre Dame man" as far back as 1928, when he was born in Milwaukee. His father, Martin Brennan, was a former Notre Dame center and fired the home with school spirit. Inevitably, Terry was drawn to Notre Dame, not only by his father's love for his alma mater, but also because his brother Jim was already playing there in 1944. Brennan's dreams of playing football for

Notre Dame became even more intense when he and his father went up to South Bend one Saturday to watch Jimmy play in a game. Terry had injured one of his knees seriously while playing at Marquette High School, and there was some doubt that he would be able to play football at all, no less at Notre Dame. But after watching his brother perform on the field, Terry was convinced of his destiny.

"If you'll fix me up with an operation on my knee, I'd like to try Notre Dame," he told his father. "I liked what I saw today."

Terry got his operation and eventually got Notre Dame, realizing a dream to play with his brother on the same Irish team. But while Jimmy was the dominating player of the two at Marquette High School, it was Terry all the way at Notre Dame. Terry Brennan was not Notre Dame's greatest back in a postwar period of superlative runners, but he was a really good one. At 17 he was Notre Dame's No. 1 left halfback, and he started 30 of 38 games in four years on the varsity. Despite two fragile knees ("Knees just aren't made right") and a relatively slim physique (165 pounds, five-foot-eleven), Brennan became one of Notre Dame's best breakaway runners and one of its most notorious touchdown threats. He scored 21 touchdowns and averaged 4.7 yards a play.

"When we needed yards, we gave the ball to Terry," points out Edward "Moose" Krause, Notre Dame's current athletic director and the line coach of Terry's playing days. And Leahy once said of his tough runner, "When it is third and four to go I don't know of a better back to get those four yards than Terence." When Brennan broke loose, which was often, he was not only good, he was spectacular. The 1947 Army game was the occasion for Brennan's most dazzling performance—a 97-yard kickoff return for a touchdown that started Notre Dame to a 27-7 victory. Leahy accorded this memorable play the proper respect when he and Brennan were photographed on the field together at the changing of orders in 1954. Leahy insisted that their picture be taken in the north end zone of Notre Dame Stadium because that was the one in which Terry scored the famous touchdown.

After Brennan graduated in 1949, he took a coaching position at Mount Carmel High School in Chicago mostly as a means of making money to go through law school at nearby DePaul University. However, his high school teams became more success-

Frank Leahy (left) and his successor, Terry Brennan, are shown on the storied turf of Notre Dame Stadium at the time of Brennan's appointment as head coach of the Fighting Irish in 1954.

ful than he imagined. In four years his Mount Carmel teams won three city football championships. Leahy, watching one of the play-offs on television, applauded the young and able coach. "I had not believed that any high school team could look so well-indoctrinated," he said.

Brennan's swift success brought him back to Notre Dame in 1953 in the newly created position of freshman coach. Some believed that the job was made especially to hold Brennan under wraps until Leahy retired. And these suspicions were confirmed the very next year when Brennan replaced the ailing

Leahy in a bittersweet setting. Leahy desperately wanted to continue, but where his foes were unsuccessful, health had beaten him down. At first Leahy heartily endorsed Brennan for the job, but their strong personalities soon clashed over a personal matter, and their relationship eventually deteriorated into a bitter feud. Milton Gross, writing for North American Newspaper Alliance at the time, surmised that their antagonism resulted from Brennan's "snub" of Leahy right after the job changed hands. "Before Brennan's first game as head coach in 1954, Leahy called to offer his help," Gross pointed out. "Frank volunteered to work as a roof spotter, but Brennan rejected the assistance. Leahy offered to spot from an end zone. Again the rejection. Instead Brennan suggested that Leahy might address the team prior to the game. Leahy did, but the next time the team was together, Brennan was alleged to have said: 'We had an intruder in our locker room last Saturday. It will never happen again while I'm coaching here.'"

Ralph Guglielmi, the Notre Dame quarterback under both Leahy and Brennan and a senior in 1954, recalls the fireworks between the two in 1954, particularly that speech from Leahy that seemed to torture Brennan: "We were playing Texas, and Leahy came into the locker room at halftime. Leahy made a speech, and I think he meant it very sincerely. He told us, 'You're not playing for me anymore, but you're playing for a great guy, Terry Brennan. It's your first game with a new coach, and you owe him a great deal.' And he really got into this talk, and we went from a tie at the halftime to beat Texas 21-7. We always had meetings the following Monday in the school auditorium, and Brennan stood up and really surprised us all. He told all the ballplayers that what happened last Saturday would never happen again. He said he would never allow anybody to come into his locker room again, and he banned Leahy from the practice field, and then in front of everybody, he challenged us individually about the situation, which was kind of immature. What happened then, I think, was we had a letdown. This really led to our downfall the following week against Purdue. Brennan probably meant no harm by it, but he certainly handled it the wrong way."

Brennan not only antagonized Leahy in his very first week on the Notre Dame job, but soon drove a wedge between himself and some of his players. After the second week of the season, when Notre Dame was beaten 27-14 by Purdue, many of the seniors were mad at the new coach, too.

"He had blamed me and some of the other seniors for that Purdue defeat in public in the newspapers," Guglielmi remembers. "I wasn't quite used to that, nor were the other ballplayers. Leahy would never do that. He would say we were outcoached, or it was one of those conditions. He would never pinpoint ballplayers. I was just a little ticked off, to be honest with you. He benched me the following game with Pittsburgh, along with five or six other seniors. Later in the game, he sent an assistant to tell me I was going to start the second half, and I told him to go to hell. If Brennan wanted me to start, I figured he should tell me himself, if he was any kind of a man."

Finally, Guglielmi and the other seniors who were in Brennan's dog house relented after another assistant came over and talked to them. "The score was pretty tight in that first half," Guglielmi says, "and this coach interceded and made sense, and we swallowed our ego and our pride and went out and played the second half. But from that time forward, there were very few words that passed between Brennan and me."

The results of Brennan's first season did not reflect any serious morale problem, even though some of the players were indeed unhappy under the vigorous new coach. The Purdue loss was the only one of the season, and the Fighting Irish went on to win nine games, most of them by substantial scores. The ever-critical Leahy was to point out later, however, that Brennan won with players that had been left him and that the 1954 Notre Dame team "was the best college football team in America." The Fighting Irish finished fourth in the national polls that year.

By 1955 Notre Dame slipped to No. 9 in the national rankings with an 8-2 record, but Brennan called it "one of my most satisfying seasons." The fact that he accomplished a good record with less talent had something to do with it. The 1955 backfield had a strong nucleus with Paul Hornung, Don Schaefer, and Jim Morse, but the line was questionable. Only captain Ray Lemek returned from the 1954 regulars, and he had a bad knee. Brennan and his assistants had to do the job with reserves from the Leahy era, and, except for losses to Michigan State and Southern California, the job was done well.

"We only had about 15 players who did all the playing," Brennan pointed out. "And finally at the end, we just pooped out in the Southern Cal game (a 42-20 loss). But even in that game, we did well in yardage. I remember one newspaperman thought they had the statistics wrong, because we gained about 625 yards to their 300 or 280, or something. We doubled their yardage and lost the game."

Notre Dame was trailing only 21-20 going into the last period when two interceptions and a fumble led to three Trojan scores. "It was the craziest game you ever saw," Brennan says. "We went down the field twice for good, long drives, got to the one-yard line of Southern Cal and fumbled the ball in the end zone. We hit passes to guys standing in the end zone, and they dropped them two times. So we were moving up and down the field all day, and kids who year long never fumbled or dropped passes did that day. It was one of those days. . .it was unbelievable. The following January, when the NCAA had its convention, they wanted to show movies of that game, they couldn't believe it. We did a good job. We just made mistakes that hurt."

One of the big reasons Notre Dame moved the ball so well that day was Hornung, one of Notre Dame's All-Americans in 1955 and probably the most valuable player on the team. Hornung was moved to quarterback because the split-T offense could exploit his versatility. Against the Trojans, Hornung was a superman. He passed for 259 yards, ran for 95 more, and kicked with unfailing efficiency. It led some observers to compare him favorably with the great George Gipp, Notre Dame's all-time triple-threat player. "That Notre Dame quarterback," said Southern Cal coach Jess Hill, "is among football's greatest."

Hornung, a brawny six-foot-two, 205-pounder, served his apprenticeship under Guglielmi in 1954. But even before that, Notre Dame-watchers knew he was going to be a surefire success. As a freshman Hornung showed flashes of poise, power, and confidence in the annual Varsity-Old Timer spring exhibition game. He outshone both Johnny Lujack and Guglielmi in his first public appearance, and a veteran Chicago newspaperman called him, "the classiest freshman football player to don a green Irish jersey in memory."

By 1955 the "Kentucky Babe" was no longer a babe. Hornung led the Irish in passing, scoring, pass interceptions, and punting. And this performance was a springboard for 1956 that catapulted him to that dizziest of individual college football honors, the Heisman Trophy. It was a distinct tribute to Hornung that he was recognized as the best college football player in the country because Notre Dame in 1956 was recognized as one of the worst teams. Heisman Trophy voters looked beneath the mountain of Notre Dame defeats (eight in ten games) and found a diamond in the rough. Despite playing most of 1956 with injury, Hornung started at three different backfield positions and led Notre Dame in eight statistical categories. And in addition to his national second-place finish in total offense, he was second in the country in kickoff returns, 15th in passing, and 16th in scoring.

Hornung carried the freight for Notre Dame through wind, rain, and dislocated thumbs. He hurt his left thumb while making a touchdown-saving tackle in the fourth game of the season yet later scored all of Notre Dame's points in a 21-14 victory over North Carolina. Against Southern Cal, he was forced to play halfback because both his thumbs were dislocated, and he was unable to handle the ball properly at quarterback. In this one the golden-haired boy returned a kickoff 95 yards for a touchdown and kept the Irish in the game all the way. But even Hornung's individual brilliance could not outshine an entire team, and the Trojans escaped with a 28-20 victory.

After watching Hornung perform miracles for Notre Dame in 1956, one observer commented: "In recent years many

Paul Hornung, Notre Dame's other "Golden Dome," fights for yardage during the Irish's 21-14 victory over North Carolina in 1956.

A familiar sight at Notre Dame in the 1950s—Paul Hornung running with the ball.

schools have had football teams named Desire. In 1956 Notre Dame had a football team named Hornung. He did everything. He ran. He kicked. He passed. He tackled. He intercepted passes. Surrounded by the walking wounded, playing for a team crippled by injuries, Hornung was the whole show."

Hornung exploded beyond his predicted potential, which was great in itself. He had been one of the most heralded of schoolboy players, and the Fighting Irish had to go to war with many of the nation's top schools for his services. Understandably, the University of Kentucky put on a sizzling, high-pressure campaign to keep Hornung in his native state. Hornung, from Louisville, had led Flaget High School to the Kentucky scholastic championship and was voted the outstanding high school football player in the state in 1952. The young star was visited not only by Bear Bryant, then University of Kentucky coach, but by the governor of Kentucky. Hornung was also romanced by Louisville, Eastern Kentucky, Western Kentucky, Purdue,

Indiana, Georgia Tech, Georgia, Florida, Auburn, Miami, Vanderbilt, Alabama, and Notre Dame. There were more, Hornung later said, but added, "I couldn't recall them all." He became an authority on college campuses.

Hornung visited Notre Dame on the weekend of the 1952 Southern Cal game with a Flaget teammate, Sherrill Sipes, and after the game met Frank Leahy in the locker room. "You lads certainly would look good in green," Leahy told them. Neither Hornung nor Sipes had been scouted personally by Notre Dame talent-finders, but on the basis of game movies, both were offered football scholarships. "I can't recall our ever having done this before," said Moose Krause, the Notre Dame athletic director.

Hornung eventually narrowed the field to Notre Dame, Kentucky, and Indiana. Finally, on July 17, 1953, he made his choice and sent a wire to Leahy: "I've finally made up my mind. My mother always wanted me to go to Notre Dame, and I've always been inclined to go there myself." No special inducement lured Hornung to Notre Dame, just the usual "room, board, tuition and laundry."

"I selected Notre Dame," Hornung later explained, "because of its religious and educational advantages. As a football player, I wanted to find out for myself if I could play with the best. Everybody knows Notre Dame signifies the best. As a quarterback, I wanted to follow in the footsteps of fellows like Carideo, Bertelli, Lujack, Tripucka, Williams and Guglielmi." Hornung also wanted to go to Notre Dame because he wanted to play under Leahy—"a helluva man." But of course the year that Hornung was eligible to play, 1954, Leahy retired and was replaced by Brennan.

Hornung's versatility was apparent right away. He had played little defense in high school, yet, when put into the annual spring exhibition game between the Notre Dame varsity and the alumni, Hornung starred on pass defense. Hornung had waited nervously for his chance, squirming on the bench for a full quarter before he was allowed to show his stuff. It seemed like an eternity before he got in, he later recalled. "The first quarter seemed so long that when it was over, I thought the half had ended, and I got up and almost started for the dressing room."

Since Guglielmi was entrenched as the quarterback, Hornung was shifted to fullback in his sophomore year and proved he was fully capable of handling that position even though he had never played it before. Used sparingly as a ballcarrier in 1954, Hornung nevertheless averaged almost seven yards a carry. He also replaced Guglielmi on occasions when the All-American quarterback needed a breather. Even though a relative unknown, Hornung displayed a variety of skills in his first year that underscored his value to the team. When Notre Dame beat Navy 6-0 midway through the season, Hornung helped the Fighting Irish out of trouble by punting from his own five yard line to the Navy 38. And later in the game, he frustrated a Navy drive by intercepting a pass deep in Notre Dame territory. When Guglielmi graduated, Hornung was pushed into the spotlight as the Notre Dame star, and Leahy predicted extravagant things for 1955. "Paul Hornung," he said, "will be the greatest quarterback Notre Dame ever had. He runs like a mower going through grass. Tackles just fall off him. His kicking—why when he reported to me as a freshman he could punt 80 yards and place-kick over the cross-bars from 70 yards."

If Leahy was exaggerating a bit, he was not far from wrong. Hornung did a lot of everything for Notre Dame in 1955. He ran for 472 yards in 92 carries and completed 46 of 103 passes for 743 yards. He became the proverbial one-man gang, and there was a general explosion of praise for the "Golden Dome," a nickname Hornung acquired for his blond hair and his establishment as a human landmark. It was a season that Hornung cherished, and for good reason.

"We had little depth," Hornung remembered later. "Sixteen men carried the load, and four of them were walking wounded. Brennan did a remarkable job to bring us through 8-2. We were worn out when we lost the finale to Southern California."

After Hornung's stunning performance against Southern Cal that day, probably his best single game at Notre Dame, he made a lot of fans—including the opposing Trojan players. So spectacular was Hornung's showing that Jon Arnett (who had scored 23 points himself for Southern Cal) called on him at a Los Angeles hotel. "Paul," Arnett said with admiration in his voice, "if you had been on our side, we'd have won 93 to 0!"

If Hornung had a fault, it was perhaps that he tried to do everything himself. Once chided about this, he offered a rebuttal. "The clubs we were playing were weak in the middle of the line. I was the closest to their weak spot, and I figured I could bust through. I think it worked." He also had 10 passes intercepted in 1955, a figure which led critics to disparage his throwing arm and led Brennan to remark at one point, "He's got to improve his passing."

This he did in 1956, even if he did have more passes intercepted (13). In his senior year Hornung completed 59 of 111 attempts for 917 yards and three touchdowns. In addition, Hornung ran for 420 yards to give him a total of 1,337 yards gained. He scored 56 points on seven touchdowns and 14 conversions. Hornung accomplished all this, pointed out an alumnus, with one of the weakest teams of recent Notre Dame vintage. "He'd go back to pass," said Angelo Bertelli, the former quarterback, "and either have to hurry his throw off balance or run with it. Most of the time he ran."

Despite his herculean accomplishments of 1956, Hornung was surprised at being named the Heisman Trophy winner. "I can't believe it," Hornung said at the time. "I didn't think I was even up for consideration." His personal rewards, however, were

Paul Hornung (left) and Coach Terry Brennan with Paul's Heisman Trophy in 1956.

dwarfed in the shadow of a losing season. "The country doesn't expect Notre Dame to lose. It was a tough pill to swallow. When you're losing, you can't be happy."

If Notre Dame was generally short of talent in 1956, there was, however, a good supply of enthusiasm. Hornung recalls: "At no time during the season did we feel we were lying down as far as spirit is concerned. We were trying in every game." Losing made a philosopher out of Hornung and his teammates. "After we lost the first one," he says, "Coach Brennan said not to worry, because every time you lost, you learned something. So I figured by the end of the season we weren't the best, but we sure must have been the smartest team in the country."

While Hornung was receiving applause, Brennan was feeling the other side of the hand. The coach got a slap in the face during the disastrous season from the student body, when he was hung in effigy from the Notre Dame Stadium wall. Authorities suppressed news of the incident, but its impact was already being felt on the Notre Dame campus. On the dummy was a sign which read: "This building and Brennan for sale—cheap."

The students were not the only ones out to get Brennan, it seemed. Frank Leahy, adding more fuel to their personal feud that was smoldering since 1954, accused the Fighting Irish of having lost their fight. Leahy's pot shot, of course, was taken at Brennan. The 28-year-old coach, firing back at his former boss, charged that Leahy had an "ulterior motive" in belittling the team. "I'm surprised that a man of Leahy's stature and intelligence would stoop to such a trick to get even with me for a personal disagreement," Brennan said. "He is mad at me and apparently has taken his anger out on the team. If Leahy's interest in Notre Dame was sincere, he wouldn't have said such things." Brennan said later, "Leahy knew what problems we had, so his criticism hurt me, hurt the team, hurt the school, hurt everybody. I never could figure the guy out." The faculty board in control of athletics made it clear that Brennan should be let go, since his three-year contract had expired. The board laid its recommendation on the desk of the school president, and while Father Hesburgh was mulling the matter over, Athletic Director Moose Krause was sounding out Joe Kuharich, the former Notre Dame player, for the head coaching job. But before Kuharich had a chance to accept it, Hesburgh had given Brennan a one-year extension on his contract.

Brennan's position at Notre Dame was on more solid

ground after the 1957 season and the startling victory over Oklahoma. The faculty board this time mechanically renewed his contract for 1958, and prospects for the season looked sublime. Brennan was now a seasoned coach with an experienced staff and a group of experienced players. Included among the excellent seniors were quarterback Bob Williams; fullback Nick Pietrosante, the Irish rushing leader of 1957 and one of the top runners in the country; and guard Al Ecuyer. Among a crop of superb juniors were Monte Stickles, the pass-catching end and field goal kicker; halfbacks Pat Doyle and Jim Crotty; and George Izo, a touted backup quarterback to Williams.

Brennan had all the potent components for a wildly successful season but for some unaccountable reason could not make the chemistry mix properly. The Fighting Irish opened with a flourish, beating Indiana and SMU, but then a demoralizing loss to Army seemed to turn the season in the other direction. The promise of spring faded in the fall, and the Irish finished with a 6-4 record, an exasperatingly poor record considering the rich talent on hand.

The anti-Brennan forces, still sizzling over that 2-8 debacle back in 1956, really got to work this time and eventually got him removed. But even though Brennan had failed in some eyes, his firing by Notre Dame was not a popular decision. The timing of the announcement, for one thing, hit many observers between the eyes. Brennan was fired during Christmas, and this especially was looked on by most as a wholly un-Christian thing to do. This "Christmas present" to Brennan, a father of four, triggered a national clamor of criticism and outrage. Notre Dame, a school that historically emphasized religion and good fellowship, had aroused violent emotions. Secondly, Brennan's overall record was not entirely disgraceful, considering the caliber of opposition that Notre Dame faced in the 1950s. The Fighting Irish had four winning seasons and finished in the Top Twenty four times during Brennan's five years there. Thirdly, Brennan was an extremely likeable, personable young man, admired by the press and most of his associates.

Newspaper feeling was strongly against Notre Dame's decision. The popular opinion of sportswriters was expressed aptly by Shirley Povich in the *Washington Post*: "Through the years, Notre Dame has stood apart as a special kind of citadel of the game that could answer all critics of big-time football. It demanded of its football players a passing grade higher than that of the non-athletes. . . .There seemed to be an immunity from such bedevilments as alumni pressure and an overweaning zeal for winning. . . .Then comes the crashing thing that Coach Brennan has been banished like a common losing coach at a state university that is insensitive to alumni howls and legislative threats. Until Notre Dame volunteers more and more enlightening facts. . .an uncomplimentary suspicion must prevail."

Coaches and players generally echoed the common newspaper sentiment. Pietrosante, for one, was bitter. "It's a pretty rotten thing," said the All-American fullback. "They don't know what they did to themselves. They didn't give him any of the breaks. They expect too much of a team that has to play a schedule like ours." Paul Dietzel, coach of Louisiana State's national champions, apparently spoke for many of the coaches when he said, "It's a disgrace to the school, and anyone taking that job now should have his head examined." Dietzel, secretary of the ethics committee of the American Football Coaches Association, added: "Here's a good coach who had a 7-3 record, then a 6-4 record, playing a very, very difficult schedule—then he gets fired. It just doesn't look good."

Edgar Hayes, sports editor of the *Detroit Times*, revealed the "inside story" of the notorious firing. Hayes claimed that a group of Knute Rockne-era alumni and the "old guard" cost Brennan his job: "A small but powerful group of alumni, headed by a Cleveland attorney, has been campaigning actively against Brennan since the close of the disastrous 1956 season when the Irish won only two of ten games. Losses this year to Purdue and Army and later to Pittsburgh and Iowa reactivated the anti-Brennan forces. This time they were able to get Father Hesburgh, if not to approve, at least to withhold his opposition to firing a coach who had four winning seasons out of five. The alumni group, which includes very few of those who were at school in the last 15 to 20 years, had a strong ally in Father John J. Cavanaugh, former president, who has traveled extensively in his duties with the Notre Dame Foundation and has been a rallying point for the anti-Brennan forces."

While the multitude of voices was raised against Notre Dame and in Brennan's behalf, there were some who applauded the decision to fire him. Leahy, an old enemy, insisted: "Notre Dame had no alternative. Brennan was dismissed because he lost control of his players. Some of his boys were bringing adverse publicity to the school, breaking training and not conducting themselves properly on road trips. Brennan was too young for the job. Coach Rockne could have come down from the heavens to give advice, and Brennan would not have listened."

Stickles, Brennan's All-American end, turned on him. "We had a helluva team in 1958," he said in later years. "Remember Nick Pietrosante? He was one of the players on that team. Thirteen of that team went into pro ball. You ask why they fired Brennan? With that team the best he could do was win six of 10 games. Yet people wonder why they fired him."

Jerry Groom, an All-American center who played with Brennan in the 1940s, noted, "evidently he wasn't big enough for the job. Terry had his chance. It wasn't a lousy deal. He's playing the role of a martyr. . ."

The sentimental view of Brennan being thrown out on his ear in the midst of Christmas was perhaps a bit overdramatized by the press. The way some newspapermen painted it, Brennan was sitting by the Christmas tree playing with his children when notified of his dismissal. Actually, it was not that callous at all. The faculty board met shortly after the final game on November 29 and voted to fire the youthful coach. On December 16, Brennan was told of the board's decision and given an opportunity to resign. But Brennan declined the offer, replying: "I don't want people to think I'm quitting under pressure."

"Is there any particular time you would like us to release the announcement of your firing?" asked Father Edmund P. Joyce, chairman of the faculty board.

"Whenever you say," Brennan answered.

"We'd like to make it as soon as possible."

"Wait until after Saturday," Brennan responded. "My boy gets off from school that day, and I'd rather have him home."

Perhaps newspapermen would not have been so quick to admonish Notre Dame for its notorious "Christmas firing" of Brennan had they dug deeper into the story and found a gentlemen's agreement wedged somewhere underneath the avalanche of criticism. Father Hesburgh later revealed that he and Brennan "mutually decided to make it before Christmas rather than after the New Year. This was decided mainly in the interest of the assistant coaches, considering the then present availability of other coaching positions that might not be available later."

So Terry Brennan was let go in a period of conflict and complexity. There were some things very clear about his dismissal. He had not won often enough to please discriminating alumni spoiled by the records of Rockne and Leahy. The alumni had exerted pressure—in the form of threats to withhold financial contributions from the university. This meant that Notre Dame was headed in a new direction, an about-face from a recent policy to keep football in its proper perspective. Now it seemed to be "win at all costs" instead of "win one for the Gipper," and Notre Dame turned for help in this new mission to an old pro, Joe Kuharich.

...And Still The Winner!

"It was just pandemonium. . .the field was totally mobbed. It was a tremendous victory for us strictly because we weren't winning that many ballgames. You know, Ernie Davis was a highly-touted All-American, and Syracuse also had John Mackey and Walt Sweeney. They had a real fine football team. . . and it was a great victory for our ballclub."—Nick Buoniconti.

Walt Sweeney could have kicked himself, and Gus Skibbie might have bitten his tongue after the 1961 Notre Dame-Syracuse game. Each had something to do with creating the most violent dispute and biggest disturbance of the collegiate football season that year.

With three seconds left to play and Syracuse winning 15-14, Notre Dame's Joe Perkowski attempted a field goal from the 46 yard line of the Orangemen. Sweeney, the Syracuse end, crashed into the Notre Dame backfield and bowled over both Perkowski and the holder, George Sefcik. For this untimely assault, Syracuse was penalized 15 yards by Skibbie, the head linesman. And Notre Dame, which had seemingly lost when its field goal attempt fell short at the final gun, was given a second shot at the goalposts from a cozier position. This time, with 0:00 showing on the clock, Sweeney did not belt anybody, but Perkowski did belt the ball through the uprights for three points that gave Notre Dame an incredible and controversial 17-15 victory.

"The way Perkowski kicked the second one," remembers Nick Buoniconti, Notre Dame's All-American guard that year, "it would have traveled 70 yards if it had to. The ball went way up in the stands. It was a hell of a kick."

Syracuse players, in shock for a while, soon were going crazy on the field. Buoniconti recalls: "They chased the officials, and one slugged an official. They were shoving and pushing. It was really a very tense moment. They really thought they got a bad deal."

This was nothing compared to the reaction from Syracuse University after the game. Officials from the eastern school cried "foul" long and loud and insisted that Notre Dame forfeit the contest. "We believe absolutely Syracuse won 15-14," said Lew Andreas, the Orangemen's athletic director. Syracuse based its position on a consensus opinion that Skibbie and his crew erred in judging the critical penalty at the end. Under the existing rules, it appeared that Notre Dame should not have been allowed an extra play after time had run out, and such distinguished football leaders as William Reed, the Big Ten Conference commissioner, and Asa Bushnell of the Eastern Athletic Conference sided with Syracuse.

Certainly, Rule 3, Section 2, of the NCAA Football Rules Interpretations seemed to support them: "A kick by Team A (Notre Dame) during a 'time expiring' down indicates that A does not want to move the ball, and a foul during the kick, including roughing the kicker, will not extend the period as the ball is not in A's possession."

"The rule, be it a good one or a bad one, could not have been much clearer," said a Syracuse official. "As long as a foul was not committed before the ball was kicked, the period should not have been extended."

Still, the score could not be changed by anyone—unless Notre Dame decided to surrender. And this, the Irish would not do. They never fought harder for a game off the field. The Reverend Edmund P. Joyce, executive vice-president of Notre Dame, believed that the key rule had been misinterpreted. Responding to the Syracuse victory claim, he said: "We are quite surprised at the developments following our last-minute victory over Syracuse. We felt and still feel that the officials made the proper decision on the field. The infraction was incurred before the clock ran out and before the ball was dead. Therefore, it seems mandatory that a penalty be invoked. It is strange that some people now feel otherwise. . ."

While the two schools were arguing back and forth, so were the nation's sportswriters. Just about every columnist of note jumped into the battle, taking sides with venom. Their tons of prose made the uproar even noisier. Red Smith, writing in the *New York Herald Tribune*, discovered an interpretation of the highly technical rule that favored Notre Dame, not Syracuse. "Now it develops that there was no error on the field, no injustice to Syracuse. On the contrary, it was Notre Dame who was fouled by Syracuse, but it was Syracuse who hollered copper." Stanley Woodward, writing in the same newspaper, disagreed violently with Smith. "As far as we are concerned," Woodward said, "we would like to renew the suggestion to Notre Dame that it withdraw as victor in this game and send the ball to Syracuse with congratulations."

Lost in all the hullabaloo of Notre Dame's "tainted" victory was the fact that the Fighting Irish had made a miraculous comeback to pull it out. This is what happened: Syracuse sophomore Bob Lelli, filling in for injured starter Dave Sarette, threw a touchdown pass to Dick Easterly in the fourth period to give the Orangemen a 15-14 lead with 10:35 left. Both offenses bogged down at this point, and the ball changed hands three times. With time running out, Syracuse had the ball and apparently the ballgame locked up. All the Orangemen had to do was keep the ball on the ground and run out the clock. But Syracuse was stopped cold—and even pushed back—with the help of Buoniconti's devastating play. On third down Lelli threw an incompleted pass. This served Notre Dame's purposes two ways—it cost Syracuse a precious down and stopped the clock, saving a few timely seconds for the Fighting Irish. On fourth and 12, Lelli counted on Ernie Davis, Syracuse's Heisman Trophy-winning back, to get the necessary yardage. But Davis could only manage five yards, and Notre Dame took over the ball on its 30 yard line with 17 seconds to go.

Frank Budka became the Notre Dame "minuteman" then. The poised sophomore went back to pass, was trapped, but struggled free and ran 21 yards to the Syracuse 49. Budka had wisely stepped out of bounds, stopping the clock with eight seconds left. Budka then hit Sefcik with an 11-yard pass to the Syracuse 38, setting up the wild ending described by one sportswriter as "unbelievable, fantastic, electrifying." Perkowski's second-chance kick touched off a joyous celebration at Notre Dame Stadium.

"The crowd of 49,246, mostly partisans of the Irish, waited for referee Tony Skover's signal and then moved onto the field in a mob to carry the victorious Irish off," noted a writer from United Press International. "The crowd wouldn't leave. It stayed in the stands and on the field after the game had ended. Irish followers were unsuccessful in their attempt to pull down the steel-based concrete goal posts. But they did keep the Irish band on the field long overtime. It was an amazing finish to a fine football game."

The score remained the same, but the rules were eventually changed to allow an extra play under parallel circumstances. This was seen as a vote in Notre Dame's favor. Admittedly weary over the whole thing, Father Joyce noted: "It seems to be the reasonable thing to do. I'm happy to learn that the situation has been clarified."

It was not surprising that Notre Dame fought so hard for a game. During the reign of Coach Joe Kuharich, victories had not been easy to come by. "Even though we had a lot of great football players and a lot of guys who went on to pro football, we were very mediocre as far as won-lost records went," points out Buoniconti, who played from 1959 through 1961 at Notre Dame and went on to star with the Miami Dolphins. "I think

With less than a minute to play in the 1961 Michigan State game, Notre Dame guard Nick Buoniconti prays on the bench. His prayers were not answered, and Notre Dame lost to the Spartans 17-7.

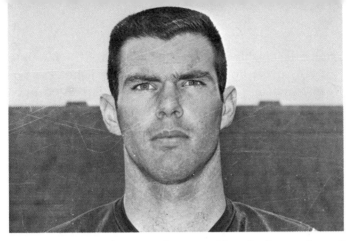

Before reaching stardom in the pros Daryle Lamonica played quarterback for Joe Kuharich at Notre Dame.

Kuharich's biggest problem was making the adjustment from pro football to college football. I think you've got to make adjustments because you're going from working with men to working with boys. In college, you get kids who are making a difficult adjustment period from high school, and they need to be handled with kid gloves and need more of a father-type image. But Joe was treating us more like professional players rather than college players. That was just his way of doing it, and it just didn't succeed in college."

Monte Stickles, who played in Kuharich's first year at Notre Dame, 1959, charged that he lacked imagination. "He uses the same old stuff," said Stickles, who became a noted pro player. "He tries to ram the ball down everybody's throat. He's too stubborn." But it was perhaps too much imagination that later got Kuharich—and Notre Dame—in trouble. During his time at Notre Dame, from 1959 through 1962, it was the consensus opinion that Kuharich had adapted the complex thinking of the professionals to the simpler college game. Kuharich, who had left the pros to join Notre Dame, tried to use complicated pro techniques with the less skilled and less mature collegians, and this resulted in an overall losing record during his four years at South Bend of 17-23.

After Kuharich's second 5-5 record in three years in 1961, he was open season for snipers. Frank Leahy fired the most direct hit when he said, "I think he handled Notre Dame like it was a professional team. In the pro leagues, you don't have to stress fundamentals, the players know them. But in college it's different. Kuharich never made the adjustment." Kuharich's inspirational leadership was questioned, too. "I don't think he got a lot out of the boys," said Leahy. "He is not the type to get a team fired up. I don't think he ever impressed upon his boys that it was a great honor to play for Notre Dame, that it is wonderful just to wear a Notre Dame uniform."

Others complained that Kuharich missed the mark widely in human relations. The *Notre Dame Scholastic* pointed to a lack of communication with his players. Newspapermen complained that he was not only hard to interview, but hard to find. "Conversing with him," said one writer, "was like dropping a stone down a deep, deep well and waiting for the sound to come back."

However, this all would have been acceptable at Notre Dame had Kuharich been a winning coach. For Kuharich was an old Notre Dame man in the very real sense of the phrase, and nothing would have pleased the school's authorities more than to have him succeed with flying colors. Kuharich was born in South Bend on April 14, 1917, and ever since the day Knute Rockne "patted me on my fanny and took me to watch the Irish practice," he wanted to be part of the Notre Dame tradition. Kuharich learned his football on the South Bend sandlots, using nothing more than an old tin can for a football. By the time he was playing football for Riley High School, he was outstanding, even though on the lighter side in weight. Dismissing his meager 150 pounds, Kuharich's coach, Forest Wood, said, "He was a scrappy, determined football player, probably the most intense kid I ever coached."

Obviously, Notre Dame thought the same thing because Kuharich was given a football scholarship by Coach Elmer Layden. And he wasted no time in making an impression on everyone in his first year. Harvey Foster, a teammate of Kuharich's, once remembered: "The freshmen had no schedule but met the varsity each week, using the offenses of the varsity's upcoming opponents. Despite Joe's size, he and another South Bend boy, Joe Reutz, became the number one guards and proved themselves difficult for the varsity to handle. What Joe lacked in size, he made up in agility and determined dedication to the game. He lived, ate and slept football and seemed to spend every waking minute thinking and talking about it."

In 1935 Kuharich became a regular guard as a sophomore and continued to grow in stature as a player, as well as in actual size. By 1937, his senior year, he was honored as an all-midwest

Joe Kuharich: He brought the professional touch to college.

player and acclaimed as a football tactician. "He had an uncanny ability to diagnose an opposing offense and impart this knowledge to his mates," said a friend. Layden agreed: "He was one of the best and smartest players I ever had at Notre Dame."

In the uncertain days preceding the Second World War, Kuharich's career followed a crazy-quilt pattern. After graduation he served as the Notre Dame freshman coach, coached at Vincentian Institute at Albany, New York, and played guard for the Chicago Cardinals for two years. Following four years in the Navy, the impatient Kuharich continued to move around like a man on the run. He finished out the 1945 season as a player for the Cardinals, became line coach of the Pittsburgh Steelers, and then moved on to the University of San Francisco, where he "settled down" for four years. An undefeated season in 1951 brought him back to the Cardinals as head coach in 1952. But in 1953 Kuharich was off and running again. He left the Cardinals organization to work as a scout for several pro teams. In 1954 he hopped to Washington to take the job as head coach of the Redskins. A successful season in 1955 won him "Coach of the Year" honors, and Kuharich stayed with the Redskins until he accepted the Notre Dame offer in December, 1958.

After Terry Brennan's turbulent years, the choice of Kuharich seemed to be ideal. Here was a popular, mellowed figure who bridged the very pages of Notre Dame history—from mascot to master of the Fighting Irish. The choice of Kuharich, perhaps, seemed a change in the Notre Dame thinking. The Notre Dame administrators, young and vigorous themselves, had gone away from youth toward age and experience. "They sought in Kuharich a man who could symbolize the old glory until such time as he was able to create a new glory," pointed out a writer. But Kuharich obviously had a time limit on his own master rebuilding plan—four years. That was the length of the contract Kuharich had signed, and the Notre Dame hierarchy felt it would be enough time for him to bring the Fighting Irish back to their former euphoric heights.

Kuharich took a pay cut to come back to Notre Dame but gleefully announced before the 1959 season: "I am flattered and proud that they decided to give me the opportunity. It always has been my hope and prayer that I could return to Notre Dame."

However, as Kuharich got down to the realities of a rebuilding year, he soon found that Notre Dame was no Shangri-la. Only 12 monogram winners were returning for the 1959 season, and Kuharich's two best backs, quarterback George Izo and halfback Red Mack, had been seriously hurt during one practice session. Kuharich's giddiness quickly faded and was overtaken by pessimism. "This will be a year of suffering for us. Suffer and sacrifice—that's all we'll be able to do."

It seemed like a prophecy come true after the first few weeks of the season. Notre Dame not only lost some games, but lost some players, too. Fullback Mike Lind and linebacker Myron Pottios were injured and lost for the year. And Jim Crotty, the team's best defensive back, was disabled for four games. Izo, one of the best passers in the country when he did play, got back into action later in the season to carry out Kuharich's high-powered, pro-type offense. The Fighting Irish were very exciting, if not highly successful—a good reason why their television replays were still drawing a big response around the country.

"Kuharich stresses offense first. . .and offense second!" said an observer. "When you score on his team, their idea is to go out and get a couple to take the lead away. He passes from his eight-yard line and keeps throwing after he gets a seven-point lead. His quarterbacks are not afraid to handle the ball on their goal line. They never kick on third down. Injuries have struck the first team, but they pour it on, win or lose."

But while people were enjoying watching Notre Dame's pro show, the Fighting Irish were not having a great time playing it. They lost five games in 1959 and needed season-ending victories over Iowa and Southern Cal to finish with a .500 season. "Any two boys can make a difference," Kuharich said of his injury-plagued squad. "In the last two games we recovered one offensive player and one two-way player (Izo and Crotty). We gained about 895 yards against Iowa and Southern California, and they gained a little more than 400 yards against us—we doubled their gain. With those two players we had a balanced team."

Kuharich's offense-minded teams were a distinct difference from those defensive squads produced during Terry Brennan's regime. It also became apparent after a while that the two coaches varied widely in their approach to life as well as their approach to football. "Joe shows his intensity more than Terry," was one observer's comment. Other comments went like this: "Kuharich goes to the pep meetings much more often than Brennan ever did. . .Kuharich leads a rather single-minded life. He coaches football and goes home. . .Terry plays golf with a certain amount of enthusiasm. Kuharich will play but not with the same interest. . .When you're with Kuharich, you feel that you're with a football coach. All he does is talk football. When you were with Terry, you talked about a variety of subjects. He wasn't consciously or subconsciously trying to twist the subject back to football. . .Joe's teams don't scrimmage as much—by quite a bit—as Terry's did."

Kuharich prepared everyone at Notre Dame for 1960 in the best pessimistic tradition of Frank Leahy. "We are not as strong now as when we started last season," he said; "1960 will be a solid question mark all the way."

It was worse than that. It was disaster with an exclamation point. At one time or another, nine boys who had been counted

Fidgety Joe Kuharich takes a sideline walk while Notre Dame engages Iowa.

on as starters were missing, plus a lot of reserves. Red Mack was out for the greater part of the year again, along with Pottios, Lind, Sefcik, Bob Scarpitto, Tom Hecomovich, John Powers, Ed Hoerster, Gerry Gray, and John Lineham. Notre Dame lost eight straight games and finished with a 2-8 record. Along with the injuries, the obvious thing that killed Notre Dame in 1960 was the lack of a strong quarterback, that crown jewel of the pro-type setting. Both Izo and Don White had graduated, and Kuharich experimented with several young hopefuls, including the eventual pro great, Daryle Lamonica. Nothing worked, and this time the alumni anxious for a return to former glory began to squirm a bit. And the Notre Dame students showed their displeasure openly with a march through campus. A small group of undergraduates walloped drums and chanted, "Down with excellence." It was an obvious blast at Notre Dame president Theodore M. Hesburgh, who had cited "a commitment to excellence" as the reason for Brennan's firing two years before.

Neither discontent by the populace nor fumbles on the field could force Notre Dame's administrators to lose faith in Kuharich. Shockingly, they gave him an unprecedented vote of confidence after the 1960 season with a three-year extension of his contract until February 1, 1966.

A great amount of injuries could excuse Kuharich from one mediocre year and another season of crushing ineptitude. But the dark fact remained that his teams had lost more games (13) in two seasons than Knute Rockne had in 13 years or Frank Leahy in 11 at Notre Dame. And Kuharich, who was hired to return the team to excellence, seemed to be going in the direction of total despair. Sportswriters, who had particularly taken umbrage with Brennan's firing, unleashed a torrent of strong words at the Notre Dame administration.

Jimmy Powers, writing in the *New York News*, was especially critical and seemed to reflect the popular feeling when he said: "Thousands of New Yorkers, loosely and somewhat inaccurately termed subway alumni, are understandably bewildered over the gyrations and inconsistencies of Notre Dame's athletic policies. A sound coach, a legitimate hero, a dedicated man of great charm, Terry Brennan, was fired a couple of years ago because the school stated its objective was 'excellence.' In his place was put a professional, Joe Kuharich. Kuharich completed a disastrous 2-8 record this year on top of a 5-5 for the lowest overall coaching record in the school's history. Taken by any measure—personality, charm, attendance or won-lost records—Kuharich comes out on the bottom. It is devoutly hoped that his superiors see in him the potential that escapes the eye of the sideline critic."

In 1961 the Notre Dame football team was like the little girl with the curl in the middle of her forehead, "very, very good or horrid. . ."

"It is hard to believe the same football team played the various parts of the schedule," wrote Joe Doyle in the *South Bend Tribune*. "One moment the Notre Dame team of 1961 seemed to be an eager, hustling squad that believed it could lick any opponent. At other times, it was indifferent, lethargic and unable to cope with anything out of the ordinary on offense or defense."

This was reflected in a 5-5 record that included the controversial victory over Syracuse. Notre Dame lost games by big scores, such as 42-21 to Iowa and 37-13 to Duke. But the Fighting Irish also won big, beating Southern California 30-0.

"One of the things that was amazing was that even though we were not playing good football in the three years I was there, we always beat Southern Cal," remembers Buoniconti. "No matter how bad we were, no matter where we played them or in what weather we played them, no matter what we did, we always ended up on the top side of those people. We played 'em in something like 10-degree weather in South Bend and beat 'em real bad. Then we went out and played 'em at Southern Cal in a pouring rain, the field was a total quagmire, and we still beat 'em."

But, obviously, beating Southern California was not the only object of the high-powered Notre Dame job. Notre Dame had to beat everyone else, and because Kuharich could not, he was let go after another 5-5 season in 1962. The pressures of winning at the end had bothered Kuharich so much that he once confided to a friend: "How did I ever end up here? I must be insane." An ally of the coach noted, "Joe just plain wanted out."

The Notre Dame job went to Hugh Devore—but not permanently. Devore, captain of the 1934 Fighting Irish team and a strong disciple of Knute Rockne, was named "interim" head coach. The personable Devore, as beloved a coaching figure who ever waved the Notre Dame colors, himself knew that he was only a stopgap measure while the search for another man was conducted. Devore, an old reliable at Notre Dame, had also been a pinch-hitter for Frank Leahy during the war years.

"I said then, and I'll say now, that I'll do whatever Notre Dame feels is best for me," said Devore, whose latest capacity had been with the freshman team prior to the 1963 season.

Devore slipped back into anonymity after a 2-7 season, although his accomplishments were quite obvious to the football wise. Notre Dame's gentle monarch had recruited big players to shore up a defensive line guilty of fourth-quarter power failures in 1963. He had improved the defense and morale, and he had collected and sharpened a group of excellent players that included quarterback John Huarte and end Jack Snow. This was all waiting for Ara Parseghian when he took over as head coach in 1964. The impatient dynamo, who had applied for the most challenging coaching job in college football, was about to embark on an odyssey of success, thanks to Devore.

Hugh Devore: "I'll do whatever Notre Dame feels is best for me."

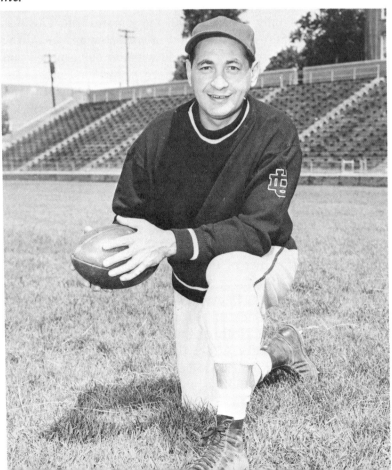

"Coaches Don't Build Houses"

"Mr. Parseghian is a little bit Napoleonic, but he sure knows what you have to do to win."—A Notre Dame player.

Ara Parseghian's first informal contact with the Notre Dame student body was made at a basketball game. He showed up as a spectator and was cheered for 10 minutes. Later there was an arranged rally at Sorin Hall, the senior dorm. This was February, and 2,500 students stood in the snow and heard the words they wanted to hear. "We will win football games," said the new coach. The rally started in an uproar and proceeded directly to bedlam, where it remained for quite a while.

Such a hysterical welcome was understandable, considering the pathetic state of Notre Dame football in the late 1950s and early 1960s. After having winning records in 63 of their first 67 seasons, the Fighting Irish went through a serio-comic era of six nonwinning years in eight. But Parseghian, an intense, vibrant man who had uplifted the football program at Northwestern, was heralded as the one who would deliver Notre Dame from the oppression of recent seasons. Notre Damers, reared on success, hoped to see it again in the era of Ara, and passions were aroused in every corner of the gorgeous campus in the winter, spring, and fall of 1964.

By the time Notre Dame rattled off nine straight victories and came within seconds of beating Southern Cal on the last day of the season, the Notre Dame populace was sure that the Fighting Irish were back where they belonged. Parseghian, as expected, was giving them something they had not had in years—excitement and triumph.

344

Ara Parseghian rides off into the sunset after a big victory.

Parseghian's achievement in his first year was all the more stunning because he accomplished a 9-1 season with practically the same material that had won but two games the year before. Parseghian's shrewd psychological sense and motivational genius had something to do with it. His indefatigable drive was another important element. But perhaps the most significant ingredient for Notre Dame's winning recipe that season was what Parseghian called "personnel alignment." He explained, "You've got to put the right man in the right job."

This preoccupied his time during 1964 when he shifted to Notre Dame after eight years at Northwestern. Parseghian made a split end out of Jack Snow, a player who had previously been used as a defensive end and sometime halfback. Coupled with quarterback John Huarte, this gave Notre Dame a devastating passing combination. Parseghian took a halfback of mammoth size, 240-pound Paul Costa, and turned him into a defensive end. This resulted in one of the strongest defensive lines in the country. He took fullback Pete Duranko and first made him a guard, then a linebacker, to shore up the backfield defense. He took the fastest halfback on the team and made a safety man out of him and made defensive halfbacks out of two of his quarterbacks. At one point during the season, Parseghian used one of his players as backup man at two positions—quarterback and split end.

Once satisfied with the alignment of players, Parseghian put them through torturous drills. Established on a command post on top of an old construction scaffold of metal tubing, Parseghian was a mercilous tyrant of all he surveyed. The players sweated under his watchful eye and wilted under his sharp tongue. Parseghian even scheduled a mile run by all players for 4 p.m. Sundays "to give them a sweat, loosen up their muscles before the Monday afternoon practice." The father of one of the players remarked with admiration: "None of the boys go astray on Saturday night; they're too tired. Parseghian gets them back to the campus and makes sure they're tired on Sunday night, too."

Parseghian's stern regimen was accepted—and even appreciated—by most of the football players. "We were waiting for something like this to happen," said fullback Joe Farrell. "You want the discipline. You want the hard work. As seniors, we were ready for him. We were tired of losing."

There were isolated cases of rebellion against the new order. When confronted by these, Parseghian at once established his supreme authority. On one occasion when one of Notre Dame's best players revolted against the Parseghian system, he was "fired" by the new coach. "You've had your chance," Parseghian told him. "As of this moment, you're off the squad."

Parseghian not only worked on their bodies, but their minds. He established a high emotional climate at Notre Dame. "This can be a successful team only if it is a proud team," he told his players. And all signs pointed to it, literally. At the entrance to the Notre Dame locker room was a huge sign in red letters that said, "Pride." On the wall of the locker room was a chart of the points scored by Notre Dame's opponents since 1946. Circled in red was the 1946 total of 24 with a note next to it: "Can you match this?"

Parseghian's ability to play on emotions was reminiscent of

346

Knute Rockne—and in fact, Parseghian probably came closer to the old Master in that respect than any other Notre Dame coach. Parseghian possessed eloquence beyond description but did not always have to speak to communicate with his players. As a friend explained, "Ara is one of those guys who can communicate through their very pores." His electric presence made locker rooms sizzle with emotion when he did speak, though. "Parseghian ranks, indisputably, as one of the most galvanic locker-room personalities since Rockne," a writer pointed out. Before one game against Purdue, Ara sent the team roaring out on the field with a bit of psychological inspiration truly worthy of Rockne.

He turned to halfback Nick Eddy and said so the whole team could hear: "Do you remember what you were doing at this time in 1951?" Before Eddy could answer, Parseghian said:

Notre Dame's latter-day Knute Rockne, Ara Parseghian.

"You were seven years old and dreaming of the day when you could play football at Notre Dame. You were seven years old—and that was the last time that Notre Dame lost to Purdue in Notre Dame Stadium." The Fighting Irish that afternoon crushed Purdue 34-15 in Notre Dame Stadium.

During his career he was not above using an old psychological play that was similar to the purest corn from the Rockne recipe book. When Parseghian was head coach of Miami of Ohio, back in 1954, he was preparing his team to play Indiana, a formidable antagonist from the Big Ten. Miami's final workout took place on Indiana's field the Friday afternoon before the game, and Parseghian brought along a set of practice uniforms that looked like hand-me-downs from Rockne's era. Wearing these old, torn uniforms, the Miami team went through the workout under the haughty stares of Indiana players, looking like a bunch of ragamuffins. The next day Miami turned up in gorgeous game uniforms and—suddenly spruced up and full of purpose—upset overconfident Indiana 6-0. As he gained more experience, Parseghian became more subtle and more sophisticated in his psychological approach. "There are great ranges to explore here," he said later at Notre Dame. "Ranges above and beyond what we realize. Emotional peaks—the ability to do things you just wouldn't realize you could do."

Along with the intangible influence of the psyche, Parseghian made some very visual influences on the field at Notre Dame. He revised the offense to such an extent that it was not recognizable from one year to the next. By 1964 Parseghian had installed a formation modeled on the professionals with a wide-open passing game. He simplified the play-calling system to make it less confusing for the players. "In the pressure of a game," he said, "you don't have time to listen to somebody yell '32' and ponder which hole is the 'three-hole' and which back is the 'two-back.' We just describe our plays in the most accurate way possible—like 'power sweep right.'" The unconventional Parseghian opened football practice to everyone in the school, not just those players on football scholarships, and got a tremendous response.

The campus vibrated with interest, and the players tingled with excitement. Remembers Snow: "Parseghian would give us a chance to show what we could do. He'd be in there with us, doing exercises, snapping the ball from center, showing us how to block and run. He told us we were good, made us believe in ourselves, gave us confidence." The coaching staff caught the Parseghian fever, too. He had brought in three of his aides from Northwestern and blended them harmoniously with the Notre Dame assistants already on hand.

"First thing," recalls offensive backfield coach Tom Pagna, "was to get the staff to believe in each other; then the squad to believe in the staff; and to believe in themselves. They developed a camaraderie. The offense cheered the defense and the reverse. You could see the feeling develop, feel the change. It began with *maybe* we can win, and it became we *are* going to win."

There was no doubt that Parseghian had serious intentions of remaking Notre Dame into a champion. Ignoring that old adage, "Coaches don't build houses," the optimistic Parseghian did just that before his squad played a single game. It was obvious that he meant to stick around a long time at South Bend.

Parseghian was in a hurry for success. He announced immediately upon his entrance to Notre Dame that he was seeking a national championship. He was denied it his first year by virtue of that loss to Southern Cal, but eventually he succeeded in winning two national titles for the Irish—in 1966 and 1973.

In a flash, Parseghian raised the Irish back to the national prominence enjoyed in the golden eras of Knute Rockne and Frank Leahy. His teams finished in the Top Ten nine of his 11 years at Notre Dame and wound up in the Top Twenty the other two. Parseghian's Notre Dame record of 95-17-4 exceeded the victories of Leahy and approached the stature of Rockne.

Parseghian's very makeup seemed streamlined for time-saving measures: black hair cropped close to his head so he could comb it with his fingers, a clip-on tie, loafers without laces, trousers with elastic waistbands. Time was his enemy, he insisted, and he beat it in a race hands down.

"You think in terms of objective and goal, and what you're trying to beat is time," he would say. "There is just so much of it. Every minute wasted is a minute lost forever. . ."

For this philosophy, Parseghian suffered in a personal purgatory. His working tempo was superhuman, and his sleeping hours were wildly irregular. Sometimes after games, it would take him 32 hours before he could relax enough to sleep. Finally, a doctor persuaded him to take some tranquilizers at one point. But even those could not fight his self-destructive body chemistry. "It's not easy. I mean I'll take one, and it'll put

A typical Saturday afternoon in fall—Notre Dame Stadium packed to the top.

me to sleep for a couple, three hours, then I get up and take another. But I find I get five, oh, 5½ hours of sleep. I get up early anyway. Five-thirty is my time that I get up during the season. Some games I may sleep late, 'til 6:30 if we've had success and it's easier sleeping."

The buildup to games created a unique torture in his system. "Before a game, his tension builds up almost to a point of suffering," explained his wife, Kathleen. "He has to choke back the tears."

It was pure irony that a man of such makeup would accept the ferocious pressures of the Notre Dame job. Parseghian insisted that it was not masochism that led him to South Bend. "I have this tendency to leave good things (Northwestern) and go on to other things that are attractive—that are attractive, I guess, because they are so tough," he explained. "The basic thing was that I said to myself, 'If I don't have the courage to take this job, then am I worthy of the one that I have? I mean, if I don't have the tenacity, the guts, the willingness to accept this responsiblity, under the so-called trying situation that exists, then am I really worthy of the job that I have?"

Notre Dame represented a symbol of success to Parseghian, and he hustled to land the coaching job. Notre Dame officials were impressed by his work at Northwestern, and more particularly impressed with the fact that he had beaten Notre Dame four straight times. Including his time at Miami, Parseghian had established a 74-41-2 record when he applied for the Notre Dame position.

Parseghian had some unsettling moments before he finally swore allegiance to the Notre Dame colors. While negotiations were going on for Parseghian's services, newspapers broke the story that he was already sewed up for the Fighting Irish family, but this was not the total truth. A press conference was called for what everyone assumed would be the announcement of his hiring, but Parseghian walked out of it and returned to Northwestern. There had been a disagreement with Father Edmund Joyce, chairman of the faculty board in control of athletics. Parseghian later laughed it off with some of his Armenian-bred humor: "Father Joyce wanted a shamrock on the new helmets, and I wanted a camel crossing the desert."

The real reason of the disagreement was never disclosed, but whatever it was, it was eventually resolved. Parseghian returned in a few days and signed a contract with Notre Dame. Moose Krause, the personable Notre Dame athletic director, introduced Parseghian to the alumni with a quip. "He should be with us a long time; after all, he signed twice."

It seemed pure destiny that Ara Raoul Parseghian had fulfilled the blind prophecy of a high school yearbook. "He will become football coach at Notre Dame," said the editor of the yearbook at South Akron High. The writer had no fact on which to base his judgment, only admiration for Parseghian's sheer intensity. Parseghian just looked like someone who was going places—fast. "I have to keep moving," Parseghian once said, and that just about summed up his life's work.

Perhaps if Parseghian's parents had known the tempo his life would take, they very likely would not have called him Ara. He was named after a ninth century B.C. Armenian king who strangled in his sleep while dreaming he was being chased by a roasted goat. During his years as a football coach, sleep was the least necessary of Parseghian's habits. An insomniac, he rarely got more than three hours at a stretch.

Parseghian was born on May 21, 1923, in Akron, Ohio, the second of three children to a French mother and an Armenian father. His mother apparently yearned for a girl, for she kept Ara in pinafores and long black curls for a painfully long time. He got out of the feminine attire finally when a sister was born two years later. Ara and his older brother, Gerard, were at first steered away from rugged boys' games and pushed toward the arts. Neither liked it very much. "My father wanted my brother—my poor brother—to be a violinist," says Ara with a grimace. Actually, the family would probably have settled for almost anything but football. Parseghian's parents regarded it as a game for ruffians, but Ara's natural inclinations eventually proved too strong for even parental rule. Parseghian tried out secretly for the South Akron High School team and finally convinced his reluctant parents to relax their militant stand against the game he loved so much. They did, and this decision ultimately led him to higher levels of football competence. After a short time at Akron University and a hitch in the navy, where he played under coaching master Paul Brown at Great Lakes, Parseghian entered Miami University at Oxford, Ohio. Here, Parseghian was honored as an all-Ohio halfback and received All-American mention in 1947, when Miami played in the Sun Bowl. After his graduation in June, 1949, Parseghian turned his back on an offer from the National Football League and joined Brown when his Cleveland team was tearing up the old All-America Conference. But a hip injury brought an end to his pro career after just one year.

Married and out of work, Parseghian went looking for employment. "There was only one thing that Ara didn't want to do," says his brother Gerard, "and that was coach. He thought coaches had to be nuts to put up with the stuff they did." Parseghian's wife, Katie, a college sweetheart, confirms this thinking. "I don't think Ara really ever thought about going into coaching in those days. I don't think he really wanted all that pressure. It was just something that evolved."

The evolution took place when Parseghian was offered the job as freshman coach at Miami under Woody Hayes. "I guess they liked the kind of work Ara did the previous spring when he was a student assistant there," says his wife. Parseghian accepted Hayes' offer—and everything happened at once. The freshman team went undefeated, and coaching "got into his blood," says his wife. Then Hayes left to coach Ohio State, and Parseghian suddenly found himself as the boss of the Miami team at the tender age of 27, the youngest head coach in the school's history. Ara stayed at Miami from 1951 through 1955 and compiled a fancy 39-6-1 record. Then he joined Northwestern at a desperate time in the school's football history. The Wildcats had won only one Big Ten game in three years. Teams were dropping off the schedule because of dwindling crowds, and players were dropping off the team because of dwindling interest. The school newspaper went so far as to suggest that the Wildcats drop out of the prestigious Big Ten Conference, but Parseghian's arrival changed this type of negative thinking. Parseghian could barely find enough players for a full-scale scrimmage at one point and suffered through an unbelievable injury jinx, but he still managed to match Northwestern's best record in 20 years. Parseghian's Northwestern teams, despite a general lack of depth through his eight years there, managed to rise to the top of the national polls at a couple of junctures and twice ran up winning streaks of six games. The Wildcats became giant-killers under their intense, fiery leader and drew national attention for several upsets, including a big one over Ohio State in 1958.

Along with the victories over Notre Dame, this stunning triumph was among Parseghian's sweetest memories at Northwestern. The Wildcats had lost all nine games the year before, and Ohio State was the Big Ten and Rose Bowl champions. "They hadn't lost in 15 games," Parseghian recalls. The memory of past humiliation spurred Northwestern on. Ohio State had routed Parseghian's team 47-6 the year before, and Ara felt that "Hayes had rubbed our noses in the dirt. I think the score was around 40-6 or 47-6, and he was playing his first ball club—his top kids!—against us for 55 or 58 minutes. In the last two or three minutes, he put in three or four ball clubs, one to go in and run one play, another to go in and run the next play. Then the next day you read where he was very tolerant with us and that he'd played 50-some boys. That irritated me—I'll be honest with you. I was very happy to beat him."

Northwestern's 21-0 victory over a far superior Ohio State team gave the Buckeyes their only defeat of the season and went down as one of the biggest upsets in Big Ten history. "We just put a man on every man's nose, guards and tackles, and let 'em hit," Parseghian says. "No tricks! No gimmicks! Just a superhuman effort! It was unbelievable!"

But Parseghian was well aware that Northwestern would not be beating Ohio State and teams of that caliber regularly. The Wildcats might rise up on occasion but would always slip backwards because of a lack of talent. This basic problem could not be cured by time. Thus Parseghian moved on to new fields at Notre Dame. The transition was not easy at first, he admits.

"There were natural transition problems that you would find at any university. Things like: understanding university policy; finding out who your helpers are; working in a new staff and assigning staff members certain recruiting territories. The job was further complicated by the fact that Notre Dame is a national institution. I knew that Notre Dame recruited on a national basis, but it was a great revelation, seeing it. It is a staggering experience to go through one week's mail."

Parseghian wasted little time getting the players he wanted—and just as quickly told them what he wanted out of them. "My first impression, he was very frank and forward," recalls safetyman Tom Schoen, a member of the first class recruited by Parseghian. "Extremely frank and forward! He outlined what he planned for X-number of years and what would be expected of us in return for the privilege of attending the university."

It was believed that Parseghian hoped to have a national champion in four years, but he was ahead of his timetable. He won it in three—and almost won it in one! The 1964 season was at once the most exhilarating and most depressing year for Notre Dame's new coach. After winning the first nine games of the year, Notre Dame had a 17-0 lead over Southern Cal at half time and the national championship all but won. But the Trojans made a remarkable comeback in the second half and pulled out a 20-17 victory in the last 93 seconds to end Parseghian's first year on a torturous note. It was easily one of the most bitter moments of his coaching career, but Parseghian gave humor that old college try. "I prefer to think of our record as 9¾ to ¼, not 9 and 1," he quipped.

By 1965 quarterback John Huarte and end Jack Snow had graduated, and the loss of one of the nation's best passing combinations slowed down the Parseghian express a bit. Opposing teams, knowing full well that Notre Dame only had a running game, stacked the line of scrimmage with eight, nine, and some-

John Huarte: Coolness under enemy fire.

times even 10 players. "On third and nine, we were in jail," said Parseghian. Still, against these odds, Parseghian's team had a 7-2-1 record, losing its two games by a mere total of 13 points. Parseghian perhaps cherished this season as much as any.

"It was a year I was really proud of because we won seven, lost two and tied one with a team that really didn't have a passing combination, so we had to play our guts out on defense," Parseghian recalls. "Our next to last game, we lost to Michigan State, 12-7, here at the stadium. Michigan State was undefeated and stayed that way (if you don't count the Rose Bowl loss). So that wasn't so bad. The final week we went down to Miami under very similar conditions to the Southern Cal trip of 1964. Hot, humid, a drastic change of climate from the cold midwest. We played to a tie. Everyone was up in arms because we didn't throw the ball more. We knew we couldn't throw. Because of our personnel, we had to play a possession-type game."

Finally, Parseghian had his national championship in 1966, although it was a bit tainted in some eyes. Notre Dame won nine games that year. But a 10-10 tie with Michigan State diminished the accomplishments of the season, and there was some opinion that the Fighting Irish did not deserve to be all alone at the top. In some quarters there were votes for co-champions. And some even went so far as to proclaim Michigan State the national champion by virtue of Parseghian's unpopular decision to play for a tie instead of a victory. In the last 75 seconds, Notre Dame had the ball on its 30 yard line but ran ball-control plays to eat up the clock instead of trying to score. This procedure, ordered by Parseghian, was greeted by boos from the stands and barbs from the press. Rushed from all sides by critics, Parseghian backpedaled and explained his reasoning. "If we had gotten field position, we would have gone for it. Back in our territory, I wasn't going to make it easy for them. For an interception would have given them a field goal shot."

It was a good thing for Notre Dame that a game still remained on its schedule. The Fighting Irish proved their excellence with a 51-0 drubbing of Southern Cal, and this sealed their position atop the wire service polls.

It was years before Parseghian could erase the bitter memory of 1964 and lose his reputation as the coach who played for a tie in the national championship game. For all his success at Notre Dame, he was sometimes branded as a man who could not win the big ones. He had lost two of three bowl games and somehow failed to complete a season without a loss or a tie through 1972. In 1973, however, Ara once and for all established himself as king of the college coaching hill. The Fighting Irish won all their games that year, including a 24-23 decision over Alabama in the Sugar Bowl that decided the national championship. Not only did Notre Dame complete a perfect season, but the Irish did it with a dramatic flair at the end, using a daring pass play deep in their territory to cement the game. The gamble, which easily could have turned in Alabama's favor had the pass been intercepted, was seen as a kind of vindication of Parseghian's distressing caution against Michigan State in 1966. The victory over Alabama was described by Notre Dame athletic director Moose Krause as "the most important game since Ara has been here."

One year later, with almost as much importance attached to their rematch in the Orange Bowl, Notre Dame beat Alabama again in a game that was staged with special dramatic effects. Notre Dame, slipping in the polls after a humiliation by Southern Cal, showed amazing resiliency by rising up to beat the Crimson Tide 13-11 and thus deny Bear Bryant's boys a national championship. This was Parseghian's last game, for he had announced his retirement after 11 years due to the exquisite pressures of the Notre Dame job. It was fitting that Parseghian went out on top, for he had started there. And it was fitting that he had given happiness to Notre Dame's followers, for he had given happiness to its players.

"He was a fantastic individual," says Terry Hanratty, one of the fine quarterbacks produced by Parseghian. "Playing for him was a real joy, both on and off the field."

Jack Snow found him communicative, a quality not discovered in any great quantity among the nation's top coaches. "He had a staff that could communicate exceptionally well with the athletes. That's probably the most important thing to have."

"The thing that impressed me most about Parseghian was that he didn't hide behind excuses," says Huarte. "In his first year, he could have made excuses for the Southern Cal loss. The way it turned out, there were about seven things that happened in the last quarter, and a lot of them were judgment situations. It would have been very easy for him to question the officiating, but he took the entire blame himself. That's what I remember more about Ara than anything else—his style and class."

Jim Seymour, an end of the late 1960s, calls Parseghian "not only one of the finest coaches I've ever been associated with, but one of the finest gentlemen. He does not forget you after you leave. I know a lot of ballplayers that have left other schools and had an empty feeling. But Ara kept in constant touch with his former ballplayers. If there was something he could help you with, he was more than willing to do it. This is what made him so unique. He's such a warm person after you get to know him; sometimes he puts on a cold front, but if you know the man, you know that he's happy for you when you're successful. Even when the chips are down, he'll go to bat for you. He's just a real beautiful person. Guys really looked up to him."

Tom Gatewood, a star receiver of the 1970s, thought of Parseghian as "the most complete college football coach in the country. . .speaking not only of his ability as a coach, but also his ability to deal with people. Our team wasn't regional in our schedule or our makeup, meaning it came from all walks of life and religion and from all parts of the country. Ara dealt with all kinds of people, and all kinds of problems came up while he was there. . .and his door was always open. There was never any standoffishness on his part. The greatest thing he gave me was the incentive to work hard, and he gave me the opportunity through an athletic grant-in-aid to achieve my athletic potential. I was a good student when I went there, but I was a better student when I left, and I was a better person as a result of him. You came into his office—and it was almost mandatory to come in and talk to him at least once a month. He'd always have a log sheet of not only my per-game catches and yardage, but he also had my academic records for the month. He was always abreast of your progress in the classrooms. He didn't want you to play for him if you weren't doing well in school. . . ."

Parseghian always felt that the "father complex" was very important in molding young players. But, actually, he became more than a second father to his players. He became a brother and a tackling dummy as well. Instead of sitting comfortably in an ivory tower, Parseghian came down into the trenches with his troops, not only rubbing elbows, but banging heads. He led calisthenics, ran pass patterns, and occasionally got racked up by his great defensive backs. "I can't coach from a tower," Parseghian once explained his seemingly masochistic impulses. "I must be in the huddle. I must be on the line. I must be in the action. I must be—I must feel a part of it."

And that, perhaps more than anything else, explained his extravagant success.

Ara Parseghian: "I must be in the huddle. I must be on the line. I must be in the action. I must feel a part of it."

No Joy In Mudville

"I still think the greatest rivalry in the country is Notre Dame and Southern Cal. They're always screwing each other up. Seems when you're going for a national championship, one team or the other will gum up the works."—Jack Snow.

A witch doctor would have had a ball in the Southern Cal dressing room. There were these half-naked young men tearing pictures of Notre Dame players off the walls, dancing on them, and chanting weird songs. They hollered and clapped and smacked each other on the back and sang blasphemous lyrics like, "Offense, offense, win one for the Gipper."

While the Trojans were brewing up this devilry, Coach John McKay was preparing more practical voodoo for the nation's top-ranked football team.

"We'll use a confusion rush," McKay said about his defensive setup. "We'll loop our tackles outside, use criss-cross stunts and play a three-deep secondary—very deep."

McKay, refusing to play sacrificial lamb to Notre Dame's 14-point favorites, also had some intricate plans for offense: "They play a split-6 defense with those big tackles slanting in. Everybody has tried to double-team their tackles, and their linebackers have taken advantage of the hole that creates to slip in and do a good job. We'll block down on the tackles with just one man and pull our guard behind him to take the linebacker. Then our ballcarrier can follow another back into the hole. We ought to be able to gouge our men through. And if we can make our inside running go, we can make our passing go."

For all these intense and complex preparations for the last

big game of the 1964 college football season, it boiled down to a simple pass play—something called "84-Z" in the Southern Cal playbook. The receiver splits wide to the left, delays for one second after the snap, sprints straight ahead for five steps, fakes outside, then cuts sharply down and across the middle of the field. The quarterback drifts straight back and throws to the spot. Craig Fertig worked the play perfectly to Rod Sherman for 15 yards and a touchdown with one minute and 33 seconds left in the game. The result was a 20-17 victory over Notre Dame in the biggest upset of the 1964 season.

The game spoiled a perfect season and denied a national championship for the Fighting Irish and burned a bitter memory into Coach Ara Parseghian's psyche. After that loss, Parseghian closed the locker room door and agonized with his team for 10 or 15 minutes before allowing anyone in. The scars still showed years later. "Be careful talking about it with Ara," a friend said a long time afterwards. "I don't think he's gotten over it yet."

"It was a big letdown," reflects Jack Snow, Notre Dame's great receiver of that season. "I thought—what a way to end up! You could see the guys' faces fall when Sherman went across for the score. The locker room was very silent, very still, a great deal of emotion. A lot of guys were crying, they were so upset. Ara didn't say much except that we had a good year and came a long way, and it was a shame that it had to end that way."

Even with that unsettling loss, Parseghian's accomplishments in his first season at Notre Dame were seen as downright miraculous. He had taken practically the same team that had lost seven of nine games under Hugh Devore the year before and smashed up through the Top Ten. After opening routs of Wisconsin, Purdue, Air Force, and UCLA, the Fighting Irish were booming toward the front of the class, and by the sixth game of the season, they had established a beachhead on top of the football world. One of the big reasons for this dramatic turnabout was the development of a great passing combination, quarterback John Huarte and Snow. Huarte had hardly enough playing time to qualify for a letter in his first two years, but Parseghian built him into the best college quarterback in the nation in 1964. By the time the season was over, the once-insecure player had set 12 Notre Dame records and tied another, winning the Heisman Trophy in the process.

Huarte's evolvement from sub to superstar was painful.

Jack Snow, one half of a great passing combination at Notre Dame.

Remembers Tom Pagna, one of the Irish coaches: "We looked for a kid with innate skills. John could throw. He had quick hands and feet, but he was not the aggressive natural leader a quarterback should be. Perhaps it had something to do with his failures of the two preceding seasons. He had to have confidence in himself before he could have the confidence of the squad. Ara told him: 'You're it. You're my quarterback.' That started his confidence flowing and his improvement. At first he would give the signal in the huddle as if it were a speech he had prepared. The time came when he barked it like an order. He learned and so did we. He had a tendency to throw off balance. We started to break him of that, but we stopped that when we realized that every quarterback has to throw off balance a good part of the time. The correct form on these things changes with every boy. It's the old story of the punter who kicks 70 yards until you start to coach him; then he kicks 30 yards."

Throughout spring training of 1964, Huarte learned to handle the ball and after a while was gliding and doing magic tricks with Parseghian's "run-action" offense. "We drilled over and over on his faking," says Pagna. "His quick hands, quick feet, poised perceptions made him an easy pupil. He became a truly great ballhandler and faker; and a leader, an intellectual-type who performed, who was followed because of what he had done and could do."

All the preparation for the season, however, seemed lost when Huarte came up with a shoulder separation. He was scheduled for an operation, but Parseghian intervened at the last moment. The coach phoned surgeons as far away as Rome to get their views and decided that the best thing would be to let the wound heal naturally. There was a 50-50 chance that way for Huarte to resume his career. Otherwise, an operation might doom him to the sidelines for 1964. Huarte agreed that it was best to let nature and exercise provide the therapy for his ailing arm and worked with Snow on summer beaches. There was naturally some apprehension when Notre Dame opened against Wisconsin. "On the way to Wisconsin," said Pagna, "I prayed that he would get off well."

None of the Notre Dame coaches or players had any doubt about Huarte's complete recovery after that game, though. Huarte hit Snow with a pass right away and then went on to complete 15 of 26 for 217 yards as the Irish walloped the Badgers 31-7.

Purdue visited Notre Dame the next week with a fine quarterback of its own, Bob Griese. The Boilermakers, who had won five of the last six games in the series, looked like spoiler-makers again when they drove 75 yards for a quick touchdown. "I'm sure there was a feeling then that the Wisconsin game was a fluke," Snow says. "But we showed 'em afterwards." Notre Dame's defense, led by 260-pound Kevin Hardy and 230-pound Alan Page, wrecked the Purdue offense and helped the Irish win going away, 34-15. "That was the big one," Snow remembers.

The new Fighting Irish were not only big and fast, they were tricky. Huarte's sleight-of-hand artistry not only fooled the opposition but the cameramen and broadcasters, who had a hard time picking up the ball. Huarte's fakery in the backfield had Ara Parseghian and his staff applauding and raving on the sidelines all season. "We were jumping jacks all year long," laughs John Ray, the defensive coach.

Against Air Force, Huarte threw a 47-yard bomb to Nick Eddy, and this would continue to be a specialty for Notre Dame's rising star. His long passes led the Irish to a 34-7 victory that day and pushed Huarte toward a Notre Dame record. By the end of the season, he would accumulate 2,062 passing yards, breaking the old mark of 1,374 set by Bob Williams in 1949. Notre Dame's rise in national standing paralleled Huarte's rise as a player. After the victory over Air Force, the Irish were raised to fourth place in the national ratings.

UCLA, featuring the nation's total offense leader in Larry Zeno, came into South Bend the fourth week of the season following impressive victories over Pitt, Penn State, and Stanford. But the Bruins did not look impressive after they left. With Huarte outpitching Zeno and Notre Dame's "Fearsome Foursome" of Page, Hardy, Tom Regner, and Don Gmitter shutting off the UCLA offense, the Irish chased the Bruins out of town with an embarrassing 24-0 defeat. Now Notre Dame was No. 2 in the wire service polls, just behind Ohio State.

On the following week Stanford proved itself incapable of handling either Notre Dame's offense or defense. Huarte set a Notre Dame record with 21 pass completions and accounted for 300 yards. The West Coast team did not make a first down until midway in the third period, and its total offense was a meager one yard rushing and 55 passing. Notre Dame ran away with it, 28-6.

When Notre Dame beat Navy and its heralded quarterback, Roger Staubach, 40-0 on the sixth weekend of the season and Ohio State barely escaped defeat at Iowa, the Irish were raised to the No. 1 ranking. The Irish then beat Pittsburgh, Michigan State, and Iowa to certify their position atop the polls. The only uneasy decision of their first nine victories came in the

Knute Rockne looks on in approval as Ara Parseghian poses with Heisman Trophy winner John Huarte.

Pittsburgh game, which Notre Dame won 17-15 with the help of a school record 91-yard touchdown pass play from Huarte to Eddy. A stunning 34-7 victory over Michigan State and smashing 28-0 triumph over Iowa set the stage for Southern Cal, a team given little chance of beating Notre Dame.

Notre Dame had a glittering 9-0 record, the best defense in the nation and the second-best offense, as well as a stack of All-American players in Huarte, Snow, linebacker Jim Carroll, and defensive back Tony Carey. The Trojans had already lost three games, and the way their coach was thinking outwardly, it looked like it was going to be four. "I studied the Notre Dame-Stanford film for six hours last night, and I have reached one conclusion: Notre Dame can't be beaten," McKay said on the Monday before the game in the Los Angeles Coliseum.

As the week grew short, McKay's pessimism enlarged, it seemed. He announced on Tuesday, "I've decided that if we play our very best and make no mistakes whatsoever, we will definitely make a first down."

And by Wednesday McKay was seen cutting into a steak with a dour expression. "The condemned man ate a hearty meal," he said.

It was all subtle bombast, of course. While McKay played his part outwardly as the underdog, he was not thinking that way. He had announced to the world: "We can't run on Notre

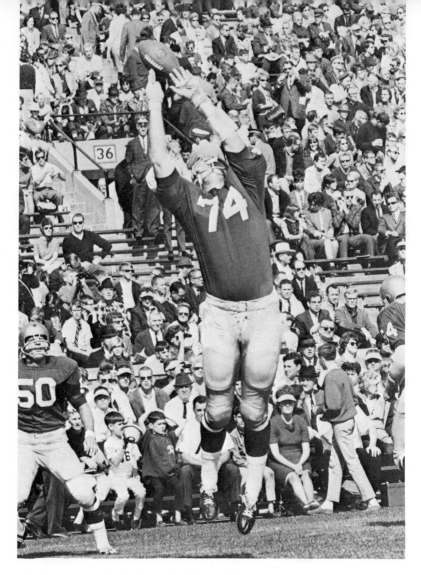

Kevin Hardy gives it that old college try.

Dame. Their tackles weigh 262 and 245, and nobody has blocked them yet. We'll have to run outside and pass." But he himself did not believe it. McKay fully expected to run inside on Notre Dame, and he had the runner to do it in little Mike Garrett. And if Garrett could make the running go, McKay reasoned, then quarterback Craig Fertig would get the aerial game off the ground.

The morning of the game portended no good for Southern Cal. At the team breakfast, linebacker Ernie Pye accidentally walked through a plate glass window and was lost to the team.

This bad luck seemed to carry over into the game. The Trojans could do nothing right in the first half. A fumble led to a 25-yard field goal by Notre Dame's Ken Ivan. A clipping penalty stalled a Trojan drive, and Huarte moved the Irish 74 yards for a touchdown, overcoming two 15-yard penalties along the way. Snow, making one of his 60 catches that year, hauled in a 21-yarder from Huarte that gave Notre Dame a 10-0 lead. Later Huarte took Notre Dame on a 72-yard drive that culminated with Bill Wolski's touchdown run. It was 17-0 Notre Dame at the half, and the Irish looked every bit like a national champion, although there was no "national championship" talk in the locker room at half time, remembers Snow.

"Ara never harped on the national championship," he recalls. "He said there was just 30 minutes left and told us to go out and finish up a great season. He said, 'We've got a good lead, we're in a good position to wind up looking good. Let's play the kind of ball we can play.'"

Parseghian, nor anyone else, expected what was to happen next. While he was giving his pep talk in the Notre Dame locker room, an amazingly confident McKay was telling his players that they could win: "Our game plan is working. Keep doing your stuff, and we'll get some points." McKay told a companion: "If we can get on the scoreboard quick, we can put some pressure on 'em. They won nine games without any duress. If we can make this thing close, they might not know how to react."

Southern Cal's inside runs worked well from the start of

With the help of Nick Eddy's running, Notre Dame crushed Iowa 28-0 for its ninth straight victory in 1964.

the second half, with Garrett and Ron Heller squeezing through huge holes created by the Trojan tackles. Fertig called a brilliant game, alternating runs and passes. Soon Southern Cal was within scoring range, and Garrett took the ball over to cut Notre Dame's lead to 17-7. Huarte rallied the Irish on a crackling drive that smashed to the Trojan nine, but a fumble curtailed it. Later a holding penalty hurt the Irish even more. They scored a touchdown, but it was nullified by the penalty.

"To my mind, that was a very questionable call," says Snow. "But I guess when things are going bad, there's not much you can do about it. We didn't get any breaks in the second half, and they did. . .and you could see them kind of eating away at us."

Now the momentum was in Southern Cal's favor, and while a wildly joyous crowd of 83,840 whooped and gasped, Fertig led the Trojans to another touchdown. "I knew we had 'em then," said McKay, extravagantly optimistic by now. "The momentum was all ours. In a situation like that, the No. 1 rating is a fairly suffocating thing."

Unable to move against the suddenly revitalized Trojans, Notre Dame was forced to punt. Garrett fielded Snow's kick and ran the ball 18 yards back to the Notre Dame 35 yard line with only two minutes and 10 seconds to go in the game. On first down Garrett cracked into the middle of the stubborn Notre Dame defense and failed to get an inch. On second down Fertig shot a pass to Fred Hill to bring the ball to the Irish 17 for a first down. Now the fans in the coliseum had raised the noise level another notch, if that was possible. Fertig threw a pass to Garrett which carried out of bounds on the 15. The scream level reached higher. On the following play Hill made a diving grab of a Fertig pass but was ruled out of bounds in the end zone. Fertig missed on the next pass, setting up a fourth-down-and-eight situation on the Notre Dame 15 with one minute and 43 seconds left.

Fertig called the "84-Z," and the play unfolded perfectly. The quarterback found Sherman clear of Tony Carey, the Irish defender, and fired a chest-high pass to the receiver for a touchdown that ruined the season for Notre Dame but provided a Hollywood ending for the delirious crowd. "I watched the way their halfback reacted, and I figured I could beat him," Sherman explained later.

"It was a tough loss," recalls Huarte, "but on the other

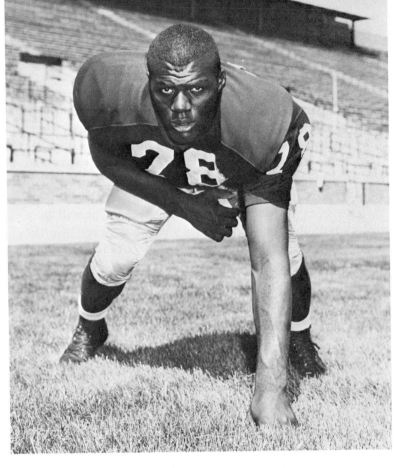

One of the "Fearsome Foursome," Alan Page.

hand, we came out of nowhere. Nobody expected Notre Dame to win as many games as we did. It was a rebuilding year for a new coach, and with all this we went roaring through the year and won nine straight games and almost won our tenth game. It was a fantastic success, a terrific, miraculous turnabout from what had taken place the previous eight years. We really captured the imagination of a lot of people. After some years of mediocrity, Notre Dame had finally come back as a first-class power. We should have gotten 98 per cent of the cake."

Notre Dame was dropped from No. 1 to No. 3 in the polls but still managed to get a slice of the "cake," anyway. The Football Hall of Fame presented the Irish with the MacArthur Bowl: "For consistency in championship performance, winning its first nine games against major colleges from East to West by an average of 21 points and leading in its 10th game for 58 minutes and 25 seconds, when Southern Cal rose to insuperable heights to win the game, 20-17, Notre Dame has been adjudged the outstanding team of the year."

But even this prestigious honor could not diminish all the pain in the Notre Dame camp. Father Theodore Hesburgh, the Notre Dame president, seemed to reflect the mood when he wrote shortly after that stunning loss to Southern Cal:

"It's dark and cold outside. I'm too old to cry and not old enough not to feel hurt. . .We can never be sure of total victory, not even of eternal salvation, until we've won it. Life goes on, the challenge remains, and it will be a really dark day and cold place here if we ever lose the desire to be No. 1 in everything we do, or lack grace and style and humanity in doing it."

The College Superbowl

"You could have dropped a bomb in the dressing room, and it wouldn't have shaken the guys. They were just sitting there, thinking back. . .not about the fact that we had tied it, but what they were reflecting on was whether they had done the job that Ara had expected, whether they had let Ara down personally because it was such a tremendous buildup, and the guys were really pumped up all week for the game."—Jim Seymour.

Notre Dame 10, Michigan State 10. No game that decided so little had so much of an impact on the college football world. For a tie, it was certainly nothing like kissing your sister, as the saying goes.

What had been heralded as a battle for the national championship fizzled to a less-than-satisfactory conclusion—and a loss in prestige for Notre Dame, a stigma for Coach Ara Parseghian, and an uproarious battle for position in the national polls.

The derision was turned toward the Fighting Irish not so much for the fact that they had played to a tie in the eagerly anticipated "game of the century" in 1966, but how they did it. Notre Dame had a chance to win it at the end but played conservatively and rode out the clock with time-consuming ground plays instead of the expected passes. And this was the coward's way out, in most eyes.

"We couldn't believe it," said George Webster, Michigan State's brutish rover back. "When they came up for their first play, we kept hollering back and forth, 'Watch the pass, watch the pass.' But they ran. We knew the next one was a pass for sure. But they ran again. We were really stunned. Then it dawned on us. They were settling for a tie."

With the ball in the vicinity of the Notre Dame 30 yard line, and time ticking away, the Michigan State players stood there with their hands on their hips, disdainfully glaring at their opponents. The Spartans on the sidelines were jeering and taunting the Irish and hollering across the field at Parseghian's solemn figure. The Spartans on the field were equally as disparaging.

"Come on, you sissies," sneered Bubba Smith, Michigan State's ferocious defensive end.

"I was saying, 'You're going for the tie, aren't you? You're going for the tie?'" said Webster. "And you know what? They wouldn't even look us in the eyes. They just turned their backs and went back into their huddle."

Parseghian, who had ordered the indistinguished strategy, later defended his views. "We fought hard to come back and tie it up. After all that, I didn't want to risk giving it to them cheap. They get reckless, and it could have cost them the game. I wasn't going to do a jackass thing like that at this point."

Thus ended the game that had been built up as the biggest affair in two decades. Not since 1946 when Notre Dame and Army played to a scoreless tie in a battle for the No. 1 ranking had a game had so much frenzy and fanfare attached to it. The attention devoted to these teams increased each week as both Notre Dame and Michigan State beat their opponents easily, and the week before the game was devoted to daily press conferences, a la Super Bowl. While the crowds of newspapermen swelled each day, both Parseghian and Michigan State coach Duffy Daugherty had to play the game over and over ahead of time. Parseghian pointed out that it looked like the match had been made in heaven since Notre Dame had an 8-0 record and was ranked No. 1, and Michigan State was 9-0 and No. 2. Daugherty said it was a shame that such games came along only every few years in college football. And both coaches said that they had told their teams that this would be one of the biggest days of their lives.

None of the Notre Dame players doubted it. When they stepped off the train in East Lansing the Friday before the game, they were a grim-looking lot. And they were made grimmer when they found out that Nick Eddy, Notre Dame's best ballcarrier, would not start. Eddy had hurt himself in a freak accident getting off the train. Terry Hanratty, the Notre Dame quarterback, remembers: "It was snowing that day and the angle of the steps coming off the train was really sharp, and the steps were a little slippery. He had a bad shoulder to begin with, and he came down and caught his shoulder on the rail and jerked it up." Sophomore Bob Gladieux was told that he would start the biggest game of the 1966 season at left halfback.

The injury jinx carried over into the game. Hanratty himself was lost to Notre Dame during the course of the vicious battle. The sensational sophomore was racked up by the six-foot-seven, 285-pound Smith early in the first quarter and suffered a shoulder separation. That brought in little Coley O'Brien, who suffered from diabetes and needed two insulin shots a day to play.

"That didn't help us any," Bubba said later. "It just let them put in that O'Brien who's slippery and faster and gave us more trouble. The other guy just sits there and waits, and that's what we wanted."

Along with Hanratty, halfback Rocky Bleier and center

Terry Hanratty takes off for some of his record-breaking yardage. During his time at Notre Dame, he surpassed George Gipp's career total.

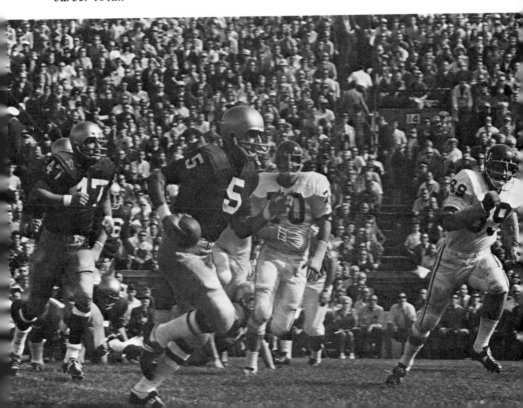

George Goeddeke also were lost to injuries, and Jim Seymour, Notre Dame's great end, recalls: "It was probably the hardest physical game we ever played in. The hitting was unbelievable, it really was. It was a very vicious game."

The passing of Jimmy Raye and the speed of Gene Washington, the Big Ten hurdles champion, had helped Michigan State sprint to a 10-0 lead early in the second quarter. A long pass from Raye to Washington set up the Spartans' first touchdown, a blast into the end zone by Regis Cavender. "I can look in a man's eyes and know whether I can beat him," said Washington after catching Raye's 42-yard bomb. "I knew I could beat those guys all day." Raye hit Washington again for 17 yards, setting up Dick Kenney's field goal.

When O'Brien came into the game for Notre Dame, the complexion changed to blue and gold. Less than two minutes after the Spartans had made it 10-0, O'Brien threw a 34-yard scoring pass to Gladieux. Then, late in the third quarter, O'Brien frantically drove Notre Dame toward the Michigan State goal line again. The Irish were denied a touchdown this time but did get a 28-yard field goal out of Joe Azzaro that tied the contest at 10-10 and sent it toward its bitter conclusion.

The look of things had changed. Michigan State, easily the better team in the first half, no longer seemed so sure of itself. Notre Dame was the dominator now, and when safety Tom Schoen picked off a wild Raye pass and brought the ball back to Michigan State's 18 yard line, it seemed surely the Irish would win. Larry Conjar plunged into Michigan State's hefty line and dug out two yards for the Irish. But on the next play, Phil Hoag and Smith cracked through into the Notre Dame backfield and nailed halfback Dave Haley for an eight-yard loss. O'Brien failed with a frantic third-down pass, and Notre Dame, instead of trying a field goal from a cozy position, had to kick from 42 yards out. Azzaro missed with 4:39 to go.

"That Haley play," Parseghian said later, shaking his head. "That was just a leakage. We leaked a guy through—blew an assignment." The coach stared at the floor. "Damn," he said.

Then there were 75 seconds left, and Notre Dame had the ball on its 30 after an aborted Michigan State drive. And there was O'Brien, heeding Parseghian's orders to run ball-control sneaks. There was no pretense at a pass, the only play that could save the day and save face for Notre Dame before the crowd of 80,011 at Spartan Stadium and a national television

374

The "Baby Bombers"—Jim Seymour (left) and Terry Hanratty.

audience.

"Boos rolled down from the stands at this un-Irish decision to settle for a draw," wrote Jesse Abramson in the *New York World Journal Tribune*.

Halfback Clint Jones, one of the Michigan State co-captains, had nothing but disdain for the Irish decision to play it safe. He reflected the mood of the Spartans when he said: "I knew they were good, and I was willing to call them great—until they did what they did at the end. I think we're the champions."

"We were the dominating ball club most of the game," said Daugherty. "Now they should rate us No. 1 and Notre Dame, 1A."

Seymour, an applauded sophomore and part of the lyrically acclaimed "Baby Bombers" team with Hanratty, had an atrocious game and a bitter aftertaste. He did not catch a pass all day, but that did not bother him as much as the final score. "It was the worst kind of depression coming off the field after working that hard and coming out with a tie," Seymour recalls. "Everybody goes back to the fact that we didn't throw the ball, but what they don't realize is that we couldn't throw the ball because they had set up a specific defense to stop the pass. . . and our quarterback was so run down because of his diabetic problem that he couldn't throw the ball more than 10 yards. And they were set for it. So why throw the ball for an interception and really hang yourself? Ara's been questioned many times about that decision and accused of not winning the big one. But there was nothing else he could do under the circumstances."

Smith, one of the more vocal Michigan State players, said he wanted to keep playing until there was a winner. But apparently few others had that much stamina. Recalls Hanratty: "Nobody can be happy with a tie. It was a helluva ballgame, but we were all so tired, I don't think anyone wanted to go into a fifth quarter."

Actually, Notre Dame did well to tie the powerful Big Ten champions that day. It was Michigan State's last game of the year, and the Spartans "could let everything hang out," as Seymour put it. Notre Dame, on the other hand, still had dangerous Southern Cal, a Rose Bowl contestant, waiting in Los Angeles for the final game of the season. "State had nothing to lose, where we couldn't afford to wreck our team," Seymour says. "I tell you, losing as many players as we did in that game, we were lucky to come out as well as we did."

The result triggered one of the biggest controversies of the year: Who was No. 1? Everybody had a say, but nobody really knew. Parseghian, of course, voted for Notre Dame and said the Irish at worst should be co-leaders with Michigan State. Daugherty, casting his ballot in the United Press International coaches' poll, split his ticket—making both Notre Dame and Michigan State No. 1.

"I still think there should be co-champions," Daugherty said.

The Irish got more first-place votes than the Spartans in the UPI poll but less overall points. On the strength of a strong second-place showing, Michigan State vaulted into first, a shade ahead of Notre Dame. The sportswriters who voted in the Associated Press poll, on the other hand, kept the Irish in front—by a whisker.

"I see no reason why we should move down," reasoned Parseghian. "After all, the No. 2 team didn't beat us."

Notre Dame got to play the last card of 1966, and it

turned out to be a blockbuster—a 51-0 grand slam over Southern Cal. The impressive victory over the bowl-bound Trojans returned the Irish to the top of the UPI poll the following week and established them as national champions everywhere except, perhaps, in East Lansing, Michigan.

"I hope we'll be pardoned for feeling we're every bit as good a team and deserving of at least an equal rating," Daugherty said, answering the decision of the polls. "It's unfortunate that you can't have co-champions because it's difficult to determine how you could possibly rate one team over another."

It is likely that, had Notre Dame not beaten Southern Cal so decisively, it would have been a doubtful champion in many eyes—not only Daugherty's.

The overwhelming importance of the Trojan game was mirrored in Parseghian's actions before and during the battle. Remembers Seymour:

"Before that game, he came into the locker room and wasn't like himself. Normally he would leave the ballplayers completely alone, except for maybe talking to the quarterbacks or the receivers about certain plays to make sure they had them down cold. But this time he came into the locker room, and after we knelt down in prayer, he went over to the blackboard and wrote down '1964' and circled it and said, 'Let's go.' He was referring to two years before when he was 9-0 and came out to Los Angeles and got beat and lost the national championship."

This game was strangely similar to the one in 1964 in some respects, but Parseghian was not about to blow another national championship.

"We're ahead 17-0 with about two minutes to go before the half," remembers Seymour, "and Ara was going nuts at this time. All he could see was that we were going in 17-0 at halftime, just like they did in 1964 and got beat 20-17. Well, the Trojans fumbled the ball, and Ara called time out. He wanted another touchdown to take into the dressing room. He called quarterback Coley O'Brien over and asked him, 'How far can you throw the ball?' And Coley said, 'Way on out to the end zone.' And Ara said, 'All right, put it up.' He told me, 'Run out there and catch it.' And that's exactly what we did, and we went ahead and kicked off, and they fumbled again, and Ara said to get another one. And we went in and got another touch-

377

down and went in leading at halftime something like 30-0. He told us at the half, 'Don't come down.' We went out for the second half and just kept going where we left off. And once he saw we had them beat good, he finally pulled out the first stringers."

It is said that Southern Cal coach John McKay never forgave Parseghian for that humiliation. "There's been no love lost between Ara and McKay," notes Seymour. But the Trojans need not have felt so bad after all, since they were beaten by Notre Dame's most-honored team in history. No fewer than 11 Notre Dame players on the 1966 team were voted on All-American first teams—halfback Nick Eddy, fullback Larry Conjar, receiver Jim Seymour, linebacker Jim Lynch, guard Tom Regner, defensive end Alan Page, defensive tackles Pete Duranko and Kevin Hardy, tackle Paul Seiler, center George Goeddeke, and defensive back Tom Schoen. In addition, Lynch

Nick Eddy runs—and it is full steam ahead for Notre Dame.

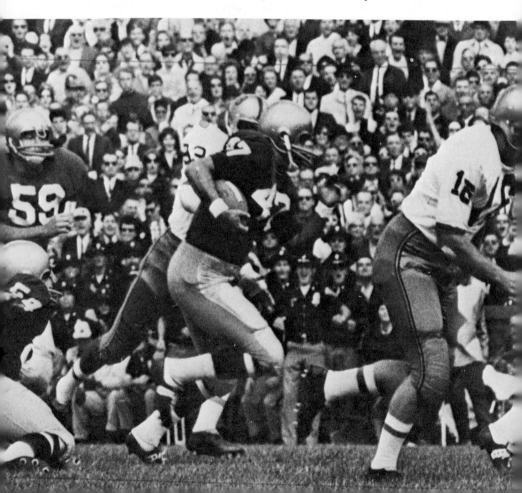

won the Maxwell Trophy as the outstanding player in the nation.

This compilation of talent compared favorably with the great Notre Dame teams of the past, and Parseghian insisted that it was the best squad he had ever coached through his 16 years in college. And so he did not mind in the least when these talented mammoths threw him into the shower at the Los Angeles Coliseum. It seemed to wash away the bitter aftertaste of the Michigan State game once and for all.

Unhooking The Horns

"I guess a defeat is good for you now and then, but I don't really recommend it."—Texas coach Darrell Royal.

Notre Dame's assignment in the 1971 Cotton Bowl seemed like something out of "Mission Impossible."

"It must stop the number one scoring team in the nation, the number one rushing team in the nation and the team with the nation's longest winning streak," said a Notre Dame press release.

Ara Parseghian, the high-strung Notre Dame coach, appeared ready to self-destruct.

"I can think of a lot of better ways to spend the holidays than trying to defense Texas' triple option," he said. "Texas is truly an awesome team. They come as close to perfection as you can get. Their execution and timing are incredible, and their lack of errors and turnovers is unbelievable."

Nothing went according to the script, though. Joe Theismann, described by one sportswriter as "a lean strip of bacon wrapped around a long straw," hit the haughty Texans with a couple of quick touchdown strikes. And the Longhorns proved entirely human with a series of costly mistakes. At the end, it was too many fumbles and too much Theismann that cost them the game and their reputation. The stinging 24-11 decision not only stopped the Longhorns' glamorous 30-game winning streak but blasted away their national championship hopes.

It turned out that Parseghian worked his miracle with "mirrors." Hoping to stop Texas' high-powered Wishbone offense, the Notre Dame coach installed a defense that reflected

Notre Dame players sweat out calisthenics prior to the 1971 Cotton Bowl game with Texas. Hard work paid off, for the Irish beat the Longhorns 24-11 on New Year's Day.

the Longhorns to a T. He later explained:

"We decided we'd have to mirror Texas to stop the Wishbone. Our people lined up in a defensive Wishbone. This forced us to play man-to-man on the run downs. If they passed, we had to take the risk. We were trying to force them to throw, and they did what we wanted them to do. We tried to make Texas play left-handed. We knew they wanted to run 90 percent of the time. So we wanted to make them pass instead of run. With our interior secondary, our people lined up in a Wishbone, too, with the secondary and the middle linebacker keying on Texas halfbacks and fullback. They had to go to the air, and we felt then the percentages were equalized, and their Wishbone running was neutralized."

This stunning defensive setup had the dramatic effect of pulling the Texas Wishbone apart. Steve Worster, the Longhorns' great runner, was shut down with 48 yards rushing, four fumbles, and a broken nose. Jim Bertelsen, another big Texas running threat, was only able to get five yards on the ground. The nation's leading rushing team was held to 216 yards on the ground, many of them by quarterback Eddie Phillips.

It was not only done with mirrors, however. Notre Dame's brute force had something to do with it, also. Texas coach Darrell Royal acknowledged: "Notre Dame was large enough physically inside that we couldn't get a crease for Worster. They were a big, tough football team. That's a lot of beef they threw at us in the middle."

Some of the "beef" belonged to Greg Marx, a 250-pound tackle. He and Mike Kadish made life unbearable for Worster, the heralded Longhorn star. "Before the game we had a slogan," Marx said. "Woo-Woo was the big man. Worster really got hit today. That was a battered Steve Worster who went off the field. Hard hitting made the breaks we got. We knew we had to make our own breaks."

While the Notre Dame line was making it rough for the Texas offense, Theismann was doing the same to the Texas defense. He ran for two touchdowns and passed for another to his favorite receiver, Tom Gatewood. "We ran good enough to keep them honest," Theismann said after the game. "If you can't run on Texas, you're in trouble."

This prestigious victory, called "one of the big moments in Notre Dame football history" by Parseghian, had a soothing therapeutic effect on the Irish. It helped heal two fresh wounds—one inflicted as recently as a month before. The Irish were out to prove that a 38-28 defeat by Southern Cal in the last game of the season was a fluke and were out to revenge a controversial 21-17 loss to Texas the year before in the Cotton Bowl.

"We thought we had the best team in the country in 1970," says Gatewood, the record-breaking Irish receiver. "We lost to Southern Cal in the rain, and we had a point to prove. We wanted one more showing before a national audience to show that we had a pretty good football team."

Perhaps even more galling than the loss to Southern Cal was the previous year's defeat to Texas. It was Notre Dame's first bowl game in 45 years, and it might have been a success except for a disputed call by the officials shortly before the end of the first half. Leading 10-7, Notre Dame was driving toward the Texas goal line when the march was stopped by a pass interception on the Texas 14. As the teams lined up for the next play, with the Longhorns in possession, a 240-pound Texas guard named Randy Stout was seen racing onto the field, waving his arms wildly. Before he reached the line of scrimmage, the ball was snapped. James Street, the Texas quarterback, was smothered by a gang of Notre Dame linemen and fumbled the ball. Notre Dame recovered on the Longhorns' six yard line with 1:57 left. The Irish fans, sensing the possibility of a touchdown, went wild. But they were soon subdued when the officials gave the ball back to Texas on the 14, first down as before. The officials ruled that there was a time out called before the play, but if there was, they were the only ones who heard it. Protests came from the Notre Dame bench, but the decision stuck, and the bizarre "twelfth man" episode eventually proved critical when Texas came from behind to win at the end. Theron P. Thomsen, a Big Ten field judge who was on the Texas side of the field, supported Stout's statement. "He signaled for a time out, and I blew the whistle before the snap," he said. The referee, Cliff Domingue of the Southwest Conference, negated the play after Thomsen advised him of the time out call. "I thought I heard a whistle," he said, "but I wasn't sure."

Notre Dame and Texas in the Cotton Bowl: Always a battle.

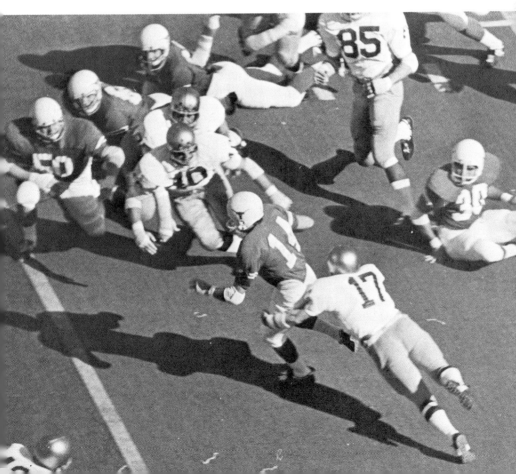

If there was a time out called, Parseghian was not sure it was legal. He was understandably agitated. "If the ball is snapped and put in play, then it's our choice. I don't know who called time out. The substitute can't call time out because he isn't in the game until he is recognized. And I asked the official on our side, 'How in Heaven's name can they keep from being penalized for having a twelfth man on the field?'"

More bitterness later came out of the game when a Texas player let go with a belated blast at the Irish. Bobby Wuensch, the Longhorns' offensive tackle, charged Notre Dame's players with unnecessary roughness after plays. "They were poor sports and always wanted to fight, and the football field is no place to fight," Wuensch said. Wuensch insisted that the Irish were not only rough with their bodies, but their mouths as well. "I couldn't believe the way they bad-mouthed Steve Worster."

These potshots at Notre Dame missed the mark by a wide margin, said Irish defensive back Chuck Zloch. "I and my teammates are surprised and appalled at his statements. The tackle said that we were trying to intimidate them after the play. There was nothing to the alleged bad stunts we were pulling on defense. There were a few words being said back and forth, but nothing that you wouldn't have in any other high-tension game. This was for the No. 1 ranking, and emotions were high. But as far as we're concerned, the charges are inaccurate."

It was the fashion to either take potshots or throw things at Notre Dame in 1969. Before the verbal blast from the Texas player, the Irish had felt the slings and arrows of Georgia Tech students. Remembering that 38-20 victory at Georgia Tech, Zloch says: "They threw everything from filled beer cans to dead fish at us. And there was nothing dirty done by the football players that provoked the Georgia Tech student body. We got some bad-mouthing from their players, but the majority of abuse came from the students who were sitting right behind our bench." At half time the students presented the Notre Dame players with their card section—the entire card section. "If those cards had hit someone, it would have been bad news. It really got bad in the second half, but nobody on our side lost his cool. We've got more class than that."

The 1969 season, though not as glamorous as the national championship year of 1966, still was a notch above 1967 and 1968, when the Irish lost two games each season. Only a 14-point loss to Purdue and a tie with Southern Cal prevented a

Joe Theismann looked like Twiggy but passed like Superman. Here he lets go a long one.

perfect season in 1969. With the hot new passing combination of Theismann and Gatewood replacing Terry Hanratty and Jim Seymour, the Fighting Irish smashed through eight opponents and set their sights on Notre Dame's first bowl game since 1925. The Cotton Bowl people were not only happy to get the Notre Dame team but also the Theismann-Gatewood team, one of the best aerial shows in college football. Their artistic association eventually obliterated the significant records established by Hanratty and Seymour from 1966 through 1968. By the time Theismann threw his last pass in the 1971 Cotton Bowl game, he had rewritten the Notre Dame record book for total offensive yards in a career (5,432), total passing yards (4,411), and touchdown passes (31). By the time Gatewood called it a career after the 1971 season, he had broken the Notre Dame record for yardage on receptions (2,283), passes caught (157), and touchdowns (19). One word—rapport—seemed to describe their happy partnership.

"Tom is a fantastic receiver," Theismann contended at the time. "He just seems to float through the secondary and has the uncanny ability to adjust his patterns with one quick step.

Joe Theismann scores, and Notre Dame beats Northwestern 35-14 in 1970.

Every quarterback should have a target like Tom to throw to."

"Joe's ability to scramble gives me the extra time I need to find an opening when my routes are blocked," Gatewood said. "He throws on the run off balance better than any quarterback I've seen."

When Theismann first showed up at Notre Dame, he was the most unlikely looking football candidate anyone had seen. Two assistant coaches, Johnny Ray and Joe Yonto, were at the South Bend airport to meet him.

Ray grabbed Yonto's arm when he saw Theismann step off the plane. "Who's that skinny kid?" he said.

"That's the quarterback Parseghian recruited."

"Oh, no," said Ray, surveying the five-foot-eleven, 148-pounder. "They're going to break his neck."

Parseghian thought so, too—until he saw him scramble. He remembers: "When he was a freshman, we sent him out to quarterback the preparation teams against the first-string defense— guys like Kevin Hardy and Mike McCoy. I thought, 'Well, this is it. They'll break him in half.' But Joe's very shifty. You never get a clean shot at him."

Theismann eventually grew an inch and gained several pounds, and the only people getting killed were Notre Dame's opponents. Although he was nicknamed "Twiggy" after the well-known skinny model of his day, Theismann never saw his slight, wiry frame as a handicap. And neither did anyone else.

"You have more agility," he said. "It makes you more shifty as a runner, and I think that a quarterback has to run and pass with almost equal ability. I enjoy running with the ball, and sometimes prefer running to passing."

Rather than become a homicide victim, as expected, Theismann became a Heisman Trophy candidate in his senior year. The Notre Dame publicity department put on a grand campaign for the All-American boy, but he fell short by a few votes. The minute that Theismann stepped on campus, Sports Information Director Roger Valdiserri had him ticketed for the Heisman.

"Son, how do you pronounce your name?" Valdiserri asked the young hopeful.

"Thees-man," said Theismann.

"Nope," Valdiserri said. "From now on, it's Thighs-man, just like in Heisman." In the pronunciation guide of the football yearbook, Valdiserri wrote "Theismann, Joe. . .as in Heisman Trophy."

From the start Theismann lived up to his terrific buildup. As a freshman he faced Notre Dame's brutal first defensive team in the annual Blue-Gold intrasquad game and gained 310 yards running and passing.

Parseghian remembers that game vividly. "This is where you find out if a kid has it. Theismann got crunched—the varsity really poured it on him. But he always popped right up. He would roll out and scramble around end, and they would bury him. I'd think, 'That is it, he is dead. This is it.' Up he would pop. The thing is, nobody ever got a clean shot at him because he squirmed around and rolled with the punch."

Groomed as a replacement for Terry Hanratty, Theismann was broken in as a punt returner and led the Irish in this department for the 1968 season. When Hanratty was injured near the end of the year, Theismann stepped in and guided Notre Dame to a 56-7 victory over Pittsburgh. He completed seven of ten passes for 153 yards and two touchdowns and ran for 38 yards and two more TDs.

"It came as a surprise to everyone but especially to me,"

Theismann recalls about his first chance as a Notre Dame quarterback. "I got a lot of help from everybody, but I really had to put my nose to the grindstone. I didn't want to blow my chance."

By the time of his senior year in 1970, the wispy Theismann was so effective that Notre Dame was leading the country in total offense. The Fighting Irish wound up with a season school record of 5,105 yards, or an average of 510 yards a game. Notre Dame's average of 92.4 plays a game was a national record. Theismann's biggest game came against Southern Cal in 1970, when he completed 33 of 58 passes for four touchdowns and a total of 526 yards.

Gatewood complemented Theismann perfectly. Remembers Mike Stock, Notre Dame's receiver coach: "Theismann to Gatewood actually developed halfway through the 1969 Purdue game. It was then that they began to exploit defenses. From that point on, they seemed to take charge. They had another outstanding game the following week against Michigan State, and they started breaking the records and giving the other defenses fits."

When Notre Dame offered Gatewood a scholarship, he almost declined it because he thought he was not good enough to play for the Fighting Irish. Then he reasoned that even if he failed at football, he could always get a good education. Actually, academics weighed as much in his selection of a college as athletics.

"I never thought I'd play," Gatewood says. "I've always been pretty insecure. I didn't know if I'd fit in. I guess I just have a low-key psyche. For a while after coming to Notre Dame, it worried me, seeing all those guys jumping around, banging lockers. I wondered if something was wrong with me. Like I slept the night before a game just like it was any other night. I never thought about it until I got in front of the crowd. And then, man, something popped. Most guys get excited by the game. I got turned on by the people. The more the better. That's the way I played. It was a release valve."

In 1969, Gatewood's sophomore season, he caught 47 passes and added six more in the Cotton Bowl game with Texas, including a 54-yard touchdown pass. Gatewood remembers that the bowl appearance had an "agony-ecstasy" type of effect on his psyche. "I was able to make the first score for Notre Dame, and the crowd was finally hushed up. I didn't have to hear that

Tom Gatewood makes one of his record-breaking receptions for Notre Dame.

'Hook 'Em Horns' noise you always hear down in Texas. And that was kind of an irony because for a split second I had a great deal of pleasure and contentment even though we lost the game. Then I was feeling very upset and dejected in the locker room after we lost it. We really made a great shot at upsetting the No. 1 team in the nation. I was just feeling very bad, looking down, and all of a sudden, I felt a tap on my shoulder, and there was the former President of the United States, Lyndon B. Johnson. He shook my hand and said, 'You played a great game. I'm sorry you lost, but good luck to you in the future.' That was the first time I ever met a President, and it was really a thrill. . ."

As a junior, Gatewood had an extraordinary season, in fact his best at Notre Dame. He caught 77 passes for 1,123 yards, both school records. Parseghian utilized Gatewood in a number of positions in 1970—not only split end. "You really have to look for Tom in our offensive formations," Parseghian noted at the time. "We split him as a tight end, we flanker him or slot him. I guess you could call him 'The Swinging Gate.'"

Gatewood's performances during the 1970 season were even more astonishing, considering the circumstances. On most occasions he was double-covered and sometimes even triple-covered.

"We tried to stop that Gatewood every way possible, but somehow he found a way to get open," said Duffy Daugherty after Notre Dame had walloped his Michigan State team 29-0. "We used a zone and a man-to-man, but he solved both."

After Gatewood helped Notre Dame beat Army 51-10 with eight receptions for 136 yards and a touchdown, three Cadet defensive backs stopped by the Irish locker room to get a closer look at the great receiver.

"We triple-covered you," they announced with awe in their voices.

"I know," said Gatewood, "and it's the greatest compliment I ever had."

Gatewood was a true thoroughbred who ran as well on a muddy track as a clear one. In fact, he seemed to play his best game on a sloppy field. In the rain and mud, he caught 10 passes for 128 yards against Southern Cal, and he had his best day in the rain against Purdue, catching 12 passes for 192 yards and three touchdowns. After Gatewood almost single-handedly led Notre Dame to a 48-0 victory over the Boilermakers in 1970, Purdue coach Bob DeMoss said: "We tried to take Gatewood away from them with double coverage, but he continually got clear. He kept turning short passes into long gainers."

With the maturity of the Theismann-Gatewood team and a brilliant defense led by tackle Mike McCoy and linebacker Bob Olson, Notre Dame completed a successful season in 1969 and accepted a bid to the prestigious Cotton Bowl. It was a new experience for all concerned.

"We knew when we accepted a scholarship that Notre

Dame would not participate in bowl games," says Walt Patulski, the Fighting Irish's brilliant defensive end. "But in my sophomore year, they decided to change the policy, and it was a big bonus for us. I don't remember hearing about it until we went into our eighth game of the season against Georgia Tech. The following week, we found out for sure."

Unlike most universities, Notre Dame left the final decision on the bowl game up to the players. Gatewood recalls: "Parseghian had such rapport with the team that he let us decide if we wanted to go or not. In a sense, he broke precedent, as far as other teams go across the country. It's usually up to the athletic board and the coaching staff. In 1969 we chose to return to a bowl game after a 45-year absence because an independent team has only one way to regain national stature—and that's in a bowl game. When we started the season, we wanted to be national champions. We had lost and tied a game already, and we didn't know how close we could come to being national champions, but we knew we were going to play the No. 1 team that was heading for the national title. . .and we wanted to play against them."

"A lot of people thought it was a joke for us to even go down there," contends McCoy, one of five Notre Dame All-Americans that year. "But they sure didn't push us around. People saw we had a good team."

Clarence Ellis, Notre Dame's fine defensive back who usually drew the other team's most troublesome pass catcher, had contained Cotton Speyrer most of the day. Then with Notre Dame winning 17-14 and the ball on the Irish 10 yard line, Speyrer made an acrobatic catch of a pass from James Street. It gave the Longhorns a vital first down, and they went in to score the winning touchdown with 1:08 left in the game.

"Clarence couldn't have played Speyrer any more perfectly," says Gatewood. "The ball was underthrown, and the receiver made a diving effort. The defensive back can't dive over a player's back and knock down the ball. So although the ball was not really thrown that good, it was perfect for that particular instance. Speyrer made a great catch, and that was it."

As Texas drove its lethal Wishbone deeper into the heart of the Irish, McCoy felt stinging frustration. "In that last drive we knew exactly where they were going to run. That's what was so frustrating. We all charged like heck but that Wishbone play hits so quick. They kept sweeping to the outside. Bob Olson did just

391

a great job. But they never did run at me. I kept screaming mentally—'Why don't you run at me? I'll take you on.' They didn't."

With the score 21-17 in favor of Texas, Notre Dame regrouped for one last attack. But the drive ended when a Theismann pass was intercepted at the Texas 14 yard line. It was one of his few mistakes of the day. Theismann broke two offensive records at the Cotton Bowl—passing for 231 yards and accumulating 279 yards in overall offense.

"It would have taken a big break for us to pull it out after Texas went ahead," says Larry DiNardo, Notre Dame's All-American guard. "They knew we had to throw so they could fall back on pass coverage, and the defensive linemen could come streaming through. A situation like that puts too much pressure on any offensive team. You'll see a team score a last-minute touchdown once in a while, but the percentages are against it. An interception is likely."

"The guys were really dejected," Gatewood remembers, "because this was our first bowl effort in 45 years. We had a lot of support, a lot of people came from Notre Dame, from all over the country in fact, to see us play. We gave them their money's worth, but it was not like coming away with a victory."

It was different the following year, though. Notre Dame returned to Dallas with revenge in mind—and got it. "The 1971 Cotton Bowl meant so much to us because we lost the year before," says Patulski. "We had a choice to go either to the Orange Bowl or the Cotton Bowl. But we had that revenge motive and voted to go back and play Texas."

Although Texas was a heavy favorite, there was a general feeling of optimism among Notre Dame players. The Fighting Irish had respect for the nation's top-ranked team but certainly not awe.

"I'd say we were bigger underdogs in this game than in our first meeting with Texas," remembers defensive tackle Mike Kadish. "Texas was strong all year, and we had just come off a loss to Southern Cal. I knew we had a good chance, but I took a lot of razzing from my friends back home. They thought the Wishbone-T would run over us. I think the loss to the Trojans made us work harder, plus the fact that we lost to Texas the year before. We knew even with the 9-1 record, if we could knock Texas off, we would have a good shot at No. 1. Besides, we wanted to put a dent in that 30-game winning streak."

Despite the loss of McCoy and Olson to graduation, Notre Dame was thought to have a better team in 1970 than 1969. Pointed out Ellis at the time: "Last year we had six sophomores starting, and with big-name seniors like McCoy and Olson there was a wide gap. A lot of us would make a big play, and nothing would be said. But Olson or McCoy would make a big play, and everybody would talk about it. It got where everybody was tight, was afraid to make a mistake. Like in the Texas game last year when Cotton Speyrer caught that pass on me. Even before I got up, I looked up, and there was Olson staring at me. I felt like I had to ask for forgiveness or something. This year we are a real unit. You know everyone's doing the job for everyone else. You don't want to make a mistake, because you know everyone's depending on you."

Parseghian's "mirror" defense installed specifically to stop the Texas Wishbone offense was not a new concept. UCLA and Baylor had used it earlier against the Longhorns with limited success.

"Essentially we played a man-for-man defense," explains Kadish. "Each of our players was assigned to take a particular member of their offense. The two tackles had their two guards, and we also were to concentrate on Steve Worster. We stayed on him all day even if he didn't get the ball."

As scientifically as the defense had been mapped out by Parseghian, there were a few unnerving moments for Notre Dame at the beginning of the game when Texas quarterback Eddie Phillips cracked the Notre Dame "mirror" for 63 yards. But as with all broken mirrors, it eventually turned into bad luck for the Texans.

"Phillips' run got us upset," Kadish says, "and we decided to play a little harder."

Texas only got a field goal out of this opening drive as Bertelsen fumbled a pitchout on what would have been an easy touchdown. It was the first of nine Texas fumbles for the day. Thereafter, Worster started fumbling—often on first down—and Theismann took advantage of the situation. He pitched a 26-yarder to Gatewood for a touchdown and scored twice on keepers of three and 15 yards. His last score was a thing of beauty—a tightrope run along the right sidelines between a horde of orange jerseys. "He danced, crawled and wiggled the last fantastic eight steps, barely staying in bounds," said a writer.

Theismann said it was the second happiest day of his life. He had been married three weeks before. Over in the dressing room, Bobby Wuensch was not as joyful. Fighting back tears, the Longhorns' offensive tackle said, "They said they were coming back and whip us. They did."

By doing so, the Irish gave Parseghian one of his most delicious moments at Notre Dame.

"I'd like to take this opportunity," said Theismann, "to ask something of the guys who say Ara can't win the big game. How do you answer what happened today?"

Joe Theismann, a "lean strip of bacon wrapped around a long straw."

Old Notre Dame Will Win Over All

"I even think the Pope could vote for us now."—Ara Parseghian.

There is the story of the defensive halfback who hollered to the bench during a game, "Hey, coach, throw us the ball."

"There *is* a ball on the field," the coach is supposed to have said.

"Yes," answered the halfback, "but they won't let us play with it."

And that is just about the story of Notre Dame's 1973 season. The Fighting Irish had the ball and would not let anyone else play with it. As a result, they won all their games and the national championship as well.

By the time the Fighting Irish got through steamrollering 10 regular season opponents, they established themselves as the greatest rushing team in Notre Dame history. The figure of 3,502 yards broke a 52-year-old record established by the fine running team of 1921 (3,430). In addition, Notre Dame broke team records for most rushes, 673; most rushes per game, 67.3; most rushing yards per game, 350.2; and most first downs rushing, 181. Notre Dame's ability to control the ball with time-gobbling ground plays helped the Irish put 358 points on the scoreboard, as opposed to only 66 for the opposition during the regular season. Then they used the same type of ball-control game to beat Alabama 24-23 in the Sugar Bowl and decide the national title.

Notre Dame's excellent rushing balance was reflected in the figures of its starting backfield. Fullback Wayne Bullock led

Fullback Wayne Bullock and quarterback Tom Clements—a winning combination for Notre Dame in 1973.

the team with 752 yards, halfback Art Best had 700, halfback Eric Penick gained 586 yards, and quarterback Tom Clements totaled 360. Significantly, this was one of the swiftest backfields that Notre Dame had in years. Penick ran the 100-yard dash in 9.5 seconds, and Best could fly at 9.7.

Most of Notre Dame's talent was packaged in young bodies. In the opener against Northwestern, the Fighting Irish started two freshmen, three sophomores, and 12 juniors. But obviously it was no detriment, for Notre Dame crushed the Wildcats 44-0 with the starting offense sitting out the second half. "We may be young," said Ross Browner, a 218-pound freshman defensive end, "but we don't play like we're young."

Notre Dame's assault embarrassed Northwestern and continued an Irish trend of winning on opening day. (They had lost but three openers since 1897.) But the pollsters were not especially impressed. They placed Notre Dame seventh in the nation. Still, Parseghian was dreaming of euphorious heights.

"It's tough to go undefeated if you don't win the first one," he said.

In the second week of the season, Notre Dame erased nightmares of past defeats by Purdue by beating the Boilermakers 20-7. Purdue coach Alex Agase had his own nightmares with the perplexing Notre Dame offense. "They give you so much misdirection," he said, "that by the time the game is over, you can't even find your way out of the stadium."

Notre Dame's only close call of the regular season came the following week, when the Fighting Irish beat Michigan State

The momentum of the Fighting Irish carried forward in the 1970s with the help of runners like Cliff Brown.

14-10. Strangely, the offense went stale in the second half—the only time that would happen all year. The four-point victory was by no means indicative of his team's strength, but Parseghian claimed that he was happy with the victory.

"Listen, I don't give a damn if we win by one point or 50," Parseghian said. "It would be a tragedy to act like we lost the football game. We've beaten Michigan State five years in a row, and I'd say that's quite an accomplishment, and it doesn't matter by how much."

The point spread no doubt satisfied the sadists the next week. Notre Dame beat Rice 28-0. And there was much more bloodletting the week after, when the Irish slaughtered Army 62-3. Then Parseghian, recalling the sting of past defeats and the taste of bitter memories, prepared for Southern Cal. The season before, Trojan running back Anthony Davis shattered the Irish with six touchdown runs as Southern Cal won 45-23, and he was a highly unpopular figure at South Bend. Before the 1973 game they taped his picture on campus sidewalks so they could walk on him. They hung Davis in effigy. And sign painters denounced him. Meanwhile, Parseghian prepared more scientific sorcery for the Southern Cal star who ran a kickoff back all the way twice against Notre Dame in 1972. Instead of kicking the ball directly to Davis, Notre Dame sent him chasing squibs to his left or his right. And by the time he could turn upfield, the Fighting Irish had shut off all routes of escape. Davis returned three kicks for 80 yards but none past the Southern Cal 35. On plays from scrimmage Notre Dame defensed Davis with equal fervor. Parseghian decided that if the Irish defense allowed the halfback 100 yards, he could not seriously hurt Notre Dame. As it was, all he got was 55 yards on 19 carries. On his first carry, Davis was only able to get two yards before being knocked down by Greg Collins, Notre Dame's 220-pound linebacker. Tom Rudnick rushed up from his defensive back position to scream, "This isn't the Los Angeles Coliseum. Welcome to South Bend."

Clearly the day was Notre Dame's, especially after Penick provided a Davis-like run in the second half. The fine halfback finished with 118 yards—50 more than USC managed—and included an 85-yard touchdown burst in his day's work. Southern Cal coach John McKay, who had been taking verbal abuse all day from the rowdy Notre Dame crowd, left the field a 23-14 loser, humming the Irish "Victory March." "There was

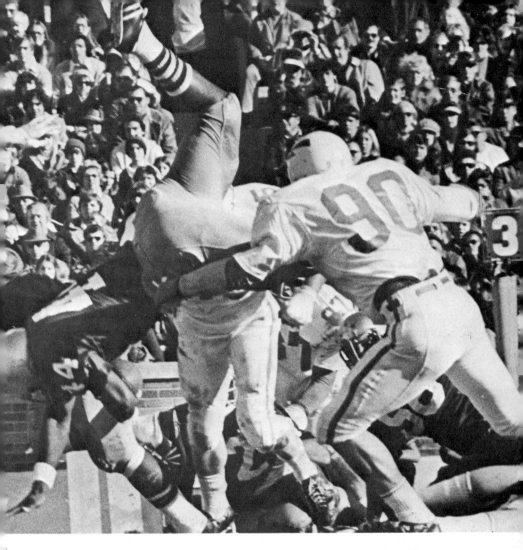

Eric Penick goes over the top against Air Force in 1973. Notre Dame won this one easily, 48-15.

nothing else to hum," he declared. The loss was the first in 24 games for his defending national champions.

Navy was an easy victim, 44-7, and Pittsburgh fell without trouble, 31-10, as Bullock had his best day of the season—167 yards and four touchdowns. Notre Dame then defeated Air Force 48-15 and Miami of Florida 44-0 to conclude the first perfect season at Notre Dame since 1949. More importantly, perhaps, it was Parseghian's first perfect season—a cherished goal that had long eluded his grasp and slipped out of his fingers in three different seasons. Significantly, he completed the undefeated, untied year in Miami's Orange Bowl—the very arena where his team had been humiliated 40-6 by Nebraska the year before in the Orange Bowl's postseason classic.

"Last year, it was a disaster," said Parseghian. "I said the next day after the Orange Bowl that we'd come back and show these people we can play football. And eleven months to the day, we came back, and hell if we didn't show 'em."

Parseghian toyed with a football in the locker room. "This ball has special significance because it's going to say 10-0. It's been an elusive goal, but we've finally got it. I would have to say it was my biggest thrill. Last season was very disappointing, but this year we had USC at home, and we wound up with a 10-0 season appropriately enough right here in the Orange Bowl eleven months to the day after our loss to Nebraska."

That victory over Miami set the stage for another of those excruciatingly dramatic "game of the century" contests that come along every few years. But somehow, this one seemed to deserve every breathless phrase of its high-powered buildup. It matched Alabama, the nation's top-ranked team, against No. 3 Notre Dame. More than 85,000 fans would be on hand in the Sugar Bowl to witness the battle for the national championship, while some 40 million more watched it on television. Who could ask for anything more, said Bear Bryant in so many words. "It's the kind of game you can sink your teeth into," noted the esteemed Alabama coach. Bryant was not distracted by so much talk about the national championship. "At Alabama, we always talk about it," he said.

It seemed like a bad omen for Alabama, though, when a flash fire in the kitchen of their hotel burned 53 steaks ordered for the pregame meal. "You can't run against Notre Dame on Rice Krispies," cracked a sportswriter.

This appeared to be the case at first. The Crimson Tide, a team with the No. 2 offensive record in college football, was downright listless in the first quarter. The Tide's first three plays from scrimmage produced a net loss of one yard. On the nine offensive plays Alabama was able to mount in the first period, the net gain was zero—compared to 118 yards and six points for Notre Dame on 20 plays. Trying to probe the bewildering Notre Dame defense, Bryant used 47 players in the first 15 minutes. Finally by the half, Bryant had solved it. The Irish led 14-10 with the help of a glittering 93-yard kickoff return by freshman Art Hunter, but Alabama had regained its composure

Tom Clements: "I held my breath for a minute, and then I saw our bench go wild, and I knew he'd caught it."

and at times taken the momentum away from the Fighting Irish. In the third period Alabama took away the lead, but Notre Dame struggled back to go ahead 21-17 on Penick's 21-yard touchdown run.

The fourth quarter was just as frantic. Fumbles abounded on the rain-slick field, but Alabama managed to hold onto the ball long enough to score the go-ahead touchdown on a nifty halfback-to-quarterback pass. Alabama kicking specialist Bill Davis missed the extra point, and it turned out to be a big miss for Alabama. It left the Crimson Tide with a 23-21 lead and opened the door for an eventual Notre Dame victory.

Clements, a quarterback criticized for not being able to win the big one, then set out to help Notre Dame win the biggest one of all. With the Sugar Bowl crowd up and whooping, the efficient quarterback drove the ball 79 yards into Alabama's gut. Three times he carried for important gains and finally lofted a 30-yard pass to Dave Casper to set the ball up on the Alabama 15 yard line. Casper made a great catch with two Alabama players beside him. "I really thought it was going to be intercepted," Clements said later. The Irish banged to the two, and on fourth down Bob Thomas kicked a field goal that gave Notre Dame a 24-23 lead.

The most unbearable drama of the painfully intense game was still to come, however. Alabama, unable to move, pinned Notre Dame at its goal line with a tremendous 69-yard punt. There were two minutes left, and Alabama's defenders stacked up to stop the Notre Dame thrust and hopefully turn the ball over to the resourceful offense in good field position. "If Bryant was a betting man," pointed out a sportswriter, "he would have to bet on his own chances." Two plays got but two yards for Notre Dame, and the Irish faced the most crucial third-down play of the game. They had to make eight yards or turn the ball over to Alabama with a punt. Parseghian called Clements over to the sidelines for strategy and suggested, "Let's pass." Clements blinked at the order. "Go ahead," said the once-conservative Parseghian. "We'll take the chance."

When Clements dropped back, he saw that Casper, his primary receiver, was covered. He had to look to the other side of the field and throw to second-string receiver Robin Weber. "After I threw, my vision was obstructed," Clements later reported. "I held my breath for a minute, and then I saw our bench go wild, and I knew he'd caught it."

Weber, all alone near Bear Bryant on the Alabama sideline, was close to a state of shock after catching the game-saving 35-yard pass. "Sure I was surprised," he said gleefully. "I'm a guy who only caught one pass all year."

That was the game. Notre Dame ran out the clock with Clements squeezing the ball hard at the end on a roll-out play.

"We played as well as we could, but Notre Dame came up with the big plays when they needed them, which meant that they did a better job of coaching than we did," said Bryant.

After the issue was decided, a sign popped up from one of the decks in venerable Tulane Stadium. It said, "God Made Notre Dame No. 1."

God, with the help of a quarterback named Clements.

Happiness at Notre Dame is being No. 1.

Winning One For Ara

"I want you to go out there and win—win not for me but for yourselves. You have won like men and lost like men. All I ask is that you play another like men. You owe me nothing. You owe one to yourselves."—Ara Parseghian.

Over a continental breakfast known facetiously as "Rolls and Rhetoric," Southern California coach John McKay was conducting his weekly interview with sportswriters before the big Notre Dame game of 1974. McKay was heard to voice profound respect for Notre Dame's nation-leading defense which had allowed a paltry average of 2.2 yards per rush.

"They do not leak," he said, "they submerge you."

Carrying his conversation into a deeper nautical vein, he equated Notre Dame's 266-pound defensive end, Steve Niehaus, to a huge fish. "He looks as big as a whale, and moves like a porpoise."

McKay added ominously, "The Irish are a lot of big guys running around hitting people. You're not going to make a lot of points on them."

McKay might have been a good coach, but he was a complete washout as a prophet. The Trojans not only scored on Notre Dame's highly-touted defense, but scored with alarming efficiency and buried the Irish under a huge mountain of points in the second half. Losing at one time by 24-0, the Trojans eventually put the haughty Irish to rout, 55-24. It was one of the most remarkable scoring blitzes in college football history.

Ara Parseghian thought he knew at least part of the reason for his team's collapse in the Los Angeles Coliseum: "Our prob-

Notre Dame's workhorse, Wayne Bullock.

lem is that we did not have a good week of preparation. It was 20 and 30 degrees all week, and we had to practice indoors almost all the time. The cold weather seems to thicken the blood or something. We've never had a good second half out here."

Probably, a better reason for the embarrassing defeat went back before the start of the season rather than just the week before. Along with the usual attrition through graduation, Notre Dame lost an unusual amount of top-flight players for the 1974 season. Eric Penick, the regular halfback, was hurt just a week prior to the conclusion of spring practice and was lost for half the season. During the summer two freak industrial accidents took away Notre Dame's starting left guard Steve Quehl and defensive back Tim Simon. Bob Zanot, the Irish's starting defensive back, was injured in a fall scrimmage and had to undergo knee surgery. And six players were suspended in a campus sex scandal.

Notre Dame had lost the heart of its defensive unit, and a tip-off on this glaring Irish weakness came in the third game of the 1974 season when they were upset by Purdue, 31-20. Victories during the season were not easily gained, despite the presence of Wayne Bullock, who was quickly establishing himself as one of Notre Dame's most proficient fullbacks. Bullock carried the ball an Irish record 36 times as Notre Dame squeezed by Michigan State 19-14. ("This is the hardest I ever worked. I carried 27 times for four touchdowns against Pittsburgh last year. But 36 times! In high school I'd regularly carry maybe 15, 16, 17 times a game. But I like football, and we had to hit at Michigan State's middle.")

The agony of putting together the pieces of Notre Dame's broken team weighed heavily on Parseghian's mind. "Our problems have been compounded almost to an unbelievable degree," he said. Other problems bothered him as well. "This has been an abnormal year for me," he noted. "Everything has been involved—the post-Sugar Bowl situation which put demands on me, the earliest season opener in our history." Parseghian's health was less than perfect, too, and he was bothered by family problems. "My daughter's wedding in September was an emotional experience," said Parseghian. "She is the girl that is afflicted with multiple sclerosis." Parseghian wanted to spend more time at home, and it bothered him that he was away from his loved ones most of the time.

On the way home from the Navy game on the eighth weekend of the season, a tough 14-6 victory over a supposedly vastly inferior opponent, Parseghian made his decision to retire from football.

"My wife knew and my brother knew of my decision," Parseghian says. "But nobody else did."

Despite the loss to Purdue, Notre Dame was invited to the Orange Bowl in a rematch of the Sugar Bowl classic with Alabama. The debacle with Southern Cal further diminished Notre Dame's stature, and some even questioned the presence of the Fighting Irish in the postseason game with the nation's top-ranked team. But not Bear Bryant, the Alabama coach who had been unlucky in bowls. Fretting over Notre Dame's monolithic team, Bryant said: "They're so big, I don't think we can move them. At least not consistently."

By this time the atmosphere was sizzling with drama and emotion. Parseghian had announced his resignation publicly and theatrically a few weeks before the game. Now Notre Dame could "win one for Ara" instead of the Gipper—a catch-phrase that was fast catching on as the big night approached in Miami. At a whimsical celebrity luncheon two days before the Orange Bowl, the emcee suggested that "if Notre Dame is going to win one for Ara, maybe Alabama ought to win one for a change." He referred to the Crimson Tide's record of seven losses and one tie in their last eight bowl games. Bryant laughed along with the others at the joke but later expressed deep fears about his offense. There had been many injuries—"the worst I ever saw. We could be great and never know it. We haven't been together enough."

Contributing to the electric scenario was dramatic news of dissension and racial problems on the Notre Dame football team. There were rumors that the players were angry at Parseghian and university authorities for suspending those six black players earlier in the year. Reports reached the stage where official denials were deemed necessary. A member of Parseghian's staff seemed to infer something was wrong when he said, "There is a different attitude on the team this year than a year ago. Last year, the boys were loose and supremely confident. It is not that they are not confident now. But there is a seriousness and determination that wasn't as obvious then."

Parseghian dismissed this disconcerting annoyance from his mind and concentrated instead on Alabama's Wishbone offense.

He set up a defense that just about dared the Crimson Tide to pass—a seven-man line and a snug secondary. It worked as Parseghian had hoped, disrupting the flow of Alabama's triple option.

"More often than not, two of the four backs blitzed, leaving only two Notre Dame players to defend against passes," noted a sportswriter. "It was virtually a nine-man rush. When the rush included a meat locker full of colossal 266-pound Steve Niehaus and 265-pound Kevin Nosbusch and 253-pound Mike Fanning hunched over hindquarter to hindquarter, not even a Wishbone with the sharp edges of Alabama's could cut through."

A fumbled punt at the Alabama 16 set up a first-quarter Irish touchdown, and an offside penalty, on a field goal attempt after a Notre Dame drive had been stopped, set up the second score. Notre Dame's defense kept guessing right, and the Irish led 13-3 in the fourth quarter.

Then came the most breathtaking part of the game. Alabama's Richard Todd threw a 48-yard touchdown pass to Russ Schamun on a fourth-and-five play and a two-point conversion pass, to cut the Notre Dame lead to 13-11. And then with 1:39 left, Todd was given one more chance. Two completions moved the ball from the Alabama 38 yard line to the Notre Dame 38. But the Irish aborted the frantic mission of the Alabamians when Reggie Barnett intercepted a Todd pass with about a minute to go.

"I had visions of tucking the ball under my arm and sailing downfield for a touchdown," Barnett said later. "But when I saw those crimson shirts coming my way, I was glad to just step out of bounds."

In the wildly joyous Notre Dame locker room, there were no signs of the supposed dissension that had been rumored so loudly before.

"We played in pain," Parseghian was saying. "I have nothing but admiration for these kids who played their hearts out when normally they could have been on the sidelines with legitimate injuries. Take Mark Brenneman, our center, for instance. He had a line fracture of a bone in his foot, and he wore a tennis shoe on that foot. He played until he aggravated muscles in his other leg and had to come out. Then there was Kevin Nosbusch, our defensive tackle. He played with a torn knee. He was in severe pain. Greg Collins insisted on playing the full game even though he had 14 stitches in his knees from a motorcycle accident last Saturday. Luckily, none of the stitches popped out. As for Wayne Bullock, he was very weak and was unable to keep anything on his stomach for five days. We told him to come out when he got weak, but he wanted to stay in there, and we tried to spell him occasionally with Tom Parise."

These vivid examples of courage underscored the grim determination of the Notre Dame players to vindicate themselves after the embarrassing loss to Southern Cal. The players, as well, wanted this last one for Ara.

"There was something superstitious, something unreal about the way we lost to Southern Cal," said halfback Al Samuels, whose runs contributed to Notre Dame's mighty upset victory over Alabama. "We had to show the country we were not as bad as we looked. I think our guys saw Southern Cal jerseys out there every time they hit an Alabama player. We know we are a better team than they are. We were determined to prove it."

Epilogue

Outlined against a blue gray January sky, the Golden Dome pokes up through a latticework of leafless trees. Heavy snow has whipped in from the north and blitzed the Notre Dame campus. It is all quiet and self-haunting now.

Dan Devine swings his car into a parking space at the Athletic and Convocation Center. He steps out and walks gingerly through the snow, his ears nearly lacerated by the biting wind. Inside the warm building, he brushes by history en route to his office—a bust of Knute Rockne here, a plaque of George Gipp there, a portrait of Frank Leahy, a game ball from a great Ara Parseghian victory.

Once settled down with a pint-sized mug of caffein-free coffee, the new coach of the Notre Dame football team reveals his feelings about taking over the most glamorous job in college sports.

"I think with no ghosts," says the bookish-looking Devine. "They keep talking to me about pressure. I just don't comprehend it. I don't think any coach would have survived 27 years if pressure affected him."

Devine was the coach picked to succeed Parseghian, Notre Dame's Armenian demigod. But Devine, a man of great experience and success himself, was not ready to emulate him—or the other Notre Dame heroes of the past.

"I am a great admirer of Ara Parseghian," he tells you, "and I have the highest regard for the legends of Knute Rockne and Frank Leahy, but if I spent my time worrying about trying to match their records I wouldn't have time to apply to my own work."

Devine admits he is "tradition and challenge-oriented," but his office reflects more challenge than tradition. Instead of Rockne, there is a painting of a leprechaun on the wall. And the only reference to the former Notre Dame coach is a plaque showing that in 1959, Devine was voted "Coach of the Year" by the Rockne Club.

Some of the dramatic events in Devine's career are represented by game balls from his time at Arizona State and Missouri and with the Green Bay Packers of the National Football League. His college record was impressive—120 victories, 40 defeats, and eight ties.

At 50, Devine looks as if he could still play as well as coach. He has maintained his high school physique of 175 pounds with no hint of fat. "Tennis, hockey, basketball, handball. . .these people around here always get you in a game," he says.

Around the lanes of travel on America's most famous college campus, there is talk that Devine can do it—as well as Parseghian did it, or those other famous predecessors. It is the House That Rockne Built, all right, but it has a new owner right now. Devine promises at least the same type of football that was prevalent under Parseghian.

"I've been basically using the same type of offense that Ara has," Devine says. "I always run the quarterback and use the sprintout pass. Our offensive philosophies are somewhat similar. I'm not a dropback-passer coach."

Devine is a rah-rah type, not adverse to bringing a little of that old college spirit into play.

"I like a hitter," he says. "I like a guy that plays. Give me 30 or 35 people that play all out, and I'll give them 100 percent. If they give me 100 percent, they're going to win. You've got to have talent. But if you don't have sacrifice, you're going to have a tough time winning."

Devine can view the sprawling Notre Dame campus from his office window. On a clear day he can see the traditional Golden Dome and gorgeous mosaics towering above the glittering new library building. There is one avante garde portrayal in granite that is particularly noticeable—Moses beckoning the Children of Israel. On the campus, irreverent students say that he is signaling, "We're No. 1." Perhaps Devine sees it the same way, too.

Appendix

NOTRE DAME'S ALL-TIME LEADERS

(Includes Regular-Season Games Only)

TOTAL OFFENSE YARDS

Career:	Plays	Yards	Avg.
Joe Theismann, 1968-70	807*	5432*	6.7
Terry Hanratty, 1966-68	731	4738	6.5
Tom Clements, 1972-74	760	4664	6.1
George Gipp, 1917-20	556	4110	7.4*
Ralph Guglielmi, 1951-54	644	3285	5.1
Paul Hornung, 1954-56	442	2747	6.2

Season:			
Joe Theismann, 1970	391*	2813*	7.2
John Huarte, 1964	242	2069	8.5
Tom Clements, 1974	310	1918	6.2
Joe Theismann, 1969	308	1909	6.2
Terry Hanratty, 1968	253	1745	6.9
Terry Hanratty, 1967	281	1622	5.8

RUSHING YARDS

Career:	Carries	Yards	Avg.	TD
George Gipp, 1917-20	369	2341*	6.3	16
Emil Sitko, 1946-49	362	2226	6.1	25
Neil Worden, 1951-53	476*	2039	4.3	29
Marchy Schwartz, 1929-31	335	1945	5.8	16
Don Miller, 1922-24	283	1933	6.8*	17
Jim Crowley, 1922-24	294	1841	6.3	15
Christy Flanagan, 1925-27	285	1822	6.4	15

Season:				
Marchy Schwartz, 1930	124	927*	7.5	9
Creighton Miller, 1943	151	911	6.0	10
Neil Worden, 1953	145	859	5.9	11
Wayne Bullock, 1974	203*	885	4.2	12
George Gipp, 1920	102	827	8.1*	8
John Mohardt, 1921	136	781	5.7	11

PASSES COMPLETED

Career:	Att.	Comp.	Int.	Pct.	Yards	TD
Terry Hanratty, 1966-68	550*	304*	34	.553	4152	27
Joe Theismann, 1968-70	509	290	35*	.570*	4411*	31*
Tom Clements, 1972-74	490	265	29	.541	3594	24
Ralph Guglielmi, 1951-54	436	209	24	.479	3117	18
Bob Williams, 1948-50	374	190	24	.508	2519	26
Angelo Bertelli, 1941-43	318	167	30	.525	2578	28

Season:	Att.	Comp.	Int.	Pct.	Yards	TD
Joe Theismann, 1970	268	155*	14	.578	2429*	16†
Tom Clements, 1974	215	122	11	.567	1549	8
Terry Hanratty, 1968	197	116	9	.589	1466	10
John Huarte, 1964	205	114	11	.556	2062	16†
Terry Hanratty, 1967	206	110	15	.534	1439	9
Joe Theismann, 1969	192	108	16†	.563	1531	13

PASSES CAUGHT

Career:

	Ct.	Yards	TD
Tom Gatewood, 1969-71	157*	2283*	19*
Jim Seymour, 1966-68	138	2113	16
Bob Gladieux, 1966-68	72	947	6
Joe Heap, 1951-54	71	1166	7
Jack Snow, 1962-64	70	1242	9
Pete Demmerle, 1974	69	1071	11

Season:

	Ct.	Yards	TD
Tom Gatewood, 1970	77*	1123*	7
Jack Snow, 1964	60	1114	9*
Jim Seymour, 1968	53	736	4
Jim Seymour, 1966	48	862	8
Tom Gatewood, 1969	47	743	8

INTERCEPTIONS

Career:

	No.	Yards
Tom MacDonald, 1961-63	15*	167
Ralph Stepaniak, 1969-71	13	179
Clarence Ellis, 1969-71	13	157
Johnny Lattner, 1951-53	13	128
Mike Townsend, 1971-73	13	86
Angelo Bertelli, 1941-43	12	60
Tom Schoen, 1965-67	11	226*
Tony Carey, 1963-65	11	130

Season:

	No.	Yards
Mike Townsend, 1972	10*	39
Tom MacDonald, 1962	9	81
Tony Carey, 1964	8	121
Angelo Bertelli, 1942	8	41

PUNT RETURN AVERAGE

(Min. 1.5 Returns Per Game)

Career:

	No.	Yards	Avg.
Nick Rassas, 1963-65	39	612	15.7*
Bill Gay, 1947-50	46	580	12.6
Andy Puplis, 1935-37	47	527	11.2
Frank Carideo, 1928-30	92*	947*	10.3
Tom Schoen, 1965-67	71	700	9.9

Season:

	No.	Yards	Avg.
Nick Rassas, 1965	24	459	19.1*
Andy Puplis, 1937	21	281	13.4
Bill Gay, 1949	19	254	13.4
Frank Dancewicz, 1945	18	240	13.3
Steve Juzwik, 1941	22	280	12.7

KICKOFF RETURN AVERAGE

Career: (Min. 0.5 Rets. P.G.)

	No.	Yards	Avg.
Paul Castner, 1920-22	21	767*	36.5*
Nick Eddy, 1964-66	14	404	28.9
Paul Hornung, 1954-56	23	663	28.8
Jim Crotty, 1957-59	16	424	26.5
Ron Bliey, 1962-63	18	440	24.4
Gary Diminick, 1971-73	30*	711	23.7

Season: (Min. 6 Returns)

	No.	Yards	Avg.
Paul Castner, 1922	11	490	44.5
Johnny Lattner, 1953	8	331	41.4
Paul Hornung, 1956	16	496*	31.0

Christy Flanagan, 1926	6	183	30.5
Chet Wynne, 1921	9	258	28.7

SCORING

Career:	TD	XPt.	FG	Pts.
Louis (Red) Salmon, 1900-03	36*	60	2	250*§
Stan Cofall, 1914-16	30	60	2	246
Gus Dorais, 1910-13	12¶	96	11	198
Ray Eichenlaub, 1911-14	30‡	0	0	176
Neil Worden, 1951-53	29	0	0	174

Season:				
Louis (Red) Salmon, 1903	15	30	0	105*
Bob Gladieux, 1968	14	0	0	84
Bob Kelly, 1944	14	0	0	84
Stan Cofall, 1916	12	12	0	84

KICK-SCORING

Career:	XPt.	FG	Pts.
Scott Hempel, 1968-70	122*	14	164*
Bob Thomas, 1971-73	98	21*	161
Gus Dorais, 1910-13	96	11	129
Joe Azzaro, 1964, 66-67	79	13	118
Bob Thomas, 1971-72	55	12	91
Ken Ivan, 1963-65	54	12	90

Season:			
Bob Thomas, 1973	43	9*	70*
Joe Azzaro, 1967	37	8	61
Scott Hempel, 1968	45*	5	60
Scott Hempel, 1969	41	5	56
Bob Thomas, 1972	34	7	55
Ken Ivan, 1965	27	7	48

PUNTING AVERAGE

Career:	No.	Yards	Avg.
Bill Shakespeare, 1933-35	91	3705	40.7*
Brian Doherty, 1971-73	134*	5333*	39.8
Paul Castner, 1920-22	84	3329	39.6
Dan McGinn, 1963-65	94	3684	39.2
Harry Stevenson, 1937-39	92	3529	38.4
George Gipp, 1917-20	96	3670	38.2

§Salmon's TD and FG were worth 5 points each.
¶Three of Dorais' touchdowns were worth 5 points each.
‡Four of Eichenlaub's touchdowns were worth 5 points each.
*Notre Dame record.
†Notre Dame record shared.

415

NOTRE DAME ALL-TIME INDIVIDUAL RECORDS

TOTAL OFFENSE
(Rushing and Passing Combined)

Plays

Game: 75—Terry Hanratty vs. Purdue, 1967 (420 yards)
71—Joe Theismann vs. Southern Cal, 1970 (512 yards)
Season: 391—Joe Theismann, 1970 (2813 yards)
310—Tom Clements, 1974 (1918 yards)
308—Joe Theismann, 1969 (1909 yards)
Career: 807—Joe Theismann, 1968-70 (5432 yards)
760—Tom Clements, 1972-74 (4664 yards)
731—Terry Hanratty, 1966-68 (4738 yards)

Plays Per Game

Season: 39.1—Joe Theismann, 1970 (391 in 10)
Career: 28.1—Terry Hanratty, 1966-68 (731 in 26)

Yards Gained

Game: 512—Joe Theismann vs. Southern Cal, 1970 (526 passing, minus 14 rushing)
420—Terry Hanratty vs. Purdue, 1967 (366 passing, 54 rushing)
Season: 2813—Joe Theismann, 1970 (384 rushing, 2429 passing)
2069—John Huarte, 1964 (7 rushing, 2062 passing)
Career: 5432—Joe Theismann, 1968-70 (1021 rushing, 4411 passing)
4738—Terry Hanratty, 1966-68 (586 rushing, 4738 passing)

Yards Per Game

Season: 281.3—Joe Theismann, 1970 (2813 in 10)
249.3—Terry Hanratty, 1968 (1745 in 7)
Career: 187.3—Joe Theismann, 1968-70 (5432 in 29)
182.2—Terry Hanratty, 1966-68 (4738 in 26)

Yards Per Play

Game: (Min. 20 plays) 13.7—John Huarte vs. Navy, 1964 (20 for 273)
Season: (Min. 1000 yards) 9.37—George Gipp, 1920 (164 for 1536)
8.55—John Huarte, 1964 (242 for 2069)
Career: (Min. 2000 yards) 7.46—John Huarte, 1962-64 (306 for 2283)
7.39—George Gipp, 1917-20 (556 for 4110)

Points Responsible For (Points scored and passed for)

Game: 35—Art Smith vs. Loyola, Chicago, 1911 (7 TDs, 5 points each)
Season: 126—John Mohardt, 1921 (scored 12 TDs, passed for 9)
124—Joe Theismann, 1970 (scored 26 points, passed for 98)
Career: 280—Joe Theismann, 1968-70 (scored 92 points, passed for 31 TDs and one 2-point conversion)
264—Terry Hanratty, 1966-68 (scored 98 points, passed for 27 TDs and two 2-point conversions)

Points Responsible For Per Game

Season: 12.4—Joe Theismann, 1970 (124 in 10)
11.8—John Huarte, 1964 (118 in 10)
Career: 10.2—Terry Hanratty, 1966-68 (264 in 26)
9.7—Joe Theismann, 1968-70 (280 in 29)

416

RUSHING

Carries

Game: 36—Wayne Bullock vs. Michigan State, 1974 (127 yards)
29—Denny Allan vs. Michigan State, 1969 (102 yards)
29—Creighton Miller vs. Northwestern, 1942 (151 yards)
Season: 203—Wayne Bullock, 1974 (855 yards)
181—Neil Worden, 1951 (676 yards)
Also holds per-game record at 18.1
162—Wayne Bullock, 1973 (752 yards)
Career: 476—Neil Worden, 1951-53 (2039 yards)
Also holds per-game record at 15.9 (476 in 30)
392—Wayne Bullock, 1972-74 (1730 yards)
369—George Gipp, 1917-20 (2341 yards)

Consecutive Carries by Same Player

Game: 8—Larry Conjar vs. Army, 1965
8—Neil Worden vs. Oklahoma, 1952

Yards Gained

Game: 186—Emil Sitko vs. Michigan State, 1948 (24 carries)
185—Marchy Schwartz vs. Carnegie Tech, 1931 (19 carries)
Season: 927—Marchy Schwartz, 1930 (124 carries)
911—Creighton Miller, 1943 (151 carries)
Career: 2341—George Gipp, 1917-20 (369 carries)
2226—Emil Sitko, 1946-49 (362 carries)

Yards Gained Per Game

Season: 103.4—George Gipp, 1920 (827 in 8)
95.4—Don Miller, 1924 (763 in 8)
Career: 86.7—George Gipp, 1917-20 (2341 in 27)
74.3—Don Miller, 1922-24 (1933 in 26)

Average Per Carry

Game: (Min. 10 carries) 17.1—John Petitbon vs. Michigan State, 1950 (10 for 171)
(Min. 5 carries) 24.4—Coy McGee vs. Southern Cal, 1946 (6 for 146)
Season: (Min. 100 carries) 8.1—George Gipp, 1920 (102 for 827)
7.5—Marchy Schwartz, 1930 (124 for 927)
Career: (Min. 150 carries) 6.8—Don Miller, 1922-24 (283 for 1933)
6.4—Christy Flanagan, 1926-28 (285 for 1822)

Touchdowns Scored by Rushing

Game: 7—Art Smith vs. Loyola, Chicago, 1911
6—Bill Downs vs. DePauw, 1905
Season: 16—Bill Downs, 1905
(Per Game) 1.7—Ray Eichenlaub, 1913 (12 in 7)
Career: 36—Louis (Red) Salmon, 1900-03
30—Stan Cofall, 1914-16
Also holds per-game record at 1.2 (30 in 25)
29—Neil Worden, 1951-53

Longest Rush

92—Bob Livingstone vs. Southern Cal, 1947 (TD)

PASSING

Attempts

Game: 63—Terry Hanratty vs. Purdue, 1967 (completed 29)
58—Joe Theismann vs. Southern Cal, 1970 (completed 33)
Season: 268—Joe Theismann, 1970 (completed 155)
215—Tom Clements, 1974 (completed 122)
210—Bob Williams, 1950 (completed 99)
Career: 550—Terry Hanratty, 1966-68 (completed 304)
509—Joe Theismann, 1968-70 (completed 290)

Attempts Per Game
Season: 28.1—Terry Hanratty, 1968 (197 in 7)
Career: 21.2—Terry Hanratty, 1966-68 (550 in 26)

Completions
Game: 33—Joe Theismann vs. Southern Cal, 1970 (attempted 58)
29—Terry Hanratty vs. Purdue, 1967 (attempted 63)
Season: 155—Joe Theismann, 1970 (attempted 268)
122—Tom Clements, 1974 (attempted 215)
116—Terry Hanratty, 1968 (attempted 197)
Career: 304—Terry Hanratty, 1966-68 (attempted 550)
290—Joe Theismann, 1968-70 (attempted 509)

Completions Per Game
Season: 16.6—Terry Hanratty, 1968 (116 in 7)
Career: 11.7—Terry Hanratty, 1966-68 (304 in 26)

Consecutive Passes Completed
Game: 10—Angelo Bertelli vs. Stanford, 1942

Consecutive Games Completing a Pass
Career: 34—Ralph Guglielmi; last 4 games of 1951, all 10 of
1952, 1953, 1954

Percent Completed
Game: (Min. 10 comp.) 81.3%—Bob Williams vs. Michigan State,
1949 (13 of 16)
78.9%—Cliff Brown vs. Tulane, 1971
(15 of 19)
Season: (Min. 100 atts.) 58.9%—Terry Hanratty, 1968 (116 of 197)
57.8%—Joe Theismann, 1970 (155 of 268)
Career: (Min. 150 atts.) 57.0%—Joe Theismann, 1968-70 (290 of
509)
55.3%—Terry Hanratty, 1966-68 (304 of
550)

Passes Had Intercepted
Game: 7—Frank Dancewicz vs. Army, 1944
Season: 16—Joe Theismann, 1969; Angelo Bertelli, 1942; John
Niemiec, 1928 (also holds per-game record at 1.8,
16 in 9)
Career: 35—Joe Theismann, 1968-70
(Per Game) 1.3—Terry Hanratty, 1966-68 (34 in 26)

Lowest Percentage Had Intercepted
Season: (Min. 100 atts.) 3.5%—Ralph Guglielmi, 1953 (4 of 113)
4.6%—Terry Hanratty, 1968 (9 of 197)
Career: (Min. 150 atts.) 4.3%—John Huarte, 1962-64 (11 of 255)
5.5%—Ralph Guglielmi, 1951-54 (24 of
436)

Attempts Without Interception
Game: 31—Frank Dancewicz vs. Navy, 1944

Consecutive Attempts Without Interception
Career: 91—John Huarte, all of 1962 and 1963 and first two games
of 1964

Yards Gained

Game: 526—Joe Theismann vs. Southern Cal, 1970
          366—Terry Hanratty vs. Purdue, 1967
Season: 2429—Joe Theismann, 1970
          2062—John Huarte, 1964
Career: 4411—Joe Theismann, 1968-70
          4152—Terry Hanratty, 1966-68

Yards Per Game

Season: 242.9—Joe Theismann, 1970 (2429 in 10)
          209.4—Terry Hanratty, 1968 (1466 in 7)
Career: 159.7—Terry Hanratty, 1966-68 (4152 in 26)
          152.1—Joe Theismann, 1968-70 (4411 in 29)

Yards Per Attempt

Game: (Min. 20 atts.)   12.8—George Izo vs. Pittsburgh, 1958
                                     (26 for 332)
Season: (Min. 100 atts.) 10.1—John Huarte, 1964 (205 for 2062)
                              9.4—Joe Theismann, 1970 (268 for 2529)
Career: (Min. 150 atts.) 9.2—John Huarte, 1962-64 (255 for 2343)
                              8.7—Joe Theismann, 1968-70 (509 for 4411)

Yards Per Completion

Game: (Min. 10 comp.) 27.4—John Huarte vs. Navy, 1964 (10 for 274)
Season: (Min. 50 comp.) 18.1—John Huarte, 1964 (114 for 2062)
                             17.8—George Izo, 1958 (60 for 1067)
Career: (Min. 75 comp.) 17.3—George Izo, 1957-59 (121 for 2095)
                             17.0—John Huarte, 1962-64 (138 for 2343)

Touchdown Passes

Game: 4—Daryle Lamonica vs. Pittsburgh, 1962
         4—Angelo Bertelli vs. Stanford, 1942
Season: 16—Joe Theismann, 1970; John Huarte, 1964; Bob Williams, 1949
Career: 31—Joe Theismann, 1968-70
         28—Angelo Bertelli, 1941-43

Touchdown Passes Per Game

Season: 1.7—Angelo Bertelli, 1943 (10 in 6)
Career: 1.08—Angelo Bertelli, 1941-43 (28 in 26)
         1.07—Joe Theismann, 1968-70 (31 in 29)

Longest Pass Play

91—John Huarte to Nick Eddy vs. Pittsburgh, 1964 (TD)

RECEIVING

Passes Caught

Game: 13—Jim Seymour vs. Purdue, 1966 (276 yards, 3 TD)
         12—Tom Gatewood vs. Purdue, 1970 (192 yards, 3 TD)
Season: 77—Tom Gatewood, 1970 (1123 yards)
         60—Jack Snow, 1964 (1114 yards)
Career: 157—Tom Gatewood, 1969-71 (2283 yards)
         138—Jim Seymour, 1966-68 (2113 yards)

Catches Per Game

Season: 7.7—Tom Gatewood, 1970 (77 in 10)
6.9—Jim Seymour, 1966 (48 in 7)
Career: 5.3—Jim Seymour, 1966-68 (138 in 26)
5.2—Tom Gatewood, 1969-71 (157 in 30)

Yards Gained

Game: 276—Jim Seymour vs. Purdue, 1966 (caught 13, 3 TD)
217—Jack Snow vs. Wisconsin, 1964 (caught 9, 2 TD)
Season: 1123—Tom Gatewood, 1970 (caught 77)
1114—Jack Snow, 1964 (caught 60)
Career: 2283—Tom Gatewood, 1969-71 (caught 157)
2113—Jim Seymour, 1966-68 (caught 138)

Yards Per Game

Season: 123.1—Jim Seymour, 1966 (862 in 7)
112.3—Tom Gatewood, 1970 (1123 in 10)
Career: 81.3—Jim Seymour, 1966-68 (2113 in 26)
76.1—Tom Gatewood, 1969-71 (2283 in 30)

Yards Per Catch

Game: (Min. 5) 41.6—Jim Morse vs. Southern Cal, 1955 (5 for 208)
24.9—Larry Parker vs. Southern Cal, 1970 (7 for 174)
Season: (Min. 20) 22.1—Jim Morse, 1956 (20 for 442)
(Min. 30) 18.6—Jack Snow, 1964 (60 for 1114)
Career: (Min. 40) 21.2—Jim Morse, 1954-56 (52 for 1102)
17.7—Jack Snow, 1962-64 (70 for 1242)

Touchdown Passes

Game: 3—Tom Gatewood vs. Purdue, 1970; Jim Seymour vs. Purdue, 1966; Jim Kelly vs. Pittsburgh, 1962; Jim Mutscheller vs. Michigan State, 1950; Bill Barrett vs. North Carolina, 1949; Eddie Anderson vs. Northwestern, 1920
Season: 9—Jack Snow, 1964
Career: 19—Tom Gatewood, 1969-71
16—Jim Seymour, 1966-68

Touchdown Passes Per Game

Season: 1.1—Jim Seymour, 1966 (8 in 7)
Career: 0.6—Tom Gatewood, 1969-71 (19 in 30)

PUNTING

Punts

Game: 15—Marchy Schwartz vs. Army, 1931 (509 yards)
Season: 67—Fred Evans, 1941 (2557 yards)
64—Johnny Lattner, 1952 (2345 yards)
Career: 134—Brian Doherty, 1971-73 (5333 yards)
122—Bob Williams, 1948-50 (4606 yards)
119—Johnny Lattner, 1951-53 (4200 yards)

Punts Per Game

Season: 7.4—Fred Evans, 1941 (67 in 9)
Career: 5.5—Fred Evans, 1940-42 (105 in 19)

Average Per Punt

Game: (Min. 5) 48.7 —Joe O'Neill vs. Pittsburgh, 1936 (7 for 341)
(Min. 10) 44.8 —Paul Castner vs. Purdue, 1921 (12 for 537)
Season: (Min. 30) 42.7 —Brian Doherty, 1973 (39 for 1664)
40.02—Bill Shakespeare, 1935 (45 for 1801)
40.00—Bill Shakespeare, 1934 (41 for 1638)

Longest Punt
86—Bill Shakespeare vs. Pittsburgh, 1935

INTERCEPTIONS

Interceptions Made
Game: 3—By 11 players. Last: Mike Townsend vs. Air Force,
                1972
Season: 10—Mike Townsend, 1972 (39 yards)
                Also holds per-game record at 1.0 (10 in 10)
             9—Tom MacDonald, 1962 (81 yards)
Career: 15—Tom MacDonald, 1961-63 (167 yards)
                Also holds per-game record at 0.6 (15 in 24)

Interceptions by a Linebacker
Season: 5—John Pergine, 1966 (72 yards)
Career: 9—John Pergine, 1965-67 (91 yards)

Yards Gained
Game: 96—Jack Elder vs. Army, 1929 (1 interception)
Season: 197—Nick Rassas, 1965 (6 interceptions)
                Also holds per-game record at 19.7
           151—Frank Carideo, 1929 (5 interceptions)
Career: 226—Tom Schoen, 1965-67 (11 interceptions)
           220—Nick Rassas, 1963-65 (7 interceptions)
                Also holds per-game record at 10.5 (220 in 21)

Average Per Return
Game: (Min. 2)   42.5—Steve Juzwik vs. Army, 1940 (2 for 85)
Season: (Min. 4) 32.8—Nick Rassas, 1965 (6 for 197)
                   30.2—Frank Carideo, 1929 (5 for 151)
Career: (Min. 6) 31.4—Nick Rassas, 1963-65 (7 for 220)
                   21.2—Paul Hornung, 1954-56 (10 for 212)

Touchdowns
Game: 1—By many players. Last: Randy Harrison vs. Navy, 1974
Season: 2—Tom Schoen, 1966; Randy Harrison, 1974
Career: 3—Tom Schoen, 1965-67

Longest Interception Return
96—Jack Elder vs. Army, 1929 (TD)

PUNT RETURNS

Punt Returns
Game: 9—Tom Schoen vs. Pittsburgh, 1967 (167 yards)
Season: 42—Tom Schoen, 1967 (447 yards)
                Also holds per-game record at 4.7
            40—Gene Edwards, 1925 (173 yards)
Career: 92—Frank Carideo, 1928-30 (947 yards)
                Also holds per-game record at 3.3 (92 in 28)
            88—Harry Stuhldreher, 1922-24 (701 yards)

Yards Gained

Game: 167—Tom Schoen vs. Pittsburgh, 1967 (9 returns)
157—Chet Grant vs. Case Tech, 1916 (3 returns)
Season: 459—Nick Rassas, 1965 (24 returns)
447—Tom Schoen, 1967 (42 returns)
Also holds per-game record at 49.7 (447 in 9)
Career: 947—Frank Carideo, 1928-30 (92 returns)
Also holds per-game record at 33.8 (947 in 28)
701—Harry Stuhldreher, 1922-24 (88 returns)

Average Per Return

Game: (Min. 3) 52.3—Chet Grant vs. Case Tech, 1916 (3 for 157)
(Min. 5) 22.0—Frank Carideo vs. Georgia Tech, 1929 (5 for 110)
Season: (Min. 1.5 rets. per game) 19.1—Nick Rassas, 1965 (24 for 459)
13.4—Andy Puplis, 1937 (21 for 281)
Career: (Min. 1.5 rets. per game) 15.7—Nick Rassas, 1963-65 (39 for 612)
12.6—Bill Gay, 1948-50 (46 for 580)

Touchdowns

Game: 2—Vince McNally vs. Beloit, 1926
Season: 3—Nick Rassas, 1965
Career: 3—Nick Rassas, 1963-65

Longest Punt Return

95—Chet Grant vs. Case Tech, 1916 (TD)
95—Harry (Red) Miller vs. Olivet, 1909 (did not score, 110-yard field)

KICKOFF RETURNS

Kickoff Returns

Game: 8—George Gipp vs. Army, 1920 (157 yards)
6—Mark McLane vs. Southern Cal, 1974 (95 yards)
6—Jack Landry vs. Michigan State, 1951 (112 yards)
Season: 16—Bill Wolski, 1963 (379 yards)
Also holds per-game record at 1.8 (16 in 9)
16—Paul Hornung, 1956 (496 yards)
Career: 30—Gary Diminick, 1971-73 (711 yards)
24—Bill Wolski, 1963-65 (559 yards)
24—Bob Scarpitto, 1958-60 (493 yards)
(Per Game) 1.1—Ron Bliey, 1962-63 (18 in 16 games)

Yards Gained

Game: 253—Paul Castner vs. Kalamazoo, 1922 (4 returns)
174—Willie Maher vs. Kalamazoo, 1923 (4 returns)
Season: 496—Paul Hornung, 1956 (16 returns)
(Per Game) 70.0—Paul Castner, 1922 (490 in 7)
490—Paul Castner, 1922 (11 returns)
Career: 767—Paul Castner, 1920-22 (21 returns)
Also holds per-game record at 29.5 (767 in 26)
711—Gary Diminick, 1971-73 (30 returns)
663—Paul Hornung, 1954-56 (23 returns)

Average Per Return

Game: (Min. 2) 74.0—Johnny Lattner vs. Penn, 1953 (2 for 148)
Season: (Min. 0.5 rets. per game) 48.3—Nick Eddy, 1966 (4 for 193)
Career: (Min. 12) 36.5—Paul Castner, 1920-22 (21 for 767)
28.9—Nick Eddy, 1964-66 (14 for 404)

Touchdowns

Game: 2—Paul Castner vs. Kalamazoo, 1922
Season: 2—Nick Eddy, 1966; Johnny Lattner, 1953; Willie Maher, 1923; Paul Castner, 1922
Career: Same as season record

Longest Kickoff Return

105—Alfred Bergman vs. Loyola, Chicago, 1911 (did not score, 110-yard field)
100—Joe Savoldi vs. SMU, 1930 (TD)

TOTAL KICK RETURNS
(Combined Punt and Kickoff Returns)

Kick Returns

Game: 10—George Gipp vs. Army, 1920 (2 punts, 8 kickoffs; 207 yards)
9—Tom Schoen vs. Pittsburgh, 1967 (9 punts; 167 yards)
Season: 43—Gene Edwards, 1925 (40 punts, 3 kickoffs; 213 yards)
42—Tom Schoen, 1967 (42 punts; 447 yards)
Also holds per-game record at 4.7 (42 in 9)
Career: 96—Frank Carideo, 1928-30 (92 punts, 4 kickoffs; 1006 yards). Also holds per-game record at 3.4 (96 in 28)
91—Harry Stuhldreher, 1922-24 (88 punts, 3 kickoffs; 724 yards)

Yards Gained

Game: 254—Willie Maher vs. Kalamazoo, 1923 (80 on punts, 174 on kickoffs)
253—Paul Castner vs. Kalamazoo, 1922 (253 on kickoffs)
Season: 559—Paul Hornung, 1956 (63 on punts, 496 on kickoffs)
Also holds per-game record at 55.9
541—Nick Rassas, 1965 (459 on punts, 82 on kickoffs)
Career: 1006—Frank Carideo, 1928-30 (947 on punts, 59 on kickoffs)
Also holds per-game record at 35.9 (1006 in 28)
797—Nick Rassas, 1963-65 (612 on punts, 185 on kickoffs)

Average Per Return

Game: (Min. 5) 22.7—Angelo Dabiero vs. Pittsburgh, 1960 (6 for 136)
22.0—Frank Carideo vs. Georgia Tech, 1929 (5 for 110)
Season: (Min. 1.5 rets. per game) 28.0—Paul Hornung, 1956 (20 for 559)
23.3—Bill Gay, 1948 (15 for 349)
Career: (Min. 1.5 rets. per game) 17.7—George Gipp, 1917-20 (38 for 671)
17.0—Nick Rassas, 1963-65 (47 for 797)

Touchdowns Scored

Game: 2—Vince McNally vs. Beloit (punt returns)
2—Paul Castner vs. Kalamazoo, 1922 (kickoff returns)
Season: 3—Nick Rassas, 1965 (punt returns)
Career: 3—Nick Rassas, 1963-65 (punt returns)

ALL-PURPOSE RUNNING

(Yardage gained from rushing, receiving and all runbacks)

Yards Gained

Game: 361—Willie Maher vs. Kalamazoo, 1923 (107 rushing, 80 punt returns, 174 kickoff returns)
357—George Gipp vs. Army, 1920 (150 rushing, 50 punt returns, 157 kickoff returns)
Season: 1512—Bob Gladieux, 1968 (717 rushing, 442 receiving, 91 punt returns, 262 kickoff returns)
Also holds per-game record at 151.2
1387—Creighton Miller, 1943
Career: 3116—Johnny Lattner, 1951-53 (1724 rushing, 581 receiving, 128 interceptions, 307 punt returns, 376 kickoff returns)
3064—George Gipp, 1917-20

Yards Per Game

Career: 113.5—George Gipp, 1917-20 (3064 in 27; 2341 rushing, 52 interceptions, 217 punt returns, 454 kickoffs)
103.9—Johnny Lattner, 1951-53 (3116 in 30)

TOTAL YARDAGE GAINED

(Yardage gained from rushing, passing, receiving and all runbacks)

Yards Gained

Game: 519—Joe Theismann vs. Southern Cal, 1970 (526 passing, 7 receiving, minus 14 rushing)
420—Terry Hanratty vs. Purdue, 1967
Season: 2820—Joe Theismann, 1970 (2429 passing, 384 rushing, 7 receiving). Also holds per-game record at 282.0
2080—John Huarte, 1964
Career: 5551—Joe Theismann, 1968-70 (4411 passing, 1021 rushing, 20 receiving, 99 punt returns)
Also holds per-game record at 191.4 (5551 in 29)
4833—George Gipp, 1917-20

SCORING

Points Scored

Game: 35—Art Smith vs. Loyola, Chicago, 1911 (7 TD, 5 points each)
30—Bill Wolski vs. Pittsburgh, 1965 (5 TD); Willie Maher vs. Kalamazoo, 1923 (5 TD); Bill Downs vs. DePauw, 1905 (6 TD, 5 points each)
Season: 105—Louis (Red) Salmon, 1903 (15 TD, 5 points each, 30 PAT)
84—Bob Gladieux, 1968; Bob Kelly, 1944; Stan Cofall, 1916
Career: 250—Louis (Red) Salmon, 1900-03 (36 TD, 5 points each, 60 PAT, 2 FG, 5 points each)

Points Per Games

Season: 11.7—Louis (Red) Salmon, 1903 (105 in 9)
11.1—Alvin Berger, 1912 (78 in 7)
Career: 10.3—Stan Cofall, 1914-16 (246 in 24)
7.1—Gus Dorais, 1910-13 (198 in 28)

Touchdowns

Game: 7—Art Smith vs. Loyola, Chicago, 1911
6—Bill Downs vs. DePauw, 1905
Season: 16—Bill Downs, 1905
Also holds per-game record at 1.8 (16 in 9)
15—Louis (Red) Salmon, 1903

Career: 36—Louis (Red) Salmon, 1900-03
            30—Stan Cofall, 1914-16; Ray Eichenlaub, 1911-14
            (Per Game) 1.3—Stan Cofall, 1914-16 (30 in 24)

First Notre Dame Touchdown

Harry Jewett vs. Michigan, April 20, 1888 (5-yard run)

2-Point Attempts

Game: 3—Joe Theismann vs. Pittsburgh, 1970; Terry Hanratty vs.
            Pittsburgh, 1966; John Huarte vs. Wisconsin and Mich-
            igan State, 1964
Season: 9—John Huarte, 1964; 6—Terry Hanratty, 1966
Career: 10—John Huarte, 1962-64; 8—Terry Hanratty, 1966-68

2-Point Attempts Scored

Season: 2—Bob Minnix, 1971; Bill Wolski, 1965

Successful 2-Point Passes

Season: 2—John Huarte, 1964 (attempted 9)

KICK-SCORING

Field Goals Made

Game: 3—Bob Thomas vs. Southern Cal, 1973 (3 attempts); Mich-
            igan State and Northwestern, 1972 (3 attempts) and
            North Carolina, 1971 (3 attempts); Gus Dorais vs.
            Texas, 1913 (7 attempts)
Season: 9—Bob Thomas, 1973 (18 attempts)
            8—Joe Azzaro, 1967 (10 attempts)
            7—Dave Reeve, 1974; Bob Thomas, 1972; Ken Ivan, 1965
Career: 21—Bob Thomas, 1971-73 (35 attempts)
            14—Scott Hempel, 1968-70 (21 attempts)
            13—Joe Azzaro, 1964, 66-67 (18 attempts)

Field Goals Attempted

Game: 7—Gus Dorais vs. Texas, 1913 (made 3)
            4—Paul Castner vs. Purdue and Nebraska, 1921
Season: 18—Bob Thomas, 1971-73 (made 9)
            14—Paul Castner, 1921 (made 4)
Career: 35—Bob Thomas, 1971-73 (made 21)
            28—Paul Castner, 1920-22 (made 6)

Longest Field Goal Made

49—Joe Perkowski vs. Southern Cal, 1961

First Notre Dame Field Goal

Mike Daly vs. Chicago, 1897 (35 yards)

Points After Touchdown Made

Game: 9—By four players. Last: Ken Ivan vs. Pittsburgh, 1965
                                              (10 attempts)
Season: 45—Scott Hempel, 1968 (50 attempts)
            Also holds per-game record at 4.5
            43—Bob Thomas, 1973 (45 attempts)
Career: 122—Scott Hempel, 1968-70 (132 attempts)
            Also holds per-game record at 4.4 (122 in 28)
            98—Bob Thomas, 1971-73 (101 attempts)

Points After Touchdown Attempted

Game: 12—Frank Winters vs. Englewood H.S., 1900 (made 9)
            10—Ken Ivan vs. Pittsburgh, 1965 (made 9)
Season: 52—Steve Oracko, 1949 (made 38)
            51—Scott Hempel, 1968 (made 45)
Career: 132—Scott Hempel, 1968-70 (made 122)
            105—Gus Dorais, 1910-13 (made 96)

425

Percent Made

Season: (Min. 20 made) 100%—Bob Thomas, 1972, (34 of 34)
95.6%—Bob Thomas, 1973 (43 of 45)
95.5%—Bob Thomas, 1971 (21 of 22)
Career: (Min. 50 made) 97.0%—Bob Thomas, 1971-73 (98 of 101)
92.4%—Scott Hempel, 1968-70 (122 of 132)

Consecutive PAT Made

62—Bob Thomas, from Nov. 6, 1971 vs. Pittsburgh to Oct. 20, 1973 vs.
Army (missed 6th attempt)
30—Scott Hempel, from Nov. 16, 1968 vs. Georgia Tech to Oct. 25,
1969 vs. Tulane

Points Scored by Kicking (PAT and FG)

Game: 13—Bob Thomas vs. Northwestern, 1972 (4 PAT, 3 FG)
12—Bob Thomas vs. Air Force, 1973 (6 PAT, 2 FG)
12—Scott Hempel vs. Purdue, 1970 (6 PAT, 2 FG)
12—Gus Dorais vs. Texas, 1913 (3 PAT, 3 FG)
Season: 70—Bob Thomas, 1973 (43 PAT, 9 FG)
Also holds per-game record at 7.0
61—Joe Azzaro, 1967 (37 PAT, 8 FG)
Career: 164—Scott Hempel, 1968-70 (122 PAT, 14 FG)
Also holds per-game record at 5.9 (164 in 28)
161—Bob Thomas, 1971-73 (98 PAT, 21 FG)

DEFENSIVE RECORDS

Tackles Made (Since 1956)

Season: 144—Greg Collins, 1974; 142—Bob Olson, 1969
Career: 369—Bob Olson, 1967-69; 295—Greg Collins, 1972-74

Tackles For Minus Yardage (Since 1967)

Season: 19—Jim Stock, 1974 (120 yards)
17—Walt Patulski, 1970 (112 yards)
Career: 40—Walt Patulski, 1969-71 (264 yards)
30—Jim Stock, 1972-74 (186 yards)

Passes Broken Up (Since 1956)

Season: 13—Clarence Ellis, 1969; 11—Tom Schoen, 1967; Luther
Bradley, 1973
Career: 32—Clarence Ellis, 1969-71; 19—Tom O'Leary, 1965-67

Opponent Fumbles Recovered (Since 1952)

Season: 5—Jim Musuraca, 1971; Don Penza, 1953; Dave Flood, 1952
Career: 7—Jim Stock, 1972-74
6—Jim Musuraca, 1970-72; Bob Scholtz, 1957-59

NOTRE DAME ALL-TIME TEAM RECORDS

(Modern College Football Records begin with the 1937 season, the advent of NCAA statistics. Notre Dame's Modern Records (indicated by MR) are also listed in categories where the all-time record was set prior to 1937. The Modern Records are not necessarily second best to the all-time mark, only the best since 1937.)

SINGLE GAME-OFFENSE

TOTAL OFFENSE

Most plays—104 vs. Iowa, 1968
Fewest Plays—31 vs. Pittsburgh, 1937
Most Yards Gained—720 vs. Navy, 1969
Fewest Yards Gained—12 vs. Michigan State, 1965
　　　　　　　　(24 passing, minus 12 rushing)
Average Per Play—12.9 vs. Kalamazoo, 1923 (36 for 464)
　　　　　　　　MR: 10.2 vs. Navy, 1949 (50 for 511)

RUSHING

Most Rushes—91 vs. Navy, 1969
Fewest Rushes—23 vs. Pittsburgh, 1937
Most Yards Gained—629 vs. Drake, 1931
　　　　　　　　MR: 597 vs. Navy, 1969
Fewest Yards Gained—Minus 12 vs. Michigan State, 1965
Average Per Rush—12.9 vs. Kalamazoo, 1923 (36 for 464)
　　　　　　　　MR: 10.0 vs. Great Lakes, 1942 (25 for 250)
Touchdowns—27 vs. American Medical, 1905
　　　　　　　　MR: 10 vs. Dartmouth, 1944

PASSING

Most Attempts—63 vs. Purdue, 1967
Most Completions—33 vs. Southern Cal, 1970
Fewest Attempts—0, Many times. MR: 1 vs. Iowa, 1945
Fewest Completions—0, Many times. MR: 0 vs. Iowa, 1945
Had Intercepted—8 vs. Army, 1944
Attempts Without Interception—33 vs. Navy, 1944
Percent Completed (Min. 20 atts.)—81.8% vs. Iowa, 1967 (18 of 22)
Most Yards Gained—526 vs. Southern Cal, 1970
Fewest Yards Gained—Minus 7 vs. Iowa, 1949
Touchdowns—5 vs. Pittsburgh, 1944

INTERCEPTIONS

Interceptions—7 vs. Northwestern, 1971; Wisconsin, 1943
Yards Gained—185 vs. Northwestern, 1971
Touchdowns—2 vs. Northwestern, 1971; Southern Cal, 1966

PUNTS

Most Punts—16 vs. Indiana, 1921; MR: 16 vs. Army, 1941
Fewest Punts—0, Several times. Last: vs. Oklahoma, 1968
Average Per Punt (Min. 5)—48.4 vs. Purdue, 1949 (5 for 242)

PUNT RETURNS

Returns—13 vs. Wabash, 1924; MR: 12 vs. Iowa, 1939
Yards Gained—225 vs. Beloit, 1926; MR: 168 vs. Pittsburgh, 1967
Average Per Return (Min. 3)—38.3 vs. California, 1965 (3 for 115)

KICKOFF RETURNS

Returns—9 vs. Iowa, 1956; Army, 1945
Yards Gained—354 vs. Kalamazoo, 1922; MR: 179 vs. Iowa, 1956
Average Per Return (Min. 3)—55.0 vs. Pennsylvania, 1953 (3 for 165)

SCORING

Points—142 vs. American Medical, 1905; MR: 69 vs. Pittsburgh, 1965
Touchdowns—27 vs. American Medical, 1905
   MR: 10 vs. Pittsburgh, 1965; Dartmouth, 1944
PAT Kicks Made—13 vs. Rose Poly, 1914; MR: 9 vs. Pittsburgh, 1965
2-Point Attempts—4 vs. Pittsburgh, 1970; Michigan State, 1964
2-Point Attempts Made—2 vs. Michigan State, 1964
Field Goal Attempts—7 vs. Texas, 1913; MR: 4 vs. Georgia Tech, 1970
Field Goals Made—3 vs. Texas, 1913; MR: 3 vs. Southern Cal, 1973;
   Michigan State, Northwestern, 1972; North Caro-
   lina, 1971

FIRST DOWNS

Total First Downs—36 vs. Army, 1974
Fewest First Downs—2 vs. Nebraska, 1917; MR: 3 vs. Pittsburgh, 1937
By Rushing—30 vs. Army, 1974
By Passing—19 vs. Southern Cal, 1970
By Penalty—5 vs. Georgia Tech, 1968

PENALTIES

Most Against—20 vs. Beloit, 1926; MR: 20 vs. Nebraska, 1948
Fewest Against—0 vs. Ohio State, 1935; MR: 1, Many times
Yards Penalized—175 vs. SMU, 1954

FUMBLES

Fumbles—10 vs. Northwestern, 1931; MR: 10 vs. Purdue, Oklahoma,
   1952
Fumbles Lost—7 vs. Michigan State, 1952

SINGLE GAME-DEFENSE

TOTAL DEFENSE

Fewest Plays—11 by Kalamazoo, 1923; MR: 27 by Carnegie Tech, 1941
Fewest Yards Gained—Minus 17 by St. Louis, 1922
   MR: 2 by Carnegie Tech, 1941
Most Yards Gained—521 by Michigan State, 1956

RUSHING DEFENSE

Fewest Rushes—8 by Kalamazoo, 1923; MR: 15 by Pittsburgh, 1968
Fewest Yards Gained—Minus 51 by Wisconsin, 1964
Most Yards Gained—411 by Michigan State, 1962
Most Yards Lost—141 by Southern Cal, 1961
Average Per Rush—Minus 1.8 by Wisconsin, 1964 (28 for minus 51)

PASS DEFENSE

Fewest Attempts—0 by Carnegie Tech, 1925; St. Louis, 1922
        MR: 1 by Iowa, 1939
Most Attempts—45 by SMU, 1951
Fewest Completions—0, Many times. Last: by Army, 1941
Most Completions—23 by SMU, 1951
Fewest Yards Gained—0, Many times. Last: by Michigan State, 1963
Most Yards Gained—338 by SMU, 1951

FIRST DOWNS

Fewest Total First Downs—0 by Wabash, 1924; Kalamazoo, 1923;
        St. Louis, 1922; Michigan State, 1921
        MR: 1 by Southern Cal, 1950; Carnegie
        Tech, 1941
Most Total First Downs—28 by Duke, 1961

FUMBLES

Most Fumbles—11 by Purdue, 1952
Most Fumbles Lost—8 by Purdue, 1952

SEASON-OFFENSE

TOTAL OFFENSE

Plays—924—1970
Plays Per Game—92.4—1970 (National Record)
Yards Gained—5105—1970
Yards Per Game—510.5—1970
Average Per Play—6.72—1921 (671 for 4512)
        MR: 6.02—1949 (722 for 4348)

RUSHING OFFENSE

Rushes—684—1974
Rushes Per Game—67.3—1973
Yards Gained—3502—1973
Yards Per Game—350.2—1973 (3502 in 10)
Average Per Rush—6.2—1921 (556 for 3430)
        MR: 5.4—1946 (567 for 3061)
Touchdowns—38—1968

PASSING

Attempts—283—1970
Attempts Per Game—28.3—1970
Completions—162—1970
Completions Per Game—16.2—1970
Percent Completed—58.3%—1968 (147 of 252)
Had Intercepted—22—1958
Lowest Percent Had Intercepted—4.4%—1953 (6 of 137)
Yards Gained—2527—1970
Yards Per Game—252.7—1970
Average Per Attempt (Min. 125 atts.)—9.5—1964 (222 of 2105)
Average Per Completion (Min. 75 comp.)—17.5—1964 (120 of 2105)
Touchdowns—18—1949

INTERCEPTIONS

Interceptions—26—1966; 1943 (including one fumble return)
Yards Gained—497—1966
Average Per Return (Min. 10)—17.8—1945 (19 for 338)
Touchdowns—4—1966

PUNTS

Most Punts—90—1934; MR: 85—1941, 1939
Fewest Punts—23—1968
Highest Average—42.4—1973 (41 for 1738)

PUNT RETURNS

Returns—66—1921; MR: 58—1939
Yards Gained—617—1939
Yards Per Game—68.6—1939 (617 in 9)
Average Per Return—18.7—1965 (25 for 468)
Touchdowns—3—1926; MR: 3—1965

KICKOFF RETURNS

Returns—49—1956
Yards Gained—1174—1956
Yards Gained Per Game—117.4—1956
Average Per Return—32.2—1922 (36 for 1160)
  MR: 27.6—1957 (25 for 689)
Touchdowns—5—1922

SCORING

Points—389—1912; MR: 376—1968
Points Per Game—55.6—1912 (389 in 7)
  MR: 37.6—1968 (376 in 10)
Touchdowns—55—1912; MR: 53—1949
Touchdowns Per Game—7.9—1912 (55 in 7)
  MR: 5.3—1949 (53 in 10)
PAT Kicks Made—49—1921; MR: 45—1968
Highest Percent PAT Kicks Made—100%—1972 (34 of 34)
2-Point Attempts—12—1964
2-Point Attempts Made—3—1971, 1970, 1965, 1958
Field Goals Made—9—1973
Safeties Scored—2—1973, 1959, 1958, 1954, 1949

FIRST DOWNS

Total First Downs—292—1968 (National Record)
First Downs Per Game—29.2—1968 (292 in 10; National Record)
First Downs by Rushing—181—1973
First Downs by Passing—106—1968
First Downs by Penalty—15—1968

PENALTIES

Most Penalties—101—1926; MR: 98—1952
Fewest Penalties—29—1939, 1937
Yards Penalized Per Game—93.3—1952
Fewest Yards Penalized—225—1939
Fewest Yards Penalized Per Game—25.0—1937 (225 in 9)

FUMBLES

Fewest Fumbles—16—1964, 1950
Most Fumbles—57—1952
Fewest Fumbles Lost—6—1941
Most Fumbles Lost—29—1952

430

SEASON-DEFENSE

TOTAL DEFENSE

Fewest Plays Allowed Per Game—37.1—1924; MR: 46.1—1937
Fewest Yards Allowed—651—1924; MR: 1275—1946
Fewest Yards Allowed Per Game—72.3—1924 (651 in 9)
    MR: 141.7—1946 (1275 in 9)
Lowest Average Per Play—1.8—1921 (468 for 843)
    MR: 2.7—1941 (481 for 1283)

RUSHING DEFENSE

Fewest Rushes Allowed Per Game—29.2—1920 (263 in 9)
    MR: 35.7—1946 (321 in 9)
Fewest Yards Allowed—495—1921; MR: 611—1941
Fewest Yards Allowed Per Game—45.0—1921 (495 in 11)
    MR: 67.9—1941 (611 in 9)
Lowest Average Per Play—1.4—1921 (365 for 495)
    MR: 1.8—1941 (340 for 611)
Yards Lost by Opponents—578—1949

PASS DEFENSE

Fewest Attempts Allowed Per Game—6.9—1925 (69 in 10)
    MR: 9.7—1937 (87 in 9)
Fewest Completions Allowed Per Game—1.6—1924 (14 in 9)
    MR: 3.0—1937 (27 in 9)
Lowest Percent Completed—21.5%—1924 (14 of 65)
    MR: 30.6%—1938 (41 of 134)
Fewest Yards Allowed Per Game—15.6—1924 (140 in 9)
    MR: 49.4—1938 (445 in 9)
Fewest Touchdown Passes—0—1931, 1924, 1922, 1921
    MR: 1—1946, 1940

PUNTS

Most Opponent Punts—119—1921; MR: 98—1939
Most Punts Had Blocked—7—1933, 1932; MR: 4—1949, 1938

PUNT RETURNS

Fewest Returns—5—1968
Fewest Yards Gained—47—1954
Lowest Average Per Return—5.0—1951 (28 for 140)

SCORING

Fewest Points Allowed—0—1903 (9 games)
    MR: 24—1946 (9 games)

FIRST DOWNS

Fewest First Downs Allowed—42—1924; MR: 61—1937
Fewest Rushing First Downs Allowed—27—1932, 1923
    MR: 40—1946
Fewest Passing First Downs Allowed—8—1924; MR: 14—1937

FUMBLES

Most Opponent Fumbles—51—1952
Most Fumbles Lost—28—1952

GENERAL TEAM
RECORDS

Won-Lost Record — Home and Away

	Won	Lost	Tied	Pct.
Home	306	54	12	.839
Away	188	77	19	.695
Neutral Sites	69	19	7	.763
Totals	563	150	38	.775

Consecutive Wins
21 (1946-48)
20 (1919-20)
20 (1929-31)

Consecutive Games Without Defeat
39 (2 ties) (1946-50)
27 (3 ties) (1910-14)
26 (1 tie) (1929-31)

Consecutive Losses
8 (1960)

Consecutive Wins At Home
39 (From Nov. 9, 1907 vs. Knox through Nov. 17, 1917 vs. Michigan State)

Consecutive Games Undefeated At Home
93 (Including 3 ties; from Oct. 28, 1905 vs. American Medical through Oct. 27, 1928 vs. Drake. Carnegie Tech ended streak with a 27-7 victory on Nov. 17, 1928)

Consecutive Games Scoring
96 (From Sept. 24, 1966; intact start of 1975 season)

Consecutive Shutouts
9 (1903)

Consecutive Games Shut Out By Opponents
4 (1933)

Consecutive Capacity Crowds at Notre Dame Stadium
48 From Nov. 14, 1964 vs. Michigan State. Ended vs. Air Force, Nov. 22, 1973

Points Scored, Half and Quarter*
Half
1st: 121—American Medical, 1905; MR: 49—Pittsburgh, 1968
2nd: 74—St. Viator, 1912; MR: 39—Pittsburgh, 1944
Quarter
1st: 35—Kalamazoo, 1921; MR: 32—Tulane, 1947
2nd: 35—Indiana, 1951
3rd: 42—St. Viator, 1912; MR: 27—Illinois, 1968; SMU, 1952
4th: 32—St. Viator, 1912; MR: 28—Illinois, 1941
*Game was divided into quarters in 1910

432

NOTRE DAME ALL-TIME FOOTBALL RECORD

Year	W	L	T
1887	0	1	0
1888	1	2	0
1889	1	0	0
1892	1	0	1
1893	4	1	0
1894	3	1	1
1895	3	1	0
1896	4	3	0
1897	4	1	1
1898	4	2	0
1899	6	3	1
1900	6	3	1
1901	8	1	1
1902	6	2	1
1903	8	0	1
1904	5	3	0
1905	5	4	0
1906	6	1	0
1907	6	0	1
1908	8	1	0
1909	7	0	1
1910	4	1	1
1911	6	0	2
1912	7	0	0
1913	7	0	0
1914	6	2	0
1915	7	1	0
1916	8	1	0
1917	6	1	1
1918	3	1	2
1919	9	0	0
1920	9	0	0
1921	10	1	0
1922	8	1	1
1923	9	1	0
•1924	10	0	0
1925	7	2	1
1926	9	1	0
1927	7	1	1
1928	5	4	0
•1929	9	0	0
•1930	10	0	0
1931	6	2	1
1932	7	2	0
1933	3	5	1
1934	6	3	0
1935	7	1	1
1936	6	2	1
1937	6	2	1
1938	8	1	0
1939	7	2	0
1940	7	2	0
1941	8	0	1
1942	7	2	2
•1943	9	1	0
1944	8	2	0
1945	7	2	1
•1946	8	0	1
•1947	9	0	0
1948	9	0	1
•1949	10	0	0
1950	4	4	1
1951	7	2	1
1952	7	2	1
1953	9	0	1
1954	9	1	0
1955	8	2	0
1956	2	8	0
1957	7	3	0
1958	6	4	0
1959	5	5	0
1960	2	8	0
1961	5	5	0
1962	5	5	0
1963	2	7	0
1964	9	1	0
1965	7	2	1
•1966	9	0	1
1967	8	2	0
1968	7	2	1
1969	8	2	1
1970	10	1	0
1971	8	2	0
1972	8	3	0
•1973	11	0	0
1974	10	2	0
Totals	563	150	38

•National Champions (9). Undefeated and Untied: 11 seasons (1889 not included).

NOTRE DAME'S LONGEST PLAYS

RUSHING

Player (Opponent-Year)	Yards
Bob Livingstone (So. California, 1947)	92
Larry Coutre (Navy, 1949)	91
Joe Heap, (SMU, 1954)	89
Ulric Ruel (Ohio Northern, 1908)	85
Paul McDonald (St. Vincent's, 1907)	85
Jack McCarthy (Drake, 1937)	85
Bob Kelly (Pittsburgh, 1944)	85
Eric Penick (Southern Cal, 1973)	85
Lou Zontini (Minnesota, 1938)	84
Emil Sitko (Illinois, 1946)	83*
Corwin Clatt (Great Lakes, 1942)	81
Larry Coutre (Tulane, 1949)	81

PASS PLAYS

Passer-Receiver (Opponent-Year)	Yards
John Huarte-Nick Eddy (Pittsburgh, 1964)	91
Terry Hanratty-Jim Seymour (Purdue, 1966)	84
Joe Theismann-Mike Creaney (Pittsburgh, 1971)	78
Paul Hornung-Jim Morse (So. California, 1955)	78
Harry Stuhldreher-Jim Crowley (Nebraska, 1924)	75
Bob Williams-Gary Myers (Navy, 1958)	75
George Izo-Aubrey Lewis (Pittsburgh, 1957)	74
John Huarte-Nick Eddy (Navy, 1964)	74
George Izo-Red Mack (Pittsburgh, 1958)	72*
Frank Dancewicz-Bob Kelly (6) lateral to Chick Maggioli (65) (Illinois, 1944)	71
Frank Dancewicz-Phil Colella (Dartmouth, 1945)	70

PASS INTERCEPTIONS

Player (Opponent-Year)	Yards
Jack Elder (Army, 1929)	96
Nick Rassas (Northwestern, 1965)	92
Jack Elder (Drake, 1927)	90
Steve Juzwik (Army, 1940)	85
Mike Swistowicz (North Carolina, 1949)	84
Art Parisien (Minnesota, 1925)	82*
Wally Fromhart (So. California, 1935)	82*
Lou Loncaric (North Carolina, 1955)	75
Fred Carideo (Purdue, 1934)	72
Paul Hornung (North Carolina, 1954)	70
Clarence Ellis (Georgia Tech, 1969)	70

FUMBLE RETURN

Player (Opponent-Year)	Yards
Frank Shaughnessy (Kansas, 1904)	107

KICKOFF RETURNS

Player (Opponent-Year)	Yards
Alfred Bergman (Loyola, Chicago, 1911)	105*†
Joe Savoldi (SMU, 1930)	100
George Melinkovich (Northwestern, 1932)	98
Arthur Bergman (Nebraska, 1919)	97
Terry Brennan (Army, 1947)	97
Nick Eddy (Purdue, 1966)	96
Dom Callicrate (Olivet, 1907)	95
Paul Castner (Kalamazoo, 1922)	95
Don Miller (St. Louis, 1922)	95
Bill Cerney (DePauw, 1922)	95
Paul Hornung (So. California, 1956)	95

Al Hunter (Alabama, 1973) 93‡

†-Playing field was 110 yards long in 1911. Bergman received the kickoff on his own goal line and was downed on Loyola's 5-yard line.

PUNT RETURNS

Player (Opponent-Year)	Yards
M. Harry (Red) Miller (Olivet, 1909)	95*
Chet Grant (Case Tech, 1916)	95
Joe Heap (So. California, 1953)	94
Joe Heap (Pittsburgh, 1952	92
John Lattner (Iowa, 1952)	86
Lancaster Smith (Pittsburgh, 1948)	85
Bob Scarpitto (So. California, 1958)	82*
Tom Schoen (Pittsburgh, 1967)	78
Frank Carideo (Georgia Tech, 1929)	75
Billy Barrett (Navy, 1951)	74
Tim Simon (Army, 1973)	73

FIELD GOALS

Player (Opponent-Year)	Yards
Joe Perkowski (So. California, 1961)	49

Player (Opponent-Year)	Yards
Bob Thomas (Miami, 1973)	47
Bob Thomas (Mich. State, 1972)	47
Bob Thomas (Northwestern, 1972)	47
Paul Castner (Rutgers, 1921)	47
Dave Reeve (Rice, 1974)	45
Bob Thomas (Southern Cal, 1972)	45
Don Hamilton (Wabash, 1909)	45
Joe Perkowski (Navy, 1961)	45
Ken Ivan (Pittsburgh, 1963)	45
Paul Castner (Rutgers, 1921)	43
Monty Stickles (Navy, 1959)	43
Monty Stickles (Georgia Tech, 1959)	43

PUNTS

Player (Opponent-Year)	Yards
Bill Shakespeare (Pittsburgh, 1935)	86
Bill Shakespeare (Navy, 1935)	75
Ed DeGree (Nebraska, 1922)	74
Bill Shakespeare (Pittsburgh, 1934)	72
Nick Pietrosante (Navy, 1957)	72
Elmer Layden (Wabash, 1924)	71
Jim Yoder (Texas, 1971)	71†
Jack Snow (Purdue, 1964)	70

†Cotton Bowl   ‡Sugar Bowl

NOTRE DAME ON NCAA TELEVISION SERIES

NATIONAL TELECASTS
(W-16, L-11, T-1)

YEAR	OPPONENT	SCORE
1952	*Oklahoma	27-21
1953	*SMU	40-14
1954	SMU	26-14
1955	Michigan State	7-21
1956	*Oklahoma	0-40
1957	Oklahoma	7-0
1958	Iowa	21-31
1959	Michigan State	0-19
1960	Northwestern	6-7
1961	*Oklahoma	19-6
1962	Oklahoma	13-7
1963	Stanford	14-24
1964	*Michigan State	34-7
1965	*Southern Cal	28-7
1966	*Purdue	26-14
1967	*Michigan State	24-12
1968	Michigan State	17-21
	Southern Cal	21-21
1969	Georgia Tech	38-20
1970	Missouri	24-7
	Southern Cal	28-38
1971	LSU	8-28
1972	Michigan State	16-0
	Southern Cal	23-45
1973	Purdue	20-7
	*Air Force	48-15
1974	Georgia Tech	31-7
	Southern Cal	24-55

REGIONAL TELECASTS
(W-8, L-8, T-1)

YEAR	OPPONENT	SCORE
1955	*SMU	17-0
	Pennsylvania	46-14
1956	Navy (Balt.)	7-33
	*Michigan State	14-47
1957	Army (Phila.)	23-21
	Iowa	13-21
1958	Purdue	22-29
	Pittsburgh	26-29
1959	Pittsburgh	13-28
1962	Navy (Phila.)	20-12
1963	Michigan State	7-12
1965	California	48-6
1966	Michigan State	10-10
1968	*Purdue	22-37
1971	*Michigan State	14-2
1973	*Southern Cal	23-14
1974	*Miami (Fla.)	38-7

Total: 45 appearances —
W-24, L-19, T-2

*Game played at Notre Dame

NOTRE DAME
BOWL GAME RECORDS

SCORING SUMMARIES

1925 ROSE BOWL — Notre Dame 27, Stanford 10

Notre Dame		0	13	7	7 — 27
Stanford		3	0	7	0 — 10

Attendance: 53,000

Team	Score S-ND	Qtr.	*Time Left	Play
Stanford	3-0	1	8:00	Cuddeback 27 FG
ND	3-6	2	13:30	Layden 3 run (Crowley kick failed)
ND	3-13	2	8:00	Layden 78 interception (Crowley kick)
ND	3-20	3	5:00	Hunsinger 20 fumble return (Crowley kick)
Stanford	10-20	3	1:00	Shipkey 7 pass from Walker (Cuddeback kick)
ND	10-27	4	0:30	Layden 70 interception (Crowley kick)

*Time approximate

1970 COTTON BOWL — Texas 21, Notre Dame 17

Notre Dame		3	7	0	7 — 17
Texas		0	7	0	14 — 21

Attendance: 73,000 — Weather: Fair, 48 degrees

Team	Score ND-T	Qtr.	Time Left	Play
ND	3-0	1	8:41	Hempel 26 FG
ND	10-0	2	14:40	Gatewood 54 pass from Theismann (Hempel kick)
Texas	10-7	2	11:12	Bertelsen 1 run (Feller kick)
Texas	10-14	4	10:05	Koy 3 run (Feller kick)
ND	17-14	4	6:52	Yoder 24 pass from Theismann (Hempel kick)
Texas	17-21	4	1:08	Dale 1 run (Feller kick)

1971 COTTON BOWL — Notre Dame 24, Texas 11

Notre Dame		14	10	0	0 — 24
Texas		3	8	0	0 — 11

Attendance: 73,000 — Weather: Fair, 52 degrees

Team	Score T-ND	Qtr.	Time Left	Play
Texas	3-0	1	11:28	Feller 23 FG
ND	3-7	1	7:58	Gatewood 26 pass from Theismann (Hempel kick)
ND	3-14	1	5:11	Theismann 3 run (Hempel kick)
ND	3-21	2	13:28	Theismann 15 run (Hempel kick)
Texas	11-21	2	1:52	Bertelsen 2 run (Lester pass from Phillips)
ND	11-24	2	0:24	Hempel 36 FG

1973 ORANGE BOWL — Nebraska 40, Notre Dame 6

Nebraska	7	13	20	0 — 40
Notre Dame	0	0	0	6 — 6

Attendance: 80,010 — Weather: Fair, 74 degrees

Team	Score N-ND	Qtr.	Time Left	Play
Neb	7-0	1	11:19	Rodgers 8 run (Sanger kick)
Neb	14-0	2	14:21	Dixon 1 run (Sanger kick)
Neb	20-0	2	12:20	Anderson 52 pass from Rodgers (Sanger kick failed)
Neb	26-0	3	11:17	Rodgers 4 run (Humm pass failed)
Neb	33-0	3	7:33	Rodgers 5 run (Sanger kick)
Neb	40-0	3	6:00	Rodgers 50 pass from Humm (Sanger kick)
ND	40-6	4	13:51	Demmerle 5 pass from Clements (Clements pass failed)

1974 SUGAR BOWL — Notre Dame 24, Alabama 23

Notre Dame	6	8	7	3 — 24
Alabama	0	10	7	6 — 23

Attendance: 85,161 — Weather: Fair, 55 degrees

Team	Score ND-A	Qtr.	Time Left	Play
ND	6-0	1	3:19	Bullock 6 run (kick failed, bad center snap)
Ala	6-7	2	7:30	Billingsley 6 run (Davis kick)
ND	14-7	2	7:17	Hunter 93 kickoff return (Demmerle pass from Clements)
Ala	14-10	2	0:39	Davis 39 FG
Ala	14-17	3	11:02	Jackson 5 run (Davis kick)
ND	21-17	3	2:30	Penick 12 run (Thomas kick)
Ala	21-23	4	9:33	Todd 25 pass from Stock (Davis kick failed)
ND	24-23	4	4:26	Thomas 19 FG

1975 ORANGE BOWL — Notre Dame 13, Alabama 11

Notre Dame	7	6	0	0 — 13
Alabama	0	3	0	8 — 11

Attendance: 71,801 — Weather: Fair, 70 degrees

Team	Score ND-A	Qtr.	Time Left	Play
ND	7-0	1	6:41	Bullock 4 run (Reeve kick)
ND	13-0	2	8:29	McLane 9 run (Reeve kick failed)
Ala	13-3	2	1:45	Ridgeway 21 FG
Ala	13-11	4	3:13	Schamun 48 pass from Todd (Pugh pass from Todd)

INDIVIDUAL RECORDS
TOTAL OFFENSE

Plays

Game:	38	Joe Theismann, 1970 (279 yards)
	34	Joe Theismann, 1971 (198 yards)
Career:	73	Tom Clements, 1973-74-75 (369 yards)
	72	Joe Theismann, 1970-71 (477 yards)

Yards Gained

Game:	279	Joe Theismann, 1970 (38 plays)
	243	Tom Clements, 1974 (27 plays)
Career:	477	Joe Theismann, 1970-71 (72 plays)
	369	Tom Clements, 1973-74-75 (73 plays)

Carries
RUSHING
Game: 24 Wayne Bullock, 1975 (83 yards)
19 Wayne Bullock, 1974 (79 yards)
Career: 43 Wayne Bullock, 1974-75 (162 yards)
32 Tom Clements, 1973-74-75 (78 yards)

Yards Gained
Game: 83 Wayne Bullock, 1975 (24 carries)
79 Wayne Bullock, 1974 (19 carries)
Career: 162 Wayne Bullock, 1974-75 (43 carries)
91 Eric Penick, 1973-74-75 (23 carries)

Attempts
PASSING
Game: 27 Joe Theismann, 1970 (completed 17)
22 Tom Clements, 1973 (completed 9)
Career: 43 Joe Theismann, 1970-71 (completed 26)
41 Tom Clements, 1973-74-75 (completed 20)

Completions
Game: 17 Joe Theismann, 1970 (attempted 27)
9 Tom Clements, 1973 (attempted 22)
9 Joe Theismann, 1971 (attempted 16)
Career: 26 Joe Theismann, 1970-71 (attempted 43)
20 Tom Clements, 1973-74-75 (attempted 41)

Yards Gained
Game: 231 Joe Theismann, 1970
176 Joe Theismann, 1971
Career: 407 Joe Theismann, 1970-71
291 Tom Clements, 1973-74-75

Touchdown Passes
Game: 2 Joe Theismann, 1970
Career: 3 Joe Theismann, 1970-71

Catches
RECEIVING
Game: 6 Tom Gatewood, 1970 (112 yards)
Career: 8 Tom Gatewood, 1970-71 (155 yards)
6 Pete Demmerle, 1973-74-75 (76 yards)

Yards Gained
Game: 112 Tom Gatewood, 1970 (6 catches)
75 Dave Casper, 1975 (3 catches)
Career: 155 Tom Gatewood, 1970-71 (8 catches)
76 Pete Demmerle, 1973-74-75 (6 catches)

Touchdown Passes
Career: 2 Tom Gatewood, 1970-71

Points
SCORING
Game: 18 Elmer Layden, 1925
12 Joe Theismann, 1971
Career: 18 Elmer Layden, 1925

Touchdowns
Game: 3 Elmer Layden, 1925
2 Joe Theismann, 1971
Career: 3 Elmer Layden, 1925

LONGEST PLAYS
Yards

	Yards	
Rush	27	Jim Crowley, 1925
Pass	60*	Joe Theismann to Jim Yoder, 1971
Interception	78*	Elmer Layden, 1925
Punt	74	Jim Yoder, 1971
Kickoff Return	93*	Al Hunter, 1974
Field Goal	36	Scott Hempel, 1971
Fumble Return	20*	Ed Hunsinger, 1925

*TD.

NOTRE DAME ALL-TIME FOOTBALL RECORD

W-L-T OPPONENT   SCORE

1887

Coach: None
Captain: Henry Luhn
L Michigan   0-8

(0-1-0)

1888

Coach: None
Captain: Edward C. Prudhomme
L Michigan   6-24
L Michigan   4-10
W Harvard School (Chi.) 20-0

(1-2-0)   30-34

1889

Coach: None
Captain: Edward C. Prudhomme
W Northwestern   9-0

(1-0-0)

1890-1891 — No team

1892

Coach: None
Captain: Patrick H. Coady
W South Bend H.S.   56-0
T Hillsdale   10-10

(1-0-1)   66-10

1893

Coach: None
Captain: Frank M. Keough
W Kalamazoo   34-0
W Albion   8-6
W DeLaSalle (S)   28-0
W Hillsdale (S)   22-10
L Chicago   0-8

(4-1-0)   92-24

1894

Coach: James L. Morison
Captain: Frank M. Keough
W Hillsdale   14-0
T Albion   6-6
W Wabash   30-0
W Rush Medical   18-6
L Albion   12-19

(3-1-1)   80-31

1895

Coach: H. G. Hadden
Captain: Daniel V. Casey
W Northwestern Law   20-0
W Illinois Cycling Club   18-2
L Indpls. Artillery (S)   0-18
W Chicago Phys. & Surg.   32-0

(3-1-0)   70-20

1896

Coach: Frank E. Hering
Captain: Frank E. Hering
L Chicago Phys. & Surg.   0-4
L Chicago   0-18
W S.B. Commercial A.C.   46-0
W Albion   24-0
L Purdue   22-28
W Highland Views   82-0
W Beloit (R)   8-0

(4-3-0)   182-50

1897

Coach: Frank E. Hering
Captain: John I. Mullen
T Rush Medical   0-0
W DePauw   4-0
W Chicago Dental Surg.   62-0
L Chicago   5-34
W St. Viator   60-0
W Michigan State (R)   34-6

(4-1-1)   165-40

1898

Coach: Frank E. Hering
Captain: John I. Mullen
W Illinois   5-0
W Michigan State   53-0
L Michigan   0-23
W DePauw   32-0
L Indiana   5-11
W Albion   60-0

(4-2-0)   155-34

1899

Coach: James McWeeney
Captain: John I. Mullen
W Englewood H.S.   29-5
W Michigan State   40-0
L Chicago   6-23
W Lake Forest   38-0
L Michigan   0-12
W Indiana   17-0
W Northwestern (R)   12-0
W Rush Medical   17-0
T Purdue   10-10
L Chicago Phys. & Surg.   0-5

(6-3-1)   169-55

1900

Coach: Pat O'Dea
Captain: John F. Farley
W Goshen   55-0
W Englewood H.S.   68-0
W S.B. Howard Park   64-0
W Cincinnati   58-0
L Indiana   0-6
T Beloit   6-6
L Wisconsin   0-54
L Michigan   0-7
W Rush Medical (R)   5-0
W Chicago Phys. & Surg.   5-0

(6-3-1)   261-73

SCORING VALUES

Seasons	Touchdown	Field Goal	Point After	Safety
1887-1897	4 points	5 points	2 points	2 points
1898-1903	5 points	5 points	1 point	2 points
1904-1908	5 points	4 points	1 point	2 points
1909-1911	5 points	3 points	1 point	2 points
1912-1957	6 points	3 points	1 point	2 points
1958 to date	6 points	3 points	1 point for kick 2 points for run or pass	2 points

1901

Coach: Pat O'Dea
Captain: Albert C. Fortin

T	South Bend A.C.	0-0
W	Ohio Medical U.	6-0
L	Northwestern (R)	0-2
W	Chicago Medical Col.	32-0
W	Beloit	5-0
W	Lake Forest	16-0
W	Purdue	12-6
W	Indiana (R)	18-5
W	Chicago Phys. & Surg.	34-0
W	South Bend A.C.	22-6

(8-1-1) 145-19

1902

Coach: James F. Faragher
Captain: Louis J. Salmon

W	Michigan State	33-0
W	Lake Forest	28-0
L	Michigan	0-23
W	Indiana	11-5
W	Ohio Medical U.	6-5
L	Knox	5-12
W	American Medical	92-0
W	DePauw	22-0
T	Purdue	6-6

(6-2-1) 203-51

1903

Coach: James F. Faragher
Captain: Louis J. Salmon

W	Michigan State	12-0
W	Lake Forest	28-0
W	DePauw (R)	56-0
W	American Medical	52-0
W	Chicago Phys. & Surg.	46-0
W	Missouri Osteopaths	28-0
T	Northwestern	0-0
W	Ohio Medical U.	35-0
W	Wabash	35-0

(8-0-1) 292-0

1904

Coach: Louis J. Salmon
Captain: Frank J. Shaughnessy

W	Wabash	12-4
W	American Medical	44-0
L	Wisconsin	0-58
W	Ohio Medical U.	17-5
W	Toledo A.A.	6-0
L	Kansas	5-24
W	DePauw	10-0
L	Purdue	0-36

(5-3-0) 94-127

1905

Coach: Henry J. McGlew
Captain: Patrick A. Beacom

W	N. Division H.S. (Chi.)	44-0
W	Michigan State	28-0
L	Wisconsin	0-21
L	Wabash	0-5
W	American Medical	142-0
W	DePauw	71-0
L	Indiana	5-22
W	Bennett Med. Col. Chi.	22-0
L	Purdue	0-32

(5-4-0) 312-80

1906

Coach: Thomas A. Barry
Captain: Robert L. Bracken

W	Franklin	26-0
W	Hillsdale	17-0
W	Chi. Phys. & Surg.	28-0
W	Michigan State	5-0
W	Purdue	2-0
L	Indiana	0-12
W	Beloit (R)	29-0

(6-1-0) 107-12

1907

Coach: Thomas A. Barry
Captain: Dominic L. Callicrate

W	Chi. Phys. & Surg. (R)	32-0
W	Franklin	23-0
W	Olivet	22-4
T	Indiana	0-0
W	Knox	22-4
W	Purdue	17-0
W	St. Vincent's (Chi.)	21-12

(6-0-1) 137-20

1908

Coach: Victor M. Place
Captain: M. Harry Miller

W	Hillsdale	39-0
W	Franklin	64-0
L	Michigan	6-12
W	Chicago Phys. & Surg.	88-0
W	Ohio Northern	58-4
W	Indiana	11-0
W	Wabash	8-4
W	St. Viator	46-0
W	Marquette	6-0

(8-1-0) 326-20

1909

Coach: Frank C. Longman
Captain: Howard Edwards

W	Olivet	58-0
W	Rose Poly	60-11
W	Michigan State	17-0
W	Pittsburgh	6-0
W	Michigan (U)	11-3
W	Miami (Ohio)	46-0
W	Wabash	38-0
T	Marquette	0-0

(7-0-1) 236-14

1910

Coach: Frank C. Longman
Captain: Ralph Dimmick

W	Olivet	48-0
W	Butchel (Akron)	51-0
L	Michigan State	0-17
W	Rose Poly	41-3
W	Ohio Northern	47-0
T	Marquette	5-5

(4-1-1) 192-25

1911

Coach: John L. Marks
Captain: Luke L. Kelly

W	Ohio Northern	32-6
W	St. Viator	43-0
W	Butler (R)	27-0

W	Loyola (Chi.)	80-0
T	Pittsburgh	0-0
W	St. Bonaventure	34-0
W	Wabash	6-3
T	Marquette	0-0

(6-0-2) 222-9

1912

Coach: John L. Marks
Captain: Charles E. (Gus) Dorais

W	St. Viator	116-7
W	Adrian	74-7
W	Morris Harvey	39-0
W	Wabash	41-6
W	Pittsburgh (S)	3-0
W	St. Louis	47-7
W	Marquette	69-0

(7-0-0) 389-27

1913

Coach: Jesse C. Harper
Captain: Knute K. Rockne

W	Ohio Northern	87-0
W	South Dakota	20-7
W	Alma	62-0
W	Army (U)	35-13
W	Penn State (R)	14-7
W	Christian Bros. (St.L.)	20-7
W	Texas	30-7

(7-0-0) 268-41

1914

Coach: Jesse C. Harper
Captain: Keith K. Jones

W	Alma	56-0
W	Rose Poly	103-0
L	Yale	0-28
W	South Dakota	33-0
W	Haskell	20-7
L	Army	7-20
W	Carlisle	48-6
W	Syracuse	20-0

(6-2-0) 287-61

1915

Coach: Jesse C. Harper
Captain: Freeman C. Fitzgerald

W	Alma	32-0
W	Haskell	34-0
L	Nebraska	19-20
W	South Dakota	6-0
W	Army	7-0
W	Creighton	41-0
W	Texas	36-7
W	Rice	55-2

(7-1-0) 230-29

1916

Coach: Jesse C. Harper
Captain: Stan Cofall

W	Case Tech	48-0
W	Western Reserve	48-0
W	Haskell	26-0
W	Wabash	60-0
L	Army	10-30
W	South Dakota	21-0
W	Michigan State	14-0
W	Alma	46-0
W	Nebraska	20-0

(8-1-0) 293-30

440

1917

Coach: Jesse C. Harper
Captain: James Phelan

W	Kalamazoo	55-0
T	Wisconsin	0-0
L	Nebraska	0-7
W	South Dakota (R)	40-0
W	Army (U)	7-2
W	Morningside	13-0
W	Michigan State	23-0
W	Wash. & Jefferson	3-0

| | (6-1-1) | 141-9 |

1918

Coach: Knute K. Rockne
Captain: Leonard Bahan

W	Case Tech	26-6
W	Wabash	67-7
T	Great Lakes	7-7
L	Mich. State (U) (R)	7-13
W	Purdue	26-6
T	Nebraska (S)	0-0

| | (3-1-2) | 133-39 |

1919

Coach: Knute K. Rockne
Captain: Leonard Bahan

W	Kalamazoo	14-0
W	Mount Union	60-7
W	Nebraska	14-9
W	Western St. Nor.	53-0
W	Indiana (R)	16-3
W	Army	12-9
W	Michigan State	13-0
W	Purdue	33-13
W	Morningside (S)	14-6

| | (9-0-0) | 229-47 |

1920

Coach: Knute K. Rockne
Captain: Frank Coughlin

W	Kalamazoo	39-0
W	Western St. Nor.	42-0
W	Nebraska	16-7
W	Valparaiso	28-3
W	Army	27-17
W	Purdue (HC)	28-0
W	Indiana	13-10
W	Northwestern	33-7
W	Michigan State	25-0

| | (9-0-0) | 251-44 |

1921

Coach: Knute K. Rockne
Captain: Edward N. Anderson

W	Kalamazoo	56-0
W	DePauw	57-10
L	Iowa (U)	7-10
W	Purdue	33-0
W	Nebraska (HC)	7-0
W	Indiana	28-7
W	Army	28-0
W	Rutgers	48-0
W	Haskell	42-7
W	Marquette	21-7
W	Michigan State	48-0

| | (10-1-0) | 375-41 |

1922

Coach: Knute K. Rockne
Captain: Glen Carberry

W	Kalamazoo	46-0
W	St. Louis	26-0
W	Purdue	20-0
W	DePauw	34-7
W	Georgia Tech	13-3
W	Indiana (HC)	27-0
T	Army	0-0
W	Butler	31-3
W	Carnegie Tech (S)	19-0
L	Nebraska	6-14

| | (8-1-1) | 222-27 |

1923

Coach: Knute K. Rockne
Captain: Harvey Brown

W	Kalamazoo	74-0
W	Lombard	14-0
W	Army	13-0
W	Princeton	25-2
W	Georgia Tech	35-7
W	Purdue (HC)	34-7
L	Nebraska (U)	7-14
W	Butler	34-7
W	Carnegie Tech	26-0
W	St. Louis (R)	13-0

| | (9-1-0) | 275-37 |

1924

Coach: Knute K. Rockne
Captain: Adam Walsh

W	Lombard	40-0
W	Wabash	34-0
W	Army	13-7
W	Princeton	12-0
W	Georgia Tech (HC)	34-3
W	Wisconsin	38-3
W	Nebraska	34-6
W	Northwestern	13-6
W	Carnegie Tech	40-19

| | (9-0-0) | 258-44 |

ROSE BOWL

W	Stanford	27-10

1925

Coach: Knute K. Rockne
Captain: Clem Crowe

W	Baylor (R)	41-0
W	Lombard	69-0
W	Beloit	19-3
L	Army	0-27
W	Minnesota	19-7
W	Georgia Tech (R)	13-0
T	Penn State (R)	0-0
W	Carnegie Tech (HC)	26-0
W	Northwestern	13-10
L	Nebraska (U)	0-17

| | (7-2-1) | 200-64 |

1926

Coach: Knute K. Rockne
Co-Captains: Eugene Edwards
and Thomas Hearden

W	Beloit	77-0
W	Minnesota	20-7
W	Penn State (R)	28-0
W	Northwestern	6-0
W	Georgia Tech (R)	12-0
W	Indiana	26-0
W	Army	7-0
W	Drake (HC) (S)	21-0
L	Carnegie Tech (U)	0-19
W	So. Calif. (2:00)	13-12

| | (9-1-0) | 210-38 |

1927

Coach: Knute K. Rockne
Captain: John P. Smith

W	Coe (R)	28-7
W	Detroit	20-0
W	Navy	19-6
W	Indiana	19-6
W	Georgia Tech	26-7
T	Minn. (S) (1:00-M)	7-7
L	Army	0-18
W	Drake	32-0
W	So. California	7-6

| | (7-1-1) | 158-57 |

1928

Coach: Knute K. Rockne
Captain: Frederick Miller

W	Loyola (N.O.)	12-6
L	Wisconsin	6-22
W	Navy	7-0
L	Georgia Tech	0-13
W	Drake	32-6
W	Penn State (R)	9-0
W	Army (U) (2:30)	12-6
L	Carnegie Tech (R)	7-27
L	So. California	14-27

| | (5-4-0) | 99-107 |

1929

Coach: Knute K. Rockne
Captain: John Law

W	Indiana	14-0
W	Navy	14-7
W	Wisconsin	19-0
W	Carnegie Tech	7-0
W	Georgia Tech	26-6
W	Drake	19-7
W	So. California	13-12
W	Northwestern	26-6
W	Army	7-0

| | (9-0-0) | 145-38 |

441

1930

Coach: Knute K. Rockne
Captain: Thomas Conley

W	S.M.U. (4:00)	20-14
W	Navy†	26-2
W	Carnegie Tech	21-6
W	Pittsburgh	35-19
W	Indiana	27-0
W	Pennsylvania	60-20
W	Drake	28-7
W	Northwestern	14-0
W	Army (R-S) (3:30)	7-6
W	So. California (U)	27-0
	(10-0-0)	265-74

1931†

Coach: Heartley W. (Hunk)
Anderson
Captain: Thomas Yarr

W	Indiana	25-0
T	Northwestern (R)	0-0
W	Drake	63-0
W	Pittsburgh	25-12
W	Carnegie Tech	19-0
W	Pennsylvania	49-0
W	Navy	20-0
L	So. Calif. (U)(1:00)	14-16
L	Army (U)	0-12
	(6-2-1)	215-40

1932

Coach: Heartley W. (Hunk)
Anderson
Captain: Paul A. Host

W	Haskell	73-0
W	Drake	62-0
W	Carnegie Tech	42-0
L	Pittsburgh (U)	0-12
W	Kansas	24-6
W	Northwestern	21-0
W	Navy	12-0
W	Army	21-0
L	So. California	0-13
	(7-2-0)	255-31

1933

Coach: Heartley W. (Hunk)
Anderson
Co-captains: Hugh J. Devore
and Thomas A. Gorman

T	Kansas	0-0
W	Indiana	12-2
L	Carnegie Tech (U)	0-7
L	Pittsburgh	0-14
L	Navy	0-7
L	Purdue	0-19
W	Northwestern	7-0
L	So. California	0-19
W	Army (U)	13-12
	(3-5-1)	32-80

1934

Coach: Elmer F. Layden
Captain: Dominic M. Vairo

L	Texas	6-7
W	Purdue	18-7
W	Carnegie Tech (R)	13-0
W	Wisconsin	19-0
L	Pittsburgh	0-19

L	Navy (R)	6-10
W	Northwestern	20-7
W	Army (4:00)	12-6
W	So. California	14-0
	(6-3-0)	108-56

1935

Coach: Elmer F. Layden
Captain: °Joseph G. Sullivan

W	Kansas	28-7
W	Carnegie Tech	14-3
W	Wisconsin	27-0
W	Pittsburgh (3:00)	9-6
W	Navy	14-0
W	Ohio St. (U) (0:32)	18-13
L	Northwestern (R) (U)	7-14
T	Army (0:29-ND)	6-6
W	So. California	20-13
	(7-1-1)	143-62

1936

Coach: Elmer F. Layden
Captain: William R. Smith
—John P. Lautar

W	Carnegie Tech	21-7
W	Washington (St. L.)	14-6
W	Wisconsin (R)	27-0
L	Pittsburgh	0-26
W	Ohio State (R)	7-2
L	Navy (U)	0-3
W	Army	20-6
W	Northwestern (U)	26-6
T	So. California	13-13
	(6-2-1)	128-69

1937

Coach: Elmer F. Layden
Captain: Joseph B. Zwers

W	Drake	21-0
T	Illinois	0-0
L	Carnegie Tech (U)	7-9
W	Navy (S) (2:00)	9-7
W	Minnesota (U)	7-6
L	Pittsburgh	6-21
W	Army (R)	7-0
W	Northwestern	7-0
W	So. California (1:45)	13-6
	(6-2-1)	77-49

1938

Coach: Elmer F. Layden
Captain: James J. McGoldrick

W	Kansas	52-0
W	Georgia Tech	14-6
W	Illinois	14-6
W	Carnegie Tech	7-0
W	Army	19-7
W	Navy (R)	15-0
°W	Minnesota	19-0
W	Northwestern	9-7
L	So. California (U)	0-13
	(8-1-0)	149-39

1939

Coach: Elmer F. Layden
Captain: John F. Kelly

W	Purdue	3-0
W	Georgia Tech	17-14
W	S.M.U.	20-19
W	Navy	14-7
W	Carnegie Tech (S)	7-6
W	Army	14-0
L	Iowa (U)	6-7
W	Northwestern (3:30)	7-0
L	So. California	12-20
	(7-2-0)	100-73

1940

Coach: Elmer F. Layden
Captain: Milt Piepul

W	Col. of Pacific	25-7
W	Georgia Tech	26-20
W	Carnegie Tech	61-0
W	Illinois	26-0
W	Army (R)	7-0
W	Navy (4:00)	13-7
L	Iowa (5:00) (U)	0-7
L	Northwestern	0-20
W	So. California	10-6
	(7-2-0)	168-67

1941

Coach: Frank Leahy
Captain: Paul B. Lillis

W	Arizona	38-7
W	Indiana (R)	19-6
W	Georgia Tech	20-0
W	Carnegie Tech (R)	16-0
W	Illinois	49-14
T	Army (R)	0-0
W	Navy	20-13
W	Northwestern	7-6
W	So. California	20-18
	(8-0-1)	189-64

1942

Coach: Frank Leahy
Captain: George E. Murphy

T	Wisconsin	7-7
L	Georgia Tech (U)	6-13
W	Stanford	27-0
W	Iowa Pre-Flight (U)	28-0
W	Illinois	21-14
W	Navy (R)	9-0
W	Army	13-0
L	Michigan	20-32
W	Northwestern	27-20
W	So. California	13-0
T	Great Lakes (S)	13-13
	(7-2-2)	184-99

442

1943

Coach: Frank Leahy
Captain: Patrick J. Filley

W	Pittsburgh	41-0
W	Georgia Tech	55-13
W	Michigan	35-12
W	Wisconsin	50-0
W	Illinois (R)	47-0
W	Navy	33-6
W	Army	26-0
W	Northwestern	25-6
W	Iowa Pre-Flight	14-13
L	Gt. Lakes(U)(0:33)	14-19
	(9-1-0)	340-69

1944

Coach: Edward C. McKeever
Captain: Patrick J. Filley

W	Pittsburgh	58-0
W	Tulane	26-0
W	Dartmouth (R)	64-0
W	Wisconsin	28-13
W	Illinois	13-7
L	Navy	13-32
L	Army	0-59
W	Northwestern	21-0
W	Georgia Tech	21-0
W	Great Lakes	28-7
	(8-2-0)	272-118

1945

Coach: Hugh J. Devore
Captain: Frank J. Dancewicz

W	Illinois	7-0
W	Georgia Tech	40-7
W	Dartmouth	34-0
W	Pittsburgh	39-9
W	Iowa	56-0
T	Navy	6-6
L	Army	0-48
W	Northwestern	34-7
W	Tulane	32-6
L	Great Lakes	7-39
	(7-2-1)	255-122

1946

Coach: Frank Leahy
New Captain Each Game

W	Illinois	26-6
W	Pittsburgh	33-0
W	Purdue	49-6
W	Iowa	41-6
W	Navy	28-0
T	Army	0-0
W	Northwestern (R)	27-0
W	Tulane	41-0
W	So. California	26-6
	(8-0-1)	271-24

1947

Coach: Frank Leahy
Captain: George Connor

W	Pittsburgh	40-6
W	Purdue	22-7
W	Nebraska	31-0
W	Iowa	21-0
W	Navy	27-0
W	Army	27-7
W	Northwestern (R)	26-19
W	Tulane	59-6
W	So. California	38-7
	(9-0-0)	291-52

1948

Coach: Frank Leahy
Captain: William Fischer

W	Purdue	28-27
W	Pittsburgh	40-0
W	Michigan State	26-7
W	Nebraska	44-13
W	Iowa	27-12
W	Navy	41-7
W	Indiana (R)	42-6
W	Northwestern	12-7
W	Washington	46-0
T	So. Calif.(0:35-ND)	14-14
	(9-0-1)	320-93

1949

Coach: Frank Leahy
Co-Captains: Leon J. Hart
and James E. Martin

W	Indiana	49-6
W	Washington	27-7
W	Purdue	35-12
W	Tulane	46-7
W	Navy	40-0
W	Michigan State	34-21
W	North Carolina	42-6
W	Iowa	28-7
W	So. California	32-0
W	S.M.U.	27-20
	(10-0-0)	360-86

1950

Coach: Frank Leahy
Captain: Jerome P. Groom

W	No. Carolina (2:40)	14-7
L	Purdue (U) (R)	14-28
W	Tulane	13-9
L	Indiana (U)	7-20
L	Michigan State	33-36
W	Navy (R-S)	19-10
W	Pittsburgh	18-7
T	Iowa	14-14
L	So. California	7-9
	(4-4-1)	139-140

1951

Coach: Frank Leahy
Captain: Jim Mutscheller

W	Indiana	48-6
W	Detroit (Nt)	40-6
L	S.M.U. (U)	20-27
W	Pittsburgh	33-0
W	Purdue	30-9
W	Navy	19-0
L	Michigan State	0-35
W	North Carolina	12-7
T	Iowa (0:55-ND)	20-20
W	So. California (R)	19-12
	(7-2-1)	241-122

1952

Coach: Frank Leahy
Captain: James F. Alessandrini

T	Pennsylvania	7-7
W	Texas (U)	14-3
L	Pittsburgh (U)	19-22
W	Purdue	26-14
W	North Carolina	34-14
W	Navy	17-6
W	Oklahoma (U)	27-21
L	Michigan State	3-21
W	Iowa	27-0
W	So. California (U)	9-0
	(7-2-1)	183-108

1953

Coach: Frank Leahy
Captain: Donald Penza

W	Oklahoma	28-21
W	Purdue	37-7
W	Pittsburgh	23-14
W	Georgia Tech	27-14
W	Navy	38-7
W	Pennsylvania	28-20
W	North Carolina	34-14
T	Iowa (0:06-ND)	14-14
W	So. California	48-14
W	S.M.U.	40-14
	(9-0-1)	317-139

1954

Coach: Terry Brennan
Co-Captains: Paul A. Matz
and Daniel J. Shannon

W	Texas	21-0
L	Purdue (U)	14-27
W	Pittsburgh	33-0
W	Michigan State (R)	20-19
W	Navy	6-0
W	Pennsylvania	42-7
W	North Carolina	42-13
W	Iowa	34-18
W	So. Calif (R) (5:57)	23-17
W	S.M.U.	26-14
	(9-1-0)	261-115

1955

Coach: Terry Brennan
Captain: Raymond E. Lemek

W	S.M.U.	17-0
W	Indiana	19-0
W	Miami (Fla.) (Nt)	14-0
L	Michigan State	7-21
W	Purdue	22-7
W	Navy (R)	21-7
W	Pennsylvania	46-14
W	North Carolina	27-7
W	Iowa (2:15)	17-14
L	So. California (U)	20-42

(8-2-0) 210-112

1956

Coach: Terry Brennan
Captain: James A. Morse

L	S.M.U. (U) (Nt) (1:50)	13-19
W	Indiana	20-6
L	Purdue	14-28
L	Michigan State	14-47
L	Oklahoma	0-40
L	Navy (R)	7-33
L	Pittsburgh	13-26
W	No. Carolina (1:16)	21-14
L	Iowa	8-48
L	So. California	20-28

(2-8-0) 130-289

1957

Coach: Terry Brennan
Co-Captains: Richard Prendergast and
Edward A. Sullivan

W	Purdue	12-0
W	Indiana	26-0
W	Army	23-21
W	Pittsburgh	13-7
L	Navy (R)	6-20
L	Michigan State	6-34
W	Oklahoma (U) (3:50)	7-0
L	Iowa	13-21
W	So. California (S)	40-12
W	S.M.U.	54-21

(7-3-0) 200-136

1958

Coach: Terry Brennan
Co-Captains: Allen J. Ecuyer and
Charles F. Puntillo

W	Indiana	18-0
W	S.M.U.	14-6
L	Army	2-14
W	Duke	9-7
L	Purdue (R)	22-29
W	Navy	40-20
L	Pittsburgh (0:11)	26-29
W	North Carolina	34-24
L	Iowa	21-31
W	So. California	20-13

(6-4-0) 206-173

1959

Coach: Joseph L. Kuharich
Captain: Kenneth M. Adamson

W	North Carolina (R)	28-8
L	Purdue	7-28
W	California	28-6
L	Michigan State	0-19
L	Northwestern (R)	24-30
W	Navy (0:32)	25-22
L	Georgia Tech (4:27)	10-14
L	Pittsburgh (R)	13-28
W	Iowa (3:25)	20-19
W	So. California (U)	16-6

(5-5-0) 171-180

1960

Coach: Joseph L. Kuharich
Captain: Myron Pottios

W	California	21-7
L	Purdue	19-51
L	North Carolina (R)	7-12
L	Michigan State	0-21
L	Northwestern	6-7
L	Navy (R)	7-14
L	Pittsburgh	13-20
L	Miami (Fla.) (Nt)	21-28
L	Iowa	0-28
W	So. Cal. (U) (R)	17-0

(2-8-0) 111-188

1961

Coach: Joseph L. Kuharich
Co-Captains: Norbert W. Roy and
Nicholas A. Buoniconti

W	Oklahoma	19-6
W	Purdue	22-20
W	So. California	30-0
L	Michigan State	7-17
L	Northwestern	10-12
L	Navy	10-13
W	Pittsburgh	26-20
W	Syracuse (0:00)	17-15
L	Iowa	21-42
L	Duke	13-37

(5-5-0) 175-182

1962

Coach: Joseph L. Kuharich
Captain: Mike Lind

W	Oklahoma	13-7
L	Purdue	6-24
L	Wisconsin	8-17
L	Michigan State (R)	7-31
L	Northwestern	6-35
W	Navy (R)	20-12
W	Pittsburgh	43-22
W	North Carolina	21-7
W	Iowa	35-12
L	So. California	0-25

(5-5-0) 159-192

1963

Coach: Hugh J. Devore
Captain: Joseph Robert Lehmann

L	Wisconsin (1:07)	9-14
L	Purdue	6-7
W	So. Cal. (U) (6:28)	17-14
W	U.C.L.A.	27-12
L	Stanford (U)	14-24
L	Navy	14-35

444

L	Pittsburgh	7-27
L	Michigan State	7-12
..	Iowa°	...
L	Syracuse (3:28)	7-14
	(2-7-0)	108-159

1964

Coach: Ara Parseghian
Captain: James S. Carroll

W	Wisconsin (R)	31-7
W	Purdue	34-15
W	Air Force	34-7
W	U.C.L.A.	24-0
W	Stanford	28-6
W	Navy	40-0
W	Pittsburgh	17-15
W	Michigan State	34-7
W	Iowa	28-0
L	So. Calif. (U)(1:33)	17-20
	(9-1-0)	287-77

1965

Coach: Ara Parseghian
Captain: Philip F. Sheridan

W	California	48-6
L	Purdue	21-25
W	Northwestern	38-7
W	Army (Nt)	17-0
W	So. California (R)	28-7
W	Navy	29-3
W	Pittsburgh	69-13
W	North Carolina	17-0
L	Michigan State	3-12
T	Miami (Fla.) (Nt)	0-0
	(7-2-1)	270-73

1966

Coach: Ara Parseghian
Captain: James R. Lynch

W	Purdue	26-14
W	Northwestern	35-7
W	Army	35-0
W	North Carolina	32-0
W	Oklahoma	38-0
W	Navy	31-7
W	Pittsburgh	40-0
W	Duke	64-0
T	Michigan State	10-10
W	So. California	51-0
	(9-0-1)	362-38

1967

Coach: Ara Parseghian
Captain: Robert P. (Rocky) Bleier

W	California	41-8
L	Purdue	21-28
W	Iowa	56-6
L	So. California	7-24
W	Illinois	47-7
W	Michigan State	24-12
W	Navy	43-14
W	Pittsburgh	38-0
W	Georgia Tech	36-3
W	Miami (Fla.) (Nt)	24-22
	(8-2-0)	337-124

1968

Coach: Ara Parseghian
Co-captains: George J. Kunz and Robert L. Olson

W	Oklahoma	45-21
L	Purdue	22-37
W	Iowa	51-28
W	Northwestern	27-7
W	Illinois	58-8
L	Michigan State	17-21
W	Navy	45-14
W	Pittsburgh	56-7
W	Georgia Tech	34-6
T	So. California	21-21
	(7-2-1)	376-170

1969

Coach: Ara Parseghian
Co-captains: Robert L. Olson and Michael Oriard

W	Northwestern	35-10
L	Purdue	14-28
W	Michigan State	42-28
W	Army	45-0
T	Southern California	14-14
W	Tulane (Nt)	37-0
W	Navy	47-0
W	Pittsburgh (R)	49-7
W	Georgia Tech (Nt)	38-20
W	Air Force	13-6
	(8-1-1)	334-113

COTTON BOWL

L	Texas (1:08)	17-21

1970

Coach: Ara Parseghian
Co-captains: Larry DiNardo and Tim Kelly

W	Northwestern	35-14
W	Purdue	48-0
W	Michigan State	29-0
W	Army	51-10
W	Missouri	24-7
W	Navy	56-7
W	Pittsburgh	46-14
W	Georgia Tech (6:28)	10-7
W	Louisiana State (2:54)	3-0
L	Southern Cal(R)(U)	28-38
	(9-1-0)	330-97

COTTON BOWL

W	Texas	24-11

1971

Coach: Ara Parseghian
Co-Captains: Walter Patulski and Thomas Gatewood

W	Northwestern	50-7
W	Purdue (2:58) (R)	8-7
W	Michigan State	14-2
W	Miami (Fla.) (Nt)	17-0
W	North Carolina	16-0
L	So. California (U)	14-28
W	Navy	21-0
W	Pittsburgh	56-7
W	Tulane	21-7
L	Louisiana State (Nt)	8-28
	(8-2-0)	225-86

1972

Coach: Ara Parseghian
Co-Captains: John Dampeer and Greg Marx

W	Northwestern	37-0
W	Purdue	35-14
W	Michigan State	16-0
W	Pittsburgh	42-16
L	Missouri (U) (R)	26-30
W	TCU	21-0
W	Navy	42-23
W	Air Force	21-7
W	Miami (Fla.)	20-17
L	Southern Cal	23-45
	(8-2-0)	283-152

ORANGE BOWL
L Nebraska (Nt)   6-40

1974

Coach: Ara Parseghian
Co-Captains: Tom Clements and Greg Collins

W	Georgia Tech	31-7
W	Northwestern	49-3
L	Purdue (U) (R)	20-31
W	Michigan State	19-14
W	Rice (3:08)	10-3
W	Army (S)	48-0
W	Miami (Fla.)	38-7
W	Navy	14-6
W	Pitt (R) (2.49)	14-10
W	Air Force (R)	38-0
L	Southern Cal	24-55
	(9-2-0)	305-136

ORANGE BOWL
W Alabama (U)   13-11

1973

Coach: Ara Parseghian
Tri-Captains: Dave Casper, Frank Pomarico (Off.)
and Mike Townsend (Def.)

W	Northwestern	44-0
W	Purdue	20-7
W	Michigan State	14-10
W	Rice (Nt)	28-0
W	Army	62-3
W	Southern Cal (R)	23-14
W	Navy	44-7
W	Pittsburgh (S)	31-10
W	Air Force	48-15
W	Miami (Fla.)(Nt)	44-0
	(10-0-0)	358-66

SUGAR BOWL
W Alabama   24-23

HEAD FOOTBALL COACHES

YEAR	COACH	WON	LOST	TIED	
1887-88-89-92-93	No head coaches	7	4	1	.636
1894	J. L. Morison	3	1	1	.750
1895	H. G. Hadden	3	1	0	.750
1896-98	Frank E. Hering	12	6	1	.667
1899	James McWeeney	6	3	1	.667
1900-01	Patrick O'Dea	14	4	2	.778
1902-03	James Faragher	14	2	2	.875
1904	Louis Salmon	5	3	0	.625
1905	Henry J. McGlew	5	4	0	.556
1906-07	Thomas Barry	12	1	1	.923
1908	Victor M. Place	8	1	0	.889
1909-10	Frank C. Longman	11	1	2	.917
1911-12	L. H. Marks	13	0	2	1.000
1913-17	Jesse C. Harper	34	5	1	.872
1918-30	Knute Rockne	105	12	5	.897
1931-33	Heartley (Hunk) Anderson	16	9	2	.640
1934-40	Elmer Layden	47	13	3	.783
1941-43, 46-53	Frank Leahy	87	11	9	.888
1944	Edward McKeever	8	2	0	.800
1945; 1963	Hugh Devore	9	9	1	.500
1954-58	Terry Brennan	32	18	0	.640
1959-62	Joseph Kuharich	17	23	0	.425
1964-74	Ara Parseghian	95	17	4	.848
		563	150	38	.790

HIGHLIGHTS OF ALL-TIME RECORD

Under Knute Rockne (1918-1930) .... Notre Dame won 105, lost 12, tied 5—.898
Under Heartley (Hunk) Anderson (1931-33) .... Notre Dame won 16, lost 9, tied 2—.640
Under Elmer Layden (1934-1940) .... Notre Dame won 47, lost 13, tied 3—.783
Under Edward McKeever (1944) .... Notre Dame won 8, lost 2—.800
Under Frank Leahy (1941-43; 1946-53) .... Notre Dame won 87, lost 11, tied 9—.888
Under Terry Brennan (1954-58) .... Notre Dame won 32, lost 18—.640
Under Joe Kuharich (1959-1962) .... Notre Dame won 17, lost 23—.425
Under Hugh Devore (1945; 1963) .... Notre Dame won 9, lost 9, tied 1—.500
Under Ara Parseghian (1964-1974) .... Notre Dame won 95, lost 17, tied 4—.848
Biggest score for Notre Dame .... 1905—Notre Dame 142, American Medical 0
Biggest score under Rockne .... 1926—Notre Dame 77, Beloit 0
Biggest score under Anderson .... 1932—Notre Dame 73, Haskell 0
Biggest score under Layden .... 1940—Notre Dame 61, Carnegie Tech 0
Biggest score under McKeever .... 1944—Notre Dame 64, Dartmouth 0
Biggest score under Leahy .... 1947—Notre Dame 59, Tulane 6
Biggest score under Brennan .... 1957—Notre Dame 54, Southern Methodist 21
Biggest score under Kuharich .... 1961—Notre Dame 30, Southern California 0
Biggest score under Devore .... 1945—Notre Dame 56, Iowa 0
Biggest score under Parseghian .... 1965—Notre Dame 69, Pittsburgh 13
Worst defeat of all time .... 1944—Notre Dame 0, Army 59
Worst defeat under Rockne .... 1925—Notre Dame 0, Army 27
Worst defeat under Anderson .... 1933—Notre Dame 0, Purdue   19
                                            1933—Notre Dame 0, Southern Cal. 19
Worst defeat under Layden .... 1936—Notre Dame 0, Pittsburgh 26
Worst defeat under McKeever .... 1944—Notre Dame 0, Army 59
Worst defeat under Leahy .... 1951—Notre Dame 0, Michigan State 35
Worst defeat under Brennan .... 1956—Notre Dame 0, Oklahoma 40
                                            1956—Notre Dame 8, Iowa   48
Worst defeat under Kuharich .... 1960—Notre Dame 19, Purdue 51
Worst defeat under Devore .... 1945—Notre Dame 0, Army 48
Worst defeat under Parseghian .... 1972—Notre Dame 6, Nebraska 40
Most points scored by
    Notre Dame at home: 142 .... (Oct. 28, 1905—ND 142, American Medical 0)
Most points scored by
    Notre Dame away from home: 69 .... (Nov. 6, 1965—ND 69, Pittsburgh 13)
Most points scored against Notre Dame at home: 51 .... (Oct. 1, 1960—Purdue 51, ND 19)
Most points scored against
    Notre Dame away: 59 .... (Nov. 11, 1944—Army 59, ND 0, in New York)
Worst defeat for Notre Dame at home .... Oklahoma 40, ND 0 (Oct. 27, 1956)
Worst defeat for Notre Dame away .... Army 59, ND 0 (Nov. 11, 1944)

NOTRE DAME
ROSTER -- 1887-1974

A

Achterhoff, Jay 1973-74
Adamonis, Stan 1937
Adams, John (Tree) 1942-43-44
Adamson, Ken 1957-58-59
Agnew, Ed 1930
Agnone, John 1945-46
Ahern, Bill 1960-61-62
Albert, Frank 1937-38-39
Alessandrini, Jack 1950-51-52
Alexander, Ben 1931-32
Alexander, Harry 1965-66
Allan, Denny 1968-69-70
Allen, Wayne 1962
Allison, Bill (Tex) 1916-17
Allocco, Frank 1972-73-74
Allocco, Rich 1974
Alvarado, Joe 1971-72-73
Ambrose, John 1919
Ames, Dick 1938
Anderson, Eddie 1918-19-20-21
Anderson, Heartley (Hunk) 1918-19-20-21
Andler, Ken 1974
Andreotti, Pete 1963-64-65
Andres, Bill 1917
Andrews, Frank (Bodie) 1916-17
Angsman, Elmer 1943-44-45
Anson, George 1894
Arboit, Ennio 1936-37
Arboit, Pete 1937-39
Archer, Art 1944
Archer, Clyde 1938
Arment, Bill 1974
Armstrong, Lennox 1911
Arndt, Russ 1922-23-24
Arrington, Dick 1963-64-65
Arrix, Bob 1952
Ashbaugh, Russell (Pete) 1941-42-46-47
Atamian, John 1962-63-64
Augustine, Charlie 1959-60
Azzaro, Joe 1964-65-66-67

B

Bach, Joe 1923-24
Bachman, Charlie 1914-15-16
Bagarus, Steve 1939-40
Bahan, Leonard (Pete) 1917-18-19
Bailie, Roy 1929-30
Bake, Tom 1974
Balliet, Calvin 1973-74
Banas, Steve 1931-32-33
Banicki, Fred 1949
Banks, Mike 1973-74
Barber, Bob 1938
Bardash, Virgil 1950-51-52
Barnard, Jack 1962
Barnett, Reggie 1972-73-74
Barrett, John 1893-94

Barrett, Billy 1949-50-51
Barry, George 1923
Barry, Norm 1917-18-19-20
Barry, Norm 1940-41
Barstow, Fred 1931-32-34
Bartlett, Jim 1949-50
Barz, Bill 1968-69-70
Bauer, Ed 1972-74
Baujan, Harry 1913-14-15-16
Beach, Joe 1933-34
Beacom, Pat 1903-04-05-06
Beams, Byron 1954-55
Bechtold, Joe 1938
Becker, Doug 1974
Becker, Harry 1933-34-35
Bednar, George 1961-62-63
Begley, Gerry 1947-48-49
Beh, Carleton 1914
Beinor, Ed 1936-37-38
Belden, Bill 1935
Belden, Bob 1966-67-68
Benda, Joe 1925-26-27
Benigni, George 1944
Bennett, Anson 1898
Bereolos, Hercules 1939-40-41
Berezney, Pete 1943-44-45
Berger, Alvin (Heine) 1911-12-13-14
Bergman, Alfred (Dutch) 1910-11 13-14
Bergman, Arthur (Dutch) 1915-16-19
Bergman, Joe (Dutch) 1921-22-23
Berkey, Ken 1916
Berta, Bill 1938
Berteling, John (Doc) 1906-07
Bertelli, Angelo 1941-42-43
Berve, Ben 1906
Beschen, Dick 1958
Best, Art 1972-73-74
Biagi, Frank 1938-39
Bianco, Don 1951
Bice, Len 1931
Bigelow, Jim 1952-53-54
Bill, Bob 1959-60-61
Binkowski, Ben 1936-37-38
Binz, Frank 1908
Bisceglia, Pat 1953-54-55
Bitsko, Mickey 1961
Bleier, Bob (Rocky) 1965-66-67
Bliey, Ron 1962-63
Boeringer, Art (Bud) 1925-26
Boji, Byron 1949-50-51
Boland, Joe 1924-25-26
Boland, Ray 1932
Bolger, Matt 1941
Bolger, Tom 1971-72-73
Bonar, Bud 1933-34
Bonder, Frank 1974
Bondi, Gus 1927-28-29
Bonvechio, Sandy 1963-64

450

Borer, Harold	1938	
Borowski, Chuck	1936	
Bosse, Joe	1954-55	
Bossu, Augie	1936-37-38	
Bossu, Frank	1968-69-70	
Bossu, Steve	1974	
Boulac, Brian	1960-61-62	
Bouwens, Seraphine	1897	
Boyle, Rich	1958	
Bracken, Bob	1904-05-06	
Bradley, Luther	1973	
Brady, Jim	1927-28	
Brancheau, Ray	1931-32-33	
Brandy, Joe	1917-19-20	
Brantley, Tony	1973-74	
Bray, Jim	1926-27-28	
Brennan, Ed	1894	
Brennan, Jim	1944-46-47	
Brennan, Joe	1909	
Brennan, Terry	1945-46-47-48	
Brennan, Terry	1967-68-69	
Brennan, Tom	1938	
Brenneman, Mark	1971-73-74	
Brent, Francis	1901	
Brew, Frank	1937-38	
Briick, Herb	1970-71-72	
Brill, Marty	1929-30	
Brocke, Jim	1963	
Brock, Tom	1940-41-42	
Brogan, John	1905	
Broscoe, Eddie	1936-38	
Brosey, Cliff	1939-40	
Brown, Bob	1895-96	
Brown, Cliff	1971-72-73	
Brown, Earl	1936-37-38	
Brown, Earl	1892	
Brown, Frank	1926	
Brown, Harvey	1921-22-23	
Brown, Ivan	1973	
Brown, Roger	1946-47	
Browner, Ross	1973	
Bruno, Bill	1934-35-36	
Brutz, Jim	1939-40-41	
Brutz, Marty	1942-46	
Bucci, Don	1951-52-53	
Buches, Steve	1968-69-70	
Buczkiewicz, Ed	1952	
Budka, Frank	1961-62-63	
Budynkiewicz, Ted	1947-48	
Bulger, Jim	1970-71	
Bullock, Wayne	1972-73-74	
Buoniconti, Nick	1959-60-61	
Burdick, Henry	1906-07-08	
Burgener, Mike	1965-66-67	
Burgmeier, Ted	1974	
Burke, Ed	1960-61-62	
Burke, Frank	1944	
Burke, John	1907	
Burke, Kevin	1956-58	
Burnell, Max	1936-37-38	
Burnell, Max	1959-60	
Burnett, Al	1945	
Burns, Bill	1962-63	
Burns, Paul	1949-50-51	

Bush, Hardy	1913-14	
Bush, Jack	1949-50-51	
Bush, Joe	1951-52-53	
Bush, Roy	1945	
Buth, Doug	1974	
Butler, Frank	1930	
Byrne, Bill (Illy)	1926	
Byrne, John	1921	
Byrne, Tom	1925-26-27	

C

Cabral, Walter	1951-52-53-54	
Caito, Leo	1960	
Caldwell, George	1932-33-34	
Callaghan, Leo	1954	
Callicrate, Dom	1905-06-07	
Cameron, Alexander	1921	
Campbell, Stafford	1889	
Canale, Frank	1931-32-34	
Cannon, Jack	1927-28-29	
Capers, Tony	1968	
Caprara, Joe	1949-50	
Carberry, Glen (Judge)	1920-21-22	
Carey, Tom	1951-52-53-54	
Carey, Tony	1964-65	
Carideo, Frank	1928-29-30	
Carideo, Fred	1933-34-35	
Carmody, James	1930	
Carney, Mike	1974	
Carollo, Joe	1959-60-61	
Carrabine, Gene	1951-52	
Carrabine, Luke	1954	
Carroll, Jim	1962-63-64	
Carter, Don	1947	
Carter, Tom	1949-50	
Cartier, Dezera	1889	
Cartier, George	1887	
Casey, Dan	1894-95	
Cash, Tony	1944	
Casper, Dave	1971-72-73	
Cassidy, Bill	1929	
Cassidy, Thaddeus	1938-40	
Castin, Jack	1960	
Castner, Paul	1920-21-22	
Cavalier, John	1936	
Cavanaugh, Tom	1895-96	
Cavanaugh, Vince	1930-31	
Cerney, Bill	1922-23-24	
Chandler, Bill	1944	
Chanowicz, Stan	1935	
Chauncey, Jim	1974	
Chevigny, Jack	1926-27-28	
Chidester, Abraham (Abe)	1893-94	
Chlebeck, Andy	1940	
Christensen, Ross	1974	
Christman, Norb	1928-29-30-31	
Church, Augie (Sonny)	1934-35	
Church, Durant	1904	
Cibula, George	1943	
Ciechanowicz, Emil	1947-48	
Cieszkowski, John	1969-70-71-72	
Ciesielski, Dick	1956-58-59	
Cifelli, Gus	1946-47-48-49	
Clark, Bill	1959-60	

Clark, Oswald 1945
Clasby, Ed 1944
Clatt, Corwin (Cornie) 1942-46-47
Clear, Eugene 1904
Clement, B. 1908
Clements, Bill 1960
Clements, Jack 1971
Clements, Tom 1972-73-74
Clifford, Jerry 1935-36-37
Clinnen, Walter 1908-10
Clippinger, Art 1910
Cloherty, John 1969-70-71
Coad, Dick 1904
Coady, Ed 1888-89
Coady, Pat 1892
Coady, Tom 1888-89
Cody. Francis (Lew) 1925
Cofall, Stan 1914-15-16
Colella, Phil 1945
Coleman, Charles 1901
Coleman, Herb 1942-43
Collins, Chuck 1922-23-24
Collins, Eddie 1926-27-28-29
Collins, Fred 1925-26-27-28
Collins, Greg 1972-73-74
Collins, Joe 1908-09-10
Collins, Leo 1966
Colosimo, Jim 1957-59
Colrick, John 1927-28-29
Conjar, Larry 1965-66
Conley, Tom 1928-29-30
Connell, Ward (Doc) 1922-23-24
Connor, George 1946-47
Connor, Joe 1935
Connor, John 1948-49
Connors, Ben 1918-19
Conway, Denny 1964-65
Cook, Bill 1912-13
Cook, Ed 1953-54
Cook, Harold 1922
Cooke, Larry 1954-55-56
Corbisiero, John 1944
Corby, Sidney 1894-96
Corgan, Mike 1937-38
Corry. Clarence 1894
Corson, Bob 1957
Costa, Don 1958
Costa, Paul 1961-63-64
Costello, Al 1932-33-34
Cotter, Bob 1969
Cotter, Dick 1948-49-50
Cotton, Forrest (Fod) 1920-21-22
Coughlin, Bernie 1922-24-25
Coughlin, Danny 1920-21
Coughlin, Frank 1916-19-20
Coutre, Larry 1946-47-48-49
Cowhig, Gerry 1942-46
Cowin, Jeff 1969
Coyne, Bob 1954
Crawley, Pat 1892
Creaney, Mike 1970-71-72
Creevey, John 1942-46
Creevey, Tom 1973
Creevy, Dick 1940-41-42

Creevy, Tom 1942
Crimmins, Bernie 1939-40-41
Criniti, Frank 1966-67-68
Cripe, Clarence 1907
Cronin, Art 1934-35-36
Cronin, Carl 1929-30-31
Cronin, Dick 1945
Crotty, Jim 1957-58-59
Crotty, Mike 1969-70-71
Crowe, Clem 1923-24-25
Crowe, Ed 1925
Crowe, Emmett 1936-37-38
Crowley, Charlie 1910-11-12
Crowley, Charlie 1918-19
Crowley, Jim 1922-23-24
Cullen, Jack 1960-61
Cullen, John 1892-93
Cullinan, Joe (Jepers) 1900-01-02-03
Cullins, Ron 1974
Culver, Al 1929-30-31
Curley, Bob 1943
Cusack, Joe 1887-88
Cusick, Frank 1942
Cyterski, Len 1951
Czarobski, Zygmont (Ziggy) 1942-43-46-47

D

Dabiero, Angelo 1959-60-61
Dahman, Ray (Bucky) 1925-26-27
Dailer, Jim 1944-47-48
Dainton, Bill 1965
Daly, Charles 1899
Daly, Mike 1896-97
Dampeer, John 1970-71-72
Danbom, Larry 1934-35-36
Dancewicz, Frank 1943-44-45
Daniels, Bert 1908
Darcy, John 1936
Daut, John 1949
Davila, Jenaro 1895
Davin, David 1954
Davlin, Mike 1944
Davis, Irwin 1933-34
Davis, Ray 1943
Davitt, Harold 1901
deArrietta, Jim 1968-69
DeBuono, Dick 1945
Dee, John 1944
DeFranco, Joe 1937-38-39
DeGree, Ed 1920-21-22
DeGree, Walter (Cy) 1916-17-19
Deinhart, Joe 1924
Demmerle, Pete 1972-73-74
Dempsey, John 1894
DeNardo, Ron 1957
Denchfield, Art 1927
Dennery, Vince 1962-63-64
DePola, Nick 1960
DePrimio, Dennis 1969-70-71
Desch, Gus 1921-22
Desmond, Bill 1902
Devine, Ed 1968
Devine, Tom 1971-72
Devore, Hugh 1931-32-33

452

Dew, Billy	1927-28
Dewan, Darryll	1970-71-72
DiCarlo, Mike	1961-62-63
Dickerson, Sydney	1889
Dickman, Dan	1967
Dickson, George	1949
Diebold, Clarence	1900
Diebold	1910
Diener, John	1906-07-08
Dillon, Dan	1903
Diminick, Gary	1971-72-73
Dimmick, Ralph	1908-09-10
DiNardo, Gerry	1972-73-74
DiNardo, Larry	1968-69-70
Dinkle, Nicholas	1892-93-94
Dionne, Louis	1908
Ditton, James	1907
Dixon, Sherwood	1916-17
Djubasak, Paul	1957
Doar, Jim	1901-02
Doarn, John	1926-27-28
Doherty, Brian	1971-72-73
Doherty, Kevin	1973-74
Doherty, Pat	1912
Dolan, Bill	1911-12
Dolan, Pat	1955-56-57
Dolan, Sam (Rosey)	1906-07-08-09
Donahue, John	1898
Donoghue, Dick	1927-28-29-30
Donohue, Pete	1967
Donovan, Bob (Smousherette)	1906
Donovan, Dick (Smoush)	1903-04-05
Donovan, Red	1918
Doody, Frank	1938-40
Dooley, Jim	1919-20-21
Dorais, Charles (Gus)	1910-11-12-13
Dorais, Joe	1915-16
Dove, Bob	1940-41-42
Downs, Bill	1905
Downs, Morris	1905
Doyle, Pat	1957-58-59
Doyle, Nick	1906
Draper, Bill	1903-04-05
Drennan, William	1922
Drew, Dave	1970-71-72
Dubenetzky, John	1974
DuBrul, Ernest	1892-93
Duffy, John	1907-08-09-10
Dugan, Bill	1907
Dugan, Mike	1957-58
Duggan, Eddie	1911-12-13-14
Duncan, Ernest	1899
Dunlay, Jim	1950-51
Dunn, Ed	1934-35
Dunphy, Ray	1912
Duranko, Pete	1963-64-65-66
Dushney, Ron	1966-67-68
Dwan, Alan	1906
Dwyer, Gene	1942
Dwyer, Pete	1908-09-10

E

Earley, Bill	1940-41-42
Earley, Fred	1943-45-46-47

Earley, Mike	1966
Eastman, Tom	1974
Eaton, Tom	1968-69-70
Eaton, Wilbur	1923-24
Ebli, Ray	1940-41
Eckman, Mike	1969
Ecuyer, Al	1956-57-58
Eddy, Nick	1964-65-66
Edmonds, Wayne	1953-54-55
Edwards, Gene (Red)	1924-25-26
Edwards, Howard (Cap)	1908-09
Eggeman, Fred	1906
Eggeman, Joe	1923
Eggeman, John	1897-98-99
Eggert, Herb	1924
Eichenlaub, Ray	1911-12-13-14
Elder, Jack	1927-28-29
Ellis, Clarence	1969-70-71
Ellis, Howard	1915
Elser, Don	1933-34-35
Elward, Allen (Mal)	1912-13-14-15
Ely, Gene	1936-37
Emanuel, Denny	1936-37
Emerick, Lou	1950
Endress, Frank	1944
Enright, Rex	1923-25
Epstein, Frank	1950
Espanan, Ray	1946-47-48-49
Etten, Nick	1962-63
Etter, Bill	1969-71-72
Eurick, Terry	1974
Evans, Fred (Dippy)	1940-41-42

F

Fagan, Bill	1897
Fallon, Jack	1944-45-46-48
Fanning, Mike	1972-73-74
Fansler, Mike	1902-03-04
Faragher, Jim	1900-01
Farley, John	1897-98-99-00
Farrell, Joe	1962-63-64
Farrell, Tom	1923
Fay, Ed	1944-45
Fedorenko, Nick	1974
Feeney, Al	1910-11-12-13
Fehr, Frank	1887-88-89
Feigel, Chuck	1948-49-50
Feltes, Norm	1922
Fennessey, John	1897
Filley, Pat	1941-42-43-44
Fine, Tom	1973-74
Finegan, Charles (Sam)	1911-12-13-14
Finneran, Jack	1937-38-39
Fischer, Bill	1945-46-47-48
Fischer, Ray	1968
Fitzgerald, Art	1944
Fitzgerald, Dick	1953-54-55
Fitzgerald, Freeman (Fitz)	1912-13-14-15
Fitzgibbons, James	1889
Fitzpatrick, Bill	1926
Fitzpatrick, George	1916-19
Flanagan, Christy	1925-26-27
Flanagan, Jim	1943
Flanigan, John (Thunder)	1917

453

Flannigan, John 1892-93
Fleming, Charles 1898-99
Fleming, Steve.. 1889
Flinn, Neil 1922
Flood, Dave 1950-51-52
Flor, Ollie 1958-59
Flynn, Bill 1945-48-49-50
Flynn, Charles 1889
Flynn, Dave 1950
Flynn, Ed 1950
Flynn, Jack 1921-22
Flynn, John... 1931-32
Fogel, John 1935-36-37
Foley, Joe 1931
Foley, Tom 1910
Ford, Bill 1960
Ford, Gerald 1943
Ford, Jim 1940
Fortin, Al 1898-99-00-01
Foster, Harvey 1936-37
Fox, Harry 1936
Fox, Roger 1966
Frampton, John 1947-48
Francis, Al 1955
Frantz, George 1915-16
Frasor, Dick 1951-52-53-54
Frawley, George 1942
Frederick, John 1925-26-27
Freebery, Joe 1967-68
Freeze, Chet 1907-08
Freistroffer, Tom 1970-71-72
Frericks, Tom 1974
Friske, Joe 1923
Fromhart, Wally 1933-34-35
Frost, Bob 1938
Fry, Willie 1973
Funk, Art 1902-03-04-05
Furlong, Nick 1902-03
Furlong, Nick 1967-68-69
Furlong, Tom 1967

G

Gaffney, John 1953-54
Galanis, John 1974
Galardo, Armando 1952-53
Galen, Albert 1895
Gallagher, Bill 1969-70-71
Gallagher, Frank 1936
Gallagher, John 1895
Gallagher, Tom 1938-39-40
Gambone, John 1973
Gander, Del 1949-50-51
Ganey, Mike 1943-44-45
Gardner, John 1968
Gargan, Joe 1912-13
Gargiulo, Frank...................................... 1959-60
Garner, Terry 1970-71-72
Garunde 1908
Garvey, Art (Hector) 1920-21
Gasparella, Joe 1944-45
Gasseling, Tom 1968-69-70
Gasser, John 1968-69
Gatewood, Tom 1969-70-71
Gaudreau, Bill 1951

Gaul, Frank 1945-47-48
Gaul, Frank 1933-34-35
Gay, Bill 1947-48-49-50
Gaydos, Bob 1955-56-57
Gebert, Al (Bud) 1928-29
Geniesse, Oswald 1924
George, Don 1953-54
Geremia, Frank 1956-57-58
Gildea, Hubert 1931-32
Gillen, Charles 1900-01-02
Gipp, George 1917 18-19-20
Girolami, Tony 1940
Glaab, John 1944-45
Gladieux, Bob 1966-67-68
Gleason, Joe (Red) 1935-36-37
Gleckler, Ed 1974
Glueckert, Charles 1922-23-24
Glynn, Ed (Cupid) 1909
Glynn, Ralph 1899-00
Gmitter, Don 1964-65-66
Goberville, Tom 1961-62-63
Goeddeke, George 1964-65-66
Goeke, John 1895
Gompers, Bill 1945-46-47
Goodman, Ron 1972-73-74
Gores, Tom 1969
Gorman, Tim 1965-66
Gorman, Tom (Kitty) 1931-32-33
Gottsacker, Harold 1936-37-38
Grable, Charles 1965
Grabner, Hank 1918
Grady, Bill 1914
Graney, Mike 1958
Grant, Chet 1916-20-21
Grau, Frank 1960-61
Gray, Gerry 1959-61-62
Greeney, Norm 1930-31-32
Grenda, Ed 1969
Griffith, Dan 1958-60
Groble, George 1954-55-56
Groom, Jerry 1948-49-50
Grothaus, Walt 1945-47-48-49
Gubanich, John 1938-39-40
Guglielmi, Ralph 1951-52-53-54
Gullickson, Tom 1974
Gulyas, Ed 1969-70-71
Gunderman, Reuben 1931
Gushurst, Fred (Gus) 1912-13
Gustafson, Phil 1969
Guthrie, Dave 1904
Guthrie, Tom 1944
Gutowski, Denny 1970-72

H

Hack, Jim 1934-36
Hadden 1895
Haffner, George 1959-60
Hagan, Lowell 1932-33
Hagerty, Bob 1966
Haggar, Joe 1970-72
Hagopian, Gary 1969
Hague, Harry 1907
Haley, Dave 1966-67

Hamby, Jim 1949-51
Hamilton, Don 1908-09
Hanley, Dan 1930-33-34
Hanley, Frank 1896-99
Hanlon, Bob 1943
Hanousek, Dick 1924-25
Hanratty, Terry 1966-67-68
Hardy, Kevin 1964-65-66-67
Hardy, Russell 1915
Hargrave, Bob 1939-40-41
Harmon, Joe 1922-23-24
Harrington, Vince 1922-23-24
Harris, Jim 1930-31-32
Harrison, Randy 1974
Harshman, Dan 1965-66-67
Hart, Leon 1946-47-48-49
Harchar, John 1973
Hartman, Pete 1972-73
Harvat, Paul 1911-12
Harvey, Tad 1937-38-39
Hayduk, George 1971-72-73
Hayes, Art 1898-99-00
Hayes, Dave 1917-19-20
Hayes, Jackie 1939-40
Healy, Pat 1959
Healy, Tom 1903-04-05
Heap, Joe 1951-52-53-54
Hearden, Tom 1924-25-26
Heath, Cliff 1938
Heaton, Mike 1965-66-67
Hebert, Carl 1955-57
Hecomovich, Tom 1959-60-61
Hedrick, Gene 1955-56
Heenan, Pat 1959
Hein, Jeff 1971-72-73
Helwig, John 1948-49-50
Heman, Dick 1945
Hempel, Scott 1968-69-70
Hendricks, Dick 1953-54
Heneghan, Curt 1966-67-68
Henley, James 1892
Henneghan, Bill 1960
Henning, Art 1906-07-08
Hepburn, Joseph 1887-88-89
Hering, Frank 1896
Herwit, Norm 1928
Hesse, Frank 1893-95-96
Heywood, Bill 1946
Hickey, Louis 1934-36
Hickman, Bill 1957
Hicks, Bill 1912
Higgins, Bill 1948-49-50
Higgins, Luke 1942
Higi, Joe 1921
Hill, Greg 1971-72-73
Hines, Mike 1941
Hoebing, Bob 1945
Hoerster, Ed 1960-61-62
Hofer, Bill 1936-37-38
Hoffman, Frank (Nordy) 1930-31
Hogan, Don 1939-40-41
Hogan, Don 1962
Hogan, John 1926
Hogan, Paul 1918

Hollendoner, Frank 1937-38
Holmes, George (Ducky) 1914-16
Holton, Barry 1917-20
Holtzapfel, Mike 1966-67-68
Hooten, Herman 1970-71
Hoppel, Leo 1936
Horan, Bill 1936
Horney, John 1964-65-66
Hornung, Paul 1954-55-56
Host, Paul 1930-31-32
Houck, George 1887
Houser, Max 1923-24
Howard, Al 1929-30
Huarte, John 1962-63-64
Huber, Bill 1942
Hudak, Ed 1947-48-49
Huff, Andy 1969-71-72
Hughes, Ernie 1974
Hughes, Tom 1954-55-56
Humbert, Jim 1969-70-71
Humenik, Dave 1961-62
Hunsinger, Ed 1922-23-24
Hunter, Al 1973
Hunter, Art 1951-52-53
Hurd, Bill 1967
Hurd, Dave 1957-58
Hurlbert, Jim 1926-27
Hurley, Bill 1926-27
Hutzell, Oscar 1906

I

Ivan, Ken 1963-64-65
Izo, George 1957-58-59

J

Jackson, Ernie 1968
James, Johnny 1922
Jaskwhich, Chuck 1930-31-32
Jeffers, Jack 1947-48
Jewett, Harry 1887-88
Jeziorski, Ron 1964-65-66
Jockisch, Bob 1967-68
Johnson, Frank (Rodney) 1945-47-48-49
Johnson, Murray 1950
Johnson, Pete 1974
Johnson, Ron 1968-70
Johnston, Frank 1949-50
Jonardi, Ray 1949-50
Jones, Bill 1926-27
Jones, Jerry 1915-16
Jones, Keith (Deak) 1911-12-13-14
Jones, Ray 1911
Joseph, Bob 1951-52
Joyce, Tom 1905
Just, Jim 1956-57-58
Juzwik, Steve 1939-40-41

K

Kadish, Mike 1969-70-71
Kafka, Mike 1974
Kane, Mickey 1920-21-22
Kantor, Joe 1961-63-64
Kapish, Bob 1949-50-51
Kapish, Gene 1953-54-55

455

Kaplan, Clarence 1929-30
Karr, Jim 1938
Kasper, Cy 1919-20
Kassis, Tom 1928-29-30
Katchik, Joe 1951
Keach, Leroy 1906
Kearns, John 1892
Keefe, Emmett 1912-13-14-15
Keefe, Frank 1926
Keefe, Larry 1924
Keefe, Walter 1904-06
Kegaly, John 1954
Kegler, Bill 1896-97
Kell, Paul 1936-37-38
Kelleher, Bill 1911-12-13-14
Kelleher, Dan 1974
Kelleher, John 1938-39
Keller, Dick 1953-54
Kelley, Ed 1895
Kelly, Al (Red) 1909
Kelly, Bob 1943-44
Kelly, Bob 1950-51
Kelly, Chuck 1974
Kelly, Gerald 1965-66
Kelly, Jim 1940
Kelly, Jim 1961-62-63
Kelly, Jim 1964-66
Kelly, Joe 1944
Kelly, Johnny 1936
Kelly, Johnny 1937-38-39
Kelly, Luke 1908-09-10-11
Kelly, Pete 1938-39-40
Kelly, Tim 1968-69-70
Kelly, Will 1916
Kenneally, Tommy 1927-28-29
Kennedy, Charles 1967-68-69
Kennedy, John 1908
Keough, Frank 1892-93-94
Kersjes, Frank 1930
Kerr, Bud 1937-38-39
Kienast, Phil 1961
Kiley, Roger (Rodge) 1919-20-21
Kiliany, Dennis 1967-68
Kineally, Kevin 1973
King, Hollis (Hoot) 1913-14-15
King, Tom 1916-17
Kiousis, Marty 1949
Kirby, Harry 1901-02
Kirby, Maurice 1893
Kirk, Bernie 1918-19
Kizer, Noble 1922-23-24
Klees, Vince 1973-74
Knott, Dan 1973
Koch, Bob 1938-39-40
Koch, Dave 1949
Kohanowich, Al 1951-52
Koken, Mike 1930-31-32
Kolasinski, Dan 1960
Kolski, Steve 1960-61-62
Kondrk, John 1970-71-72
Kondrla, Mike 1968
Konieczny, Rudy 1965-66
Kopczak, Frank 1934-35-36
Koreck, Bob 1959-60

Kornman, Russ 1972-73-74
Korth, Howard 1938-40
Kos, Gary 1968-69-70
Kosikowski, Frank 1946-47
Kosky, Ed 1930-31-32
Kostelnik, Tom 1962-63-64
Kovalcik, George (Jake) 1936-38
Kovatch, John 1939-40-41
Kowalski, George 1914
Kozak, George 1931
Krall, Rudy 1944
Krause, Ed (Moose) 1931-32-33
Krivik, Stan 1945
Krupa, Ed 1942-43
Kuchta, Frank 1956-57
Kucmicz, Mike 1965-66
Kudlacz, Stan 1941-42
Kuechenberg, Bob 1966-67-68
Kuffel, Ray 1943
Kuh, Dick 1948
Kuharich, Joe 1935-36-37
Kulbitski, Vic 1943
Kunz, George 1966-67-68
Kuppler, George 1898-99-00
Kurth, Joe 1930-31-32
Kurzynske, Jim 1945
Kutzavitch, Bill 1961

L

LaBorne, Frank 1931-32-33
LaFollette, Clarence 1923
Laiber, Joe 1939-40-41
Lally, Bob 1947-48-49
Lamantia, Pete 1966
Lambeau, Earl (Curly) 1918
Lambert, Steve 1968
Lamonica, Daryle 1960-61-62
Lanahan, John 1940-41-42
Landolfi, Chuck 1967-68
Landry, Jack 1948-49-50
Laney, Tom 1973-74
Lantry, Joe 1906
Larkin, Art (Bunny) 1912-13-14
Larkin, Ed 1938
Larson, Fred (Ojay) 1918-20-21
Larson, John 1911
Lasch, Bob 1953-54
Lathrop, Ralph (Zipper) 1911-12-13-14
Lattner, Johnny 1951-52-53
Lauck, Chick 1966-67-68
Lautar, John 1934-35-36
Lavin, John 1966-67-68
Law, John 1926-27-28-29
Lawrence, Don 1956-57-58
Lawson, Tom 1967-69
Layden, Elmer 1922-23 24
Layden, Mike 1933-34-35
Leahy, Bernie 1929-30-31
Leahy, Frank 1928-29
Leahy, James 1968
LeBlanc, Joe 1911
Lebrau, John 1944
LeCluyse, Len 1946-47
Leding, Mike 1931-32

456

Lee, Al 1938-40
Lee, Jack 1951-52-53-54
Lee, Jay 1911
Lehmann, Bob 1961-62-63
Lemek, Ray 1953-54-55
Lennon, Peter 1898
Leonard, Bill 1945-47
Leonard, Bob 1938-39-40
Leonard, Jim 1931-32-33
Leppig, George 1926-27-28
Lesko, Al 1945-48
Levicki, John 1934-35-36
Lewallen, Brian 1968-69
Lewis, Aubrey 1955-56-57
Lieb, Tom 1921-22
Liggio, Tom 1960-61
Likovich, John 1974
Lillis, Paul 1939-40-41
Lima, Chuck 1955-56-57
Limont, Mark 1944
Limont, Paul 1942-43-46
Lind, Mike 1960-61-62
Linehan, Ed 1892
Linehan, John 1960
Lins, George 1896-97-98-99-00-01
Listzwan, Tom 1928
Littig, Edward 1897
Lium, John 1966
Livergood, Bernie 1922-23-24
Livingstone, Bob 1942-46-47
Loboy, Alan 1963-64
Lockard, Frank (Abbie) 1917-18
Locke, Joe 1927-29
Lodish, Mike 1957-58-59
Logan, Les 1920-21-22
Lombardo, Camilo 1918
Loncaric, Lou 1954-55-56
Lonergan, Frank (Happy) 1901-02-03
Long, Harry 1963-64-65
Longhi, Ed 1936-37-38
Longo, Tom 1963-64-65
Loop, Paul 1958
Lopienski, Tom 1972-73-74
Loula, Jim 1960
Lower, Harold 1912
Lozzi, Dennis 1972-73
Luecke, Dan 1960
Luhn, Henry 1887
Lujack, Johnny 1943-46-47
Lukats, Nick 1930-32-33
Lyden, Mike 1943
Lynch, Dick 1955-56-57
Lynch, Ed 1907-08-09
Lynch, Jim 1964-65-66
Lynn, Brad 1937
Lyon, Francis 1896

M

MacAfee, Ken 1974
MacDonald, Tom 1961-62-63
Maciag, Dick 1970-72
Mack, Bill (Red) 1958-59-60
Maddock, Bob 1939-40-41
Madigan, Edward (Slip) 1916-17-19

Maggioli, Achille (Chick) 1943-44
Magevney, Hugh (Red) 1921
Maglicic, Ken 1962-63-64
Magnotta, Mike 1959-60
Mahaffey, Tom 1931-32
Mahalic, Drew 1972-73-74
Maher, Willie (Red) 1921-22-23
Mahoney, Dick 1930-31
Mahoney, Gene 1927
Mahoney, Jim 1948-49
Malone, Grover 1915-16-19
Malone, Mike 1968
Maloney, James 1887
Maloney, Jim 1908-09
Maloney, John 1938
Mangialardi, Fred 1951-52-53
Manzo, Lou 1958
Marchand, Gerry 1950
Marelli, Ray 1925-26
Mariani, John 1970-71-72
Marino, Nunzio 1944
Markowski, Joe 1953
Marquardt, Clarence 1938
Marr, John 1934-35-36
Marsico, Joe 1966
Martell, Gene 1953-54-55
Marshall, Walt 1935-36-37
Martin, Bill 1910
Martin, Bob 1952-53
Martin, Dave 1965-66-67
Martin, Jim 1946-47-48-49
Martin, Jim (Pepper) 1934-35-36
Martin, Mark 1968
Martin, Mike 1970
Martz, George 1944
Marx, Greg 1970-71-72
Maschmeier, Tom 1974
Massey, Bob 1930
Massey, Jim 1969
Masterson, Bernie 1938
Mastrangelo, John 1944-45-46
Mathews, Lee 1908-09-10
Mathews 1914
Mattera, Vince 1963-64
Mattes, Francis 1888
Matthews, Ed 1938
Matz, Paul 1951-52-53-54
Mavraides, Menil (Minnie) 1951-52-53
Maxwell, Joe 1960-61-62
Maxwell, Joe 1924-25-26
May, Paul 1965-66
Mayer, Frank 1925-26
Mayl, Gene 1921-22-23
Mazziotti, Tony 1933-34-35
Mazur, John 1949-50-51
McAdams, Vince (Bennie) 1926
McAvoy, Tom 1905
McBride, Bob 1941-42-46
McBride, Mike 1972-73
McCabe, Harold (Dinger) 1925-26
McCarthy, Bill 1951
McCarthy, Bill 1934-35-36
McCarthy, Frank 1927
McCarthy, Jack 1935-36-37

457

McCarthy, William	1895	Melady, Eugene	1887-88
McCarty, Pat	1936-37	Melinkovich, George	1931-32-34
McCormick, Nevin (Bunny)	1936-37	Mello, Jim	1942-43-46
McCoy, Mike	1967-68-69	Menie, Tom	1970-71
McDermott, Ed	1902-03	Meno, Chuck	1956
McDermott, Frank	1921	Mense, Jim	1953-54-55
McDermott	1892	Mergenthal, Art	1944
McDonald, Angus	1896-98-99	Merkle, Bob	1964
McDonald, Paul	1907-08	Merlitti, Jim	1967-68-69
McDonnell, John	1954-55-56	Mertes, Al	1906-07-08
McDonough, Joe	1938	Meschievitz, Vince	1950
McGannon, Bill	1938-39-40	Meter, Bernie (Bud)	1942-43-46
McGee, Coy	1945-46-47-48	Metzger, Bert	1928-29-30
McGehee, Ralph	1946-47-48-49	Metzger, Harry	1912
McGill, Mike	1965-66-67	Meyer, John	1963-64
McGinley, John	1956-57	Michels, Andrew	1940
McGinn, Dan	1963-64-65	Michaels, Bill	1947
McGinnis, Dan	1910-11-12	Michuta, John	1933-34-35
McGinnis, John	1942	Mieszkowski, Ed	1943-45
McGlew, Henry (Fuzzy)	1900-01-02-03	Mikacich, Jim	1959-60-61
McGoldrick, Jim	1936-37-38	Milbauer, Frank	1922-23
McGovern, George	1936	Miles, Frank (Rangy)	1918
McGrath, Bob	1936	Miller, Creighton	1941-42-43
McGrath, Chester (Mugsy)	1910-11	Miller, Don	1922-23-24
McGrath, Frank	1923	Miller, Earl	1918
McGrath, Jack	1926-27-28	Miller, Edgar (Rip)	1922-23-24
McGraw, Pat	1970-71-72	Miller, Fred	1926-27-28
McGuff, Al	1932	Miller, Gerry	1922-23-24
McGuire, Bob	1917	Miller, Harry (Red)	1906-07-08-09
McGuire, Mike	1974	Miller, Howard	1921
McGurk, Jim	1945-46	Miller, John	1914-15-16
McHale, John	1940	Miller, Ray	1911-12
McHale, John	1968-69-70	Miller, Steve	1934-35-36
McHugh, Tom	1951-52-53	Miller, Tom	1940-41-42
McInerny, Arnold	1915-16	Miller, Walter	1915-16-17-19
McIntyre, John	1938-39	Miller, Ward	1916
McKenna, Jim	1935	Millheam, Curtis (Duke)	1931
McKeon, Tom	1889	Millner, Wayne	1933-34-35
McKillip, Leo	1948-49-50	Mills, Rupert (Rupe)	1913-14
McKinney, Charles	1926-27	Milota, Jim	1954-56
McKinley, Tom	1966-67-68	Minik, Frank	1960-61-62
McLane, Mark	1974	Minnix, Bob	1969-70-71
McLaughlin, Dave	1941	Miskowitz, Lew	1973
McLaughlin, Tom	1911-12-13	Mittelhauser, Tom	1963
McLaughlin, Pat	1974	Mixon, Leo	1922
McMahon, Joe	1934-35-36	Modak, Dan	1949-50
McMahon, Johnny	1936-37-38	Mohardt, Johnny	1918-19-20-21
McManmon, Art	1929-30	Mohn, Bill	1918
McManmon, John	1924-25-26	Monahan, Bill	1897-98-99
McMullan, John	1923-24-25	Monahan, Tom	1960
McMullan, John	1953-54-55	Mondron, Bob	1955
McNally, Vince	1925-26	Montroy, Jack	1928
McNamara, Regis	1929-30-31	Monty, Tim	1966-67-68
McNeill, Chuck	1941	Mooney, Al	1937-38-39
McNerny, Larry	1903-04-05	Moore, Dan	1925-26
McNichols, Austin	1946	Moore, Elton	1973-74
McNulty, Mike	1898-99	Morales, Alfred	1916
McNulty, Paul	1922	Morgan, Larry (Red)	1917
McSorley, John	1926-27	Morgan, Steve	1910-11-12
Meagher, Jack	1916	Moriarity, Mike	1906-08-09
Meagher, John	1888	Moriarty, George	1933-34-35
Meeker, Bob	1963-64-65	Moriarty, Kerry	1974
Megin, Bernard	1936	Moritz	1896
Mehre, Harry	1919-20-21	Morrin, Dan	1971-72-73

458

Morrison, James 1894
Morrison, Paul 1938
Morrissey, Joe................................ 1926-27-28
Morrissey, Rockne 1952-53
Morse, Jim.................................... 1954-55-56
Morse 1894
Mortell, John 1938
Mosca, Angelo 1956
Moynihan, Tim 1926-27-28-29
Mudron, Pat 1968-70
Muehlbauer, Mike 1957-58-59
Mueller, Art 1934
Muessel... 1893
Mulcahey, Jim 1937
Mullen, Jack 1894-95-96-97-98-99
Muller, Nick 1962
Mullins, Larry (Moon) 1927-28-29-30
Mundee, Fred 1934-35-36
Munger, Harold 1911-12
Munro, Jim 1954-55-56
Munson, Frank 1905-06-07
Murphy, Dan 1904
Murphy, Denny 1960-61-62
Murphy, Emmett 1930-31-32
Murphy, Fred.................................. 1892
Murphy, Gene................................ 1921-22
Murphy, George 1940-41-42
Murphy, Jerry 1916
Murphy, Johnny 1936-37
Murphy, John 1908
Murphy, John................................. 1894-95-96
Murphy, Tim 1921-22-23
Murphy, Tom 1950-51-52
Murphy, Tom 1927-28-29
Murray, Joe.................................... 1897-98
Murray, John 1961-62
Murrin, George 1925-26-27
Musuraca, Jim 1970-71-72
Mutscheller, Jim 1949-50-51
Myers, Gary 1956-57-58

N

Naab, Dick 1959-60-61
Nadolney, Romanus (Peaches) 1918
Nagurski, Bronko 1956-57-58
Nash, Joe....................................... 1926-27-28-29
Nash, Tom...................................... 1968-69
Naughton, David 1897
Naughton, Mike 1971-72-73
Nebel, Ed 1958-59
Neece, Steve 1973-74
Neff, Bob 1940-41-42
Neidert, Bob 1968-69-70
Nelson, Patrick 1887
Nemeth, Steve 1943-44
Nickel, Russ 1936
Nicola, Norm 1962-63-64
Nicula, George 1953-54-55
Niehaus, Steve 1972-73-74
Niemiec, John 1926-27-28
Niezer, Charles 1897
Nightingale, Chuck 1970
Nissi, Paul 1960
Noon, Tom 1926

Noppenberger, John 1923
Norri, Eric 1966-67-68
Nosbusch, Kevin 1972-73-74
Novakov, Dan 1969-70-71
Novakov, Tony 1973-74
Nowack, Art 1953
Nowers, Paul (Curly) 1912-13
Noznesky, Pete 1954-55
Nusskern, John 1949
Nyere, George 1901-02-03

O

Oaas, Torgus (Turk) 1910-11
Oberst, Gene 1920-22-23
O'Boyle, Harry 1924-25-26
O'Brien, Coley............................... 1966-67-68
O'Brien, Dick 1940-41
O'Brien, Johnny (One Play) 1928-29-30
O'Brien, Johnny 1938-39-40
O'Brien, Tom 1956
O'Connor, Bill (Bucky) 1942-46-47
O'Connor, Bill (Zeke) 1944-46
O'Connor, Dan 1968
O'Connor, Dan............................... 1902
O'Connor, Paul (Bucky) 1928-29-30
O'Connor, Phil 1945
Odem, James 1914-15
O'Donnell, Hugh 1914-15
O'Donnell, John 1972-74
O'Donnell, Leo 1914
Odyniec, Norm 1956-57-58
O'Flynn, Ed 1906
O'Hara, Charlie.............................. 1960-61-62-63
O'Hara, Francis 1896
O'Hara, Joe 1916-19
O'Leary, James 1907
O'Leary, Tom 1965-66-67
Olosky, Marty 1961-62-63
O'Loughlin, Bill 1936-37-38
Olson, Bob 1967-68-69
O'Malley, Dom 1899-00-02
O'Malley, Hugh 1966
O'Malley, Jim 1970-71-72
O'Meara, Walt 1938-39-40
O'Neil, Bill 1911
O'Neil, Bob 1951-52
O'Neil, John 1904
O'Neill, Bob.................................. 1938-39
O'Neill, Hugh 1916
O'Neill, Joe 1934-35-36
Opela, Bruno 1945
O'Phelan, John 1903
Oracko, Steve................................. 1945-47-48-49
O'Regan, Tom 1887
O'Reilly, Chuck 1936-37
O'Reilly, Martin 1940
Oriard, Mike 1968-69
Osterman, Bob 1939-40
Ostrowski, Chet 1949-50-51
O'Toole, Dan 1970-71-72
Owen, Tom 1918
Owens, Bill 1957

459

P

Page, Alan 1964-65-66
Paine, Bob 1907-08
Palladino, Bob 1943
Palmer, Ralph 1895-96
Palumbo, Sam 1951-52-53-54
Panelli, John 1945-46-47-48
Paolone, Ralph 1950
Papa, Bob 1964
Papa, Joe 1938-40
Parise, Tom 1973-74
Parisien, Art 1925-26
Parker, Larry 1970-71
Parker, Mike 1971-73
Parry, Tom 1944
Parseghian, Mike 1974
Pasquesi, Tony 1952-53-54
Paterra, Frank 1951-52
Patten, Paul 1940-41
Patton, Eric 1969-70-71
Patulski, Walt 1969-70-71
Payne, Randy 1974
Pearson, Dudley 1917-19
Peasenelli, John 1940-42
Penick, Eric 1972-73-74
Penman, Gene 1962
Penza, Don 1951-52-53
Pergine, John 1965-66-67
Perko, John 1943
Perkowski, Joe 1959-60-61
Perry, Art 1949-50
Peters, Marty 1933-34-35
Peterson, Elmer 1940
Petitbon, John 1949-50-51
Pfefferle, Dick 1932-34-35
Pfeiffer, Bill 1961-62-63
Phelan, Bob 1919-20-21
Phelan, Jim 1915-16-17
Philbin, Dave 1916-17
Philbrook, George 1908-09-10-11
Phillips, Denny 1961-62-63
Phillips, John 1918
Piccone, Cammille (Pic) 1942
Pick, John 1900-01
Piel, Ed 1901
Piepul, Milt 1938-39-40
Pierce, Bill 1930-31-32
Pietrosante, Nick 1956-57-58
Pietrzak, Bob 1958-59-60
Pilney, Andy 1933-34-35
Pinn, Frank 1954
Pivarnik, Joe 1931-32-33
Pivec, Dave 1962-63
Plain, George 1938
Pliska, Joe 1911-12-13-14
Ploszek, Mike 1974
Poehler, Fred 1951-52
Pohlen, Pat 1973-74
Pojman, Henry 1933-34-35
Polisky, John (Bull) 1925-26-27
Pomarico, Frank 1971-72-73
Pope, Al 1969
Porter, Paul 1945
Poskon, Dewey 1967-68-69

Postupack, Joe 1939
Potempa, Gary 1971-72-73
Potter, Tom 1945-46
Pottios, Myron 1958-59-60
Powers, John 1897
Powers, John 1917
Powers, John 1959-60-61
Prelli, Joe 1924-25-27
Prendergast, Dick 1955-56-57
Prokop, George 1918-19-20
Prokop, Joe 1940-41
Provissiero, John 1928
Prudhomme, Edward 1887-88-89
Pszeracki, Joe 1973-74
Puntillo, Chuck 1957-58
Puplis, Andy 1935-36-37

Q

Quehl, Steve 1972-73
Quinlan, Mike 1892
Quinn, Jim 1926
Quinn, Steve 1965-66-67
Quinn, Tom 1966-67-68

R

Raba, Elmer 1945
Racanelli, Vito 1967
Race, Joe 1935-36-37
Raich, Nick 1953-54
Rakers, Jim 1962-63
Rankin, George 1969-70
Ransavage, Jerry 1926-27-28
Rascher, Norb 1932
Rascher, Norb 1960-62
Rassas, George 1938-40
Rassas, Kevin 1966-67
Rassas, Nick 1963-64-65
Raterman, John 1969-70-71
Ratkowski, Ray 1958-59-60
Ratterman, George 1945-46
Rausch, Lorenzo 1914
Ray, John 1944
Ready, Bob 1951-52-53-54
Reagan, Bob 1921-22-23
Reedy, Joe 1925
Reese, Frank 1921-23-24
Reeve, Dave 1974
Regner, Tom 1964-65-66
Reid, Don 1967-68-69
Reilly, Clarence 1924
Reilly, Jack 1928
Reilly, Jim 1967-68-69
Rellas, Chris 1943
Renaud, Charles 1943
Reynolds, Frank 1956-57-58
Reynolds, Lawrence 1908
Reynolds, Paul 1951-52-54-55
Reynolds, Tom 1967
Rhoads, Tom 1965-66
Riffle, Chuck 1937-38-39
Rigali, Bob 1952-53
Rigali, Bob 1924-25
Riley, Charlie 1925-26-27
Rini, Tom 1958-59

Riordan, Will 1941
Rively, Clair 1939
Roach, John 1923-24-25-26
Roach, Tom 1932-33
Robertson, Bob 1935
Robinson, Jack 1932-34
Robinson, Tyrone 1972
Robst, Paul 1951-53
Roby, Charles 1892-93
Rockne, Knute 1910-11-12-13
Rogenski, Steve 1936-38
Rogers, John 1930-31
Rohan, Andy 1973-74
Rohrs, George 1931
Ronchetti, Pete 1916-17
Ronzone, Matt 1934
Roolf, Jim 1971-72
Rosenthal, Jacob (Rosy) 1894-95-96
Roth, Jesse 1908
Rovai, Fred 1944-45-46
Roy, Norb 1959-60-61
Royer, Dick 1956-57-58
Ruckelshaus, John 1925
Rudnick, Tim 1971-72-73
Ruell, Ulric 1908
Ruetz, Joe 1935-36-37
Rufo, John 1974
Ruggerio, Frank 1943-44-45
Russell, Bill 1945-46
Russell, Marv 1973-74
Rutkowski, Ed 1960-62-62
Rutkowski, Frank 1974
Ruzicka, Jim 1967-69
Ryan, Billy 1907-08-09-10
Ryan, Jim 1917
Ryan, Jim 1965-66
Rydzewski, Frank 1915-16-17
Rykovich, Julie 1943
Rymkus, Lou 1940-41-42

S

Sabal, Al 1957-58-59
Sack, Allen 1964-65-66
Sadowski, Ed 1936
Saggau, Bob 1938-39-40
Saggau, Tom 1948
Salmon, Louis (Red) 1900-01-02-03
Salmon, Joe 1911
Salvino, Bob 1954
Samuel, Al 1972-73-74
Sanders, Cy 1918-19
Sanford, Charles 1889
Sarb, Pat 1973
Sauget, Dick 1964
Savoldi, Joe 1928-29-30
Sawicz, Paul 1973
Sawkins, Edward 1887-88
Scales, Ed 1973
Scanlan, Ray 1906
Scannell, Bob 1954-55-56
Scarpitto, Bob 1958-59-60
Schaack, Ed 1892
Schaaf, Jim 1956-57-58
Schaefer, Don 1953-54-55

Scharer, Eddie 1924-25
Schilling, Joe 1936
Schillo, Fred 1892-93-94-96-97
Schiralli, Angelo 1966
Schiralli, Rocco 1932-33-34
Schivarelli, Pete 1969-70
Schlezes, Ken 1970-71-72
Schmid, Charles 1940
Schmidt, Oscar 1894
Schmitt, Bill 1906-07-08-09
Schneider, J. S. 1899
Schnurr, Fred 1966
Schoen, Tom 1965-66-67
Scholtz, Bob 1957-58-59
Schrader, Jim 1951-52-53
Schramm, Paul 1954-55-56
Schreiber, Tom 1944-45
Schrenker, Henry 1938-40
Schrenker, Paul 1933-34
Schultz, Herb 1927
Schulz, Clay 1959-60-61
Schumacher, Larry 1967-68-69
Schuster, Ken 1944
Schwartz, Charles 1929
Schwartz, Marchy 1929-30-31
Scibelli, Joe 1958
Scott, Vince 1944-45-46
Seaman, Neil 1957-58
Seaman, Tom 1950-51-52
Secret, Bob 1961
Sefcik, George 1959-60-61
Seiler, Leo 1960
Seiler, Paul 1964-65-66
Selcer, Dick 1956-57-58
Seyfrit, Frank (Si) 1920-21
Seymour, Jim 1966-67-68
Shakespeare, Bill 1933-34-35
Shamla, Dick 1934
Shanahan, George 1918
Shannon, Dan 1951-52-53-54
Sharkey, Ed 1974
Sharp, Art 1913-14
Shaughnessy, Frank (Shag) 1901-02-03-04
Shaughnessy, Rodney 1921
Shaw, Lawrence (Buck) 1919-20-21
Shay, George (Dinny) 1927-28-29
Shaughnessy, Tom 1914
Shea, Bill (Red) 1920-21
Sheahan, Jim 1968
Sheehan, Clarence 1903-04-05-06
Sheeketski, Joe 1930-31-32
Shellogg, Alec 1936-37
Shellogg, Fred 1936-37
Sheridan, Benny 1937-38-39
Sheridan, Phil 1938-39-40
Sheridan, Phil 1963-64-65
Sherlock, Jim 1960-61-62
Shields, Bob 1926
Shulsen, Dick 1955-56-58
Signaigo, Joe 1943-46-47
Silver, Nate 1902-03-04-05
Simmons, Floyd 1945-46-47
Simon, Jack 1961-62-63
Simon, Tim 1973

461

Simonich, Ed 1936-37-38
Sinnott, Roger 1893
Sipes, Sherrill 1954-55-56
Sitko, Emil 1946-47-48-49
Sitko, Steve 1937-38-39
Skall, Russell 1947
Skat, Al 1943
Skoglund, Bill 1966
Skoglund, Bob 1944-45-46
Skoglund, Len 1935-36-37
Slackford, Fred (Fritz) 1915-16-19
Slafkosky, John 1961-62
Slager, Rick 1974
Slovak, Emil 1945-46
Smith, Art 1911
Smith, Bill 1933-34
Smith, Dick (Red) 1925-26
Smith, Gene 1973
Smith, Gene 1948-49-50
Smith, Glen 1910-11
Smith, Howard 1927
Smith, John (Clipper) 1925-26-27
Smith, Lancaster (Lank) 1946-47-48
Smith, Maurice (Clipper) 1917-18-19-20
Smith, Pete (Red) 1921
Smith, Scott 1970-71
Smith, Sherman 1972-73-74
Smithberger, Jim 1965-66-67
Snell, Ed 1936
Snowden, Jim 1961-63-64
Snow, Jack 1962-63-64
Snow, Paul 1966-67-68
Snyder, Jim 1943
Solari, Fred 1933-34-35
Spalding, Tom 1917
Spaniel, Frank 1947-48-49
Springer, Frank 1887-88
Staab, Fred 1930
Stanczyak, Al 1945
Standring, Jay 1968-69
Stange, Gus 1922-23
Stanitzek, Frank 1954
Stanley, Basil 1917
Stansfield, John 1910
Statuto, Art 1943-44-46-47
Steenberge, Pat 1970-71
Steiner, Art 1902-03
Steinkemper, Bill 1934-35-36
Stelmazek, Ed 1945
Stenger, Brian 1966-67-68
Stepaniak, Ralph 1969-70-71
Stephan, Jack 1974
Stephan, Leo 1914-15
Stephens, Clay 1961-62-63
Stephens, Jack 1952
Stevenson, Harry 1937-38-39
Stevenson, Martin 1912
Stewart, Ralph 1944
Stickles, Monty 1957-58-59
Stilley, Ken 1933-34-35
Stine, Raleigh (Rollo) 1917-18
Stock, Jim 1972-73-74
Stoudt, Clement 1900
Strohmeyer, George 1946-47

Stroud, Clarke 1950
Studebaker, John 1893-94
Studer, Dean 1954-55-56
Stuhldreher, Harry 1922-23-24
Sullivan, Bob 1938
Sullivan, Danny 1936-37
Sullivan, Ed 1955-56-57
Sullivan, Eddie 1940
Sullivan, George 1943-44-46-47
Sullivan, Joe 1933-34
Sullivan, John 1937-38
Sullivan, Larry 1940-41-42
Sullivan, Tim 1971-72-73
Sullivan, Tom 1908
Sullivan, Tom 1963-64-65
Susko, Larry 1972-73
Swatland, Dick 1965-66-67
Swearingen, Tim 1967-68
Sweeney, Bob 1973-74
Sweeney, Chuck 1935-36-37
Swendsen, Fred 1969-70-71
Swistowicz, Mike 1946-47-48-49
Swonk, Frank 1897
Sylvester, Steve 1972-73-74
Szatko, Greg 1972-73
Szot, Denis 1962-63
Szymanski, Dick 1951-52-53-54
Szymanski, Frank 1943-44

T

Talaga, Tom 1963-64-65
Taylor, Bob 1951-52-53
Taylor, James 1896
Tereschuk, John 1970-71
Terlaak, Bob 1930
Terlep, George 1943-44
Tharp, Jim 1943
Theisen, Charles 1936-38
Theismann, Joe 1968-69-70
Thernes, Matt 1934-35
Thesing, Joe 1937-38-39
Thomann, Rick 1969-70-71
Thomas, Deane 1948
Thomas, Frank 1920-21-22
Thomas, Bob 1971-72-73
Thornton, Pete 1964-65
Tobin, George 1942-46
Tobin, John (Red) 1932-33
Toczylowski, Steve 1944
Todorovich, Mike 1943
Toneff, Bob 1949-50-51
Tonelli, Mario 1936-37-38
Torrado, Rene 1967
Toth, Ron 1956-57-58
Townsend, Mike 1971-72-73
Townsend, Willie 1970-71-72-73
Trafton, George 1919
Traney, Leon 1945
Trapp, Bill 1969-70-71
Traver, Les 1959-60-61
Tripucka, Frank 1945-46-47-48
Trombley, Cliff 1925
Trumper, Ed 1943
Tuck, Ed 1966-67-68

Tuck, Sweeney	1938	Wetoska, Bob	1956-57-58
Twomey, Ted	1928-29	Wheeler, Lucian	1895

U

Urban, Gasper 1943-46-47

V

Vainisi, Jack 1945
Vairo, Dom 1932-33-34
Vangen, Willard 1946
Van Huffel, Al 1965-66
Van Rooy, Bill 1930
Van Summern, Bob 1945
Varrichione, Frank 1951-52-53-54
Vasys, Arunas 1963-64-65
Vaughan, Charles 1911
Vaughan, Pete 1908-09
Vejar, Laurie 1931-32
Vergara, George 1922-23
Vezie, Manny 1926-27-28-29
Viola, Gene 1959-60-61
Virok, Ernie 1945
Vlk, George 1928-29-30
Voedisch, John (Ike) 1925-26-27
Voelkers, John 1913-14-15

W

Wack, Steve 1968
Wadsworth, Mike 1963-64-65
Wagner, Earl 1899
Waldorf, Rufus 1904-05-06
Waldron, Ronayne 1943
Wallace, John 1923-24-25-26
Wallner, Fred 1948-49-50
Walls, Bob 1974
Walsh, Adam 1922-23-24
Walsh, Bill 1895
Walsh, Bill 1945-46-47-48
Walsh, Bob 1941
Walsh, Bob 1946
Walsh, Charles (Chile) 1925-26-27
Walsh, Earl 1919-20-21
Ward, Gilbert (Gillie) 1914-16
Ward, Bob 1955-56-57
Warner, Jack 1940-41
Washington, Bob 1971-72-73
Wasilevich, Max 1973
Washington, Dick 1953
Waters, Fred 1897
Waybright, Doug 1944-47-48-49
Webb, Bob 1940
Webb, Mike 1970-71-73
Weber, Robin 1973-74
Webster, Mike 1963-64
Weibel, John 1922-23-24
Weidner, Fred 1934
Weiler, Jim 1973-74
Weithman, Jim 1950-51-52
Welch, Bob 1944
Wendell, Marty 1944-46-47-48
Wengierski, Tim 1966
Westenkircher, Joe 1944
Weston, Jeff 1974

Whelan, Ed 1950
Whelan, Jack 1951-52
Whelan, Jim 1925
Whipple, Ray 1915-16
White, Bob 1945
White, Carl 1911
White, Don 1957-58-59
White, Eddie 1925-27
White, Jim 1942-43
White, Richard 1918
Whiteside, Bill 1949-50
Wightkin, Bill 1946-47-48-49
Wilcox, Percy 1920
Wilke, Bob 1934-35-36
Wilke, Henry 1957-58-59
Wilke, Roger 1959-60-61
Wilkins, Dick 1955
Williams, Bo 1928
Williams, Bob 1956-57-58
Williams, Bob 1948-49-50
Williams, Cy 1910
Williams, George 1959-60-61
Williams, Scott 1969
Williams, Ted 1938
Wilson, George 1953-54-55
Winegardner, Jim 1966-67-68
Winsouer, Paul 1935-36
Winter, Frank 1898-99-00-01
Wisne, Gerald 1966-67-68
Witchger, Jim 1968-69-70
Witteried, George 1916
Wittliff, Phil 1968
Witucki, Jack 1954
Woebkenberg, Harry 1974
Wojcihovski, Vic 1934-35-36
Wolf, Louie 1915
Wolski, Bill 1963-64-65
Wood, Fay 1907-08
Wood, Greg 1962
Worden, Neil 1951-52-53
Wright, Harry 1940-41-42
Wright, Jim 1968-69-70
Wright, Tom 1970
Wujciak, Al 1973-74
Wunsch, Harry 1931-32-33
Wynne, Chet 1918-19-20-21
Wynne, Elmer 1925-26-27

Y

Yarr, Tommy 1929-30-31
Yeager, Leslie (Dutch) 1915-16
Yoder, Jim 1969-70
Yonakor, John 1942-43
Yonto, Joe 1945
Young, Jacob 1907
Young, John (Tex) 1933
Yund, Walter 1911-12

Z

Zajeski, Ben 1953-54
Zalejski, Ernie 1946-48-49
Zambroski, Tony 1949-50-51

Zancha, John 1949-50
Zanot, Bob 1972-73
Zappala, Tony 1973-74
Zehler, Bill 1945
Zeitler, Charles 1893-94-95
Zenner, Elmer 1935-36
Ziegler, Ed 1967-68-69
Zielony, Dick 1969-70
Ziemba, Wally 1940-41-42
Zikas, Mike 1969-70-71
Zilly, Jack 1943-46
Zimmerman, Jeff 1967-68
Ziznewski, Jay 1968
Zloch, Bill.. 1963-64-65
Zloch, Chuck 1968-69-70
Zloch, Jim 1972-73
Zmijewski, Al 1946-47-48-49
Zoia, Clyde 1917
Zontini, Lou 1937-38-39
Zubek, Bob 1966
Zuber, Tim 1970
Zuendel, Joe 1938
Zurowski, Dave 1964-66
Zwers, Joe 1935-36-37